Windows Home Server For Dummies

Cheat Sheet

P9-EGN-664

Eight Home Server Improvements You Need Right Now

1. **Stick a second hard drive on your server.** Windows Home Server needs two or more hard drives on the server in order to perform all the backups you paid for. The second hard drive needn't be fancy. (See Chapter 18.)

2. **Turn on duplication for your server's shared folders.** (See Chapter 5.)

3. **Enable the** Guest **account.** The Guest account does more than you think. For example, it can help your Xbox 360 pull music and videos off the server. (See Chapter 4.)

4. **Set up Remote Access.** If you ever need to log on to your home network from Patong or low Earth orbit, you'll be glad you have it. (See Chapter 10.)

5. **Back up your recorded TV shows.** (See Chapter 7.)

6. **Turn off other backup programs on Vista and XP machines.** With Windows Home Server in place, you won't need NTBackup or Vista's Automatic Backup programs. (See Chapter 12 for how to give them the axe.)

7. **Get offsite storage.** Windows Home Server can't protect your data if your house burns down or your server decides to eat all its disks. Offsite backup isn't automatic, but it can be free. (See Chapter 15.)

8. **Have Windows XP or Vista transfer photos directly from your camera to the server.** Cut out the middleman. It's easy. (See Chapter 9.)

Where to Go for Home Server Help

The official Windows Home Server forum: `forums.microsoft.com/windowshomeserver`

The official Windows Home Server blog: `blogs.technet.com/homeserver`

Microsoft's Knowledge Base: `support.microsoft.com/search/?adv=1`

Philip Churchill's MS Windows Home Server blog: `mswhs.com`

Terry Walsh's We Got Served blog: `wegotserved.co.uk`

Home Server blog (in German): `home-server-blog.de`

My AskWoody site: `AskWoody.com`

For Dummies: Bestselling Book Series for Beginners

Windows Home Server For Dummies®

Ten Gotchas They Don't Teach in WHS School

1. **If you forget the server's password, you're in deep dreck.** See Chapter 19 for help.

2. **You can't change your own password unless you know the server's password.**

3. **You can't let other people look at your shared folders unless you know the server's password.** Ditto, ditto, and ditto.

4. **You can back up a PC over a wireless connection every night like clockwork, but you have to physically connect the computer to your network to restore data to that PC from a backup.** (See Chapter 13.)

5. **You can only restore to a hard drive that's bigger than (or the same size) as the original.** (See Chapter 13.)

6. **Windows Home Server isn't a Media Server.** If you expect to stream videos or music stored on your server to your Xbox, you have to connect the Xbox to a separate, bona fide Media Server computer, which then talks to the server. (See Chapter 8.)

7. **You can't get at previous versions of files in shared folders if you're running Windows Vista Home Basic or Premium.** (See Chapter 17.)

8. **Windows Home Server maxes out at ten user names.** (See Chapter 4.)

9. **You can hang a printer on your server, but usually it's a pain.** If Windows Home Server includes your printer driver, it'll be easy, but if you need to *install* a driver, you're in for a tussle. (See Chapter 17.)

10. **You can't use Remote Access to control a computer running Windows XP Home, Vista Home Basic, or Home Premium.** (See Chapter 11.)

Three Ways to Use WHS You Might Not Have Considered

1. **Restore a computer that the kids (or somebody) screwed up.** The Restore CD can get you back to an earlier working state. (See Chapter 13.)

2. **Automatically upload photos from the server to Flickr.** (See Chapter 21.)

3. **Run uTorrent on the server.** Most of the time, your Windows Home Server just sits there, doing nothing. Why not do something useful with it — such as downloading Torrents from the Internet? (See Chapter 21.)

For Dummies: Bestselling Book Series for Beginners

Windows® Home Server

FOR

DUMMIES®

Windows® Home Server

FOR

DUMMIES®

by Woody Leonhard

Author of *Windows Vista™ All-in-One Desk Reference For Dummies*
and *Windows Vista™ Timesaving Techniques For Dummies*

Wiley Publishing, Inc.

Windows® Home Server For Dummies®

Published by
Wiley Publishing, Inc.
111 River Street
Hoboken, NJ 07030-5774
www.wiley.com

Copyright © 2008 by Wiley Publishing, Inc., Indianapolis, Indiana

Published by Wiley Publishing, Inc., Indianapolis, Indiana

Published simultaneously in Canada

WILEY

About the Author

Curmudgeon, critic, and perennial "Windows Victim," **Woody Leonhard** runs a fiercely independent Web site devoted to delivering the truth about Windows and Office, whether Microsoft likes it or not. With up-to-the-nanosecond news, observations, tips, and help, `AskWoody.com` has become the premier source of unbiased information for people who actually use the products.

Starting at the dawn of Windows 3.0, Woody has written more than 40 books, drawing an unprecedented six Computer Press Association awards and two American Business Press awards. Woody was one of the first Microsoft Consulting Partners and is a charter member of the Microsoft Solutions Provider organization. He's widely quoted — and reviled — on the Redmond campus.

Woody moved to Phuket, Thailand, seven years ago. He lives in Patong with his wife, Duangkhae (better known by her Thai nickname "Add"); his father, George; and his ornery all-American beagle, Chronos. Add and a crew of 30 run Khun Woody's Bakery and three Sandwich Shoppes in Phuket — one each in Patong, Laguna, and Chalong. If you're ever in Phuket, feel free to drop by for the best bagels in Asia.

Dedication

To Duangkhae T. Leonhard. May our future be as happy as our past.
August 26, 2007, Le Meridien, Phuket, Thailand

Author's Acknowledgments

I would like to thank my wondrous agents, Claudette Moore — who's been with me since the beginning — and Ann Jaroncyk, who keeps it all running; Becky Huehls, who got all the hard work, including the nail-biting task of ensuring that edits finished in time for me to make my wedding; Steve Hayes, Melody Layne, and Tiffany Ma, who championed the cause of a *For Dummies* guide to a mass-market server; Jason Dossett, who kept me honest; Barry Childs-Helton for the tremendous copy edit; and Patrick Redmond and all the production folks who turned my keyboard clicks into the tome you have in your hands.

Thanks, too, to Mike Craven (`theofficemaven.com`), Terry Walsh (`wegotserved.co.uk`), and Philip Churchill (`mswhs.com`) for all their help and support.

Publisher's Acknowledgments

We're proud of this book; please send us your comments through our online registration form located at www.dummies.com/register/.

Some of the people who helped bring this book to market include the following:

Acquisitions and Editorial

Project Editor: Rebecca Huehls

Acquisitions Editors: Melody Layne, Steve Hayes, and Tiffany Ma

Sr. Copy Editor: Barry Childs-Helton

Technical Editor: Jason Dossett

Editorial Manager: Leah P. Cameron

Editorial Assistant: Amanda Foxworth

Sr. Editorial Assistant: Cherie Case

Cartoons: Rich Tennant (www.the5thwave.com)

Composition Services

Project Coordinator: Patrick Redmond

Layout and Graphics: Carl Byers, Carrie A. Cesavice, Reuben W. Davis, Joyce Haughey, Melissa K. Jester, Christine Williams

Proofreaders: David Faust, John Greenough, Sossity R. Smith

Indexer: Broccoli Information Management

Anniversary Logo Design: Richard Pacifico

Publishing and Editorial for Technology Dummies

   Richard Swadley, Vice President and Executive Group Publisher

   Andy Cummings, Vice President and Publisher

   Mary Bednarek, Executive Acquisitions Director

   Mary C. Corder, Editorial Director

Publishing for Consumer Dummies

   Diane Graves Steele, Vice President and Publisher

   Joyce Pepple, Acquisitions Director

Composition Services

   Gerry Fahey, Vice President of Production Services

   Debbie Stailey, Director of Composition Services

Contents at a Glance

Introduction 1

Part I: Getting Windows Home Server to Serve 7
Chapter 1: Bringing Windows Home Server to Life.............................9
Chapter 2: Installing the WHS Software 27

Part II: Setting Up the Network 37
Chapter 3: Bringing Computers into the Home Server Fold 39
Chapter 4: Adding Users and Controlling Passwords.........................55
Chapter 5: Using Built-In Shared Folders...75

Part III: Making the Most of Multimedia 95
Chapter 6: Sharing Music and Videos..97
Chapter 7: Recording and Playing TV 113
Chapter 8: Streaming with the Xbox 129
Chapter 9: Nailing Down Your Photos 141

Part IV: Sharing in the Wild 163
Chapter 10: Starting Remote Access..165
Chapter 11: Using Remote Access 189

Part V: Backing Up...205
Chapter 12: Running Backups..207
Chapter 13: Restoring a Dead Computer from Backup......................229
Chapter 14: Restoring Files from Backup 241
Chapter 15: Backing Up the Server 255

Part VI: Staying Alive and Well 265
Chapter 16: Monitoring System Health..267
Chapter 17: Breaking into the Server 277
Chapter 18: Adding and Retiring Drives 293
Chapter 19: Repairing and Recovering the Server 305

Part VII: The Part of Tens **319**

Chapter 20: Top Ten Health Traps Triaged 321

Chapter 21: Ten More Tricks with Windows Home Server 331

Index **341**

Table of Contents

Introduction *1*

About This Book 1
Foolish Assumptions 2
How This Book Is Organized 2
    Part I: Getting Windows Home Server to Serve 3
    Part II: Setting Up the Network 3
    Part III: Making the Most of Multimedia 3
    Part IV: Sharing in the Wild 3
    Part V: Backing Up 3
    Part VI: Staying Alive and Well 4
    Part VII: The Part of Tens 4
Icons Used in This Book 5
Where to Go from Here 5

Part 1: Getting Windows Home Server to Serve *7*

Chapter 1: Bringing Windows Home Server to Life 9

What Can You Do with Windows Home Server? 10
    Backing up and restoring 10
    Sharing folders 11
    Managing disks 12
    Accessing your network from far afield 14
    Keeping the home fires burning 15
    Streaming media 16
How Do You Control Windows Home Server? 16
    Welcome to the Console 16
    What happens behind the scenes 18
Knowing Windows Home Server's Limitations 19
    What Windows Home Server won't do 20
    Tapping into previous versions of a file 21
What Hardware Do You Need? 22
Choosing a Great Windows Home Server 24
Positioning the Server in Your Home or Office 26

Chapter 2: Installing the WHS Software 27

Do You Need to Install Windows Home Server? 28
Preparing to Install 29
Installing Windows Home Server 31

Part II: Setting Up the Network *37*

Chapter 3: Bringing Computers into the Home Server Fold .... .39
    Kick-Starting the Network 39
    Installing Windows Home Server Connector
        on a Windows XP Machine 42
    Installing Windows Home Server Connector
        on a Windows Vista Machine 46
    Configuring Windows Home Server 49

Chapter 4: Adding Users and Controlling Passwords .... .55
    Understanding User Control...56
    Raising the Bar for Passwords...57
    Adding New Users the Smart Way..60
    Using the Guest Account...65
    Synchronizing Passwords...68
    Changing Passwords the Old-Fashioned Way................................71
        On the server 71
        In Windows XP 72
        In Windows Vista 73

Chapter 5: Using Built-In Shared Folders 75
    Organizing Files with Shared Folders 76
    Finding the Shared Folders 77
        Opening shared files on the server 78
        Pinpointing each user's shared folder 79
    Controlling Access to Shared Folders 80
        Experiencing folder permissions firsthand............................80
        Changing shared folder permissions 82
    Controlling Shared Folders from the Console 84
        Creating new shared folders 86
        Usin' your noggin with sharin'..89
    Duplicating Shared Folders..90

Part III: Making the Most of Multimedia *95*

Chapter 6: Sharing Music and Videos 97
    Sharing from A to Z to PC to PC 98
    Playing From (and With) the Server 102
    Ripping to the Server...107
    Sharing C.R.A.P. Music on the Network...110

Chapter 7: Recording and Playing TV 113

Understanding Windows Home Server and Recorded TV.....................114
Storing Shows on Your Server..115
Creating a shared home for recorded TV...........................115
Moving recorded TV to the server....................................118
Recording TV directly to the server 124
Viewing TV Shows Stored on the Server..................................125
Why WHS Doesn't Back Up Recorded TV 126

Chapter 8: Streaming with the Xbox 129

Using an Xbox in Server Land 130
Getting Your Xbox to Play with the Server 131
Using a Media Center PC to Stream to an Xbox 137
Connecting an Xbox to a Media Center computer 137
Playing media files with a connected Xbox 139

Chapter 9: Nailing Down Your Photos 141

Using the Windows Tools..142
Modifying XP for Shared Photos 144
Viewing photos in the shared Photos folder 144
Moving photos from your camera to the shared Photos folder....148
Modifying the screen saver to use the shared Photos folder.......153
Modifying Vista for Shared Photos 155
Viewing photos in the shared Photos folder 155
Moving photos directly from your camera
to the shared Photos folder..156
Creating a screen saver from the shared Photos folder...............159

Part IV: Sharing in the Wild...*163*

Chapter 10: Starting Remote Access 165

Remote Access — the Good, the Bad, and the Really Frustrating.........166
An Overview of Remote Access Setup 167
Setting up the Server 169
Configuring Your Router 171
Establishing a Permanent Domain Name................................176
Spreading Out the Welcome Mat..179
Getting Connected for the First Time — or Maybe Not 182
My Encounter with the Seventh Ring..185

Chapter 11: Using Remote Access **189**

    Logging on to Your Windows Home Server Remotely.....................190

    Accessing Shared Folders 192

        Uploading files 194

        Downloading files 196

    Getting into the Windows Home Server Console.............................197

    Pulling Puppet Strings on Your Home Network's Computers 199

        Reviewing the ground rules 200

        Getting logged on 201

Part V: Backing Up *205*

Chapter 12: Running Backups **207**

    Mired in Myriad Backups 208

        Backing up files on network computers 208

        Backing up shared folders with Folder Duplication 212

        Shadow copies in Windows Home Server 214

        Understanding what Vista is backing up 214

        Checking Windows XP for backup routines 215

    Unraveling the Mess 216

    Setting Up Server Backups That Serve You 217

        Backing up on your time 218

        Choosing what gets backed up 220

        Keeping backups 222

    Checking That Backups Run Smoothly 224

Chapter 13: Restoring a Dead Computer from Backup **229**

    Dealing with Home Computer Restore Restrictions.......................230

    Restoring a Hard Drive 231

    Rolling Your Own Home Computer Restore CD 238

Chapter 14: Restoring Files from Backup **241**

    Restoring a Backed-Up File 242

    Restoring a Shared Folder File with Windows XP,
        Media Center, or Tablet PC..246

    Restoring a Shared Folder File with Vista Business,
        Enterprise, or Ultimate 250

Chapter 15: Backing Up the Server **255**

    Mapping Out Windows Home Server Storage 256

    Using Folder Duplication...257

    Making Offsite Backups of Shared Files 258

        Copying files to an external drive 259

        Choosing an online backup provider...263

Part VI: Staying Alive and Well.................*265*

Chapter 16: Monitoring System Health 267

Understanding the Network Health Indicator 268
What Can Go Wrong? 271
How to Fix Health Problems 272

Chapter 17: Breaking into the Server 277

Deciding to Break In..278
Logging On to the Server with RDP 280
Attaching a Printer with RDP..283
Restoring a Previous Version of a Shared File with RDP.....................286
Giving Your Server a Permanent IP Address 290

Chapter 18: Adding and Retiring Drives 293

Knowing When and What to Feed the Maw 294
Adding a New Internal Hard Drive 297
Adding a New External Hard Drive 300
Retiring an Old Drive Safely...302

Chapter 19: Repairing and Recovering the Server 305

Dealing with Lost Passwords...306
Fixing a Broken Server Hard Drive..308
    Primary versus secondary drives 309
    Replacing a broken secondary drive 310
    Repairing the primary drive..313

Part VII: The Part of Tens.................................*319*

Chapter 20: Top Ten Health Traps Triaged 321

No Spyware Protection..322
Backup Warning...323
Backup Warning, New Hard Drive 325
Backup Error..325
Backup Server Error 326
Storage Status, Not Enough Room 327
Storage Status, Failing Hard Drive 328
Passwords Do Not Match 329
Updates Are Ready..329
Antivirus Out of Date...330

Chapter 21: Ten More Tricks with Windows Home Server **331**

Installing (and Uninstalling) Add-Ins 332
Launching Programs from Windows Home Server Console...................334
Changing Your Remote Access Page with Whiist....................................335
Running uTorrent on the Server 336
Wake on LAN for Home Server 336
Uploading Photos to Flickr with PhotoSync...337
Streaming Away from Home with WebGuide 337
Streaming to Your TiVo...338
Streaming to Your Phone with LobsterTunes..338
Finding More Add-Ins..339

Index *341*

Introduction

*W*hen I first heard that Microsoft was working on a new, supposedly dumbed-down version of Windows Server for use by mere mortals, I let out a groan. Literally. Years ago, Windows Small Business Server had the same original premise that Windows Home Server has today — a trimmed-down version of Windows Server for people who don't wear white lab coats. I worked on the first beta versions of Small Business Server, and I carry emotional scars about it to this day. So it was with great trepidation, and more than a little skepticism, that I installed an early beta test copy of Windows Home Server on my own home network. I came away more than a little amazed.

Windows Small Business Server rates as a snarly, Byzantine, overwhelming glob of software that any sane person avoids like anopheles mosquitoes. Installing a gigantic Windows Server program like Exchange Server on your home network is like parking the *QE II* in your driveway. The average home user needs the fancy Windows Server Web hosting (and its ubiquitous security holes) like a jogger needs a wheelbarrow. Windows Server in *my* home? No way. I've got better ways to waste my time, ya know?

Fortunately, Windows Home Server is different. Way different. In fact, the only similarity I can find between Windows Server and Windows **Home** Server is the name.

If you have a network at home or in your small office, and you haven't yet tried Windows Home Server, you're in for a treat. It's the first Microsoft product I know about that goes in slick, with very little fuss, and performs useful tricks right out of the box. You don't need a Ph.D. in Windows Server Arcana. In fact, if you never do anything more than stick the WHS box on your network and forget about it, you can sleep better at night, knowing that your data's backed up. And you needn't lift a finger.

About This Book

This book shows you how to get Windows Home Server to peacefully coexist with your network — and what to do with WHS once it's in. In usual

For Dummies fashion, I show you how to accomplish what you want to do with a minimum of fuss and a maximum of clarity — one very straightforward step at a time — and I promise I won't put you to sleep in the process.

In addition to showing you what you need to know today, in this book I also try to lay the groundwork for your future Adventures in Home Server Land, fully realizing that new killer applications could arrive any day. That's because Windows Home Server rates as more than an operating system — it's a *platform*. (At least, that's what Microsoft's marketing department calls it.) I fully expect that WHS will take on a life of its own as more and more software developers discover that a home network can do more than turn on the Jacuzzi every afternoon and warn you when you're running out of milk. We're just beginning to see applications appearing that are designed specifically for Windows Home Server — the nascent platform is just beginning to, uh, plat. These are exciting times, and WHS is an exciting product!

The Cheat Sheet at the beginning of the book lists my choices as the most important things you need to know about WHS. Tear it out, tape it to your monitor, pass it around to other folks with home networks, and be sure to tell 'em Woody shares their pain.

Foolish Assumptions

I assume that you already have a home or small office network, and that you know how to use either Windows XP or Windows Vista — possibly both — depending on what kind of computers inhabit your network.

If you have an Xbox 360 and you want to use it with Windows Home Server (believe me, you do!), I assume you know how to get your Xbox cranked up.

If you're running Windows Small Business Server, you can follow along here, too: I won't tell you anything in particular about SBS, but Windows Home Server backs up SBS-connected PCs like ringin' a bell.

How This Book Is Organized

You can read the book from front to back, or you can dive right into the chapter of your choice. Either way works just fine. Any time a concept is mentioned that isn't covered in depth in that chapter, you'll find a cross-reference to another chapter to find out more. If you're looking for something specific, check out either the table of contents or the index.

Part I: Getting Windows Home Server to Serve

If you haven't yet bought a Windows Home Server, look at this part for a few key considerations — and limitations. If WHS didn't come preinstalled on its own box, I show you how to install it. Then I step you through setting up the box and plugging it in.

Part II: Setting Up the Network

Here you find out how to get WHS going for the first time — and you *don't* set up WHS from the WHS computer itself. Discover the art of plugging computers into the grid, adding users, establishing passwords wisely, adding printers, and using the built-in shared folders.

Part III: Making the Most of Multimedia

This is the part that puts the WOW in WHS: getting music, photos, videos, recorded TV, and movies to work across your WHS network. Discover what you can and can't do (Digital Rights Management — what I call "C.R.A.P. music and movies" — will drive ya nuts). This part is also where I explain how to hook up an Xbox to play music and TV shows stored on your Windows Home Server.

Part IV: Sharing in the Wild

Another whiz-bang feature of WHS is shared folders. Here you find out how to control access to the shared folders, and set up Remote Access, so you can log on to your WHS network and any computer on the network, from anywhere in the world.

Part V: Backing Up

B-o-r-i-n-g. Backup elicits snores until the very moment your hard drive dives into the bit bucket. That's when you'll wish you had read this part. WHS contains a remarkably smart, capable, hands-off backup system. Spend a few minutes getting to know it. Then remember this part of the book the next time your computer crashes, or the kids completely screw up one of their machines.

Part VI: Staying Alive and Well

It's 10:00. Do you know where your children are? WHS won't tell you that much, but it will tell you whether their PC has its antivirus programs up-to-date, or if the latest backup failed because the cat chewed the USB cable. This part also talks about getting into the WHS box, adding and retiring hard drives, and the like.

Part VII: The Part of Tens

So you gotta ask yourself, why isn't this Part X? I dunno. Sometimes life doesn't quite turn out the way you planned, eh? This part is my favorite part because it points you in new directions, giving tantalizing glimpses into the new kinds of WHS application software currently being built in a garage near you. Life is short. Eat dessert — and read the Part of Tens — first.

Icons Used in This Book

While perusing this book, you'll notice some icons in the margins screaming for your attention. Each one has a purpose.

When I'm jumping up and down on one foot with an idea so absolutely cool that I can't stand it anymore — that's when I stick in a Tip icon. You can browse through any chapter and hit the very highest points by jumping from Tip to Tip.

You don't need to memorize the stuff marked with this icon, but you should try to remember that this icon indicates something special that you need to know in future WHS endeavors.

Achtung! ¡Cuidado! Anyplace you see a Warning icon, you can be sure that I've been burnt — badly — in the past. Mind your fingers. These situations are really, really mean suckers.

If your hat's propeller doesn't work very well, you can skip these snippets. But if you want to understand the *why* behind the *how*, these icons point the way.

Here's how I call out the inside story — pointed facts that Microsoft might find embarrassing, school-of-hard-knocks advice, the kind of straight (sometimes politically incorrect) talk that shows you what's really happening. Hit my Web site, AskWoody.com, for the latest.

Where to Go from Here

If you want your voice to be heard, you can contact the publisher of the *For Dummies* books by clicking the Contact Us link on the publisher's Web site at www.dummies.com or by sending snail mail to Wiley Publishing, Inc., 10475 Crosspoint Boulevard, Indianapolis, IN 46256.

You can contact me at woody@AskWoody.com. I can't answer all the questions I get — man, there ain't enough hours in the day! — but I take some of the best and post them on AskWoody.com frequently.

Speaking of AskWoody.com, drop by! I bet you'll be pleasantly surprised by the straight story, and coverage of important news items that you can't find anywhere else. And I have hundreds of volunteers who have written more than half a million answers to computer questions, all accessible by clicking the Ask A Question tab on my Web page.

Confused about where to go next? Well, you can flip the page. Or you can flip a coin. Or you could hire a hundred monkeys and have them sit down at a hundred PCs and see how long it takes them to come up with the first chapter.

Part I
Getting Windows Home Server to Serve

The 5th Wave   By Rich Tennant

"Okay, make sure this is right. 'Looking
for caring companion who likes old movies,
nature walks and quiet evenings at home.
Knowledge of configuring a Windows Home
Server with a Vista laptop and XBox 360,
a plus.'"

In this part . . .

Windows Home Server makes a great slave, but a horrible master.

As long as you stick to the prescribed installation procedure — described here in loving detail — your Windows Home Server box will purr like a kitten, and you'll never have to deal with the Byzantine underbelly of the beast. At least, WHS's sharp fangs won't appear until you try to do something strange, like set up an old printer. Follow the rules here and you only see the Dr. Jekyll persona of the server; with a little luck, you'll never even know that Mr. Hyde hides deep inside.

This part of *Windows Home Server For Dummies* takes you on a guided tour of Windows Home Server, its features and foibles, and then escorts you through choosing and installing the WHS box itself. If you bought WHS as a shrink-wrapped, standalone product (as opposed to buying it preinstalled on a new PC), this part also shows you how to get WHS installed on the PC of your choice.

Chapter 1

Bringing Windows Home Server to Life

In This Chapter

▶ Making great things happen with Windows Home Server

▶ Dealing with WHS's limitations

▶ Controlling Windows Home Server with a "headless horseman" console

▶ Choosing a fabulous Windows Home Server — cheap

▶ Sticking the Home Server box in your home or small office

▶ Installing the shrink-wrapped version of Windows Home server

*A*s a first approximation, you should think of your Windows Home Server as a washing machine.

Okay, okay. It's a washing machine with a LAN cable and a gaggle of hard drives. Picky, picky. I'm pushing the analogy a bit. But in many ways, your Windows Home Server box just sits there. No keyboard to soak up spilled coffee. No mouse accumulating gunk on its slick little feet. No 27-inch widescreen LCD monitor with Dolby 7.1 surround sound and an independently powered subwoofer that pushes more air than a Lear Jet.

Naw, *it just sits there*.

Once you get the hang of it, and customize the software in a couple of ways, your Windows Home Server sort of fades into the background. Then you needn't lift a finger. You can completely forget about it. Until the day the hard drive on one of your PC dies, or you discover that one bit in your magnum opus flipped and Word can't read it anymore, or you're vacationing on Mt. Denali and the boss calls to say she needs that report you left back at the house *right now*, or the kids invite a friendly little rootkit to take up residence on the family computer.

That's when you'll thank your lucky stars that Windows Home Server's sittin' in the background doin' its thing.

I can't recall any Microsoft product (except for Notepad, maybe) that works so well, so easily, with so little fuss, right out of the box. If you have two or more computers networked together — doesn't matter if you only use them to send email and surf the Web, or print cross-stitch patterns and play Gears of War — some day, in some way, Windows Home Server will save your bacon.

What Can You Do with Windows Home Server?

For a little box that just sits there, Windows Home Server covers some very important bases. But it doesn't try to cover *all* the bases. That's part of the genius of Windows Home Server: Its designers didn't try to solve every problem, didn't cater to every wish list, didn't let the ugly Windows Server 2003 genie — the guy inside WHS with Robin Williams's voice and Hannibal Lecter's soul — out of the bottle.

From my point of view, Windows Home Server does just six things — and each one rates its own section . . .

Backing up and restoring

At the top of the feature heap, Windows Home Server backs up all the data on all your computers (see Figure 1-1). Automatically. No setup wizards, other than a very simple hook-up program. No weird jargon.

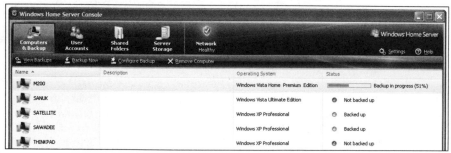

Figure 1-1: Windows Home Server backups are a breeze.

Here's what you can expect if you use WHS as your backup central:

- ✔ **If you need to retrieve an old copy of a file, WHS makes it easy.** I talk about the ins and outs in Part V.

- ✔ **WHS Backup lets you restore an entire hard drive.** This ain't your father's backup program: if one of the PCs on your network suddenly loses its C: drive — or you get clobbered by a virus, or a rogue Windows automatic update freezes your Windows XP machine tighter than a penguin's tail feathers — WHS's computer restore feature (Chapter 13) lets you bring back an earlier version of the entire hard drive with very little fuss.

- ✔ **If you shell out the shekels and put two or more hard drives in your WHS computer, Windows Home Server *mirrors* backup data:** Separate, individually recoverable copies of the backup reside on more than one hard drive. That way, if one of the WHS computer's hard drives fail, you can resurrect everything. Try doing that with your one-button-backup hard drive.

- ✔ **The backup program itself packs lots of smarts.** For example, if you have the same file on two different drives, or even on two different computers, WHS only maintains one backup. In fact, if pieces of files are duplicated across multiple machines, only one copy of each piece — each Lego block, if you will — gets stored. WHS maintains a table that keeps track of which piece goes where on what machine.

    Very slick.

Sharing folders

Any server worth its salt lets you store folders on the server and get at those folders from other computers on the network. That's the premise behind *shared folders*.

If you've struggled with shared folders in Windows XP or Vista (or even Windows 98 or Windows for Workgroups 3.11, for that matter), you have no doubt become conversant with \\really\convoluted\folder\names. Heaven help ya if you want to look at the photos of your summer vacation three years ago, and can't remember if they're sitting on the TV room computer's D: drive, or the bedroom's C:\Documents and Settings\Bill\Desktop\Vacation Pics folder.

Windows Home Server creates a small set of pre-defined folders for you, and you can readily add more. People using your network can easily find the folders — and (if you give them permission) stick stuff in the folders and take stuff out. The great saving grace about WHS shared folders: they sport simple names like, oh, Photos or Music (see Figure 1-2). None of this \\computername\drive\folder\subfolder garbage.

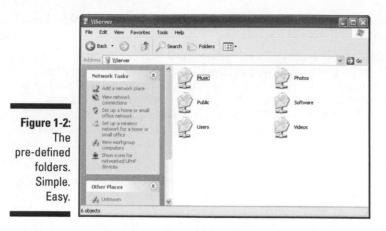

Figure 1-2:
The
pre-defined
folders.
Simple.
Easy.

As the Reverend C.A. Goodrich famously wrote in 1827, *There is as much meaning in the old adage, and the observance of which let me urge you as a remedy for every degree of evil I advert to — "Have a place for every thing, and keep every thing in its proper place."* Maintaining one shared location for everything, and keeping everything in its place, can simplify your life tremendously, whether you advert to degrees of evil or not. (Could somebody please tell me how to advert to a degree? Sounds like fun.)

When your Great Aunt Martha wants to look at your family photos, she can sit down at any computer on the network, and she can see this folder called `Photos`. *Mirabile dictu*, that's where the photos reside. Auntie Martha doesn't have to know the name of the computer that contains the photos, the drive they're on, or any other computer arcana. They're just there.

As you get more adept at using WHS, you'll discover that you can create new shared folders, grant access permissions, and the like (see Chapter 5). But straight out of the box, the folders suddenly appear out of thin air — and they make sense.

Managing disks

Windows Home Server takes care of disk management behind the scenes so you don't have to.

You'll never know, or care, which drive on the WHS computer holds what folders, or which files.

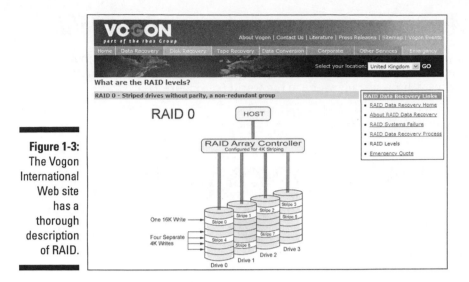

Figure 1-3:
The Vogon
International
Web site
has a
thorough
description
of RAID.

If you have more than one hard drive on your WHS computer, backups get mirrored automatically. Computer geeks tend to think of that as a *RAID* feature — Redundant Array of Inexpensive Disks, see Figure 1-3 — but WHS doesn't use RAID technology. RAID's too complicated for most home users to maintain, and it's married to specific kinds of hardware.

The Windows Home Server approach to highly reliable data storage works with plain, everyday hard drives, and the kinds of hard drive controllers you find on any PC these days. It's all done with smoke and mirrors — and some smokin' good programming. No fancy hardware. Nothing to break down. The following list takes a closer look at what you don't have to worry about:

- In the WHS world, disk drive volumes and folders get extended as needed and you don't have to fuss with the details.

- Individual folders can and do reside on two or more disks. You needn't deal with any of it.

- When the WHS machine starts running out of disk space, it tells you. Install another drive (see Chapter 18) and the drive is absorbed into the collective, Borg-style: more space becomes available, and you don't need to care about any of the details.

  Okay, you *do* have to do one thing: When you run out of space, you have to add more. But disks are cheap and easy to install.

Accessing your network from far afield

If you so desire, Windows Home server can open up your entire home or small office network so you can log on to any computer on your network from any browser, anywhere in the world (see Figure 1-4).

Figure 1-4:
Log on to any of your home computers from Atchafalaya to Timbuktu.

That sounds scary, but (at least at this point) the security looks mighty good.

WHS's *Remote Access* feature takes a little while to set up (see Chapters 10 and 11), but once it's in place, you can

- ✔ Log on to your server.
- ✔ Upload or download files from a specific folder.
- ✔ Use any pre-ordained PC on your network as if you were sitting right in front of it. (Give or take a little time for a slow connection, anyway.)
- ✔ Let other people log on to your home network and retrieve files in specially designated folders. (If you're clever and set restrictions properly, that is.)

Geeks might be reminded of something called an *FTP server*, which performs a similar function, allowing people to get into a folder from the Internet and send files to the folder or retrieve files from it. Part of Remote Access acts like FTP, but it employs an entirely different technology: Windows Home Server doesn't use FTP.

Having your own Internet-accessible repository can be really handy, and keep casual surfers from leafing through your private pics. Instead of posting pics of your new toddler, uh, toddling, on photo-sharing sites such as Flickr or dotPhoto or Webshots, you simply stick the pics in a shared folder on your own Windows Home Server and give all your family and friends the Web address and password that'll let 'em in.

Keeping the home fires burning

Windows Home Server constantly monitors all the computers on your network and gives you a concise, centralized "health report" (see Figure 1-5).

Windows Vista computers on your home or small office network keep WHS abreast of the current status of patches and virus signature file updates. Vista computers also notify the WHS server if they're running out of disk space. Windows XP and Vista machines both keep WHS apprised of their backup status.

For a thorough look at the warnings on offer — and what to do about them — see Chapters 16 and 20.

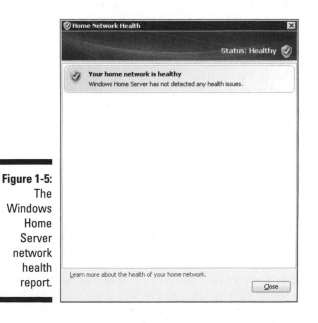

Figure 1-5:
The Windows Home Server network health report.

Streaming media

Windows Home Server doesn't provide the media streaming capabilities that you find in Windows Media Center Edition, or Windows Vista Home Premium or Ultimate. However, if you treat your server nicely and discover how to say "please" (see Part III), it will hold your media collection, and feed the collection to a Media Center or Home Premium PC. If you have an Xbox 360, you can connect it to your Media Center or Vista Home Premium (or Ultimate) PC, and that PC, in turn, can pull the media off the server.

How Do You Control Windows Home Server?

Windows Home Server was designed from the ground up to run on a "headless" computer. That means, quite simply, that a fully functional WHS server can survive with a LAN cable, a power cord, and absolutely nothing else sticking out of the machine.

Many WHS servers don't have a CD drive. Some don't even have a rudimentary video card.

If you buy Windows Home Server in a shrink-wrapped package, you'll need to connect a CD drive, keyboard, mouse and monitor to the server box long enough to get the WHS software loaded. (See Chapter 2 for details.) But once WHS comes up for air the first time, you can unplug all that accoutrement, and strip the machine down to its LAN cable, power cord, and nothing else. WHS won't mind a bit.

Welcome to the Console

You control Windows Home Server through a program *that doesn't run on the WHS server*. Windows Home Server Console runs on one of the computers on your network. In fact, you can run the Console from *any* Windows XP or Windows Vista computer on your network.

As soon as you have your Windows Home Server set up and plugged into the network, the Console setup goes something like this:

1. Stick the Windows Home Server Connector CD into any computer on the network and run the Connector setup program (see Figure 1-6).

   The Connector setup program searches your network to see if it can find a Windows Home Server.

2. If the setup program determines that it's never been run before on this particular network, it steps you through the seven steps necessary to get the WHS server box going (see Chapter 3 for details).

   You have to enter a product key (unless the WHS software came pre-installed and pre-validated), give the server a name, create a super-password, help WHS phone home and update itself, and generally bring WHS up to snuff.

3. Once the Connector setup program has the WHS box's seatbelt fastened, it puts all the networking goodies on the PC, gets the backup software going, and then installs the Windows Home Server Console (see Figure 1-7).

Figure 1-6:
Run the
Connector
setup
program on
every PC
on your
network.

Although it's true that Windows Home Server works with Macs and various flavors of Unix/Linux PCs, you have to interact with the server manually: Microsoft doesn't supply anything like a Connector CD or the Home Server Console for Macs or Unix/Linux PCs.

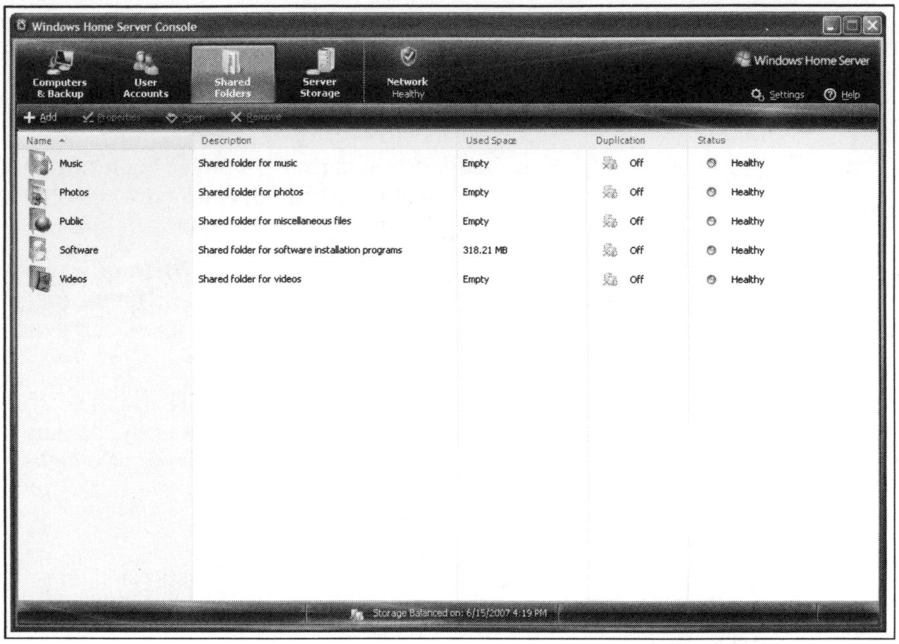

Figure 1-7:
The WHS
Console
controls the
server
remotely.

What happens behind the scenes

The installer program on the Windows Home Connector CD accomplishes
much, much more than doing the initial setup of the Windows Home Server,
uh, server and cranking up the Windows Home Server Console. Behind the
scenes, when you run the CD on your Windows XP or Vista computer, the
Connector installs and configures dozens of programs that tie deep into the
guts of Windows XP or Vista.

So while you may believe that you're controlling Windows Home Server, in
fact its minions latch onto your PC and every PC you add to the WHS network, tying it all together.

That isn't necessarily bad. But it does mean that your PCs will pick up a
bunch of software they've never had to run before.

Perhaps most notably, the Windows Home Connector CD installs a gigantic
program on Windows XP computers called the .NET Framework. (.NET
Framework is baked into Windows Vista, so the Connector doesn't have to
install it.) .NET Framework has a reputation for being big, slow and buggy,
although it's been getting better. ("Buggy?" you ask. Well, yes. Take a look at
Microsoft's Security Bulletin MS07-040, if you're looking for examples.)
Whether you like it or not, when you connect a Windows XP computer to a
Windows Home Server network, you get .NET Framework.

In addition to installing new software, the Connector CD is responsible for establishing hundreds of default settings. In my experience, it performs the job admirably well.

Behind-the-scene activities include these:

- ✓ **Defining backup locations:** Unless you change the settings (see Chapter 12), the Windows Home Server Connector backs up most of the data files on all the hard drives inside your PC. It does not back up system files, although it does back up USB-attached external drives. Surprisingly, it does not back up recorded television programs.

- ✓ **Linking to initial shared folders:** These include basics such as Photos and Music. Your Windows XP or Vista machine suddenly acquires new shortcuts on the desktop that point to the shared folders on the server.

- ✓ **Turning off remote access:** You have to go into WHS and quite deliberately give it permission to grant access to your network from the Internet (see Chapter 10).

The Connector CD also installs the programs necessary to monitor your system's health, and keep the WHS server apprised of the computer's condition.

Once you've finished running the Connector CD on a specific PC, it's your responsibility to

- ✓ Tell the WHS server about users on the PC (at least if you want to allow the users to work with the WHS server — see Chapter 4).

- ✓ Set up shared folders on the server for users on the PC (Chapter 5).

- ✓ Add printers to the server (Chapter 17).

- ✓ If you have Windows XP Media Center or Vista Home Premium (or Ultimate), unlock shared media folders and enable the Guest account so other computers on your network can get to them via the WHS server (Chapter 6).

Knowing Windows Home Server's Limitations

Have you ever bought a new product and discovered — an hour or a day or a week down the road — that it can't do what you need it to do? Hey, I sympathize. Been there. Done that.

I wanted to carve out a small part of this book to explain what Windows Home Server *doesn't*.

What Windows Home Server won't do

By and large, WHS can do anything you would expect a server to do, and much more. But there are a few shortcomings that you should understand before you knock yourself silly trying to accomplish the impossible:

- ✔ **Windows Home Server only supports ten users (plus the Guest account).** You can have ten different user names on your network — and that's all she wrote. If you need to allow more than ten people to use your network (remember *The Brady Bunch*? I was trying to forget it, too . . .), they'll have to start sharing user names.

- ✔ **Windows Home Server only supports ten PCs on the network.** Perhaps surprisingly, you can put two WHS servers on the same network, and you can even stick a WHS server on a Small Business Server network. But you can't have more than ten PCs connected simultaneously to a single WHS server.

- ✔ **You can't use a laptop as a Windows Home Server.** That's a real pity because, all other things being equal, a laptop with a dead screen would be an ideal candidate for a server.

- ✔ **Only NTFS-formatted drives get backed up.** Chances are good that all of your network's hard drives use the newer NTFS file system, instead of the old Windows 98-and-earlier FAT. Windows Home Server won't even try to back up a non-NTFS drive, so if you have a USB "thumb" drive that's formatted with FAT, it won't make the cut. You have to format your thumb drive with NTFS first. (For details, consult your thumb drive manufacturer's Web site.)

- ✔ **Windows Home Server won't back up laptops running on battery power.** Windows Home Server's automatic backup will back up any Windows XP or Vista computer, but it won't back up a laptop unless the laptop's plugged into the wall. That makes sense: Backups can draw a lot of power, and the last thing you need is to have your laptop's battery die in the middle of a backup.

- ✔ **WHS won't give the full health report on a computer running Windows XP.** When WHS reports on computers attached to the network, it only shows the backup status of Windows XP machines; there's no attempt to show the status of updates or other indicators from the Windows Security Center. By contrast, Windows Vista machines report whether the firewall is enabled, whether the antivirus software is up to date and working, and whether Windows Update is set to update Windows automatically.

- ✔ **Remote access to a computer doesn't work with certain versions of Windows.** If you want to run WHS's Remote Access to reach into your network from the Internet and run one of the computers on your home (or small office) network, the computer that's being suborned — the one that acts like a puppet while you pull the strings from afar — must be running Windows XP Professional, Windows Vista Ultimate, Vista Business, or Vista Enterprise. Alas, XP Home, Vista Home Basic, and Vista Home Premium aren't sufficiently endowed. In other words, XP Pro, Vista Ultimate, Vista Business, and Vista Enterprise PCs can play Pinocchio to your puppeteer. All the other operating systems don't have strings that can be pulled.

Tapping into previous versions of a file

Windows Home Server supports "previous versions," but the feature probably doesn't work the way you think it does.

If you have Windows Vista Business, Enterprise, or Ultimate, you already have a shadow-copy feature, and it works on all files and folders on your Vista computer. Once a day, usually around midnight, these versions of Vista take a snapshot of all the files on your computer that you've changed during the previous day and store the snapshots — creating what is commonly called a *shadow copy*. Anytime you mess up a file that's located on your Business, Enterprise, or Ultimate computer, you can right-click the file, choose Properties, then click the Previous Versions tab and bring back any earlier snapshot of the file.

That's a very powerful capability, which I discuss at length in *Windows Vista Timesaving Techniques For Dummies* (Wiley Publishing, Inc.). Installing WHS doesn't turn off the feature you've already paid for — but the Vista Business, Enterprise, and Ultimate shadow-copy feature works only on files located on the Vista PC. Files stored on your Windows Home Server, uh, server don't inherit the shadow copying capability from Vista Business, Enterprise, or Ultimate.

Here's where things get complicated.

Windows Home Server keeps shadow copies, but only for files stored in shared folders on the server. WHS doesn't reach into your Windows XP or Vista computer to make shadow copies, but it does make shadow copies of your data files on the server. It automatically takes snapshots of all the altered shared files and folders *on the server* twice a day — at noon and midnight every day. But the method and the relative ease of access differ — depending on what version of Windows XP or Vista your computer is running:

 ✔ **If you run Windows XP Service Pack 2 (either Home or Pro),** you can use this Windows Home Server "previous versions" capability to easily bring back one of the snapshots, using a Previous Versions. (See Chapter 14.)

 ✔ **If you run Vista Business, Enterprise or Ultimate,** you can get at the previous versions of files on the server using the same technique.

 ✔ **If you have Windows Vista Home Basic or Premium** — and you probably do — you can still get at the snapshots of server files, but retrieving them is cumbersome and error prone (again, see Chapter 14).

While WHS does, technically, support "previous versions," the previous-version snapshots get taken twice a day, on a fixed schedule. They only cover files on the server — there's no independent "previous versions" support for files on the rest of the network's PCs, even if they're backed up every night. Retrieving the previous versions of files on the server is easy with Vista Business, Enterprise, or Ultimate — or, for that matter, with Windows XP. Paradoxically, it's considerably more difficult with Vista Home Basic or Premium.

What Hardware Do You Need?

Microsoft publishes a set of minimum hardware requirements for Windows Home Server. As is the case with most Microsoft minimum requirements, you can stretch things a bit and still run the product reasonably well.

Don't even *think* about installing Windows Home Server in your home or office unless you have a functioning network. If you're going to try to reach into your home network from afar, using WHS's Remote Access capability, you also need a reasonably fast Internet connection (ADSL, cable, satellite, whatever). Specifically:

 ✔ WHS won't help you set up a network. You need to have one working before you can install WHS. (If you need help setting up a network, see my *Windows Vista All-In-One Desk Reference For Dummies* or *Windows XP All-In-One Desk Reference For Dummies*.) Microsoft designed WHS to go on an existing network with two or more PCs, but you really need to have only one PC on the network in order to get WHS to work.

 ✔ I hate to burst any bubbles here, but running a crossover cable between two PCs doesn't count as a functioning network. Sorry, Charlie.

 ✔ The network's *router* (you can call it a *hub* or a *switch*) must have at least one available jack on the back, so you can plug in your WHS server. Although it may be physically possible to configure a WHS server using a wireless network connection, you could go insane trying.

✔ I know people who have tried to put a WHS server on a network that uses a dial-up Internet connection. They use Windows' Internet Connection Sharing to get onto the Internet. You may think of such people as Luddites; I think of them as deluded. They pull hair out of their heads in massive clumps.

If you buy WHS pre-installed on a computer, skip the rest of this section entirely: every recent computer is capable of running Windows Home Server, and the one you bought will no doubt work well.

On the other hand, if you're going to install WHS on your own computer, you need to pay attention to a small handful of specific details. Many of us *woosh-goons* (that's what I call WHS aficionados) stick WHS on an old PC, one that was destined to accumulate dust anyway. Re-using old hardware is good for the environment and for the pocketbook. Most old — nay, ancient — computers can run WHS quite well, if you keep these few things in mind:

✔ **Make sure all your WHS hardware has Windows 2003 drivers.** Some people report success installing Windows XP drivers on a Windows Home Server box, but others find themselves in the seventh ring of Server Hell. If you have an old PC with an obscure network card, hop over to the card manufacturer's Web site and download the Windows 2003 driver. Can't find a Win2K3 driver? Then replace the hardware. Life's too short.

✔ **Get 512 MB of memory.** If you already have more than 512 MB of memory on your designated WHS server, think about scalping it, and using it on another computer. Bone-stock WHS doesn't need more than 512 MB; you'll never notice the difference if you get more (so why get it?). Of course, if you intend to add new programs to your server — something to monitor the quantity of milk curdling in the fridge, turn on the fog lights in the bathroom, and bring the Jacuzzi to a slow boil, simultaneously — you might need more memory.

✔ **You need to boot from a DVD — once.** A WHS server needs a DVD drive like a surfer needs a Great White. After you have WHS installed on an old PC, the DVD drive just takes up space. But if you use a removable (say, USB) DVD drive to install WHS, you need to make sure that your old computer can boot from the DVD drive. (*D'oh!*)

✔ Just like points on *Whose Line Is It Anyway*, **the graphics card, keyboard, mouse, and monitor don't matter.** You use them once to get the PC set up and then (so far as the server is concerned) you can throw them away.

The other, official minimal requirements are — truly — minimal. Every PC made in the last five (maybe ten) years should be able to handle the load: a Pentium 3 running at 1 GHz; an 80GB hard drive; a network adapter; and the motherboard has to follow the ACPI power-saving spec.

Choosing a Great Windows Home Server

If you're in the market for a new Windows Home Server computer — or if you're going to cobble something together with the Frankenstein pieces sitting around your house — you may be pleasantly surprised to find that WHS doesn't need much at all. You may be equally surprised to find that spending a few extra zlotys on some unexpected pieces of hardware can make a big difference in how well your system works.

From my (admittedly jaded) experience, these bits and pieces make a real difference in how well WHS works now, and will work in the future:

- ✔ **Cooling:** Really. WHS servers typically pack a lot of hot components inside a small box, and you need to keep them cool. With WHS up 24/7, and many WHS servers stuck inside stuffy closets, heat can rapidly become enemy #1. Recent studies show that hard drives aren't as sensitive to heat as once thought (see "Failure Trends in a Large Disk Drive Population" at `labs.google.com/papers/disk_failures.pdf`), but other parts of your computer will wear out faster — if they don't melt down literally — when they run hot. The solution? Fans. Lots of them. You might even consider putting a high-quality desk fan next to the box, to keep cool air flowing.

- ✔ **Multiple hard drives:** Given a choice between one big hard drive and two small ones, go for two — or, better, three — smaller drives. WHS works better when it has two drives to "mirror" data stored on the server, and it works best with the system itself stuck on a third drive. You can always add more hard drives later, but you'll get maximum protection from the get-go if you start with two or more drives.

  If you stick USB hard drives on your WHS server, don't attach them to USB hubs — you know, those cheap little gizmos that let you turn one USB port into four or eight. USB hubs work fine for mice and electric coffee warmers, but they're really slow when two or more attached pieces of equipment are vying for attention. One USB hub controlling two overworked drives performs about as well as one guy playing both parts in *Dueling Banjos*.

- ✔ **UPS:** Nope, we're not talking big brown trucks here. No matter where you live, no matter how reliable your power supply, you need an *uninterrupted power supply* (UPS), both to keep the WHS server running in the event of a power hiccup, and to minimize weird power disruptions.

✔ **Fast Ethernet:** You can run WHS on a plain-Jane 100Mbps Ethernet network connection (also called 100Base-T or, confusingly, "fast Ethernet"). But if you start streaming videos, you're going to want the fastest Ethernet you can find — which usually means 1 Gbps (which also goes by the names "Gigabit Ethernet" and "1000Base-T"). Buying a 1Gbps Ethernet card for your WHS server isn't enough; your network's router (hub, switch) has to support a 1-gigabyte-per-second speed, too.

If you stick a 1Gbps card in your server, it won't do much good unless the other PCs on your network can run at 1 Gbps, too. From what I've seen, moving up to 1 Gbps doesn't make much difference with backups — they take all night anyway. But it can make a difference if you're streaming high definition TV shows or movies to, say, an Xbox, and it most certainly will make a difference if you stream more than one video at a time.

If you're into the little things, you can also add the following bits and pieces, but you probably won't notice much difference:

✔ **More USB 2 controllers:** Here's one they don't teach in Windows school. At times, WHS handles massive amounts of data, particularly when performing its daily backups, streaming multimedia, or copying big bunches of files. If you have two or more hard drives attached to your computer with USB cables (see the preceding), and they're both connected to the same USB controller inside the computer, the controller itself can present a significant bottleneck. The solution? Get more controllers. One controller per USB connection isn't a bad idea at all.

Alternatively, if techie language doesn't intimidate you, consider using external SATA hard drives. External SATA hard drives are just like regular *internal* SATA hard drives, except the hard drive's connectors and electrical thingies dangle out of your computer. External SATA doesn't bog down as badly as USB.

✔ **Faster drives:** For most people, most of the time, most WHS disk activity takes place at night. If your WHS server runs from 3:00 to 3:12 a.m. backing up the computers on your network, but a faster hard drive would cut the job down so it completed at 3:10 a.m., well, pardon me if I snore. But if you commonly stream videos on your WHS server, you should consider picking up faster hard drives.

There are several arcane and confusing variations, but if you first choose the technology (most likely Serial ATA inside your computer and either external SATA or IDE if you want to hang the drive out the back), and then briefly consider rotation speed (10,000 rpm runs faster than 7,500 rpm, but built-in caching can — and does — make a huge difference), you should be able to make a good decision. If you want the latest unbiased reviews, consult Tom's Hardware at tomshardware.com.

✓ **A cool-looking case:** No joke. If your WHS box looks cool, you're more likely to keep it somewhere that you can see it — so you're more likely to notice weird disk activity with the concomitant blinking lights. Besides, the top of your desk is cooler than your closet, eh?

Note that I didn't say anything about processor speed, or memory, or PCI slots, SCSI drives, SD card readers, cache, fingerprint readers, webcams, sound cards, video cards, or any of a million other hardware niceties than can make a difference with Windows XP or Vista machines. WHS doesn't use 'em, doesn't know, doesn't care. If you're going to use your server for something more than WHS, you may need more oomph — hey, it takes a lot of cycles to control a gig watt Christmas light display — but for standard WHS stuff, the processor and memory you have are good enough.

Positioning the Server in Your Home or Office

You should take these factors into consideration when you pick a place to stick your Windows Home Server server:

✓ **Plan on plugging the server into a router.** If you have only one router (typically, the one connected to your cable or DSL line), that limits locations — but not as much as you might think. You can run a LAN cable up to 300 feet or so (say, 90 meters) with no ill effect, providing you don't bend the cable too abruptly.

✓ **Heat is your enemy.** Dust, too. If dust bunnies live next to your WHS box, they'll move inside in fairly short order. And they'll, uh, procreate, in accordance with their essential bunny nature. Put the server someplace where it'll stay clean and cool.

✓ **You never need to touch the server.** If you bought your server with WHS pre-installed, you only need to plug it into an electrical outlet and your router. That's it. Yeah, you should vacuum out the box every few months, but that's the extent of it. (If you install WHS on your own hardware, you need to touch it just long enough to install the software, but that's all she wrote.)

✓ **But you do need a UPS.** It's an unfortunate fact of life. You can't plan on balancing your Windows Home Server on a 2 x 4, unless you reserve a spot nearby for an uninterruptible power source. Remember that UPSs generate a substantial amount of heat.

✓ **If you can, stick it on your desk.** Especially if you get one that looks like ET's glowing hockey puck. Otherwise you'll have to drag all your friends and neighbors over to the closet to look at the dern thing — a time-honored recipe for disaster. (Google "Fibber Magee's closet" for appropriate warnings.)

Chapter 2

Installing the WHS Software

· ·

In This Chapter

▶ Figuring out whether you need to install Windows Home Server

▶ Getting ready for the installation

▶ Following all the steps for a complete installation

▶ Deciding what to do next

· ·

*M*ost people buy Windows Home Server pre-installed on a, uh, Windows home server.

Ya gotta love the terminology.

If you find this all very confusing, you're simply exhibiting a bit of common sense that didn't manifest itself in the way Microsoft's marketeers chose the product's name.

Here's the source of the semantic confusion:

✔ A *server* is a computer — a box that you plug into the wall and strap onto your network — that stores folders that are shared among all the computers on the network, controls access to the shared folders, maybe runs a printer or two, and performs other feats of magic. Microsoft doesn't make or sell the hardware components called servers.

✔ *Windows Home Server*, on the other hand, is a specific computer *program*, developed by Microsoft, that makes a computer work like a server. Microsoft sells copies of Windows Home Server to PC manufacturers who stick the program inside their boxes and peddle the resulting PCs as Windows Home Server home servers, give or take a Department of Redundancy Department hiccup. HP, for example, buys a copy of Windows Home Server, modifies it a bit (with Microsoft's blessing), sticks it in a specific kind of PC, and sells the result as the HP MediaSmart Server.

Microsoft designed Windows Home Server so PC manufacturers could bundle the program with their own hardware, and sell complete home servers, hardware, software, and all. The HPs of the world buy Windows Home Server in quantities of hundreds of thousands, as Microsoft intended from the beginning.

As we went to press, Microsoft had also vowed to sell Windows Home Server to people who assemble their own systems. The precise definition of a "system builder" seems to be open to wide interpretation, but it seems clear that at least some copies of Windows Home Server will be sold separately, not bundled pre-installed on complete PCs.

If you bought Windows Home Server, the software, and it isn't already installed on a computer, this chapter's for you.

Do You Need to Install Windows Home Server?

If you bought a Windows Home Server home server — which is to say, if you bought a computer with Windows Home Server already installed — you can skip this chapter and move on to Chapter 3, where I describe how to set up WHS so it'll work on your home or office network.

On the other hand, if you bought Windows Home Server — just the software — and it hasn't yet been installed on a computer, this chapter takes you through the steps necessary to get WHS installed.

When you finish this chapter, Windows Home Server is installed on a computer destined to become a server, but *you still have to set it up* — the topic of the next chapter.

If you've ever installed Windows XP or Windows Vista on a computer, this two-phase approach may seem a bit awkward: after all, by the time you're done installing Vista on a PC you're well and truly done — with the language chosen, a user name picked out, the clock set — you can boot your computer and run it till the cows come home.

Life isn't so simple with WHS.

First, you have to install Windows Home Server on a PC. Then you have to connect the PC to your network. Once it's connected, you need to get at least one of the other PCs on the network to recognize the new Home Server. Finally, you use the networked computer to log on to your server and run seven setup steps — described in the next chapter — that prepare the Home Server to do its job.

Don't be intimidated. It's easy if you follow along here.

Preparing to Install

So you're staring at a computer, a handful of DVDs marked "Windows Home Server," a network router begging for one more cable, and you're wondering, "Why didn't I follow my wife's advice and just buy a pre-configured Windows Home Server PC?"

I feel your pain. Been there. Done that. Sorry, honey.

Whatever your motives for taking the Home Server trail less traveled, a bit of preparation now can save a whole lot of headache down the diverged road.

Here's how to get ready:

1. **Make sure you have a PC that can handle Windows Home Server.**

   Hardware requirements are minimal — almost any PC built in the past five years will suffice (see Chapter 1 for details), but you can't install WHS on a laptop computer, and you must have a functioning LAN connection.

   Your newly anointed server must have a DVD drive and the computer must be told to boot from that drive. A USB DVD drive is okay, but only if your computer can be cajoled into booting from it.

   Depending on the proclivities of the computer you've chosen, you may have to go into the system's BIOS to tell it to boot from CD. (*BIOS* — Basic Input/Output System — is the low-level program that runs immediately after you turn on your computer.) Instructions for each computer differ, but in general you have to press Del or Esc (or possibly F1 or F12) while the computer is booting in order to get into the BIOS and confirm the setting. If you aren't sure how to tell your PC to boot from the CD, go to the manufacturer's Web page and search on "boot from CD."

2. **Double-check your current network.**

   All the computers on your network should be talking to each other, and you must have at least one free slot on your router, to plug in the new server. (See Chapter 1 for detailed requirements.)

   At least one of the computers on your network must be assimilated into the Borg — er, at least one of the computers on your network must be ready, willing, and able to run the Windows Home Server connection software. (Presumably you'll want to run the connection software on all your networked PCs, but at the very least you need one.) The good news: Any Windows XP or Vista machine will suffice.

3. **Verify that you have all the DVD/CDs that you will need.**

   WHS consists of three DVD/CDs — the *Installation DVD* includes the programs you need to put on the server; the *Connector CD* contains the program that you need to put on all the other (non-server) computers on your network; and the *Restore CD* is there for emergency re-installation if a hard drive dies.

   There's no sense in putting WHS on a computer unless you have the software necessary to get it completely set up — so, at a bare minimum, you need the Installation DVD and the Connector CD.

4. **If you're the paranoid type (and I am), get the latest BIOS version.**

   Every manufacturer has a slightly different method for updating, or *flashing*, the BIOS. To get the right instructions for your computer, boot it and watch the screen for the motherboard manufacturer's name and model number. Then go to the manufacturer's site and follow the instructions.

   You'll find it easier to flash the BIOS if you already have Windows running on the designated server machine. (Note that you can install Vista on a computer for up to 30 days with no need to validate, so you can legally slap any copy of Vista on a computer long enough to get the latest BIOS, and then install Windows Home Server over the top of the trial version of Vista. Since Windows Home Server is a bona fide operating system in all regards, and it wipes out Vista, you'll never be required to activate Vista.) Figure 2-1, for example, shows the instructions for upgrading the ASUS P5PE-VM motherboard using Windows.

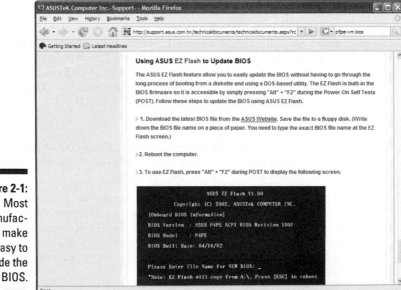

Figure 2-1:
Most manufac-turers make it easy to upgrade the BIOS.

5. **If you have any unusual hardware, make sure you have drivers on hand.**

Windows Home Server ships with built-in support for most network cards, USB controllers, and the like — but occasionally unusual (and brand new) hardware leaves the installer with a case of the willies. Although Windows XP drivers for most types of hardware will work, you'll have the greatest luck with Windows Server 2003 drivers. Check the hardware manufacturer's site for details.

Installing Windows Home Server

With the computer up to snuff, as discussed in the preceding section, it's time to install Windows Home Server.

Here's the easiest way:

1. **Reserve about four hours for the entire process.**

After you have the mouse, monitor, and keyboard set up, and you figure out how to boot from the DVD drive, you only need to interact with the computer for about five minutes at the beginning of the installation process. The WHS installer takes about an hour to copy files (more or less, depending on the speed of your DVD drive), but then it takes another hour booting and re-booting and re-re-booting, and a considerable amount of time downloading updates. By the time you shut the computer down and remove the cables, plan on at least three elapsed hours, and don't be surprised if it takes four.

2. **If your computer has more than one hard drive, consider disconnecting all but the drive that you want to end up as your "primary" Windows Home Server hard drive.**

Usually you want your largest and/or fastest hard drive to become the "primary." You can let WHS choose its own primary drive, if you like, but it's easy to reconnect other drives later.

3. **Disconnect any external USB or FireWire-connected hard drives.**

Windows Home Server is supposed to cancel the installation if it detects any external hard drives. Microsoft made it that way to prevent you from shooting yourself in the foot. The reason is simple: *When WHS takes on a new hard drive, all the data on the drive is irretrievably deleted.* Better to take it one step at a time. If you have any drives that sit outside your designated server, you need to disable them for now. Simply pull the USB or FireWire plug. Don't worry — you'll have a chance to bring them into the fold later (see Chapter 18).

4. **Attach a keyboard, mouse, and monitor to the server, and plug your LAN cable into the router.**

   Any old keyboard, mouse, and monitor will do. As soon as you're done installing WHS, you can yank all of them — you will never use them again, unless something really horrible happens to your server.

   The LAN cable has to be connected so that the installer will find the connection and install any drivers that may be necessary to get you connected to your network.

5. **Turn on the power. Put the Installation DVD in your DVD drive, and boot from the Installation DVD.**

   Chances are good you have to "Press any key to boot from the DVD drive." You know you're on the right track when you can see the message, "Windows is Loading Files."

   After a fair amount of time, you see the Aurora lights so familiar to Windows Vista users, and a notice that "Setup is initializing." A blink or 52 later, you see the first Windows Home Server Setup screen.

6. **Click Next.**

   The WHS installer scans your computer, looking for hard drives. It presents the results of the scan in the Load Additional Storage Drivers panel shown in Figure 2-2.

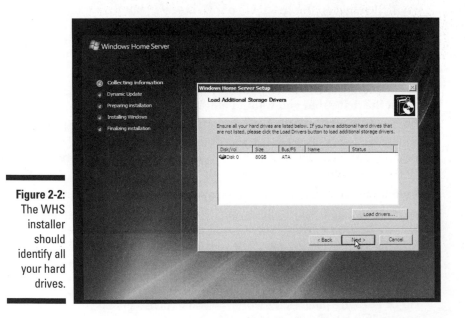

Figure 2-2:
The WHS installer should identify all your hard drives.

7. **Make sure all your built-in hard drives (and their drivers) are accounted for.**

   Depending on what you find, you have one of two ways to go:

   • If you know you have a hard drive inside your computer that isn't listed in the Load Additional Storage Drivers dialog box, click the button marked Load Drivers — and prepare yourself for a bumpy ride.

   • If the Installer found all your hard drives, click Next.

   While the WHS installer recognizes almost all modern hard drives, there are some exceptions. The Load Drivers routine asks you to choose a driver manually for your recalcitrant hard drive. That's relatively easy if you know in advance that you're going to need the driver, *and* you had the foresight to download the Windows 2003 driver from the hard-drive manufacturer's Web site. It's a real pain in the neck if you need to use another computer to go searching for the driver, transfer it to a USB key drive, and bring it back to this installation step.

   After you click Next, the WHS installer asks you to choose a type of install (that's tech-speak for "installation"; see Figure 2-3).

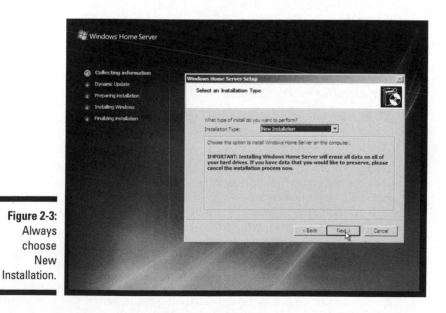

Figure 2-3:
Always
choose
New
Installation.

8. **If you're installing Windows Home Server (as opposed to trying to repair a botched system), pick New Installation and click Next.**

   The installer asks you to choose your time and currency formats and keyboard input method.

9. **Choose the time, currency, and keyboard settings that come closest to what you like (English/United States for me, but you may prefer Ozzie Ozzie Ozzie), and click Next.**

   Microsoft's infamous, inane End User License Agreement appears next. A paragon of legalistic ambiguity and inscrutable conflicting clauses, it's only slightly less dense than the U.S. Tax Code.

10. **Read the EULA in fine detail and memorize the important parts because there's a test at the end. (Okay, okay. I'm kidding.) Click I Accept the Agreement Under Penalty of Sitting Through Another Ballmer Keynote (assuming you do, of course), then click Next.**

    No, really, just read it and click. Otherwise WHS won't install.

11. **If you have a 25-character product key for WHS, type it in the next dialog box. If you don't have a product key, you can still install WHS and use it for 30 days without activating it. (After 30 days, your computer rolls over and plays dead — you can get data off the computer, but that's about it.) Click Next.**

    Even if you type in a product key, the installer does *not* activate your copy of WHS. That's a separate step you need to undertake after the system is up and working.

    The installer asks you to type in a "memorable" name for the WHS computer.

12. **If you can't stand the default name (SERVER), type in a name of your own choosing. Click Next.**

    The dialog box says you can use up to 15 characters, letters, numbers, or hyphens for the name, but no spaces. In my experience, using hyphens in a computer's name begs for problems. Stick to letters and numbers — or, better, just use SERVER. That's kinda like calling your dog DOG. He doesn't mind. (My dog figures that's his name anyway.)

    The installer puts up a stern warning, advising you that all the data on your hard drive will be blasted to, uh, bits (Figure 2-4).

    If you made it this far expecting to save some data on that hard drive, you qualify as one of the world's few trusting souls, and should seriously consider entering a nunnery. I salute you. Most of the rest of us figure the data's hosed anyway.

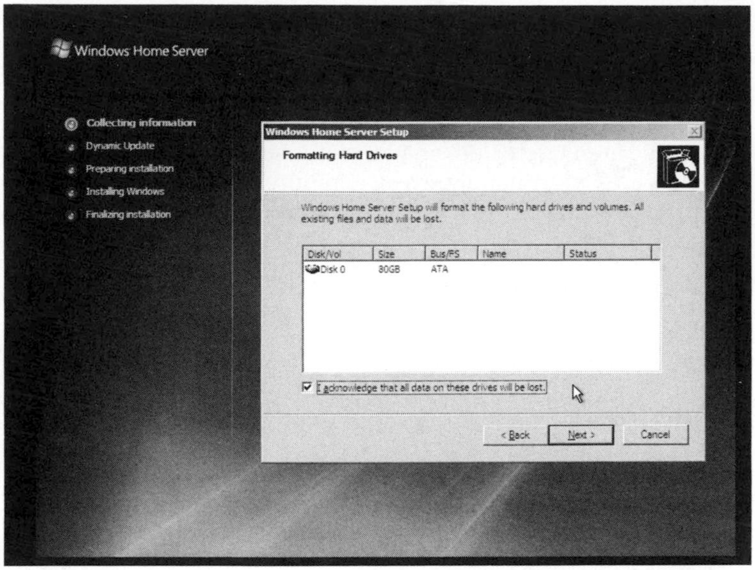

Figure 2-4:
Installing
WHS really
does wipe
out
everything
on your hard
drive.

13. **When you're ready, go ahead and check the box marked I Acknowledge that the Installer Will Blow Away All the Data on These Drives (or something really similar), and click Next.**

    The installer is now ready to start copying files.

14. **In the Ready to Install Windows Home Server screen, click Start.**

    True to its word, the installer bumps and grinds for more than an hour (on a typical PC), copying files, rebooting four (five? six?) times, running a CheckDisk, and taking another hour or so with cleanup and installing updates — all the while not asking for any input from you at all — and in the end brings up a designer screen that says "Welcome."

    You are now at the point where most Windows Home Server users start: exactly where you'd be if you bought WHS pre-installed on a computer. If you like, you can continue with the WHS installation from this point by clicking the Welcome arrow and following along in Chapter 3.

    I prefer to take down the scaffolding at this point and continue with setup the same way everybody else does. To get back on a level playing field with all the other WHS folks, follow Steps 15 and 16.

15. **Do *not* click the arrow marked Welcome. Instead, if you can, click Start⇨Turn Off Computer. If you can't get the Start button to respond, wait for the hard drive light on the front of your computer to stop blinking, and then simply turn off your computer using the On/Off switch (you may have to hold it down for 15 seconds or so).**

16. **Disconnect the mouse, keyboard, and monitor. You won't be needing them anymore. Eviscerate the DVD drive, too — chances are good you'll never need it again.**

Older hardware might pause during the boot process if a keyboard and/or mouse aren't detected, so you might have to dig into the BIOS and disable the trap. Unfortunately, every computer is different, so you may have to struggle with your computer manufacturer's Web site to get complete instructions.

Congratulations. Your server is installed and ready for setup. Finish the WHS setup by continuing in Chapter 3.

Part II
Setting Up
the Network

The 5th Wave   By Rich Tennant

UBER-USER DWAYNE GRANTZ CHALKS
UP BEFORE PUTTING WINDOWS HOME
SERVER THROUGH ITS PACES.

In this part . . .

The first time I installed a test copy of Windows Home Server — plugged in the server and ran the Connect CD on a randomly chosen guinea-pig home-office PC — I remember asking myself, "Is that *it*?" Surely, I figured, I must've missed something. It couldn't be that simple.

I mean, we're talking *Microsoft* here, right? The place where nobody can say "straightforward" in one syllable?

I'm here to tell ya: Yes, Virginia, there *is* a Santa Claus. I can hear him chanting "Ho, ho, ho!" every time I see that green status light, telling me that all the computers on my network are backed up and sleeping sound in their beds, with visions of sugarplums dancing in their heads.

Many months of wrangling with WHS have taught me a few tricks, which I pass on in this section. But the bottom line remains: For almost all of the networks, almost all of the time, getting WHS to work rates as a first-class joy.

Chapter 3

Bringing Computers into the Home Server Fold

In This Chapter

▶ Getting the server plugged into the network

▶ Connecting your first home (or office) PC

▶ Finalizing setup on the server

▶ Figuring out what to do next

*W*ith the Windows Home Server box ready to roll (as discussed in Chapter 2), you're just a few minutes away from convincing all the computers on your network to join in the fray.

Follow along closely and you'll be amazed at how easy Microsoft has made it to bring all the Windows Home Server goodies into your home or home office.

Kick-Starting the Network

Whether you bought a new PC with Windows Home Server preinstalled, or you installed the Windows Home Server software on a PC you already own (see Chapter 2), at this point you should have a WHS PC ready to be set up. In addition, you should have

> ✔ **A network:** Your network (Microsoft calls it a *workgroup*) should consist of two or more PCs running Windows XP (any version) or Windows Vista (any except 64-bit versions), where all the computers on the network can "see" all of the other computers. The computers all must be able to read data from the Windows Home Server's Connector CD, whether the data comes in from the computer's own CD drive, from a USB attached CD drive, or from a shared drive or network location.

You can verify the visibility of PCs on a network by choosing Start⇨My Network Places in Windows XP, or Start⇨Network in Windows Vista. If Windows doesn't respond with a list of all the computers, refer to Doug Lowe's *Networking For Dummies*, from Wiley, for troubleshooting details.

While Microsoft recommends that you have at least two PCs on the network, in fact Windows Home Server will work with just one networked home or office PC (although it's considerably more difficult to make sure the network is actually working unless you have two communicating PCs). You can stick more than ten PCs on the network, but WHS will only recognize — and only back up — ten PCs at most.

✔ **A place to plug your server into the network:** This is usually an available jack on your router (or switch or hub) that you can use to connect your new Windows Home Server computer.

All the home or office PCs on your network can use wireless networking, but the Windows Home Server computer should be physically plugged into the router. Some people report success running Windows Home Server on a wireless computer, but the potential for occasional glitches in the wireless signal (and the need for a wireless driver) can drive you nuts.

✔ **A reasonably fast Internet connection that's working:**

Microsoft suggests you have a broadband connection — knowing full well that there's no universally accepted definition of the term *broadband*. Suffice to say that a dial-up modem just doesn't cut the mustard, unless you're only going to use Windows Home Server for backups, but almost anything else should work well enough.

✔ **The Windows Home Server CD:** This disc may be marked Connector CD or Connector Software CD.

That's the program you need to run on all the computers on your network.

To get your Windows Home Server network going, follow these steps:

1. **Plug your Windows Home Server into the network's router (or switch or hub), plug the power cord into the wall, and turn it on.**

   Listen for the sound of angels shouting *Hosanna*. If you don't hear them, well, you didn't connect the server's sound card, did you?

2. **Pick one PC on the network to use as your guinea pig.**

   If you have a Windows Vista computer, use it. The Vista connector software goes in faster than the Windows XP connector — although both the Vista and XP flavors (at least in my experience) run without a hiccup.

3. **Depending on whether your guinea-pig PC runs Windows XP or Windows Vista, follow the steps in one of the two following sections to install the Windows Home Server Connector software.**

The installation procedures are nearly identical, but I broke them out into separate sections in this chapter to minimize any confusion.

4. **As soon as you connect, the server itself offers up the Windows Home Server setup screen (which should look more or less like Figure 3-1). Go to the last section in this chapter ("Configuring Windows Home Server") to run through the server setup steps.**

Figure 3-1: When the Connector software is connected on the first PC, you see this configuration page from the server.

You need to run the setup program only once; you might as well do it as soon as you put the connector software on the first home or office PC.

5. **One by one, install the connector software on each of the remaining home or office PCs.**

Follow the steps in the appropriate section in this chapter.

6. **Take two aspirin and call me, uh, I mean, check the Console in the morning.**

You can check it from any computer on your network. You should see a green light with backups for all your computers, run automatically overnight. (Like magic.) If backup doesn't work, look at Part V in this book for a wide array of troubleshooting tips.

Two servers, one network

Although I wouldn't recommend it for casual use, it *is* possible to put *two* Windows Home Server computers on the same network. Each home or office computer on the network gets associated with one (and only one) server. You might want to do that to separate the computers into distinct groups for remote access (see Part IV), if you want to back up different computers' data onto different servers, or if you have more than ten computers on your network.

The easiest way to set up two separate servers is by powering down one of them while you install Windows Home Server Connector on one set of PCs, and then powering down the other server while you install the connector software on a different set of PCs. Whichever server is functioning when the connector software was installed becomes the server associated with that particular PC.

Installing Windows Home Server Connector on a Windows XP Machine

Every home or office PC on your network that you want to put under the control of your Windows Home Server server has to be running a specific program called the Windows Home Server Connector. The WHS Connector for Windows XP differs slightly from the version for Windows Vista. Installation steps for the two are almost identical, but I've listed (and repeated) the steps for each version separately in this chapter, so there's no room for doubt.

This section covers installing WHS Connector on a Windows XP machine. The next section covers installing WHS Connector on a Vista PC.

The same Windows Home Server Connector program works with both Windows XP Home and Windows XP Pro. There's one significant operational difference between Home and Pro — you can use Remote Access to connect to a Windows XP Pro machine, but WHS's Remote Access doesn't work on a Windows XP Home machine. (See Part IV.) Other than that, you will see very few differences.

Windows Home Server Connector for Windows XP runs on top of a big (some would call it "bloated") Microsoft system called .NET Framework. When you install WHS Connector on a Windows XP machine, .NET Framework comes along for the ride. (No need to install .NET Framework on Vista computers because it's "baked in" — or should I say half-baked in? — as part of the operating system itself.) That's why installing Windows Home Server Connector on a Windows XP machine may take considerably longer than installing it on a Vista machine.

If you have the Windows Home Server Connector CD in hand, follow these steps to get your Windows XP machine connected to the server:

1. **Follow the steps in the preceding section, "Kick-Starting the Network," to get your Windows Home Server server hooked up to your network.**

   Pay particular attention to the part about ensuring that Windows can "see" all the other computers on the network.

2. **Make sure your Internet connection is working.**

   Fire up Firefox (getfirefox.com) or Internet Explorer (if you must) and verify that the WHS Connector installer can get online if it needs to.

3. **Make Windows show you file name extensions.**

   Every Windows PC should show file name extensions — the short (usually three-letter) part of the file name after the period, such as .com or .zip or .exe. If you get stuck in deep doo-doo and can't see your files' full names, you could dig yourself into a cavernous hole very quickly.

   To show filename extensions in Windows XP, click Start⇨My Documents, then choose Tools⇨Folder Options⇨View. Uncheck the box marked Hide Extensions for Known File Types (shown in Figure 3-2). While you're at it, consider selecting the option to Show Hidden Files and Folders. Click OK.

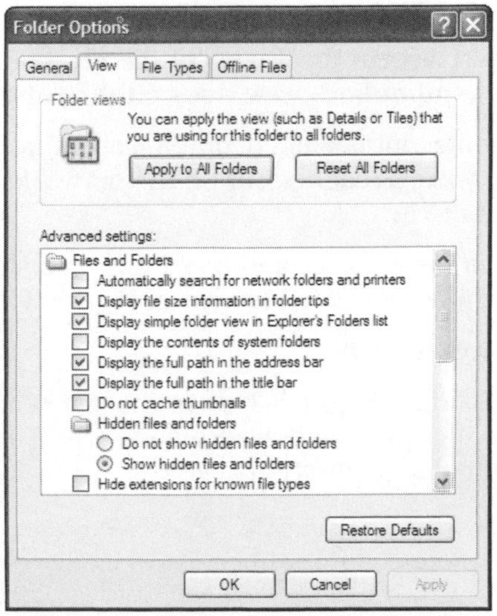

Figure 3-2:
Make Windows XP show you the full names of all your files.

4. **Insert the WHS Connector CD into your home or office PC's CD drive.**

   If the PC doesn't have a built-in CD drive, or you don't feel like futzing with a CD, you can try to run the Connector software directly from the server. Click Start⇨My Network and look for a computer called Server. If you can connect to the server (and you probably can), go to the server's shared folder called Software\Home Server Connector Software, and run the program called Setup.exe. If you can't connect to the server and don't have a built-in CD drive, you may have to monkey around a bit with a USB attached drive. Should such shenanigans prove necessary, just run the Autorun.inf file on the CD.

5. **If you don't already have .NET Framework installed on your Windows XP PC, you need to click through the wizard that appears to guide you through the process of installing .NET Framework 2.0.**

   The installation is straightforward (click Next and then *I approve* on the voluminous License Agreement) but time-consuming and, uh, tedious.

6. **When the .NET Framework installer finishes, it "highly recommends" that you download and install the latest service packs and security updates. Believe me, there are many, but that's a battle to fight another day. Click Finish and be done with it for now.**

   After you click Finish at the end of the .NET Framework installer wizard, you have to wait a minute or two or three before the Windows Home Server Connector installer springs to life.

7. **Click Next in the installer.**

   The installer offers a densely-worded, intractable (and probably unen-forceable) End-User License Agreement — the sort you've likely come to expect but will probably never grow accustomed to.

8. **Select the button marked I Accept the Terms of the License Agreement (although I didn't read it and nobody else does either), and click Next.**

   The installer can take awhile, but it's much, much faster than the .NET Framework installer. The wizard reaches out on the network, finds your home server and connects to it.

9. **If this is the first time you have connected any PC to your home server, you see the customizing wizard shown in Figure 3-3.**

   You have two possible ways to go here:

   • If you see the dialog box in Figure 3-3, go to the last section in this chapter (called "Configuring Windows Home Server") and continue with the server's initial configuration.

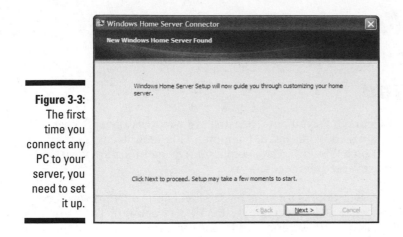

Figure 3-3:
The first
time you
connect any
PC to your
server, you
need to set
it up.

- • If you don't see a dialog box like that in Figure 3-3, don't worry, your server's already set up. Continue with Step 10.

10. **If your server's already set up, you see a dialog box that asks for the Windows Home Server password. That's the password you provided when you first setup up WHS (see Step 4 in the last section of this chapter, the one called Configuring Windows Home Server). Type in the password and click Next.**

 The Windows Home Server Connector advises you, first, that you're joining Windows Home Server (which means the Connector program sets everything up with the server so they can talk to each other) and, second, that it's configuring your backup.

11. **When the Connector advises you that it's done configuring the backup, click Next.**

 You see a dialog box that says the Connector Configuration is complete, and that your computer will be automatically backed up every day between 12:00 a.m. (which is to say, midnight) and 6:00 a.m.

12. **Click Finish.**

 You're now ready to run the Connector CD on the next PC on your network.

When you finish running the Connector CD on all your home or office PCs, continue with Chapter 4 to establish user accounts.

Installing Windows Home Server Connector on a Windows Vista Machine

The preceding section tells you how to install the Windows Home Server Connector program on a Windows XP computer. This section covers the same ground, but on a Windows Vista computer. The methods are very similar, but there are several differences.

Windows Home Server Connector runs on 32-bit versions of Windows Vista. If you don't know what a 32-bit version is, don't worry about it. The 64-bit versions of Vista are pretty esoteric, and by the time they become commonplace, Microsoft will no doubt figure out how to get the Connector to run on them, too.

With the Windows Home Server Connector CD in hand, follow these steps to get your Windows Vista machine connected to the server:

1. **Follow the instructions in the first section in this chapter, entitled "Kick-Starting the Network," to get your Windows Home Server server hooked up to your network.**

   Pay particular attention to the part about ensuring that Windows can "see" all the other computers on the network.

2. **Make sure your Internet connection is working.**

   Fire up Firefox (getfirefox.com) or Internet Explorer (if you must) and verify that the WHS Connector installer can get online if it needs to.

3. **Make Windows show you file name extensions.**

   It bears repeating: *Every* Windows PC should show filename extensions — the short (usually three-letter) part of the filename after the period, such as .com or .zip or .exe. If you get stuck in a problem and can't see your files' full names, you could end up in Vista-less limbo-land very quickly.

   To show file name extensions in Windows Vista, click Start⇨Documents. Press the Alt key, and then choose Tools⇨Folder Options⇨View. Uncheck the box marked Hide Extensions for Known File Types (Figure 3-4). While you're at it, consider selecting the option to Show Hidden Files and Folders (might as well know what they're up to). Click OK.

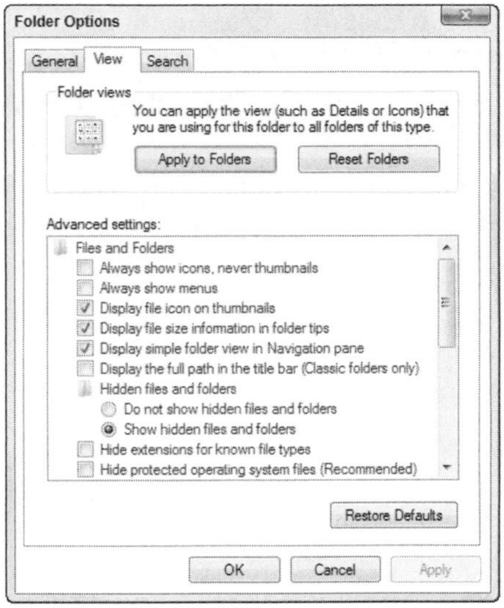

Folder Options

General | View | Search

Folder views

You can apply the view (such as Details or Icons) that
you are using for this folder to all folders of this type.

[Apply to Folders]   [Reset Folders]

Advanced settings:

Files and Folders
- ☐ Always show icons, never thumbnails
- ☐ Always show menus
- ☑ Display file icon on thumbnails
- ☑ Display file size information in folder tips
- ☑ Display simple folder view in Navigation pane
- ☐ Display the full path in the title bar (Classic folders only)
- Hidden files and folders
  - ○ Do not show hidden files and folders
  - ● Show hidden files and folders
- ☐ Hide extensions for known file types
- ☐ Hide protected operating system files (Recommended)

[Restore Defaults]

[OK]   [Cancel]   [Apply]

Figure 3-4:
Make Vista
show you
the full
names of all
your files.

4. **Insert the WHS Connector CD into your home or office PC's CD drive.**

   Vista responds by showing you an AutoPlay dialog box.

   If you don't want to mess around with CDs, try to run the Connector
   software directly from the server. Click Start⇨Network and look for
   a computer called `Server`. If you can connect to the server (and you
   probably can), go to the server's shared folder called `Software\Home
   Server Connector Software`, and run the program called `Setup.exe`.
   If you can't connect to the server and don't have a built-in CD drive, you
   may have to monkey around a bit with a USB attached drive, or
   you might copy the contents of the CD onto a USB key drive. Should
   such shenanigans prove necessary, just run the `Autorun.inf` file on
   the CD.

5. **In the AutoPlay dialog box, click the link that says Run Setup.exe
   Published by Microsoft Corporation. If you're confronted by a User
   Account Control message, click Continue.**

   Ain't high-level security wunnerful?

   Vista welcomes you to the Windows Home Server Connector program.

6. **Click Next.**

   The installer offers a densely-worded, intractable (and probably
   unenforceable) End-User License Agreement.

7. Select the button marked I Accept the Terms of the License Agreement (okay, I didn't read it; nobody else does, either), and click Next.

In its magical fashion, the wizard reaches out on the network, finds your home server, and connects to it.

8. If this is the first time you have connected any PC to your home server, you see the customizing wizard shown in Figure 3-5.

Here comes another choice:

- If you see the dialog box in Figure 3-5, go to the last section in this chapter, called "Configuring Windows Home Server," and continue with the server's initial configuration.

- If you don't see a dialog box like that in Figure 3-3, don't worry, your server's already set up. Continue with Step 9.

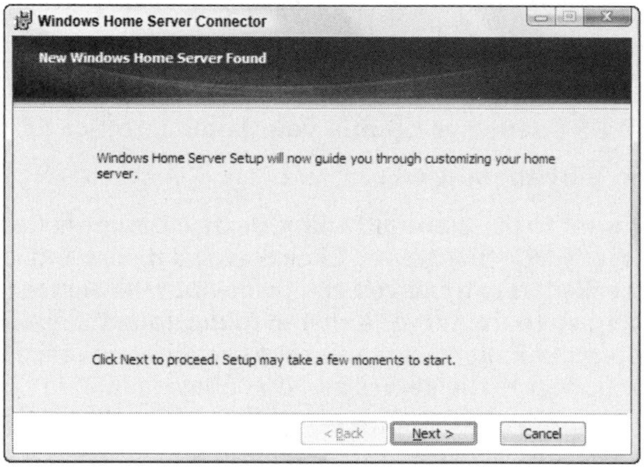

Figure 3-5:
The first time you connect any PC to WHS, you need to set it up.

9. If your server's already set up, you see a dialog box that asks for the Windows Home Server password. That's the password you provided when you first setup up WHS (see Step 4 in the next section). Type in the password and click Next.

The Windows Home Server Connector advises you, first, that you're joining Windows Home Server (which means the Connector program sets everything up with the server so they can talk to each other) and, second, that it's configuring your backup.

10. **When the Connector advises that it's done configuring the backup, click Next.**

    You see a dialog box that says the Connector Configuration is complete, and that your computer will be automatically backed up every day between 12:00 a.m. (that is, midnight) and 6:00 a.m.

11. **Click Finish.**

    You're now ready to run the Connector CD on the next computer on your network.

When you finish running the Connector CD on all your home or office PCs, continue with Chapter 4 to establish user accounts.

Configuring Windows Home Server

The first time you run the Connector CD on any PC connected to a new home server, you see an offer to customize the server, like that shown in Figure 3-3 (for Windows XP) or 3-5 (for Windows Vista).

Some people find this a bit confusing, but it makes sense when you realize that the server runs "headless" — it doesn't have its own keyboard, mouse, and monitor, poor thing. The first time the server detects that a PC has connected to it, the server — working through the PC that's just been connected — asks for you to supply a minimal amount of customizing information, just enough to get the server up and running . . . and protected.

Follow these steps to work through your home or office PC, and get the server set up right:

1. **When you see the wizard panel shown in Figure 3-3 or 3-5, click Next.**

    Windows Home Server shows you its setup screen, with a Welcome button (refer to Figure 3-1).

    If you installed WHS on your own computer, following the instructions in Chapter 2, you may recognize the screen in Figure 3-1 — except now, though the wonders of WHS Connect, it's showing on a home computer, not the server itself.

2. **Click the right-arrow next to Welcome.**

    The Windows Home Server customizer asks you to give the home server a name (see Figure 3-6).

A strong password

I know, I know. You already have about ten thousand passwords, and the last thing you need is another one. You don't want to futz with a "strong" password because you'll have to write it down, and then the kids could find it. (Or, more and more frequently in this day and age, the kids don't want to write it down because their parents can find it.)

Strong passwords are particularly important with Windows Home Server because sensitive data can be stored on the server and, perhaps most importantly for home users, remote access to the server can be altered by anyone who knows the password.

Mark Burnett, writing in the book *Perfect Passwords* (Syngress, December 2005), has come up with a method that I use for creating

new, strong passwords that *even I can remember*. Mark has spent years analyzing passwords and the means used to crack passwords, and come up with a simple rule of thumb: use a password at least 15 characters long, consisting of three or more words separated by punctuation, with one or more of the words misspelled. Brilliant. Easy.

So, for example, you might use `Windows? Home?Server?passwurd` or `Yet! Another!Bloody!Pword`. If you go one step farther and slightly obfuscate the Password Hint (say, `WHSpasswurd?` or `YAB!Pword`), it's going to be mighty difficult to crack (provided, of course, you don't use these actual examples — but you knew that) and comparatively easy to remember.

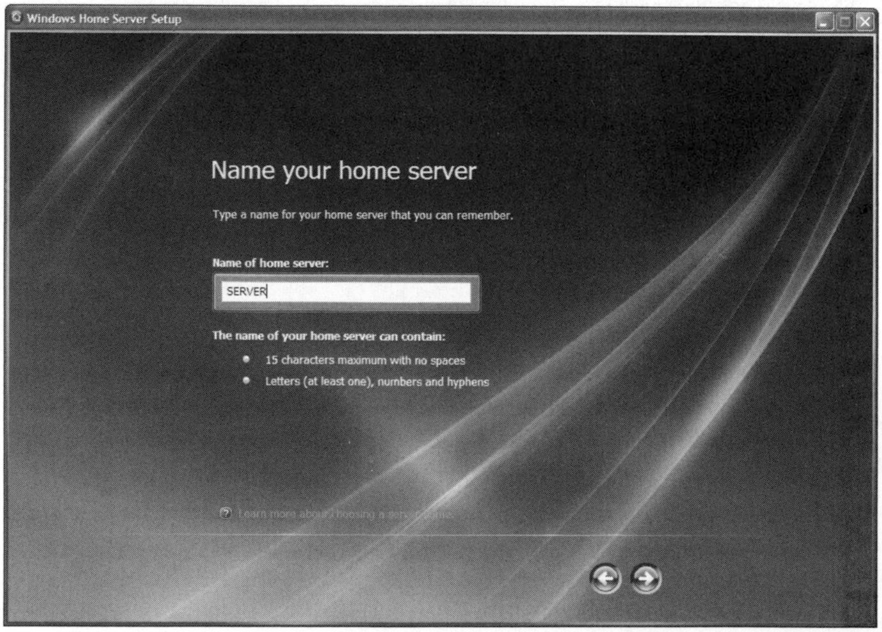

Figure 3-6:
Type in a name for the server.

3. **If you can't stand the default name (**SERVER**), type in a name of your own choosing. Click the right-arrow.**

   The Setup Wizard says you can use up to 15 characters, letters, numbers, or hyphens for the name, but no spaces. In my experience, using hyphens in a computer's name just begs for problems. Stick to letters and numbers — or, better, just use SERVER. A rose by any other name. . . .

   The Setup Wizard asks you to type a strong password that you can remember, per Figure 3-7.

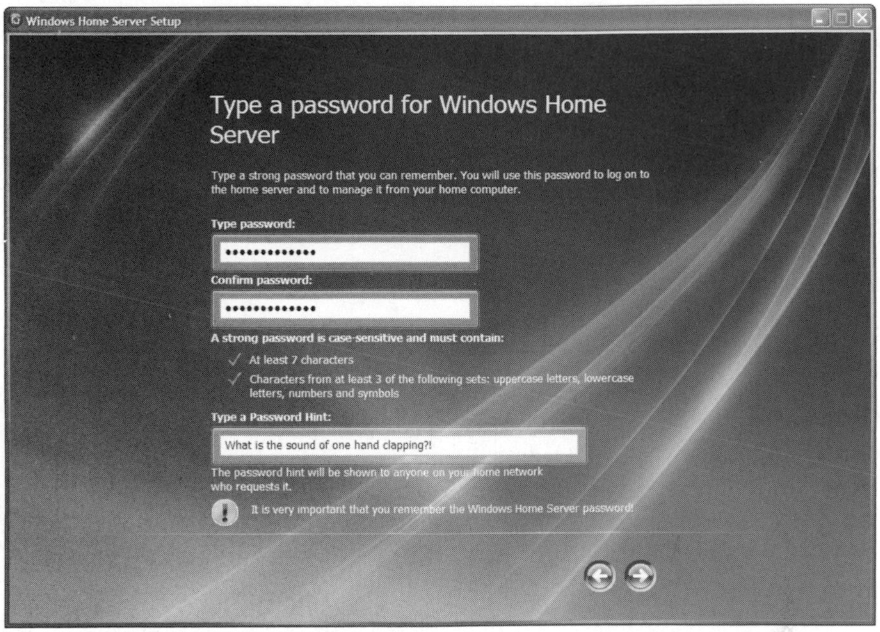

Figure 3-7:
Strong passwords are very important, particularly on your server.

4. **Take the time to figure out a strong password that you can remember (see the sidebar "A strong password," as well as the Setup Wizard's tip), type the password twice, and type in a Password Hint that anyone can see. Click the right arrow.**

   If you forget the password, see Chapter 19.

   The WHS Setup Wizard asks if you want to turn on Automatic Updates. See Figure 3-8.

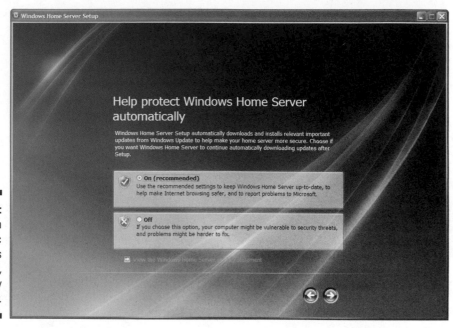

Figure 3-8:
I turn on
Automatic
Updates
for WHS,
but only
begrudgingly.

Personally, I turn on automatic updating for Windows Home Server, although I strongly recommend that you *don't* use automatic updating on Windows XP or Windows Vista.

Why the caveat? Two reasons. First, I don't log on to my WHS server all that often, and I don't want to miss a patch for lack of trying. Second, the WHS team hasn't (yet) delivered a screwed-up patch. Compare that track record with, say, the Internet Explorer 6 patch effort, which seems to get screwed up once a month.

I may change my opinion, though, as WHS gets older. Check my Web site, AskWoody.com, to see whether recent events have given me sufficient reason to switch.

5. **If you're feeling lucky, choose the button marked On to turn on WHS automatic updating (for both the server software and Internet Explorer). If you're a tad more skeptical than I — or you've been to my Web site and have reason to change your mind — then choose Off. In either case, click the right arrow.**

The WHS Setup Wizard asks whether you want to participate in Microsoft's Customer Experience Improvement Program.

6. **I never participate in Microsoft's automated tracking programs. I don't feel comfortable leaving my personal details in Microsoft's giant database. You may feel differently, but if you don't trust Microsoft, don't think twice about choosing the No button. Click the right arrow.**

The Setup Wizard asks for your permission to automatically send crash logs to the Microsoft mothership (but before you grant any such thing, take a look at Figure 3-9 and the step that follows).

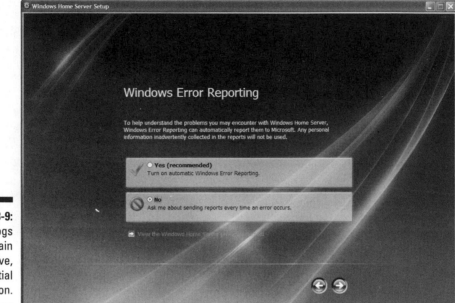

Figure 3-9:
Crash logs
can contain
sensitive,
confidential
information.

7. **Decide whether you want to send crash records to Microsoft —
   and when you've decided, click the right arrow.**

   Here's what you need to know first:

   • If you're willing to let Microsoft's automatic Dr. Watson program
     phone home with details about every crash you encounter, choose
     Yes, but realize that a complete dump of everything in memory —
     possibly including sensitive information — will go automatically into
     Microsoft's database.

   • If you choose No, you will be asked each time WHS crashes whether
     it's okay to send an error report. (One guess which option I choose.)

   Windows Home Server warns you that it is ready to download updates.

8. **Click the right arrow.**

   WHS reaches out to the Internet, downloads the latest versions of all of
   its components, re-boots the server (yes, you can reboot the server from
   a connected home or office PC), and re-emerges in its latest and greatest
   form.

   When WHS finishes the Setup Wizard, and configuration is complete, you
   see the message shown in Figure 3-10.

Figure 3-10:
Windows
Home
Server
reporting for
duty, your
majesty!

9. **Click the right arrow next to Start, type in the server's password, and you're ready to get down to business.**

   Get all the home or office PCs on your network set up with the Connector CD, and then move on to adding new users, in Chapter 4.

Chapter 4

Adding Users and Controlling Passwords

In This Chapter

▶ Making your life easier by judiciously choosing user names

▶ Weighing the pros and cons of passwords

▶ Setting up user names and passwords

▶ Changing user names and passwords

*W*indows Home Server boasts many simple, no-effort features that work precisely as you would expect, with little or no interaction required on your part. User names and passwords aren't among them.

You already know that everybody who logs on to one of the computers on your home or office network should have a password. That's what the security experts say. That's what the books and magazines and Web sites say. Yada yada yada. You should also know that nobody — and I mean *nobody* — locks down a home network as stringently as the security experts would like.

Windows Home Server's Remote Access capabilities — which you can use to log on to your home or office network from any Internet café, anywhere in the world — tend to, uh, *focus your mind clearly* on security concerns. If you turn on Remote Access (see Chapter 13), your old lackadaisical approach to user names and passwords makes almost as much sense as hanging a sign on your front door saying, "We're away on vacation but the key is under the mat."

Take a few minutes to understand how Windows Home Server enforces security on your home or office network. Forewarned and forearmed, you will find that a reasonable level of security isn't nearly as difficult, or as onerous, as you probably imagined. Just follow the steps in this chapter.

Understanding User Control

Windows Home Server doesn't interfere with the user accounts you already have set up on the PCs in your home or office network. If you put Administrator accounts with godlike capabilities and no passwords on all your PCs, WHS won't lift a finger to stop you. (But it's a *really bad idea*.)

WHS looks out for number one — for the Windows Home Server box itself. If you want to get into the server, you have to follow the server's rules. If you want to do anything else on the network, well, that isn't the server's responsibility.

Windows Home Server gets into the account-and-password-control mess in three ways:

- ✔ Anybody who wants to read from or write to shared folders on the server has to be given explicit permission. (See Chapter 11 for details on setting up shared folders.)

- ✔ Anybody who wants to log on to your network from the Internet, using Remote Access, has to be given explicit permission. (See Chapter 13 for details on Remote Access.)

- ✔ In a very roundabout way, you can tell WHS to sync the password on the server with the password on each home or office computer. (See the section "Adding New Users the Smart Way" later in this chapter.)

In all other respects, WHS doesn't interfere with user accounts or passwords, sharing settings, the type of account you set up (Administrator or Limited under Windows XP; Administrator or Standard under Vista), or any other account or password details — on any of your home or office computers. It turns a completely blind eye to anything you want to do.

Almost everyone, almost everywhere, calls a user name a "user name." (Or maybe a "username," but you get the idea.) Confusingly, Windows Home Server insists on calling a user name a "logon name." Windows Vista calls the same thing a "user account name." Windows XP calls it a "user name." Don't be confused. "Logon name," "logon ID," "login name," "user name," "user account name," and "username" all refer to the same thing — the name on the account, the name you click on the Welcome screen to get into the computer.

Windows Home Server lets you set up a maximum of ten different user names, er, user account names, uh, logon names. In addition, there's always an account called Administrator, and one called Guest. Those are both special accounts, which I discuss later in this chapter.

After working with a zillion different combinations, I've come to the conclusion that it's always best to use precisely the same user names on the server as you have on each of your home or office PCs, and it's best to make sure the passwords on the server match passwords on the home or office PCs. So, for example, if one of your PCs has a user named `BillyG` with a password of `go!getem!MSFT!`, you should also put a user named `BillyG` with the same password on the server.

Okay, that isn't a requirement — Windows Home Server won't fall over and play dead if there's a user name on a PC that isn't set up on the server. But it makes your life (and BillyG's life) much easier in myriad ways. For example, if the password on the home or office PC matches the password on the server, then BillyG won't have to type in a new password every time he tries to get into a shared folder on the server.

Raising the Bar for Passwords

Windows Home Server lets you specify rather crude minimum requirements for all new passwords that are established on the server. (Geeks call that a *password policy*.) To set your own password policy, follow these steps:

1. **On any home or office networked PC, double-click the Windows Home Server icon (down in the notification area next to the time). Then type the server's password and press Enter.**

   The Windows Home Server Console appears.

2. **In the Windows Home Server Console, click the Settings icon in the upper-right corner, and then click Passwords on the left.**

   The Console shows you its Passwords pane, per Figure 4-1.

3. **If you aren't at all concerned about restricting access to shared folders, choose the Weak policy. If you have — or plan to have — sensitive information stored in the shared folders, choose the Strong policy. Otherwise, just leave the setting on Medium, which is the default.**

   For a more complete description of the Weak, Medium, and Strong password policies, see Table 4-1.

4. **Click OK.**

   The policy you choose takes effect for all new passwords stored on the server. It doesn't change any existing passwords on the server, and it doesn't touch any settings on any of your network's home or office PCs.

Figure 4-1:
You can
choose from
three
different
password
policies.

Table 4-1	Password Policy Details	
Policy	*Restriction*	*Typical uses*
Weak	Accounts on the server aren't required to have any password, and the ones with passwords have no restrictions in force.	A home network where you aren't too worried about anybody deleting files on the server.
Medium	Accounts on the server are required to have passwords, and the passwords must be at least five characters long.	Not much security is needed, but you want to make it a little bit difficult to get into some shared folders, mostly to prevent people from accidentally messing up other folks' data.
Strong	Accounts on the server are required to have passwords, the passwords must be at least seven characters long, and each password must have at least three of the following: uppercase letters, lowercase letters, numbers, or symbols	If you have sensitive information on the server that other people shouldn't see; this is also the setting for any account used for Remote Access.

I talk about choosing strong passwords in Chapter 3 (see the sidebar "A strong password"). The best advice I know for picking a good password is to use a password at least 15 characters long, consisting of three or more words separated by punctuation, with one or more of the words misspelled. `Once?u?get?used?to?it` (no, that isn't my real password), coming up with new passwords and remembering them is remarkably easy.

A word of caution about "Medium" passwords. People are frequently surprised to learn that their favorite, pet password — the one that nobody would *ever* guess, not in a million years — is in fact being used by uncountable legions of other people. If you decide to settle on Medium passwords, make sure that everyone using your network has seen the list in Table 4-2. The passwords in that table were extracted from a computer virus that made the rounds a couple of years ago. The virus used these specific passwords to try to break into machines — and it was amazingly successful. (No, I didn't include the four-letter words of primarily Anglo Saxon origin that are also exceedingly common.)

Table 4-2	The Most Common (Printable) Passwords			
0	000000	00000000	007	1
110	111	111111	11111111	12
121212	123	123123	1234	12345
123456	1234567	12345678	123456789	1234qwer
123abc	123asd	123qwe	2002	2003
2600	54321	654321	88888888	a
aaa	abc	abc123	abcd	Admin
admin	admin123	administrator	alpha	asdf
computer	database	enable	foobar	god
godblessyou	home	ihavenopass	Internet	Login
login	love	mypass	mypass123	mypc
mypc123	oracle	owner	pass	passwd
Password	password	pat	patrick	pc
pw	pw123	pwd	qwer	root
secret	server	sex	super	sybase
temp	temp123	test	test123	win
xp	xxx	yxcv	zxcv	

Adding New Users the Smart Way

As long as you only need ten user names for your entire network, setting up the server with all your user names shouldn't take long at all.

Note that there's no overwhelming reason to limit yourself to a "one person = one user name" rule. If fewer than ten people are using your home or office network, it's (arguably) simpler to give each user his or her own user name. If you have more than ten people who need to use your network, you'll have to figure out who gets doubled up. Security experts would have you believe that shared user names lead you down the road to ruin. Bah.

The biggest problem I see with shared user names arises when one of the people sharing the name changes the password — and forgets to tell the other(s). *That* can give you a giant-size headache, and there isn't much you can do about it.

Certainly if you have sensitive data on your server, you should give each person who accesses your network a separate user name — and you should tell the server to demand Strong passwords. But in most cases, particularly on home networks, that's just an unnecessary pain in the neck.

Conversely, there's no reason to limit yourself to just one user name. You may feel more comfortable using two different user names — one for administrative jobs on the home PC that require an account with Administrator privileges; the other for daily use *without* the full power of an administrator (in Windows XP, that's a Limited Account; in Vista it's a Standard Account).

Creating an account on the server is completely separate from creating an account on a home or office computer. You can readily start a new account on a networked home computer, and never put that account on the server. You can create a new account on the server, and never put it on any of the networked computers. On Windows XP computers, you need to be concerned about the difference between Administrator and Limited accounts. On Vista computers you similarly have to balance Administrator versus Standard accounts. On Windows Home Servers, there's no distinction — no second-class citizens. Either your user name is recognized, or it isn't.

Here's the easy and fast way to bring your list of users on the server up to speed:

1. **Follow the steps in the preceding section to set your server's password policy.**

   In almost all cases (except for user names that will access the network from the Internet), Strong passwords are overkill. On the other hand, Weak passwords can be problematic if you have shared data that's even a little bit sensitive.

2. **One by one, go to each computer on your network.**

   If you add users from one computer, then from the next, then from the next, you're less likely to overlook a user name — particularly one that isn't used very often.

3. **Get to the Windows Welcome screen and make a note of every user name on the computer.**

   You may have to click Start⇨Log Off⇨Log Off (in Windows XP), or Start⇨right wedge⇨Log Off (in Vista) to bring up the Welcome screen. Write down the precise name. Spelling counts!

   If you encounter a computer with no user accounts, or a computer with just one account that logs on automatically, you need to find the name associated with the automatically-logged-on account.

   • In Windows XP, you can set a user name to log on automatically with the TweakUI PowerToy, available at

      www.microsoft.com/windowsxp/downloads/powertoys/xppowertoys.mspx

   • In Vista, a user gets logged on automatically if there is only one user name on the computer, and that account has no password.

   • If you get logged on automatically and there is no Welcome screen, click Start and look for the user name at the top of the Start menu.

If the only user name you can find on a computer is Administrator, *don't* try to add an account called Administrator to your Windows Home Server box. Life's too short — and if you don't confuse WHS, at the very least you'll confuse yourself. Ditto for made-up names that came pre-installed on the computer like Customer or Satisfied Dell Customer. Take a few minutes to set up a real account on your home or office computer. Here's how:

   a. Log on to the computer with an account that has administrator privileges.

      In Windows XP, click Start⇨Control Panel⇨User Accounts, and then click the link to Create a New Account.

      In Vista, click Start⇨Control Panel and, under the User Accounts and Family Safety icon, click the link to Add or Remove User Accounts.

   b. Make yourself a real, personalized account and use it proudly. (Even if you *are* a Satisfied Dell Customer.)

With a list of all the valid user names on the home or office computer in your hot little hands, you're ready to make those names known to the server.

4. **Log on to the home or office computer.**

You can use any kind of account — the account you use to log in doesn't need to have Administrator privileges.

5. **Double-click the Windows Home Server icon in the system tray, down near the clock.**

The Windows Home Server Console appears.

6. **Click the User Accounts tab at the top.**

The WHS Console lists all the accounts that have been set up on the server. If you haven't yet set up any accounts, the WHS Console just shows the Guest account.

7. **In the upper-left corner, click the plus-sign icon that says Add.**

Windows Home Server, working inside the WHS Console, brings up the Add User Account dialog box shown in Figure 4-2.

8. **In the box marked Logon Name, type the first user name that you jotted down in Step 3.**

If you like, you can also type in the user's real (meatspace) first name and last name — or use Phineas Fahrquahrt, for that matter.

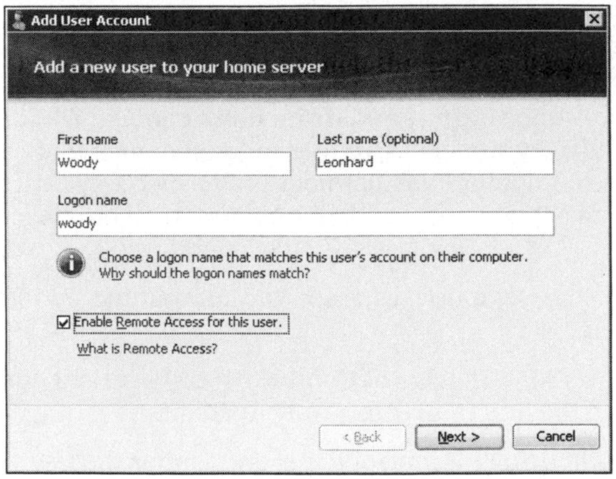

Figure 4-2:
Add a new user name, er, logon name.

Add User Account	
Add a new user to your home server	
First name	Last name (optional)
Woody	Leonhard
Logon name	
woody	

Choose a logon name that matches this user's account on their computer. Why should the logon names match?

☑ Enable Remote Access for this user.
What is Remote Access?

< Back   Next >   Cancel

Capitalization doesn't matter. If the home PC has a user name of Phineas and the server log on name comes out phineas because you forgot to capitalize the P, you shouldn't have any problems.

9. **If you want this specific user name (logon name) to be able to use Remote Access, check the box marked Enable Remote Access for this User.**

Realize that if you check the box, Windows Home Server will require you to provide — and use — a Strong password for this particular user name, *every time* you use the user name.

Not to worry. Remote Access, in general, doesn't work until you turn it on. (See Chapter 13 for details.)

10. Click Next.

Windows Home Server asks you to type in a password, per Figure 4-3.

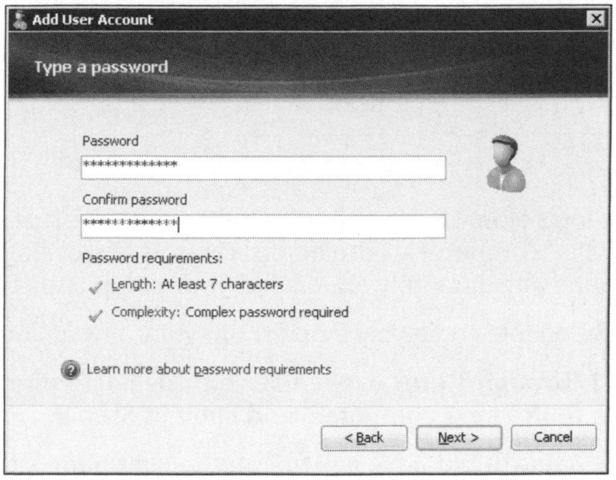

Figure 4-3:
The
password
has to meet
your
established
criteria.

You will save yourself a bit of headache in the future if you type in the same password for the server that's already in effect on the home or office computer. (See the section "Changing Passwords the Old-Fashioned Way" for details.)

11. Type in a password that passes muster. (See Table 4-1 for details.) Click Next.

WHS asks you to establish access rights to the currently available shared folders, as in Figure 4-4.

12. Consider which rights you wish to grant to this user name, and choose the buttons accordingly. Click Finish.

Keep in mind that Full access includes the ability to delete files, although you can retrieve a shadow copy "previous version" if the original gets munged (see Chapter 21).

13. Marvel as WHS checks off a list as it creates the account, sets access to shared folders, creates a new shared folder for the new user name, and (if so instructed) enables Remote Access for the user name. Click Done.

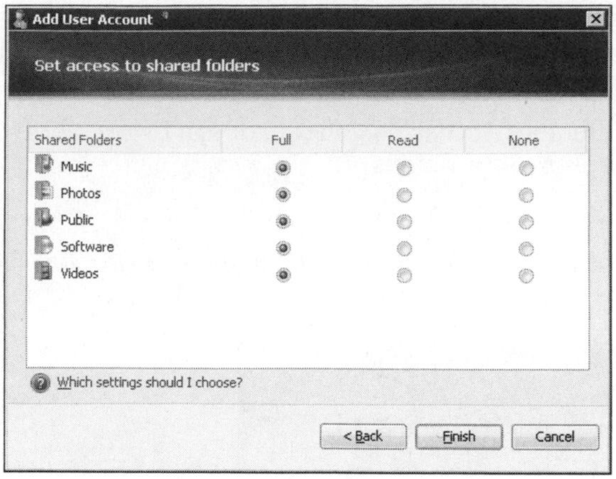

Add User Account ✕

Set access to shared folders

Shared Folders	Full	Read	None
Music	●	○	○
Photos	●	○	○
Public	●	○	○
Software	●	○	○
Videos	●	○	○

Which settings should I choose?

[< Back] [Finish] [Cancel]

Figure 4-4:
You can
set basic
access
rights for
shared
folders.

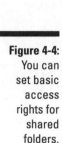

Note how Windows Home Server didn't change the user's password on the home or office computer — the computer you're working on hasn't been changed one iota. It merely channeled your commands to the server.

When the WHS Console comes back up for air, your new account appears.

14. **Repeat Steps 7 through 13 for every user on this particular computer. Then move on to the next computer, and start at Step 3.**

Sooner or later, you should have a list of all the user names that are allowed to log on to your Windows Home Server. (See Figure 4-5.)

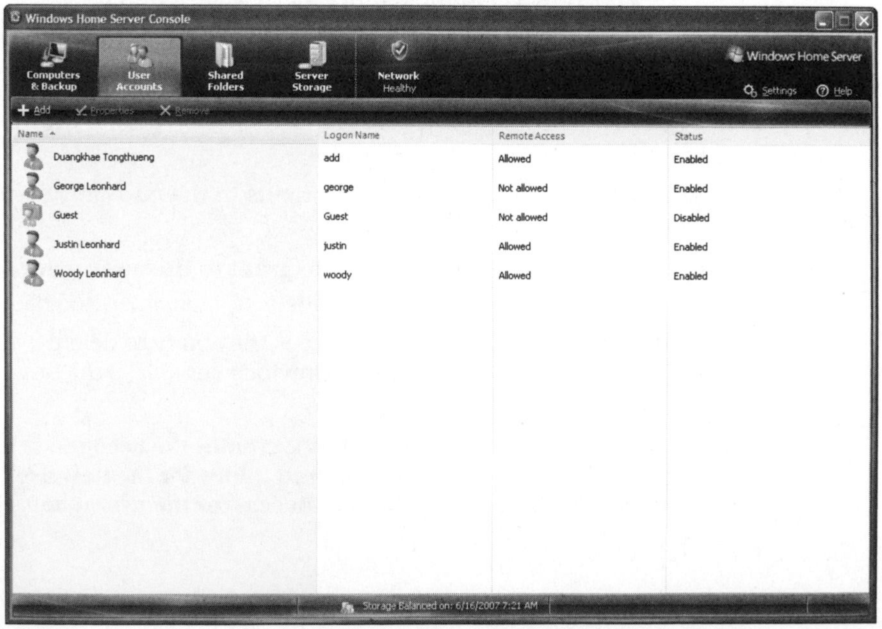

Windows Home Server Console _ □ ✕

Computers & Backup | User Accounts | Shared Folders | Server Storage | Network Healthy | Windows Home Server
Settings Help

✚ Add   Properties   ✕ Remove

Name ▲	Logon Name	Remote Access	Status
Duangkhae Tongthueng	add	Allowed	Enabled
George Leonhard	george	Not allowed	Enabled
Guest	Guest	Not allowed	Disabled
Justin Leonhard	justin	Allowed	Enabled
Woody Leonhard	woody	Allowed	Enabled

Storage Balanced on: 6/16/2007 7:21 AM

Figure 4-5:
My
Windows
Home
Server user
names.

Using the Guest Account

Every version of Windows in the past decade or so has harbored a built-in account called Guest.

Because of some poor implementation decisions in earlier versions of Windows (including Windows XP) — and a whole lotta miscommunication — the Guest account has been vilified, denigrated, spat upon, and railed against like a tree-hugger at a paper-pulp convention. Pity the poor Guest.

Most people don't realize that the Guest account lives a double life. On the one hand, it's a handy, catch-all account that works great if you want to give house guests access to parts of your server, without giving away full access to everything on the network.

On the other hand, the Guest account has been trusted with behind-the-scenes duties that make it a crucial part of running some networks. You may be surprised to know that the best way to give an Xbox 360 full access to Windows Media Center capabilities — drawing on media stored on your Windows Home Server — hinges on enabling the lowly Guest account. (See Chapter 9 for details.)

The Guest account is always there. But unless you specifically "enable" it, the account stays hidden, or at least buried deep.

If you enable the Guest account, you usually don't give it a password. That makes it easy for your actual *guests* — your 90-pound Aunt Mildred, or the 800-pound Media Center gorilla — to get onto your server and rumble around a bit. Security folks don't like that. They shudder at the idea of an unprotected account of any sort — and one with a perfectly predictable name like Guest certainly does pose an inherent security risk.

Personally, I enable the Guest account. Your situation may differ. You may be afraid that someone will sit down at a computer connected to your (possibly wireless) network, log in as Guest, and finger your files like King Kong and Fay Wray. It could happen. So if you decide to enable your Guest account — particularly if you enable it *and don't assign a password* — make sure you understand the consequences.

With that warning, here's how to enable the account called "Guest":

1. **On any home or office networked PC, double-click the Windows Home Server icon, down in the notification area next to the time. Type the server's password and press Enter.**

   You see the Windows Home Server Console.

2. **Click the User Accounts tab.**

   You see a list of all user names that are valid on the server.

3. **Double-click the line marked Guest.**

   The Properties for Guest dialog box appears, as in Figure 4-6.

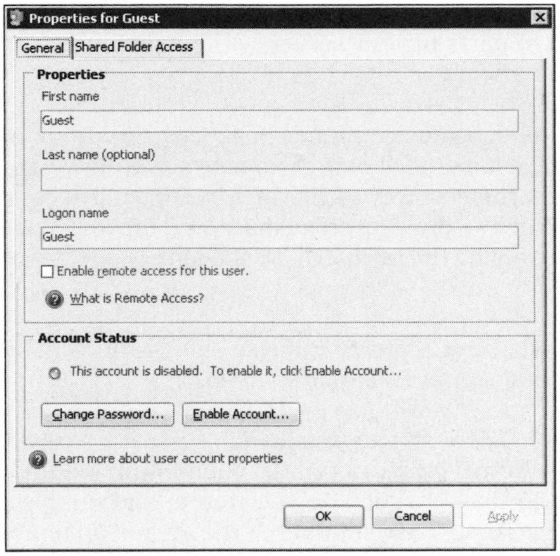

Figure 4-6:
Enable the
Guest
account
through this
dialog box.

4. **At the bottom, click the button marked Enable Account.**

   The Enable Guest Account Wizard splash screen appears.

5. **Click Next.**

   The wizard asks whether you want to establish a password for the Guest account, as in Figure 4-7.

6. **Create a password if you like, and click Next.**

   (To my mind, putting a password on the Guest account is like inviting guests into your house and then locking all the bathrooms. But your situation may differ.)

   The Enable Guest Account Wizard asks which folders the Guest account should be able to access. (See Figure 4-8.)

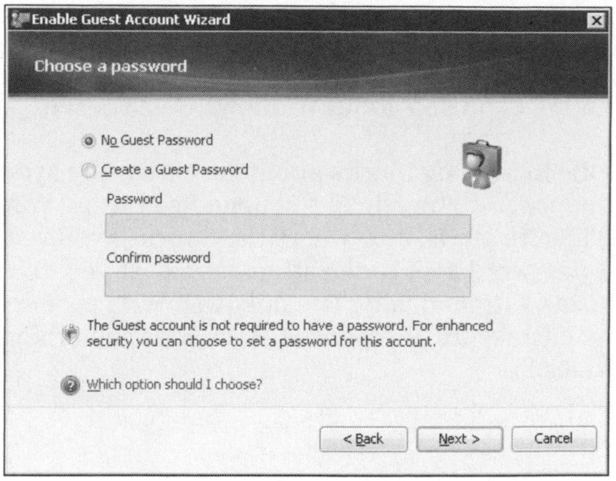

Figure 4-7:
Put a
password
on the Guest
account if
you must.

This is where the password-less Guest account should differ from other accounts on the server. In my situation, I give the Guest account Read access to all built-in shared folders, but no access at all to any other folders.

7. Choose whatever restrictions feel right for you and then click Finish.

Windows Home Server enables the account called "Guest" on the server.

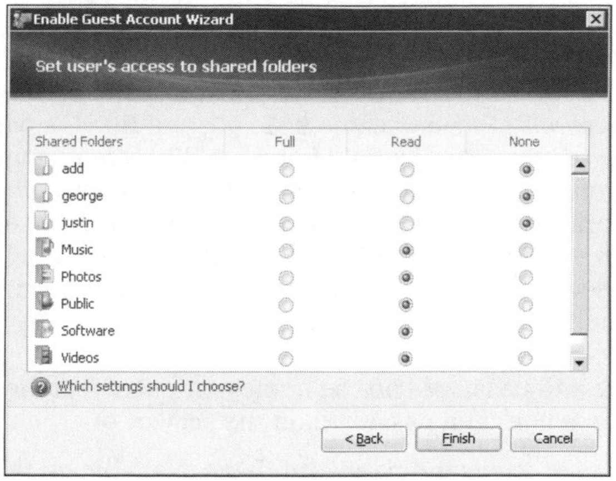

Figure 4-8:
Don't go
overboard
on giving
the Guest
account
access to
everything.

8. Click Done.

The Guest account takes its rightful place among the other accounts, which you know because its status changes to Enabled in the Windows Home Server Console.

Synchronizing Passwords

Lots of people I know get confused about Windows Home Server passwords.

Many of them read the marketing blurbs about automatically synchronized passwords (that's supposed to be one of the benefits of using Windows Home Server, eh?) but can't figure out how or where they work. If you've been having trouble figuring out password synchronization, let me let you in on a little secret: *Nothing* happens automatically. The only way WHS passwords can confuse you is if you mistakenly believe that WHS does something tricky with passwords. It doesn't.

Let's look at the basics.

Your server has a list of user names and passwords. Each of the home or office computers on your network has its own list of user names and passwords. They're separate lists — so changing the password on the server, or on any of the home or office computers, doesn't do squat to the password(s) on any other computer. There's no ripple. Not even a splash.

In one sense that's nice, because it keeps everything simple: Passwords don't go bump in the night; the only way a password on any computer can get changed is if you (or someone else) manually changes it. But in another sense, it's a pain in the neck: If your user name sits on six different computers, plus the server, and you want to change your password, you have to change it manually — seven different times.

It's important to keep all the passwords in sync. If your network has an account on several computers with the user name BillyG, and BillyG's password on the server is go!getem!MSFT!, it would behoove BillyG to change the password on *all* the computers to go!getem!MSFT!. Here's why: If you log on to one of your home or office computers with a user name that's been set up on the server, and then you try to access the data on the server (using, for example, the Shared Folders on Server icon on your home computer's desktop), Windows Home Server won't let you in unless

> ✔ The user name and password on the home computer matches the user name (er, logon name) and password on the server; or

> ✔ You provide a user name and password that's available on the server, using a dialog box like the one shown in Figure 4-9.

In short, even if your user name is known on both the home PC and the server, getting at data on the server when the two passwords don't match qualifies as a monumental, time-sucking pain in the neck.

Figure 4-9:
If the PC
and server
passwords
don't match,
you see
this box.

> **Connect to server** [?][X]
>
> Connecting to Server
>
> User name: 🛡 SANUK\woody ▾
> Password: ●●●●●●●●●●●●
> ☐ Remember my password
>
> [OK] [Cancel]

Microsoft's marketing material would have you believe that Windows Home Server includes an automatic routine to help you keep all your passwords — on all your network's computers — in sync. In fact, the assistance on offer doesn't do much at all. It's really only useful if you want to change your account's password *on the server* but don't know the password for the server itself.

Follow along here to see the extent of WHS's password synchronization:

1. **Using the steps in the section "Adding New Users the Smart Way," make sure your user name is available on the server.**

   When you set up the user name, you also establish a password.

2. **Log on to one of the computers on the network that recognizes your user name.**

   You may have to provide a password, which may or may not match the password that's on the Windows Home Server.

   If you log on with a user name (er, logon ID) that's already set up on the server, but the passwords don't match, the Windows Home Server icon in the notification area may advise you that "Passwords do not match / Windows Home Server needs your current password."

3. **Right-click the Windows Home Server icon, in the notification area, near the system clock.**

   See the line marked *Update Password*?

   • If the line marked Update Password is grayed out, then the password on this computer (the password you just typed in order to log on to this computer) matches the password on the server. Breathe a sigh of relief and — if you still want to change your password — go on to the next section. This particular Windows Home Server utility can't help you.

• If the line marked Update Password is not grayed out, the password you just typed in order to log on to this computer is *not* the same as the password on the server. Unlucky you. Choose the line that says Update Password.

Your computer shows you the Update Password dialog box, per Figure 4-10.

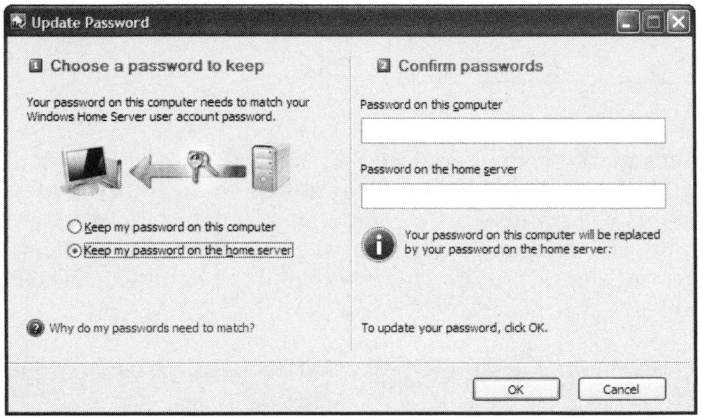

Figure 4-10: To update a password, you must know the passwords.

Ignore the gibberish in the dialog box about how your password on this computer needs to match the Windows Home Server's password. Rubbish. Synchronizing passwords will make it easier and faster to get at files on the server, and in some cases it may allow you to log on to this computer remotely. That's it.

4. Decide how you want to make the passwords match.

• If you want to copy the password on the current computer to the server — so the server's password matches the password you just typed to log on to this computer — select the line marked *Keep My Password on This Computer.*

• If you want to copy the password on the server, so it becomes the password on this computer too, select the line marked Keep My Password on the Home Server.

5. Type the password you just used to get into this computer in the top box. Type the password for this account on the server in the bottom box. Click OK.

Yes, you must type in *both* passwords in order to make the change — but (perhaps surprisingly) you don't need to know the Windows Home Server's password.

If Windows Home Server successfully changes the password — either copying this computer's password to the server or vice versa — you see a green check mark and a confirmation notice in the Update Password dialog box.

6. **Click Close.**

It's important to realize that you just changed the password on precisely one computer. If you need to change passwords on other computers, you have to log on to each of those other computers and repeat this process.

That's the whole automatic-password-synchronization shtick. It's the only way to change your account's password on the server if you don't know the server's password. Except for that one (very specific) situation, it's a hard way to do something that's normally very easy (as described in the next section).

Changing Passwords the Old-Fashioned Way

The preceding section should've had you wondering, "Where's the Clara Peller?" er, "Where's the Beef?"

I'll forgive you if you decide to forego the wonders of WHS automation and simply change your passwords manually. It's easy. If you want a new password for your account and you want them to match, simply change your user password on the server, and then change your user password in XP or Vista. The following sections walk you through the steps for doing just that.

On the server

To change the password for an account on the server, follow these steps:

1. **Pick any home or office computer and log on to it with any account.**

You can use an account with Administrator privileges, or a Limited (Windows XP) or Standard (Windows Vista) account. Doesn't make any difference.

2. **Double-click the Windows Home Server icon in the notification area, near the system clock.**

You see the WHS Console logon dialog box.

3. **Type the server's password and click the right-pointing arrow.**

   The Windows Home Server Console appears.

4. **Click the User Accounts icon at the top.**

   A list of users defined on the server appears. Refer to Figure 4-5, earlier in this chapter.

5. **Right-click the name of the account you want to change and then choose Change Password.**

   The Change Password dialog box appears, as in Figure 4-11.

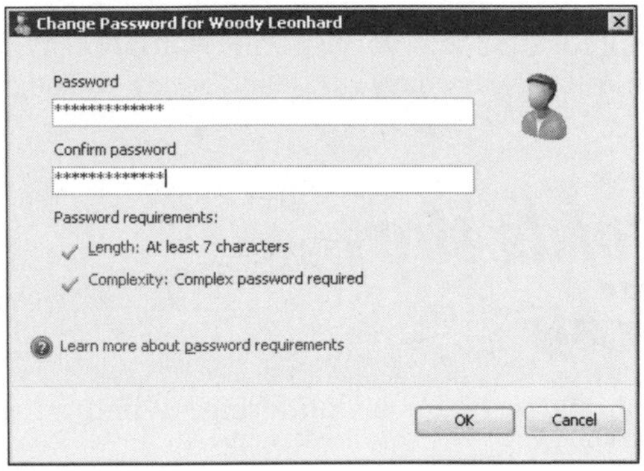

Figure 4-11:
Change an account's password here.

6. **Type the new password twice.**

   If there are any requirements imposed by the password policy currently in effect (see the "Raising the Bar for Passwords" section, earlier in this chapter) — or if you're changing the password on an account that is authorized to use Remote Access (which automatically requires a Strong password) — you need to type in a sufficiently complex password.

   Note that you *don't have to type in the old password.* Using this approach, you can modify every user's password with impunity.

7. **Click OK.**

   The new password comes into effect immediately.

In Windows XP

Here's how to change the password for an account on a Windows XP machine:

1. **Make sure you're logged on to the Windows XP computer with an account that has Administrator privileges.**

2. **Click Start⇨Control Panel⇨User Accounts, click the account that you want to change, and then click the link to Change the Password (or Create a Password, if the account doesn't have a password).**

3. **Type the new password twice.**

   Heed the warning about resetting passwords and losing encrypted files. For more details see my *Windows XP All-In-One Desk Reference For Dummies*, published by Wiley.

4. **Click Change Password, then X-button out of the User Accounts dialog box.**

   That's all it takes.

In Windows Vista

Changing the password for an account on a Windows Vista machine is almost the same as in Windows XP:

1. **Make sure you're logged on to the Vista computer with an account that has Administrator privileges.**

2. **Click Start⇨Control Panel. Under the icon marked User Accounts and Family Safety, click the link to Add or Remove User Accounts.**

3. **Click Continue to get through the $#@! User Access Control dialog box.**

4. **Click the name of the account you want to change, and then click the link to Change the Password (or Create a Password, if the account doesn't have a password).**

5. **Type the new password twice.**

   Heed the warning about resetting passwords and losing encrypted files. For more details see my *Windows Vista All-In-One Desk Reference For Dummies*, published by Wiley.

   Bonus points if you click the link that says How to Create a Strong Password. It seems that Windows Vista's definition of a Strong Password and Windows Home Server's definition of a Strong Password are quite different.

6. **Click Change Password, then X-button out of the User Accounts dialog box.**

   Synchronizing this way works pretty well, wouldn't you say?

Chapter 5

Using Built-In Shared Folders

In This Chapter

▶ Getting into the shared folders from Windows XP, Vista, and other computers

▶ Figuring out what to put and where to put it

▶ Controlling access to the shared folders

▶ Turning on the nearly-magical Folder Duplication feature

▶ Understanding the benefits — and limitations — of shared folders

*W*indows Home Server creates locations — you can call them *shared folders* — where people using the network can stick stuff.

Here's the Norman Rockwell version: When your Great Aunt Matilda comes over for dinner and she wants to look at your family photos, she can sit down at any computer on the network and see this folder called Photos. *Mirabile dictu*, that's where the photos reside. Click, click, click and in ten seconds flat she's looking at snapshots of Billy Jr. graduating from preschool or fabled search companion Rover eating the family cat.

Life's rarely that simple, eh? I don't know about your Great Aunt Matilda, but mine gets intimidated as soon as she sits in front of a computer. She'd be much more comfortable holding up the mouse and speaking into it, "Computer, show me the family photos, %$#@ it!" But we're still a long way from that point. Even Scotty on the *Enterprise* had trouble conversing with a recalcitrant mouse (in *Star Trek IV: The Voyage Home*), so I shouldn't expect too much from Aunt Matilda.

In the real Windows Home Server world, in order to get to the shared folder with pictures of Billy, Aunt Matilda has to log on to a computer on the network, locate and double-click the shortcut on the desktop called Shared Folders on Server, provide a user name and password that passes muster, and double-click the Photos folder. Only then can she finally start spelunking through the shots.

If you set up things the right way, WHS makes much of this simpler than it's ever been before. You don't need to figure out which computer holds the photos, for example — they're on the server, where they should be, of course. Don't need to know which drive, or the share name of the drive, or any of that arcana. By gathering up everything worthy of sharing and sticking it on the server, you can take great advantage of the old adage "a place for everything and everything in its place." Sounds corny, but it works.

This chapter explains what you can do to minimize Aunt Matilda's angst and to keep things organized, so the right people on your network stand a fighting chance of finding whatever it is you're trying to share — and the wrong people don't even get close.

Organizing Files with Shared Folders

Every Windows Home Server, uh, server includes six shared folders. The following list explains the intended use of each one:

- **Music:** All the songs you have that can be played on every computer in the network, or downloaded to an MP3 player by *every* computer on the network. It doesn't make much sense to stick music that's locked in to one specific computer in this folder. (See Chapter 6 for details.)

- **Photos:** Pictures that you want to make available to anybody on the network. If you have photos of a wild office party that you don't want the kids to see, stick them in a different, custom shared folder, where it's easier to limit access to specific user names. (See "Creating new shared folders" later in this chapter for details.)

- **Public:** The "all other" category that typically includes documents, spreadsheets, and other kinds of files you want to make easily available. If you want to keep all your shared documents together in the Public folder, but limit access to some of them, consider using document passwords on the sensitive documents. For example, in a small office network, you could put all the financial documents in a single folder hanging under the Public folder, but lock the payroll spreadsheets with passwords. That way you always know where to find the spreadsheets — but only folks with the password can look at them.

- **Software:** Generally companies that make software destined to be installed on Windows Home Server boxes encourage you to store the software in this folder. That makes it easier to transfer the software from one of your home or office computers onto the server, so the setup program can be run from the server.

Contrariwise, the Software folder makes a great place to stick all the software you want to install on multiple computers on the network: Firefox, your antivirus program, RoboForm, and the like. Download the software on any of your network's computers, copy or move it to the shared Software folder, and you can install it on any computer with just a couple of clicks.

✔ **Users:** This is a special folder that contains one subfolder for each user account (to use Windows Home Server's terminology, each "logon name") that's been set up on the server. (I talk about the Users folder in the section called "Pinpointing each user's shared folder" later in this chapter.)

✔ **Videos:** Similar to the Photos shared folder, where you can put your home videos. Of course if you have a stash of ripped DVDs (legal ones, of course), downloaded videos destined to be played with Windows Media Player or the Xbox 360, and recorded TV shows, you'll probably find it worthwhile to stick 'em in a different folder. That reduces the number of files that Media Player has to scan. (See Chapter 6 for details.)

I say "intended use" quite deliberately. There's nothing particularly magical about any of the folders that requires you to use them just one way. You can stick photos of trustworthy politicians in the Music folder, if you like, or the latest version of Doom XII in the Videos folder. Windows Home Server doesn't police the contents of the folders. They were constructed by the WHS Gods to help you keep your server's house in order. You can use them as intended, modifying the meanings of the folders to suit your tastes. (Do FLV files downloaded from YouTube qualify as videos? I dunno. Up to you.) You can ignore the folders entirely if you like.

But you'll make your life — and the lives of the people who use your network — much simpler if you figure out what kinds of files you want to put in the built-in shared folders, and stick to your decision. This makes things easier in part because the six folders come built into WHS. You can't delete them, so you might as well use them. If your shared folder needs go above and beyond these six folders, you can create your own shared folders, too. (See "Controlling Shared Folders from the Console" later in this chapter for the details.)

Finding the Shared Folders

When you run the WHS Connector CD on a Windows computer — Windows XP or Vista — a new shortcut called Shared Folders on Server appears on the desktop of each user's computer. Here's a quick tour . . .

Opening shared files on the server

The Shared Folders on Server shortcut is each user's gateway to the shared folders, and it works as follows:

1. **Double-click the Shared Files on Server shortcut.**

   Windows Explorer appears (see Figure 5-1) and shows all the highest-level shared folders stored on the server.

   For the shortcuts to work, the user must be logged on to the Windows XP or Vista computer with a user name and password that match one of the entries on the WHS server.

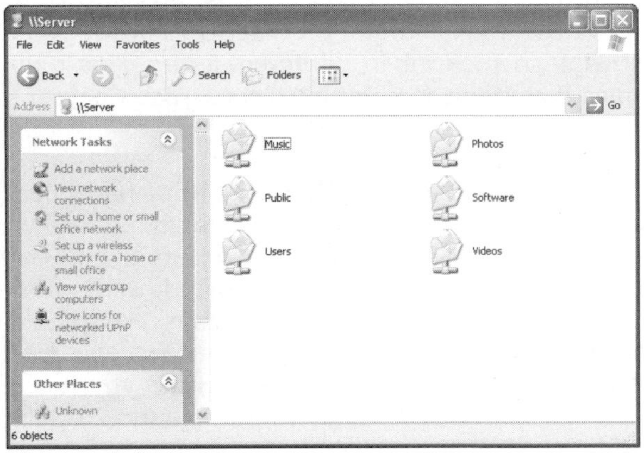

Figure 5-1:
All the shared folders appear if the user name and password match.

2. **If you click the shortcut but see a challenge dialog box like the one in Figure 5-2, you can do either of the following:**

   • Type in a user name and password that's been entered on the server (doesn't matter if the user name and password work on the home or office computer — they have to work on the server)

   • See whether the Guest account has been enabled on the server (see Chapter 4): simply type Guest as a user name (while leaving the Password box blank), and then click OK or press Enter.

   You'll see the dialog box shown in Figure 5-2 if the current user logged on to the home or office computer with a user name that doesn't appear on the server, or if the password that the current user entered doesn't match the password stored on the server.

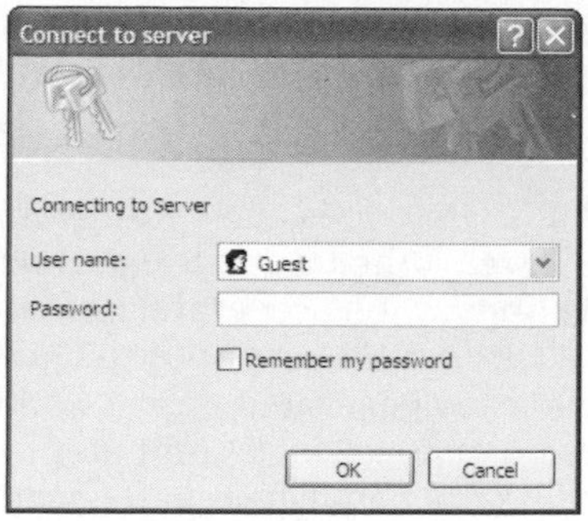

Figure 5-2:
Windows
wants to
know: Who
Goes
There?

Connect to server dialog box

For more information about getting into shared folders, see the section "Controlling Access to Shared Folders," later in this chapter.

Pinpointing each user's shared folder

When you add a new user account (er, "logon name") to the server, Windows Home Server automatically creates a folder with that user's name (see Chapter 4). The user's folder gets whisked into the shared folder called Users.

Unless somebody — you or another user with Administrator privileges — changes the folder's access permission (see the next section), the only user who can get into the automatically generated user folder, read from it, or change anything in it, *is* the current user.

In Figure 5-1 (earlier in this chapter), you see the highest-level shared folders on my Windows Home Server. In Figure 5-3, you can see how WHS has set up individual folders underneath the Users folder for each user (er, logon name) that's been added to the server.

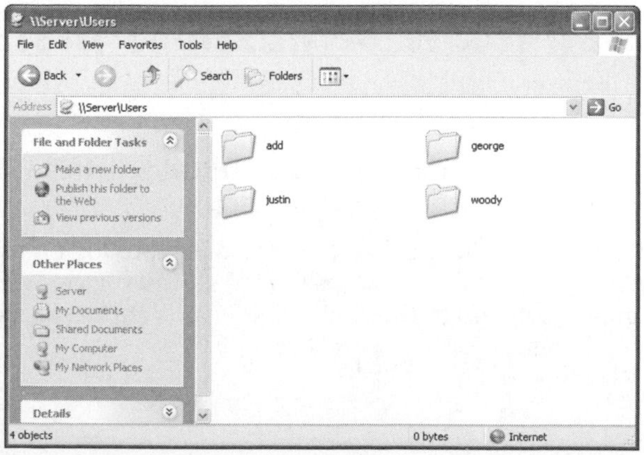

Figure 5-3:
Each user
account on
the server
gets its
own auto-
matically
generated
folder.

\\Server\Users window showing folders: add, george, justin, woody

Note that there's no folder for the account called Guest: Even though the Guest account is enabled on the server in Figure 5-3, there is no automatically generated Guest folder.

The automatically generated user folder that does exist, however, can be of some use — even if it isn't shared — even if the user is the only account that can get into it. For example, if Justin hops among several different computers on the network, and he has files that he doesn't want other people to see, he can stick those files in his automatically generated Justin folder on the server, and be able to get to his files no matter which computer he uses on the network. (He can also get to his files from anywhere in the world by using Remote Access; see Part IV.) Unless somebody changes the defaults, other people using any of the computers on the network can't get into his folder.

"Shared" folders don't have to be shared with anyone but yourself. Which brings me to the heart of the next section.

Controlling Access to Shared Folders

You might be tempted to think that all the folders you can get to from the Shared Folders on Server icon are, in fact, shared folders, and therefore accessible to you. D'OH! They aren't. Just because you can *see* a shared folder doesn't mean that you can get into it. Under normal circumstances, the folders called Music, Photos, Public, Software, and Videos are accessible to you. But you can't get into the individual Users folders (except your own) until somebody takes the initiative to make them accessible to you.

More than that, you don't have the ability to add new folders to the Shared Folders collection on the server; you can't even add a new folder to the Users folder on the server. The only place where you rule is *inside* your own Users folder. And even then, you don't have complete control.

Experiencing folder permissions firsthand

Take this guided tour of shared folders:

1. **Log on to your home or office computer. Double-click the Shared Folders on Server shortcut on your desktop.**

   • If the user name and password that you used to log on match a user name (er, "logon name") and password stored on the WHS server, you immediately go to the shared folders, as shown earlier in this chapter in Figure 5-1.

- If the user name and password that you used to log on don't match perfectly with a user name and password on the server, you get the challenge dialog box in Figure 5-2. Type a valid user name and password (which is to say, type a logon name and password known to the server) and click OK. You see the server's shared folders, per Figure 5-1.

2. **Double-click the** Music **folder. See how you can get at the files inside? Do the same for the** Photos, Public, Software, **and** Videos **folders.**

   Unless you've changed something, all the users who are known to the server (except the Guest account) have full read-and-write access to the contents of all those five folders.

3. **Double-click the** Users **folder.**

   You see a set of folders, one for each of the users who are set up on the server.

4. **Right-click a blank spot inside the** Users **folder, and choose New⇨Folder.**

   Windows XP or Vista advises you that you can't create a new folder by displaying a message that says Unable to create the folder. Access is denied.

5. **Double-click your own folder. Now right-click and choose New⇨Folder.**

   See how Windows Home Server lets you add subfolders in your own folder?

6. **Go back up to the** Users **folder, and then randomly double-click other user folders.**

   Chances are good that you can get into some of the automatically created user folders, but you can't get into others. If you can get into a folder, it means somebody specifically granted you access. You may have *read-only access*, in which case you can open any file in the folder. Or you may have *read-write access*, which means you can open, modify, or delete any file in the folder, create new subfolders, or save completely new files in the folder.

7. **Click the X button to get out of the server's shared folders.**

   Return your seats and tables to their upright positions.

When you add a new folder, it inherits the security restrictions of the parent folder. So, if a user has permission to create new subfolders in the Music folder and so creates a new folder under the shared Music folder called \John Fogerty, any user who can access the Music folder can also access the John Fogerty folder. Any user who can change or delete files in the Music folder can also change or delete John Fogerty. (I bet when John figures that out, he won't be too happy about it.)

Changing shared folder permissions

To change access permissions for a shared folder on the server, follow these steps:

1. **Working from any computer on the network, double-click the Windows Home Server icon in the system tray, down near the clock.**

   You see the Windows Home Server Console screen.

2. **Type the server's password in the indicated box, and then press Enter.**

3. **When the Windows Home Server Console comes up, click the Shared Folders icon at the top.**

   The WHS Console brings up a list of shared folders on the server, as in Figure 5-4.

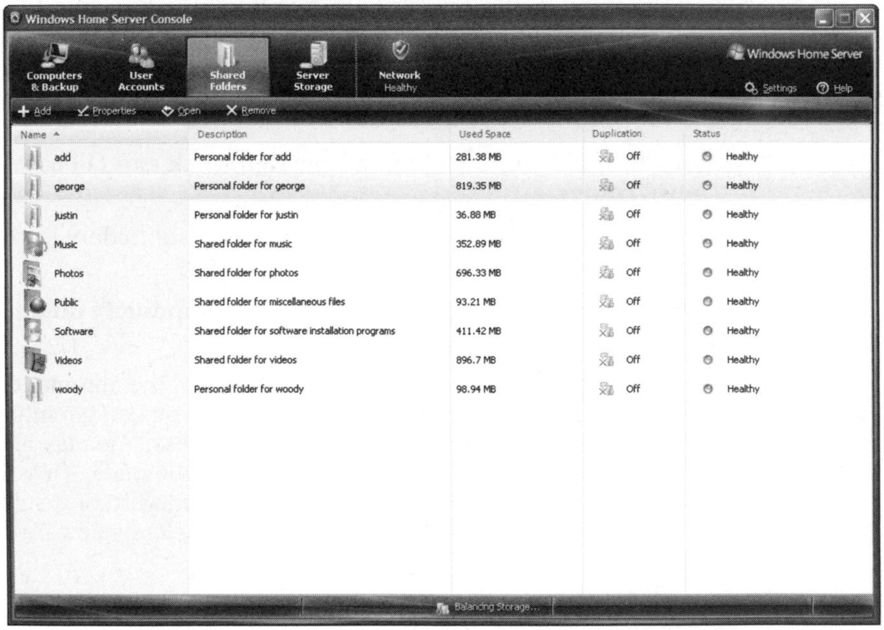

Windows Home Server Console
Computers & Backup
User Accounts
Shared Folders
Server Storage
Network Healthy
Windows Home Server
Settings
Help
Add
Properties
Open
Remove
Name
Description
Used Space
Duplication
Status
add
Personal folder for add
281.38 MB
Off
Healthy
george
Personal folder for george
819.35 MB
Off
Healthy
justin
Personal folder for justin
36.88 MB
Off
Healthy
Music
Shared folder for music
352.89 MB
Off
Healthy
Photos
Shared folder for photos
696.33 MB
Off
Healthy
Public
Shared folder for miscellaneous files
93.21 MB
Off
Healthy
Software
Shared folder for software installation programs
411.42 MB
Off
Healthy
Videos
Shared folder for videos
896.7 MB
Off
Healthy
woody
Personal folder for woody
98.94 MB
Off
Healthy
Balancing Storage...

Figure 5-4: Your server's shared folders.

If you're accustomed to looking at the server's shared folders by clicking the Shared Folders on Server icon on your desktop (as shown earlier in this chapter in Figure 5-1), this list won't look right: There's no Users folder. WHS allows you to set access permissions easily for five of the built-in shared folders — `Music`, `Photos`, `Public`, `Software`, and `Videos` — but it doesn't help you set permissions for any subfolders sitting inside those five built-in folders. WHS also makes it easy to set permissions for each of the automatically generated user folders, but it doesn't do anything to help with the Users folder itself — or with any subfolders inside the user folders. What you see in Figure 5-4 is a list of the folders you can change through the Console.

4. **Double-click the folder you want to change (or right-click the folder and choose Properties).**

   The WHS Console brings up the General tab of the Properties dialog box for the shared folder.

5. **Click the User Access tab.**

   You see the access permissions that have been granted for the folder, as shown in Figure 5-5.

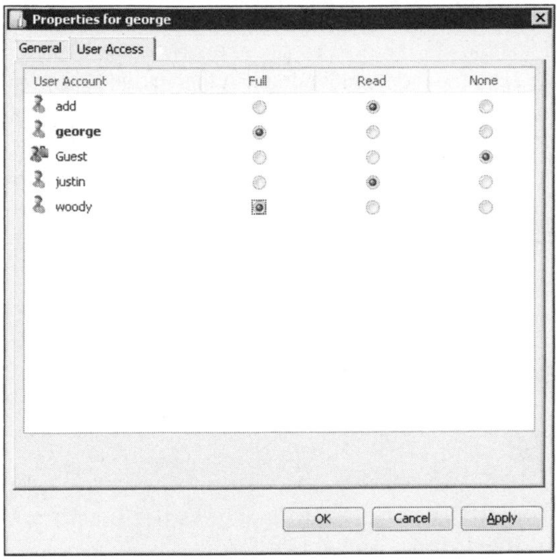

Figure 5-5: Access permissions for the folder called george.

The dialog box in Figure 5-5 is far from a paragon of clarity. To understand what it means, start at the top. The title bar at the top of the box tells you which shared folder you're setting access permissions for. In this case, it's the folder called george. Along the left, Windows Home Server lists all the users (er, "logon names") that are known to the server. The Guest account appears on the list whether you've enabled it or not (see Chapter 4). The name of the user who owns the folder appears in bold: thus **george** is in bold on the left side.

Each user has exactly one of three available access settings: Full, Read, or None. (I define those permissions more fully in Table 5-1.) You change access permissions for a specific user name (er, logon name) by selecting one of the radio buttons to the right of the user name.

6. **When you're happy with the User Access settings for this folder, click OK.**

The changes take effect immediately. If anybody on your network is looking at a shared folder when access permission change, they may see spurious Access Denied errors. Tell them to log off and log back on again, and the error should go away.

Table 5-1	Access Permission Levels
Level	*What it means*
Full	The indicated user can do anything with the files in the folder: open, modify, save, over-write, delete, or blast with a bituminous bit blotter. That user can also add and delete sub-folders within the shared folder.
Read	The indicated user can only open (and copy) files in the folder. If the user modifies the file, it has to be saved elsewhere — WHS won't allow the user to save the modified file back in this folder. Similarly, the user cannot delete files in the folder, create new files in the folder, or add (or delete) subfolders under the main shared folder.
None	Zip. Nada. The indicated user can't get into the folder; can't even pop in to have a look at the filenames.

Controlling Shared Folders from the Console

In the preceding section, I talk about setting access permissions for shared folders, using the Windows Home Server Console.

Working from the Console, you can do more than just set access permissions. In particular, you have these powers:

✓ **You can create your own custom shared folders on the server.** After they're created, the new shared folders have all the properties of the other shared folders — so, for example, you can set access permissions on your new folders in the same way you set them on any other folders. Custom shared folders can serve many purposes. You can put, say, R-rated music in a custom shared folder — and adjust the access permission levels accordingly. You can set up a separate folder with pictures that can be seen by anyone with Remote Access privileges on your computer (see Part IV), so grandpa and grandma can see pics of your latest vacation trip without bumping into inopportune shots of the car accident.

Shared folder naming requirements are a bit more restrictive than those found in Windows XP and Vista. A new shared folder's name can contain letters, numbers, spaces, periods (.), hyphens (-), or underscores (_). The last character must be either a letter or a number.

✔ **You can delete any shared folders except the five built-in folders** (Music, Photos, Public, Software, **and** Videos). You can rename the other folders, too, although I don't recommend it; life in server-land is complicated enough without puzzling over renamed folders.

✔ **You can look at a histogram showing the space taken up by files in the folder.** To do so, right-click the folder and choose View History. WHS shows you a graph of the total space occupied by all files in the folder, as in Figure 5-6.

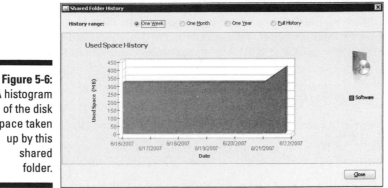

Figure 5-6: A histogram of the disk space taken up by this shared folder.

✔ **You do pretty much anything that requires full access.** For example, you can copy data into or out of shared folders, look at the contents of the folders, change the structure of the folders, or perform high-level tasks such as moving a subfolder from one shared folder to another. In effect, working from the WHS Console, you have complete access permission to everything. Simply click the shared folder that you want to get into, and then click the Open link on the menu bar.

In order to set up custom shared folders — or change just about any detail regarding any kind of shared folder, whether WHS created the folder or you made it yourself — you need to know the server's password. Without the server's password, you can work inside your own shared folder; and you can get into the built-in shared folders for music, photos and the like; but that's about it, unless somebody has taken the initiative to grant you permission to monkey around with some other shared folder. If you have delusions of grandeur about setting up a great sharing scheme, but you don't have the server's password, you're outta luck.

Creating new shared folders

Let's say you have your own small business. Your home network (which just happens to be your office network) gets used by several folks with prying eyes and not a whole lotta horse sense, if you know what I mean.

More than that, let's say that you need to store something — oh, invoices, maybe, or tax records, or business proposals — that you want several people to be able to access from anywhere on the network, but you don't want every Tom, Dick, or BillyG (or his little sister) to be able to look at, modify, or delete them.

Perfect. You have a classic need for a custom folder.

Notice that I didn't mention whether the folder would include spreadsheets or PDF files or glowing paisley wormhole extensions. With rare exception, when you create a new custom folder, your number-one thought should revolve around access. Or, to look at it a little more accurately and less naively, *denying* access.

Follow these steps to create a new custom folder:

1. **Log on to any computer on your home or office network.**

   It doesn't matter if the user name and password that you use are known to the server or not. But you *do* need to know the server's password.

2. **Double-click the Windows Home Server icon down in the notification area, next to the system clock.**

   Windows Home Server invites you to log on.

3. **Type in the server's password and press Enter.**

   The server's password is the one you set up when you first installed the server. See Chapter 3 for details, or Chapter 19 if you forgot the password altogether.

4. **At the top, click the Shared Folders icon.**

   You should see something like Figure 5-1, which appears at the beginning of this chapter. I describe the columns, their sources and their meanings in Table 5-2.

5. **Click the + Add icon at the upper left.**

   The Add a Shared Folder Wizard invites you to add a shared folder, per Figure 5-7.

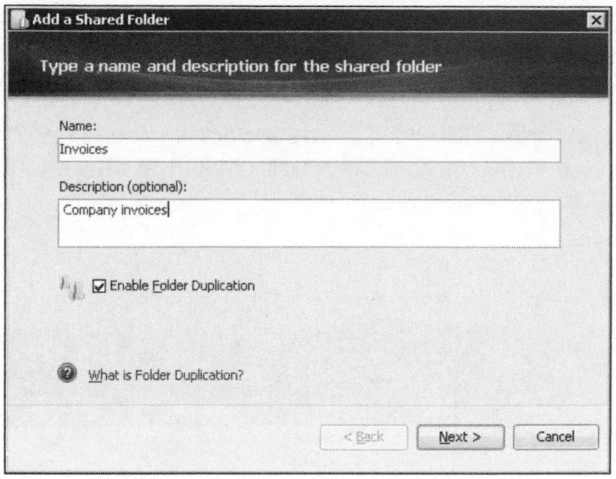

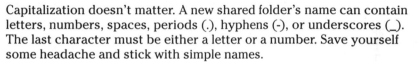

Figure 5-7:
Create a
new custom
shared
folder.

6. **Type a name for the folder.**

   Capitalization doesn't matter. A new shared folder's name can contain
   letters, numbers, spaces, periods (.), hyphens (-), or underscores (_).
   The last character must be either a letter or a number. Save yourself
   some headache and stick with simple names.

   Try to make the name both short and descriptive. Other people will be
   able to look at the name, and they should be able to decide at a glance
   if the files they seek reside in the folder.

7. **Type a description if you like. If you want to duplicate the folder (see
   "Duplicating Shared Folders" later in this chapter), and you probably
   do, check the box marked Enable Folder Duplication. Click Next.**

   Windows Home Server asks you set access permission levels, as in
   Figure 5-8.

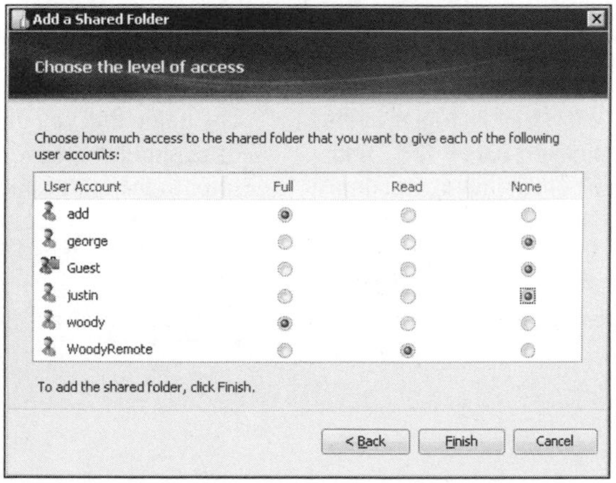

Figure 5-8:
Set access
permissions
for the new
folder.

8. **Follow the guidelines in the section "Changing shared folder permissions" earlier in this chapter, and set each user's access to Full, Read or None. Click Finish. When the wizard finishes, click Done.**

   Your new shared folder appears, ready for action (see Figure 5-9). It also shows up when anyone on your network clicks the Shared Folders on Server icon, on their desktop.

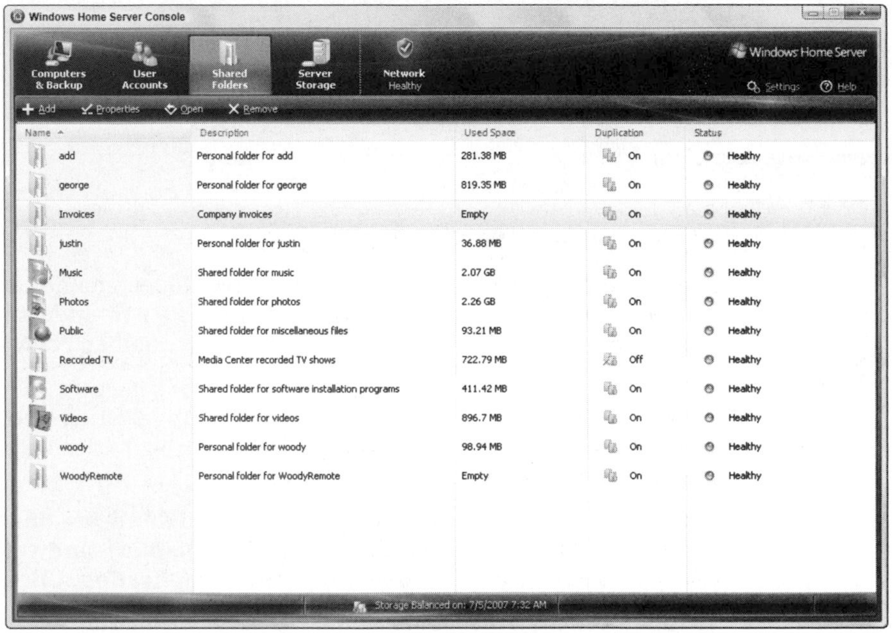

Figure 5-9: The new shared Invoices folder appears, loaded for bear.

Table 5-2	Shared Folders Characteristics	
Column	*Where It Comes From*	*What It Means*
Name	The five built-in folder names are generated by WHS and can't be changed; personal folder names are generated by WHS but you *can* change them; custom folder names are chosen by you	The name that you use throughout the network to refer to the folder, such as \\SERVER\Photos. Capitalization doesn't matter.

Column	Where It Comes From	What It Means
Description	Built-in folder descriptions generated by WHS, but you can change them; you provide custom folder descriptions	Not very helpful, really — the descriptions only appear here.
Used Space	Generated and maintained by WHS	The amount of space taken up by the original files. Doesn't include Duplicate Folder space.
Duplication	Originally all folders have Folder Duplication turned Off, but you can turn on any ones that you like.	See the section "Duplicating Shared Folders" for details.
Status	Generated and maintained by WHS.	Unless you're running out of disk space, or there's been a catastrophic disk failure, this will always read `Healthy`.

You can probably imagine situations where mixing home and office computers on a single network can get really complicated, really fast. In general, it's much more secure to keep personal computers separate from business computers, and vice versa. In practice, that may not be, uh, practical, but you need to be ever mindful of the possibility that little Billy might over-write your invoices, and plan accordingly. Peer-to-peer "workgroup" networks will never be as secure as locked-down "domain" corporate networks. Don't expect Windows Home Server to give you the kind of locked-down security that comes part and parcel with big, expensive corporate networks.

Usin' your noggin with sharin'

Windows Home Server's default permissions work just fine, for most networks, most people, most files, most of the time.

Once in a very blue moon you may decide to change permissions for a built-in folder, specifically to keep a recalcitrant user from deleting files or folders on the server that shouldn't be deleted (or modified). You may also feel compelled to change access permissions if one of the users on your network has a nasty habit of running Trojans or other programs that make mincemeat out of shared files and folders. But in general, granting Full access to the built-in folders and no access at all to users' folders makes a lot of sense, and helps to keep shared data in the built-in folders, where it belongs.

Because WHS permissions can only be assigned at the highest level — access permissions on a shared folder apply to all files and sub-folders inside the folder — the access blocking game boils down to a question of creating custom shared folders whenever you want to grant access to a limited group of people, and keep others out — or at least prevent them from clobbering the files.

Here are the rules I follow, both to simplify my life and to keep my data safe:

- ✔ Keep the default access settings on all the built-in and automatically created folders, unless there's an overwhelming need to lock someone out.

- ✔ When you need to share files among a small group of people and keep others out, create a custom shared folder, and *only grant access to people who absolutely have to get in*. If you waiver from the straight and narrow, you will frequently find that copies of confidential files end up in public places.

- ✔ If you have a truly confidential file — payroll records, for example — don't rely exclusively on shared folder access restrictions. Lock the file, too. Most office programs these days have very thorough encryption capabilities. Use them.

- ✔ Be very, very cautious granting access to your user folder — and to other users' folders, too. It's easy to forget when you're in a hurry that many moons ago you allowed somebody else permission to get into your personal shared folder. A quick click of the mouse can have far-reaching ramifications. Everybody needs some privacy. Keeping your personal folder private makes a whole lotta sense.

Duplicating Shared Folders

Windows Home Server includes a sophisticated — almost magical — capability known as *Folder Duplication*.

To a first approximation, Folder Duplication mirrors the data in a folder on two (or sometimes more) hard drives. By maintaining mirror images, any single drive can turn belly-up, and Windows Home Server will still be able to reconstitute all the files in the folder.

Folder duplication isn't the same as a backup or a "previous version" capability. These are the key differences:

✔ Windows Home Server backs up all the files on the network's Windows XP and Vista computers once a day (see Chapter 12). You can use the backups to restore an older version of a file (see Chapter 14) or if you need to revive an entire dead drive (see Chapter 13).

✔ WHS takes "previous version" snapshots of its own shared folders twice a day, and you can bring back the previous version of a file rather easily (Chapter 14).

✔ Folder duplication, on the other hand, works almost immediately. You can't get at the individual duplicated files. Folder duplication comes into play only if one of the hard drives on the server dies.

If you've ever heard of RAID — Redundant Array of Inexpensive Disks — and how a properly configured RAID system can lose a hard drive and continue without missing a beat, Windows Home Server's Folder Duplication performs a similar function, but in a very different way. Whereas RAID requires specific, dedicated hardware, Folder Duplication is baked into Windows Home Server — it doesn't require anything but plain-vanilla, everyday hardware. Some RAID systems can recover from a calamitous drive failure in the blink of an eye. Folder Duplication recovery takes awhile (see Chapter 15), but in the end it works, and works well.

You have to tell Windows Home Server that you want to enable folder duplication on specific shared folders; you don't get Folder Duplication automatically.

Folder Duplication makes it easier to sleep at night. Why? You can safely stick your family photos in Windows Home Server's Photos shared folder, turn on Folder Duplication for the Photos folder, and if one of the hard drives on your server turns belly-up, another copy is sitting around ready to (automatically!) take its place. (Like I said, magical.)

To enable folder duplication you must:

✔ Have two or more hard drives. Folder duplication doubles the amount of space required to store the files in a specific folder, because complete copies are kept on more than one hard drive.

✔ Turn on Folder Duplication for each shared folder that you want to duplicate, using the upcoming steps.

✔ Wait while the system works. The initial Folder Duplication run takes a long time. While you're waiting, Windows Home Server slows down significantly — but believe me, it's worth the wait.

If you have two or more drives on your Windows Home Server, and there's enough space to duplicate the data in your chosen shared folders, follow these steps to get Folder Duplication working:

1. **Log on to Windows Home Server's Console from any computer on the network.**

   Use the icon in the system notification area, near the clock. You'll need the server's password.

2. **Click the Shared Folders icon at the top of the Console.**

   You see a list of all shared folders on the server.

3. **Double-click the name of the folder that you want to duplicate.**

   The Properties dialog box for the folder appears, as in Figure 5-10.

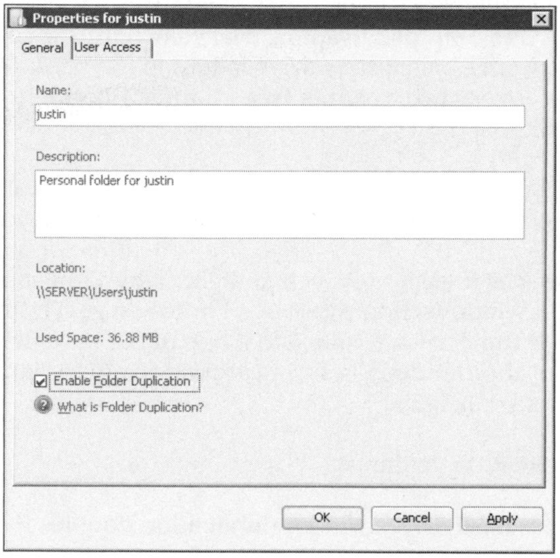

Figure 5-10:
Enable
Folder
Duplication
on the
shared
folder called
justin.

4. **Check the box marked Enable Folder Duplication. Then Click OK.**

   Windows Home Server responds by showing the Duplication status (in the Duplication column, shown in Figure 5-11) is On. It also indicates that duplication is underway by showing a Balancing Storage line at the bottom of the Console.

5. **Wait.**

   Depending on the size of the folder, the initial duplication run can take a few minutes or a few hours.

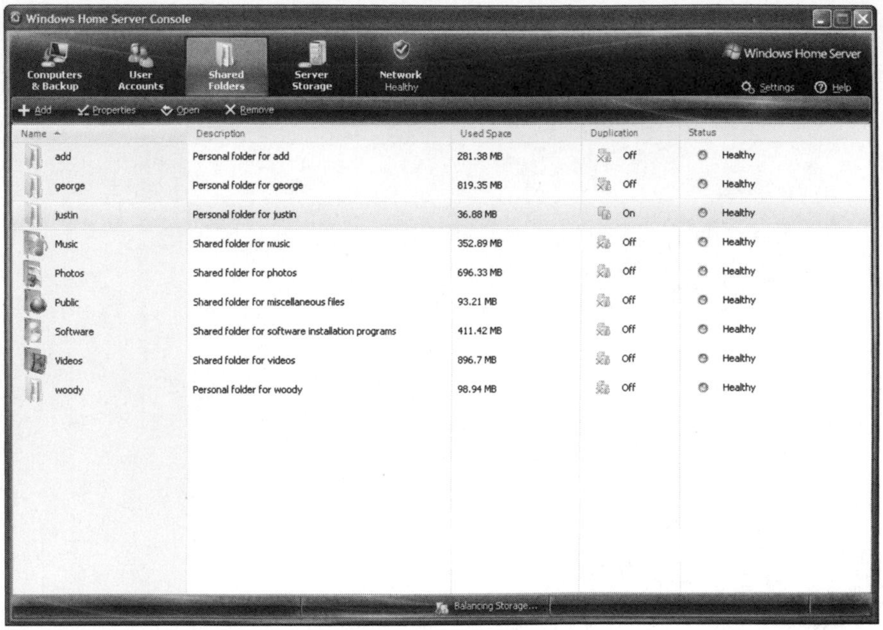

Figure 5-11:
The Console
shows
which
folders have
duplication
turned on.

I strongly recommend that you turn on Folder Duplication for every shared folder on your server, except the folders that contain stuff you can replace easily (such as, oh, downloaded programs or copies of installation CDs). If you don't have enough disk space, go out and buy more. It's really that important.

Part III
Making the Most of Multimedia

The 5th Wave   By Rich Tennant

"My guess is, they just figured out how to set up streaming
multimedia on Windows Home Server."

In this part . . .

Media-savant Windows Home Server makes a great location to store all of your music, videos, recorded TV shows, pictures, and ripped movies (legal ones, of course). You don't have to worry about outgrowing the hard drive on one (or more) of your home PCs, don't need to go searching through all your network's hard drives to find the right one — and, if you do it right, you don't need to worry about backing up your family photos or recorded TV shows.

That said, WHS exhibits quite a few rough spots when it comes to multimedia — Windows Media Player can lock out your account if you don't treat it with respect; backing up recorded TV shows takes some sleight of hand; using your Xbox to full advantage can pose some significant challenges.

This section takes you through the basics — including several surprising changes that can make a real difference in how well you can use Windows Home Server with various media. It also points out (free!) programs you can employ to smooth over the rough spots.

If multimedia under Windows Home Server has you befuddled, this part should unfuddle you. Or at least fuddle you less.

Chapter 6

Sharing Music and Videos

. . . .

In This Chapter

▶ Taking advantage of shared folders

▶ Making Windows work with shared media folders

▶ Understanding the limitations

▶ Working around the limitations

. . . .

S o you finally have WHS set up, users identified, and backups running. Good. Now for the first question on your mind (or at least, the first question on *my* mind):

Can I finally stick my music and videos on the server and get at them from all of my computers?

The answer is a resounding yes. And no. Well, sorta.

In general, you can put your media wherever you like. But whether you can actually *use* the media stored in a centralized location depends on your setup — and on the restrictions that apply to particular media.

That's what this chapter is all about.

Recorded TV shows pose particular problems, uh, "opportunities" (see Chapter 7), and the Xbox 360 and other Media Center Extenders have their own foibles (see Chapter 8). Photos work similarly, but there are some specific hoops to jump through, which I describe in Chapter 9.

In this chapter, I confine the discussion to PC-to-PC music and video shenanigans. In keeping with the basic KISS tenets (Keep It Simple, Socrates) — to which I adhere religiously — I urge you to set up simple PC-to-PC sharing via your Windows Home Server connection and get comfortable with it *before* you try to record TV or use your Xbox. So before you get bogged down in the arcane worlds of *streaming* (where your Xbox or other Media Extender box can channel music that's actually being played on a different computer) and *Media Library Sharing* (installing the plumbing that allows you to stream), the next section offers a few tricks you should consider.

Sharing from A to Z to PC to PC

Chances are pretty good that you already have your home or small office network set up to share music or videos. In a typical scenario, you can play media stored on Computer A on Computer B simply sitting down at Computer B, opening the files stored on Computer A, and running them through Windows Media Player or iTunes or maybe even Winamp.

Now that you have Windows Home Server installed, you can copy or move all your media over to the server, so everybody on the network knows where to go to find the latest Norah Jones album or Black-Eyed Peas video. In addition, with Folder Duplication enabled, you can have Windows Home Server create near-instantaneous backups of all your media files,

That part's easy. Here's an organized way to move your network's media files en masse:

1. **Make sure you have enough space on your Windows Home Server box. If you don't have enough room, don't even start moving media to the server. Wait until you've installed enough hard drive space to do the job right, the first time.**

   If you don't know off the top of your head how much music you've accumulated, go around to all the computers on your network, look in the Music and Videos folders, and count the bytes. In Vista, don't forget the Public\Public Music and Public\Public Videos folders. (In Windows XP, look for My Music and My Videos folders, both for individual users and in the Shared Documents folder.)

   If you want to have Windows Home Server maintain copies of all your music and videos, WHS needs twice the original space: if you want WHS to keep duplicates of all your music, for example, and you've accumulated 200 GB of songs, the server needs 400 GB to store two copies.

   If WHS has already successfully completed a backup of that 200 GB of music from your home computer, it already has a copy of the music, but *it isn't smart enough to know* that a copy of the music already sits inside the server. The 200 GB of backup will cycle off your server eventually (when the backup gets old enough), or you can go in and tell WHS to delete the backup entirely, thus telling it to dump the 200 GB on the next Sunday night during a cleanup run (see Chapter 12). But for the short term, if you enable Folder Duplication, you need 200 GB for the music, another 200 GB for the duplicate copy — and the old 200GB backup just sits there.

2. **If you haven't yet enabled Folder Duplication for the server's shared** `Music` **and** `Videos` **folders, and there's any way you can afford the disk space necessary to keep backup copies of your music and videos, turn on Folder Duplication.**

   I have full details of how to do that in Chapter 5. The short version: Go to any computer on the network; double-click the Windows Home Server console button in the notification area, near the clock; type in the server's password; click the Shared Folders icon. Look at the Duplication column for the `Music` and `Videos` folders. If either says Off (meaning Folder Duplication is not enabled), right-click the folder and choose Properties. Check the box marked Enable Folder Duplication, and then click OK.

   While you're in the WHS Console anyway, consider turning on Folder Duplication for your Photos, Public and Software shared folders, too.

3. **If you're going to use an Xbox or other Media Center Extender product, if you're going to put recorded TV on your server, or if you have a lot of purchased or otherwise locked-up media, turn on the server's Guest account.**

   For an in-depth explanation of the `Guest` account — and why you may not want to enable it — see Chapter 4. The short version: inside the Windows Home Server Console, click the Users icon. Look in the Status column and see if the `Guest` account is disabled. If it is, right-click the Guest icon and choose Enable Guest Account (see Figure 6-1).

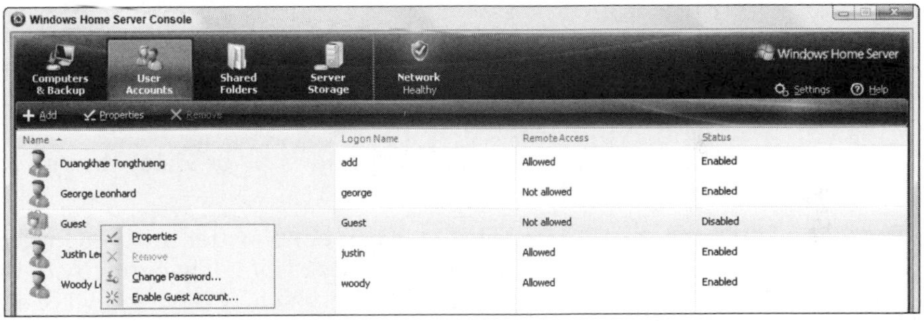

Figure 6-1:
Enabling
the
Guest
account.

When you enable the `Guest` account, WHS steps you through a wizard. You do not want a password on the `Guest` account, but you do want it to have Read access to all the folders that contain media you want to be able to stream across the network.

I explain in Chapters 7, 8, and 9 how the `Guest` account comes into play, but the basic idea is that enabling the `Guest` account, without a password, may let computers in your network get into the server without forcing you to log on manually.

4. **One by one, log on to each computer on your network. Navigate to the appropriate** Music **or** Videos **folder.**

   Don't forget the Shared Documents (Windows XP) or Public (Windows Vista) music and video folders!

5. **Select the music or videos that you want to put on the server, right-click them and choose Copy.**

   You can choose Cut if you're a more trusting soul than I. Far better to copy and delete in two separate steps, unless you're feeling lucky.

6. **On your desktop, double-click the Shared Folders on Server icon.**

   If you see a security challenge, as in Figure 6-2, type in any user name (er, logon ID) and password that's been set up on the server. The user account must have Read/Write access to the appropriate shared folder (see Chapter 5).

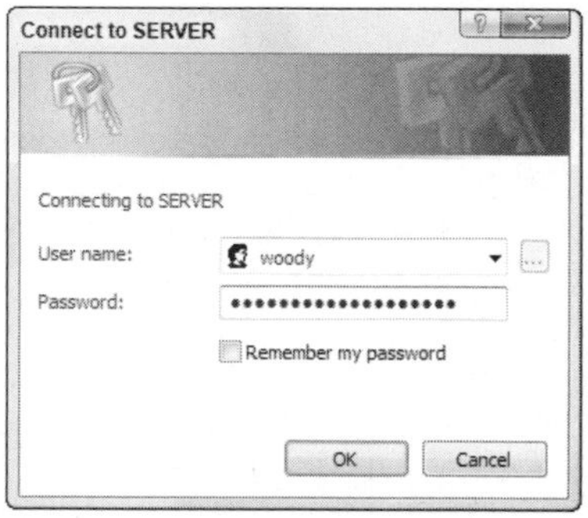

Figure 6-2:
The server
wants to
know who
you are.

Connect to SERVER

Connecting to SERVER

User name: 👤 woody ▼ [...]

Password: ••••••••••••••••••

☐ Remember my password

[OK]   [Cancel]

Windows Explorer (in either Windows XP or Vista) shows you the shared folders.

You can transfer music to the server no matter how you logged on to your Windows XP or Vista computer, by responding correctly to the security challenge shown in Figure 6-2. But you may have a devil of a time playing that music unless the user name and password you use to log on to your Windows XP or Vista machine precisely match a user name (er, logon ID) and password on the server. I talk about this surprising restriction later in this chapter, in the section called "Playing From (and With) the Server."

7. **Double-click the folder into which you wish to copy (probably Music or Videos), and then right-click and choose Paste.**

   That copies the selected music or video files into the correct location on the server.

DRM and C.R.A.P. Music

Many of the problems you will encounter with Windows Home Server and media sharing have to do with Digital Rights Management (DRM). ZDNet Executive Editor David Berlind calls it C.R.A.P. music (and video): Content Restriction, Annulment, and Protection. CRAP, er, DRM restricts how you can play music that you've bought.

Ian Rogers at Yahoo! Music hit the nail on the head when he said, "Digital Rights Management doesn't add any value for the artist, label (who are selling DRM-free music every day — the Compact Disc), or consumer. The only people it adds value to are the technology companies who are interested in locking consumers to a particular technology platform." Microsoft and Apple are the two foremost purveyors of DRM. If you buy music from either, you're paying for . . . well, you get the idea.

Most of the music you buy online these days is (rights-wise, anyway) CRAP. If you put CRAP music or videos on your server, you may not be able to play them unless you register the *playing* computer with Microsoft (for protected WMA audio and WMV video files) or Apple (for protected AAC audio and M4P video). I explain how to register your home or office computers in this chapter, in the section "Sharing CRAP Music on the Network."

Before you buy another song or video, make sure you understand the restrictions imposed by the seller. They aren't pretty. Most damningly, the rules can be — and have been — changed after the purchase; what you can do with music you buy today may not be allowed tomorrow. CRAP is like that: Microsoft and Apple can reach into your music and video files and enforce new restrictions, without your knowledge or consent.

If you find yourself stuck with a ton of music that won't play or videos that won't, uh, vid, then you may be able to convert them into an unlocked format. Google is your friend. The technology changes constantly, with legal action, threats of criminal prosecution, and legislation that puts the "drac" back in draconian. Just remember that activities deemed illegal in some jurisdictions are quite legal in others.

In the end, you're smartest to stick with audio and video formats that can't be locked: good ol' MP3. If you buy an audio CD and rip it into MP3 format, that MP3 file remains blissfully free of any restrictions, now or in the future. If you rip a movie into MP4 format, that video file can't be encumbered — but then again, it may be illegal to rip a DVD into *any* format, in the U.S. anyway. Sounds like a good excuse to take a vacation in the Caribbean, *eh, matey*?

8. **If all goes well, go back to the original files or folders and delete them.**

   If you have enough room on your home or office computer's hard drive, a copy of the files will go into the Recycle Bin, where they can be retrieved if something goes bump in the night.

9. **Repeat Steps 4 through 8 for each computer and each music- or video-bearing user account on your network.**

   That's what it takes to reliably and safely transfer all your music and videos to the server.

Playing From (and With) the Server

With all your music safely transferred to the shared Music folder on the server, whop Windows Media Player upside the head and tell it to look on the server for music and videos. (iTunes and Winamp require similar whopping.)

Windows Media Player has a hard time understanding that you've moved massive amounts of music from one computer to another: it will continue to look in the old location(s) for years (if not millennia), come up empty, and incessantly interrupt you, asking for guidance at the most inopportune times. I've developed a technique for resetting WMP that's only appropriate if you have well and truly moved *all* your music from *all* your home or office computers onto the server. Not to put too fine a spin on it, you have to start over with a clean slate, delete your entire WMP library, and rebuild it again from scratch. If you only own ten albums, it'll take a few minutes. If you have 200 GB of music, it's best to wait until you can leave the computer to its own devices overnight — and don't be too surprised if it's still chugging away the next morning.

Here's how to give Windows Media Player amnesia, so it forgets where all your network's music *used* to be stored, and tell it to rebuild its library in a new place, pointing to the shared Music folder on the server:

1. **Wait.**

   Wait until you're absolutely certain that all the music on your home or office computers has made the transition to the shared Music folder on the server. Resetting the Windows Media Player library takes time and a whole lotta disk activity. There's no sense starting until you've moved all the music files from your network, and Windows Home Server has had time to duplicate the folder.

2. **Log on to a home or office computer, using an account name and password that match the server.**

   The account name (er, logon ID) on the server must have Read/Write permission for the shared Music folder (see Chapter 5). If you haven't changed any of the access permissions for any of the server's folders, there's no need to worry — any account on the server (except the Guest account) has Read/Write access to the folder.

   Windows Home Server seems to have conniption fits if the password on the home or office computer doesn't match the password on the server.

   As we went to press, trying to use Windows Media Player 11 to access music in your server's shared Music folder really goes bonkers unless the account name and password that you used to sign in to your home or office computer matches an account name (er, logon ID) and password on the server. That account name has to have at least Read access to the shared Music folder. (See Chapter 5 for details on Read access to shared folders.) The situation's so bad that trying to play music with WMP 11 where the passwords don't match may result in a message that the server's account has been "locked out." If you get that message, realize it isn't your fault — it's caused by a dumb design decision — and you need to reboot both the server and your home or office computer to get the account working again. (See Chapter 16 for information on rebooting the server.)

3. **Make sure you're using Windows Media Player 11 or later.**

   Windows Vista customers already have WMP 11 or later. If you use Windows XP and you aren't sure which version of WMP haunts your computer, start Windows Media Player, hold down the Alt key, and click Help⇨About Windows Media Player. The version number should be 11.0 or later. If it isn't, go to

   ```
   www.microsoft.com/windows/windowsmedia/player/11/default.aspx
   ```

   Click the button to download and install WMP 11.

   WMP 11 employs a bevy of settings that affect how the media player works — and how much information Microsoft collects about you in the process. (See my *Windows Vista Timesaving Techniques For Dummies*, Techniques 26 and 27, for details.) Whatever you do, resist the urge to install URGE, Microsoft's CRAP-infested music-peddling site.

4. **Double-click the Shared Folders on Server icon on your desktop. Make sure you can get into the server's shared `Music` folder.**

   You may be presented with the Connect to Server security challenge shown earlier in this chapter as Figure 6-2.

5. **Start Windows Media Player. Click the Library button, so you can see everything in WMP's library.**

   WMP should look something like Figure 6-3.

Figure 6-3:
Preparing to give Windows Media Player amnesia.

6. **Click any song, and then press Ctrl+A.**

   That should select all the songs in the Library.

7. **Right-click any of the selected songs and choose Delete.**

   WMP responds with an `Are you sure?` dialog box.

8. **In the dialog box, select the Delete From Library Only radio button and click OK.**

   WMP 11 deletes all the library entries — but it doesn't delete the music itself. That can take awhile, so be patient. When the library's been cleared out, WMP looks empty, like Figure 6-4.

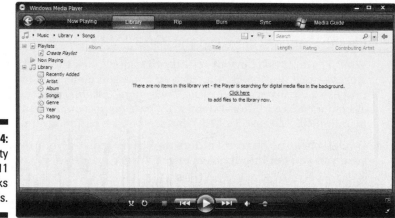

Figure 6-4:
An empty WMP 11 library looks like this.

9. **In the middle of the screen, where it says Click Here to Add Items to the Library, click the Click Here link.**

   WMP watches over folders that you specify, adding new music to its library when you stick new music in the monitored folders, and deleting items from the library when they're deleted from the folders. WMP invites you to add folders to the list of folders that it monitors (see Figure 6-5).

10. **Click Add.**

    This gets a bit confusing.

    The Add Folder dialog box (see Figure 6-6) lists the folders that you can add to the collection of folders that WMP 11 monitors. Fair enough. You might think you could easily add the shared `Music` folder on the server by clicking through on the Shared Folders on Server shortcut that's sitting on your Desktop — but you can't. Windows Media Player's Add Folder dialog box doesn't show any shortcuts!

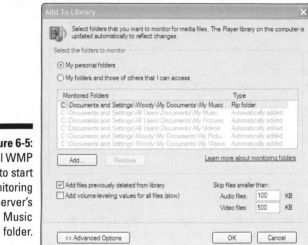

Figure 6-5:
Tell WMP
to start
monitoring
the server's
Music
folder.

Figure 6-6:
To add the
server's
Music
folder,
you have
to find it.

To make things even more confusing, the Windows Home Server computer
probably isn't listed under your usual network. As shown in Figure 6-6,
I expect all the computers on my home office network to be included in
the network called Patong. Windows Home Server marches to a different
drummer, though. Unless you've gone through some Herculean efforts to
change it, your WHS server is in a network called Workgroup.

11. **In the Add Folder dialog box, double-click your way down to**
Desktop\My Network Places\Entire Network\Microsoft
Windows Network\Workgroup\Server\Music. **Then click OK.**

12. **If you want to use WMP to play videos on the server, too, double-click your way down to** Desktop\My Network Places\Entire Network\ Microsoft Windows Network\Workgroup\Server\Videos. **Then click OK.**

13. **When you're through adding folders, back in the Add to Library dialog box (see Figure 6-5), click OK.**

    WMP starts scanning the server's Music folder (and Videos folder if you chose it, too), adding songs (and videos) as it encounters them. If you have a huge music collection, this process can take quite awhile — hours in some cases. You can click Close in the message box, which shows a progress bar, and the dialog box disappears. But indexing continues in the background, and your computer will be positively sluggish for quite some time.

14. **When Windows Media Player 11 finishes rebuilding its index — this time including all the music on the server, and not including any music that's been moved off the network computers — click Close if you haven't already, and you see the server's music, ready and readily available, as in Figure 6-7.**

With WMP 11 pointing to the server, you're ready to play anything you like from the shared Music and/or shared Videos folder on the server. The only hitch: Make sure the user name and password that you use on your home or office computer matches one on the server. It ain't nice to mess with Mother Home Server.

Figure 6-7:
WMP back and rarin' to go. . . .

Ripping to the Server

By far the best way to add new music to your collection is by simply ripping an audio CD. If you rip correctly (and I show you how in this section), the music remains blissfully unencumbered by rights restrictions. Hey, you bought it, you can use it. No questions, no after-the-fact manipulations, no inane requirements, now or in the future.

If you've followed the steps in the preceding sections and set up Windows Media Player so it retrieves music from your server's shared `Music` folder, you should definitely spend a few extra minutes and set up WMP so it *rips* music (which is to say, it copies music from an audio CD onto your computer) into your server's shared `Music` folder.

If you have a ripping program other than WMP (iTunes, Winamp, Nero, or any of dozens of others), the specific steps to make the program rip to the shared folder vary — *mutatis mutandis* — but the general tune remains the same. And if you rip DVDs, I salute you! At least, I salute you until the laws in the U.S. change so there's no question that ripping DVDs is illegal. Then I'll have to salute you surreptitiously. One thing's for sure: We haven't heard the end of it.

Here's how to tell Windows Media Player 11 to rip music — correctly — into the server's shared Music folder:

1. **Go to any computer on your network, log on with a user name and password that match one known to the server, and start Windows Media Player 11 (or later).**

   See the preceding section for dire warnings about using accounts (or, more precisely, passwords) that aren't known to the server — and for instructions on installing Windows Media Player 11, if you haven't upgraded already.

2. **Click the small down-arrow underneath the Rip tab (you have to hover your mouse over the Rip tab to see the arrow), and choose More Options.**

   WMP 11 responds with an Options dialog box.

3. **In the Rip Music to This Location box, click Change.**

   You see a Browse for Folder dialog box that looks almost exactly like the one in Figure 6-6, shown earlier in this chapter.

   As I explain in the preceding section, this dialog box is a bit confusing because you can't simply use the shortcut on the desktop to get into the server's shared `Music` folder. Instead you have to navigate the long way, surprisingly through the network called `Workgroup`.

4. **In the Add Folder dialog box, double-click your way down to**
   `Desktop\My Network Places\Entire Network\Microsoft`
   `Windows Network\Workgroup\Server\Music`. **Then click OK.**

   WMP returns to the Options dialog box, with the rip location changed to
   `\\Server\Music`.

5. **Click the down-arrow to the right of the Format box.**

   By default, Windows Media Player 11 rips into WMA format, Microsoft's
   proprietary, lockable, evil method for taking over the audio universe.
   Okay, I exaggerated. But only a little bit.

6. **Choose MP3.**

   Take a moment to consider the Audio Quality setting at the bottom of the
   dialog box. Most people find 128 Kbps to work fine as a quality setting —
   it's "CD Quality" and certainly suffices for a run-of-the-mill MP3 player.
   But if you commonly play music on a good stereo system (or over a pair
   of expensive headphones), you may want to jack up the quality to 256
   Kbps or even higher. That doubles the size of the ripped files, but if you
   have Windows Home Server, you have nearly-infinite storage anyway,
   right? Okay, I exaggerated again. But only a little.

   My settings are shown in Figure 6-8. When I rip specifically for my iPod
   or a USB key drive to play in the car, I go into this dialog box (via the
   down-pointing arrow on the Rip tab) and throttle back the audio quality.

7. **When you're happy with your rip-to-server settings, click the Devices tab.**

   WMP shows you a list of all the hardware devices on your system.

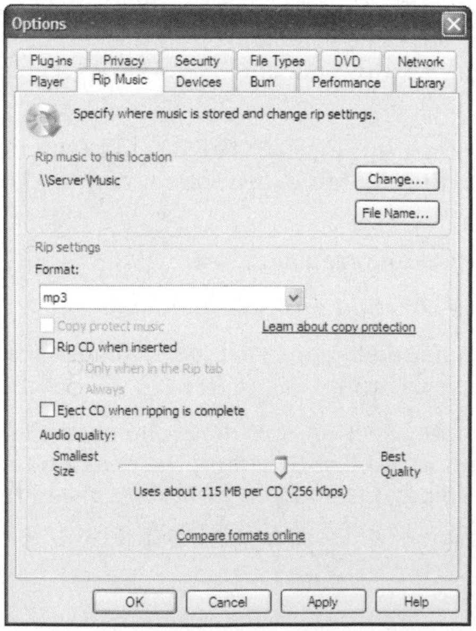

Figure 6-8:
My high-
quality
rip-to-server
settings.

8. **Click your CD or DVD drive, and then click the Properties button.**

   WMP lets you set options for ripping and playback on the CD or DVD drive.

9. **Check the box(es) that say Use Error Correction, and then click OK twice.**

   WMP is now ready to rip audio CDs — correctly — to your server's shared Music folder.

10. **Put an audio CD in your CD/DVD drive, and click the Windows Media Player Rip tab.**

    WMP shows you the songs on the album and, if it can find the album in the URGE database, pastes a picture of the album cover next to the album's title. (If you try to rip an obscure album, as I do in Figure 6-9, you just get a generic CD picture.)

11. **Down on the lower right, click the Start Rip button.**

    WMP rips the album to your shared Music folder.

If you follow this procedure, every time you rip an album, you find unencumbered MP3 files stuffed away in WMP's automatically generated folders, inside the server's shared Music folder — right where you would expect them. As an added benefit, any other computer on your network that has Windows Media Player set up to monitor the shared Music folder will also "see" the new album — and you don't have to do a thing.

To rip another audio CD, go back to Step 10. Piece o' cake.

Figure 6-9:
Windows Media Player automatically rips into the shared Music folder.

Sharing C.R.A.P. Music on the Network

There are precious few ways to share DRM-encumbered music on your home or office network, but one approach warrants a brief mention. Why? Because many of you have already bought DRM "protected" music from the iTunes store, and you probably didn't realize that it could only be played on one computer.

Except, well, not exactly.

You can pay to "upgrade" your tunes from CRAPpy to unencumbered by paying Apple an additional amount of money for each song. To see how, look at www.itunes.com for details about "iTunes Plus." If you moved a bunch of your iTunes music onto your server's shared Music folder, and don't want to pay extra to play the songs on other computers on your network, a little-known iTunes Store feature may be of use. Read on . . . .

Music that you buy on iTunes can be copied anywhere — you can hand out copies of the songs at your friendly local flea market by the zillions, and Apple won't get excited. But (as Apple assures you repeatedly) five computers at a time can play a specific song. Unfortunately, it isn't quite that simple. With apologies to Paul Harvey, here's the rest of the story . . . .

When you sign up for the iTunes Store, the computer you're using gets branded with an iTunes Store account number. When you buy songs using that computer, each of the songs gets branded with the same account number. In order to play the song, the brand on the computer and the brand on the song have to match.

If you know the iTunes Store account's password, you can use the iTunes software to brand any other computer with the same account number. But at most five computers can be branded with the same account number at the same time.

Get that?

Here's an example. Say you buy a song at the iTunes Music Store with an account number of myaccount@someplace.com and password 123456789. You stick a copy of the song in your Windows Home Server's shared Music folder. When the original computer — the one you used to buy the song — tries to play the song, it warbles like a bird, no problem. But when a different computer on your home network tries to play the song, iTunes asks for authorization.

The person using the other computer has to type in myaccount@ someplace.com and password 123456789. Immediately, the computer is "branded" with that account number. (Apple calls it "authorizing.")

Both of the computers branded with the same account number can play songs branded with the same account number — see the pattern here? — but they can't play iTunes Store-acquired songs with different account numbers. The brand applies to the whole computer, so one person using the computer can't have a different brand from that of another person using the same computer.

If another computer on your network tries to play the iTunes Store branded song, the person who tries to play the song has to provide the same account number and password, myaccount@someplace.com and 123456789. That computer then immediately becomes branded with myaccount@someplace. com. You can buy new music with that computer, and it, too, will be branded with myaccount@someplace.com.

Here's the rub: Whenever you brand a computer, iTunes phones home and determines how many computers have the same brand. At most five computers, at any one time, can be branded with the same account number.

To deauthorize a computer — remove the brand — go into iTunes, click Store⇨Deauthorize Computer, pick Deauthorize Computer for Apple Account. In the resulting dialog box (see Figure 6-10), type in your Apple ID and password, and click OK. That frees up one of the five available slots.

Other DRM-encumbered music services may work similarly. Rules and requirements change — and music services come and go like the wind. If you want to buy legitimate, unencumbered MP3 files, check out eMusic.com, and stop worrying about DRM.

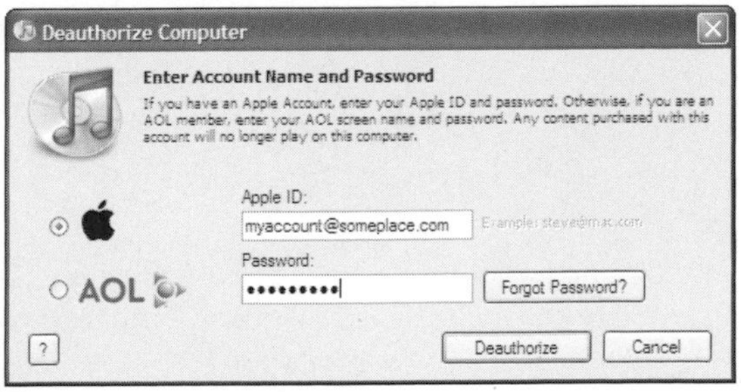

Figure 6-10: Remove a computer so it doesn't count in the five-account limit.

Deauthorize Computer
Enter Account Name and Password
If you have an Apple Account, enter your Apple ID and password. Otherwise, if you are an AOL member, enter your AOL screen name and password. Any content purchased with this account will no longer play on this computer.
⦿ 🍎   AOL ▷
Apple ID:
myaccount@someplace.com   Example: steve@mac.com
Password:
•••••••••
Forgot Password?
[?]   Deauthorize   Cancel

Chapter 7

Recording and Playing TV

In This Chapter

▶ Getting recorded TV shows onto the server

▶ Playing recorded TV shows stored on the server

▶ Backing up recorded TV

S etting up Windows Media Center so it records and plays back TV shows rates as a black art, with twists and turns that vary depending on your computer hardware, your software, and the specific nuances of your cable or satellite TV feed. I don't try to cover any of that in this book. If you don't yet have your computer hooked up to record TV, or you need help setting up a PC or an Xbox to play TV, refer to *Windows XP Media Center Edition 2004 PC For Dummies*, by Danny Briere and Pat Hurley (also from John Wiley) for Media Center specifics and *Windows Vista All-in-One Desk Reference For Dummies*, which I also wrote, for details on Windows Media Center in Vista.

This chapter takes you through the steps necessary to introduce Windows Home Server into your TV, uh, experience.

 Storing recorded TV shows on your Windows Home Server couldn't be simpler: you click and drag the recorded TV file (a so-called DVR-MS file) into any convenient shared folder. If you want to play the recorded TV show on the same computer that recorded it, go into the shared folder and double-click the file. Windows Media Player obliges and runs the TV clip, no problem.

Some recorded TV shows will play on other computers on your network (if those computers have Media Center Edition and/or certain flavors of Vista). Other shows, the victims of Digital Rights Management (you can call it CRAP TV; see Chapter 6), will only play on the same computer that recorded it.

If you want to do anything even slightly more complicated than manually moving recorded TV files and playing them in Windows Media Player, well, strap on your hip waders, bucko. That's what this chapter is all about.

Understanding Windows Home Server and Recorded TV

Remember when you saw your first Media Center computer? If you're an old-timer, you probably first set eyes on the venerable, Windows XP-based Media Center Edition, on a oversized, noisy desktop PC. If you're new to the PC-based TV recording game, you may have first seen Media Center running as a regular program on a Windows Vista Home Premium or Vista Ultimate machine. Unless you live a charmed life, it only took a day or two or three to hook together your new Media Center savvy PC, the TV, and the cable or satellite receiver. Soon after you probably started recording TV shows.

By now, your disk probably runneth over with DVR-MS files.

When you finally put together your home network, you may have discovered that other computers on your network can (under certain circumstances) play recorded TV shows or other video files stored on a Media Center computer. Through the miracles of *Media Library Sharing* and the proclivities of Windows Media Player 11 (or later), the library on one Media Center PC can be shared to any other computers on your network.

If you suddenly found yourself sitting with a surfeit of cash and an inexplicable masochistic streak, you may have also bought an Xbox (or some other so-called "media center extender") and spent another scintillating day or week or month trying to figure out how to get it to work with your Media Center computer. You learned the joys of *streaming*, where the Xbox acts as a relay station between the Media Center computer and your TV.

Once you finally have it all figured out, you buy a Windows Home Server. Now, instead of worrying about streaming and Media Library Sharing — thorny enough when only two computers are involved — you get to sit in the middle of a *three*-way competition — Vista versus the Xbox versus Windows Home Server — where Windows Home Server doesn't even speak the same language.

Boy howdy, life's never been so complicated.

Windows Home Server doesn't include any version of Windows Media Center and it isn't Media Center compatible. You can't use your server the same way you use a Media Center PC: WHS doesn't stream media files, and it won't share the media library, for starters. All too frequently, WHS gets in the way of many media-sharing activities that most home-network folks crave.

One big problem: you can't use an Xbox to directly get at media files stored on a Windows Home Server server. In particular, you can't use an Xbox to directly play recorded TV shows stored on the server. Instead, you have to set up a Media Center computer (Vista Home Premium, Ultimate, or Windows XP-based Media Center Edition) in the middle — the Xbox talks to the Media Center computer, which draws media files from the server.

Okay. I lied a little bit. In fact, some people have been able to get Media Center working under Windows Home Server. It's kinda like building a bicycle with a wheel and two crutches, and praying that the nuts don't come loose, but it can be done. Guru Richard Miller describes his experiences at `thedigital lifestyle.com/cs/forums/thread/2608.aspx`.

Follow the nostrums here to get around the more egregious server problems. If you have trouble recording or playing back recorded TV — trust me, you aren't alone! — check out *Windows XP Media Center Edition 2004 PC For Dummies*.

Storing Shows on Your Server

If you're adding Windows Home Server to the TV-recording circus that's shooting bits and flying bytes across your network, the first step is getting the blasted files from your computer to your server. If you're just getting started, you need to set up a shared folder on your server for recorded TV, which I discuss in the following section. After that, I explain the best TV-show-transferring tricks I know.

Creating a shared home for recorded TV

Before you try to move recorded TV shows to your server, you need to create a shared folder to store them. For historical reasons (and to increase your chances of making other programs work with your shared recorded TV shows), it's a good idea to call the shared folder `Recorded TV`, which is the folder name Microsoft chose eons ago for recorded TV in the original Windows XP Media Center Edition.

Follow these quick steps to make a shared `Recorded TV` folder that anybody on your network can get into:

1. **Go to any computer on your network. Right-click the Windows Home Server Console icon and choose Windows Home Server Console.**

   You need to log on to the Console in order to set up a shared folder that you can use for recorded TV shows.

2. **Type the Server's password and press Enter.**

   Windows Home Server brings up the Console (see Figure 7-1).

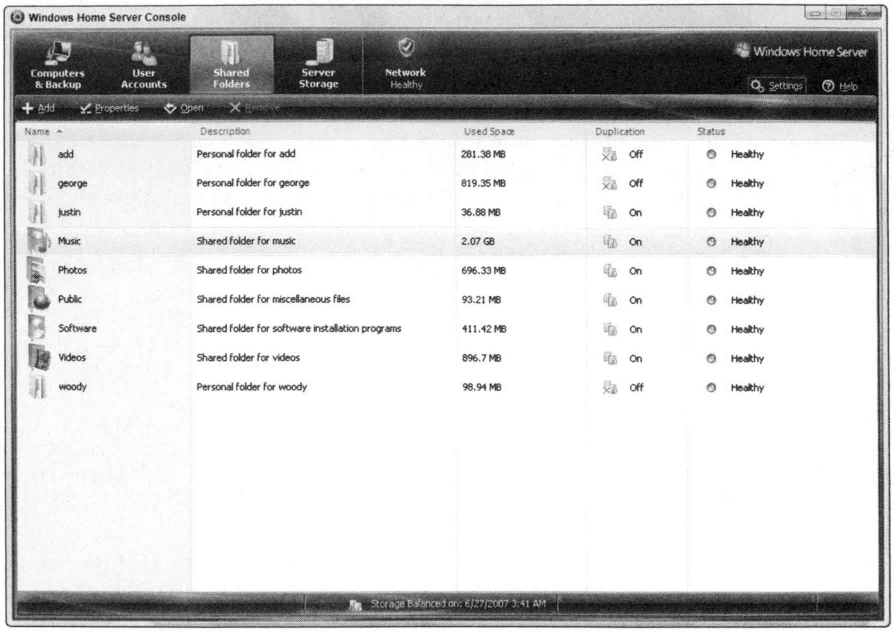

Figure 7-1:
Look for a
shared
folder called
Recorded
TV. (Your
Console
might have
one; this
Console
doesn't.)

3. **Click the Shared Folders icon, up at the top.**

• If you already have a shared folder called Recorded TV you're done with this exercise; jump down to the next section.

• If you don't have a Recorded TV folder, click the Add icon near the upper-left corner.

Windows Home Server invites you to Add a Shared Folder (per Figure 7-2).

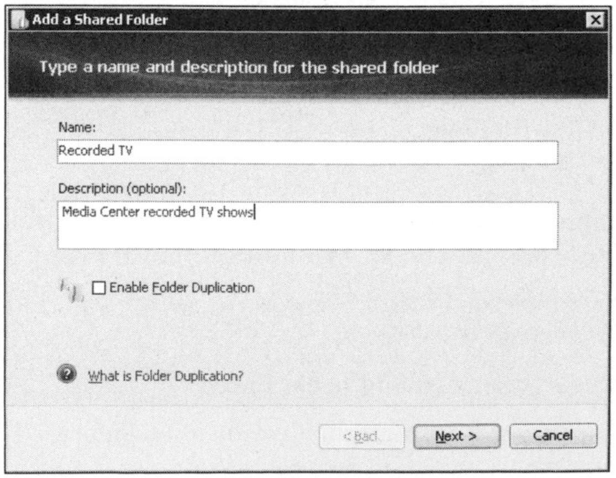

Figure 7-2:
If a
shared
folder called
Recorded
TV doesn't
exist,
create it.

4. **Type the name Recorded TV in the top box, and give the shared folder a reasonable description if you like.**

   You'll make your life much simpler if you use the name Recorded TV, precisely.

5. **If you have lots and lots of hard-drive space on your server, check the box marked Enable Folder Duplication. If you don't have acres of unused space, uncheck the box. Then click Next.**

   See Chapter 5 for an explanation of Folder Duplication, which automatically keeps a second copy of each file in the folder.

   WHS asks you what level of access you want to grant to each of the user accounts that are known to the server (see Figure 7-3).

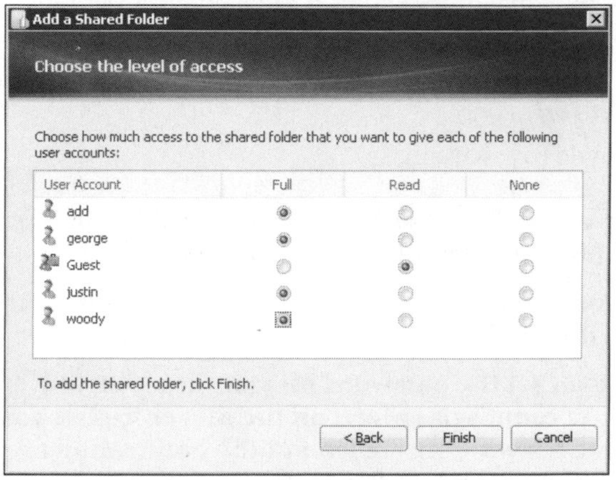

Figure 7-3:
Give
everybody
Full access,
and the
Guest
account
read-only
access.

6. **Give Full access to any user who may want to add recorded TV to the server, and Read access to everyone else. Click Finish.**

7. **When the wizard finishes adding the shared folder, click Done.**

   A shared folder called Recorded TV should be visible in your server's Shared Folder list (see Figure 7-4).

Figure 7-4:
There
it is —
a central
repository
for
recorded
TV shows.

Moving recorded TV to the server

With your shared folder set up, you're ready to move your recorded TV files to the server. I suggest you do this not only when you initially add Windows Home Server to your network, but on an ongoing basis. (You *can* record directly to the server, but in my opinion, life's too short to mess with it, as I explain in the next section, "Recording TV directly to the server.")

The easiest (and cheapest) way I've found to move recorded TV shows (DVR-MS files) from my Vista machine to a shared folder on Windows Home Server utilizes a free program from Microsoft called SyncToy.

SyncToy runs completely independently of Windows Home Server. It can be trained to move DVR-MS files from the place that Windows Media Center's TV recorder sticks such files into a shared folder on the Windows Home Server machine.

Downloading SyncToy

Here's how to get SyncToy working:

1. **Log on to one of the Windows Media Center Edition or Vista Home Premium (or Ultimate) computers on your network.**

   In order to transfer recorded TV files, SyncToy must run on the computer that recorded the TV show.

2. **If you haven't yet set the password on your home or office computer to match your account's password on the server, right-click the Windows Home Server Console icon in the notification area (next to the clock) and choose Update Password.**

   If the Update Password choice is grayed out, your passwords match already. Believe me, using SyncToy is much simpler if the passwords match.

3. **Crank up your favorite Web browser and go to the following site:**

   ```
   www.microsoft.com/windowsxp/using/digitalphotography/prophoto/synctoy.mspx
   ```

   Yes, even if you have Vista, you go to the Windows XP digital-photography site.

4. **On the right, click the Download link and follow the instructions to download SyncToy's** `Setup.msi` **file. When that's downloaded, run the file.**

   The SyncToy Setup Wizard appears (see Figure 7-5).

5. **Click Next.**

   There's another 250,000 word End User License Agreement. Click the link that says, in effect, *I read this all very thoroughly and agree with everything you say, yessiree Bob.* Then click Next.

6. **Accept all the defaults (which is to say, continue clicking Next for as long as you can). The actual installation takes a while, so sit back and relax. When the Wizard says you're done, click Close.**

   It's a rather abrupt ending.

Running a synch

With SyncToy downloaded to your computer, follow these steps to tell the toy how to shuffle your files from one folder to another:

1. **Click Start ➪ All Programs (or Start ➪ Programs in Windows Media Center Edition) and choose SyncToy.**

   You get a pesky dialog box begging you to sign up for the Customer Experience Improvement Program (Recommended). Think a moment . . . .

2. **If you really want to send details about your files to Microsoft, select Yes. Otherwise select No. Click OK.**

   SyncToy shows you its welcome screen, per Figure 7-6.

   SyncToy uses a very simple, very effective metaphor for specifying which folders you want to sync and how — the "left folder" (which, Saints be praised!, appears on the left) and the "right folder" (I bet you figured that one out already).

3. **Click the button marked Create New Folder Pair.**

   SyncToy asks you to choose the "left" folder, as in Figure 7-7.

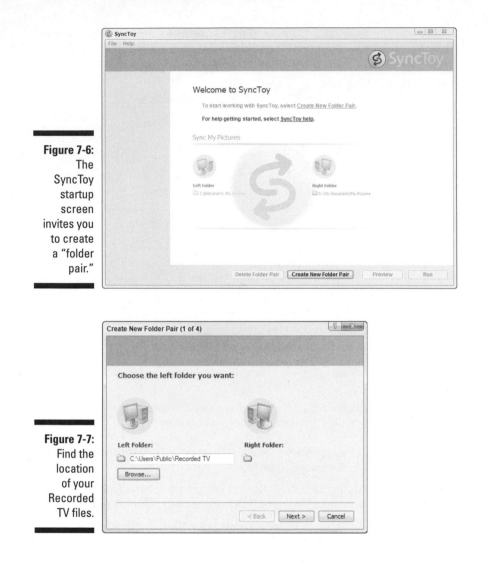

Figure 7-6: The SyncToy startup screen invites you to create a "folder pair."

Figure 7-7: Find the location of your Recorded TV files.

4. **Click the Browse button and browse to the location of your Recorded TV files; after you find them, Click Next.**

   • If you're using Windows Media Center Edition, they're located in your `\Shared Documents\Recorded TV` folder.

   • If you have Vista, they're in `\Public\Recorded TV`.

   SyncToy asks you to find the "right" folder, as in Figure 7-8.

5. **Click the Browse button. In Windows XP, you need to navigate to** `Microsoft Windows Network\Workgroup\Server`. **In Vista, it's comparatively simpler because you can find the Server computer**

under the Network icon (as shown in Figure 7-8). In either case, click once on Recorded TV, then click OK.

The "right" folder should read `\\SERVER\Recorded TV`, as in Figure 7-8.

6. **Click Next.**

SyncToy asks you how you want to synchronize, per Figure 7-9.

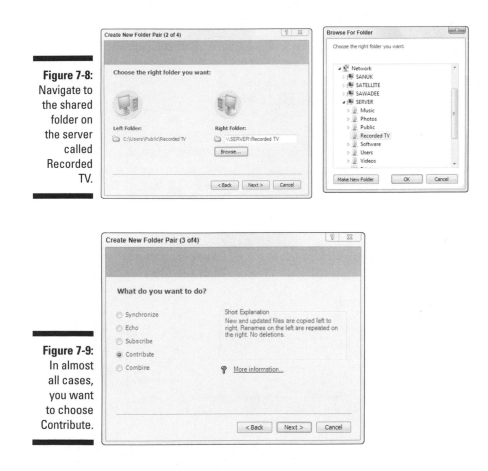

Figure 7-8: Navigate to the shared folder on the server called Recorded TV.

Figure 7-9: In almost all cases, you want to choose Contribute.

7. **Choose Contribute if you want SyncToy to copy new recorded TV shows from the home or office computer onto the server. Click Next.**

"Contribute" is a good choice because you can delete a recorded TV show from the home computer, and it will remain on the server. To get a recorded TV show off the server, you have to delete it manually.

SyncToy asks you to give your folder pair a name (see Figure 7-10).

8. **Type an appropriate name in the box and click Finish.**

The main SyncToy screen appears, ready to run your sync (see Figure 7-11).

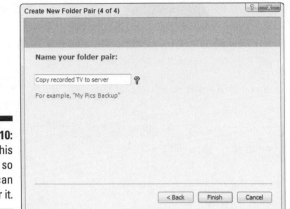

Figure 7-10:
Name this
sync so
you can
remember it.

Figure 7-11:
SyncToy is
ready to
back up
your
recorded TV
shows to
the WHS
server's
shared
Recorded
TV folder.

9. **To make sure you got the settings right, click the button marked Preview.**

   SyncToy shows you exactly what it's going to copy, and where, as in Figure 7-12.

10. **If you feel comfortable with your choices, click the Run button.**

    SyncToy does a credible job of keeping you informed about the progress of the copy. That progress can take a long, long, long time.

SyncToy, PowerToy?

Some folks at Microsoft would have you believe that SyncToy is one of the Windows PowerToys. (The PowerToys, you may know, constitute a rag-tag collection of free, officially unsupported Windows add-ins built and distributed exclusively by Microsoft that performs all sorts of cool tricks.) In fact, SyncToy was developed quite independently of the other PowerToys. It was updated to work with Windows Vista many months before Microsoft dribbled a handful of Vista add-ons out the door. Microsoft can call SyncToy a PowerToy, I s'pose, but they can call a tomato a power tool, too. Makes as much sense.

When it's done copying, SyncToy gives you a summary of any problems it may have encountered. Chances are good you have a few files in `TempRec` folders — temporary holding places for recordings in progress — that didn't make it across. Not to worry.

11. **Click Done.**

    Next time you want to copy your recorded TV shows to the server, click Start⇨All Programs⇨SyncToy and run the sync again.

It takes a while to set up SyncToy, but once you have it going, it works very well indeed.

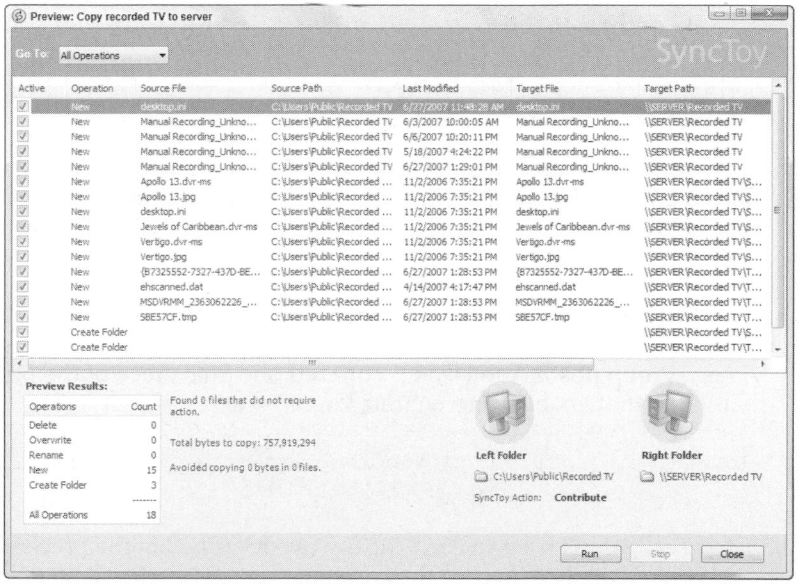

Figure 7-12:
SyncToy says that it's going to copy more than 700 MB.

Recording TV directly to the server

Microsoft has also made it devilishly difficult to record a TV program directly to any computer other than the Vista Home Premium (or Ultimate) or Windows Media Center Edition computer that's showing the TV program. You can record to your own computer, but heaven help ya if you want to record onto any other computer on your network — much less your server.

It's *possible*, mind you. But it isn't easy.

You can try to get Windows, Media Center, and Windows Home Server to co-operate and recognize each other if you feel strongly that you should be able to

✔ Record TV directly to your Windows Home Server server and/or

✔ See recorded TV shows sitting on the server listed where they belong inside Windows Media Center

You also need to have a lot of time on your hands and high tolerance for pain.

The operative term: *try*. I know many people who have been able to get the hacks to work. I know many who have failed. And I'll be hanged if I can figure out why this works in some cases but not in others. Worse, many times, it'll work for a while and then quit working, or it won't work and then magically *start* working. Must be something in the water.

Mike's Digital Home blog on The Green Button kicked off the Media Center sharing craze with this post:

```
thegreenbutton.com/blogs/mike/archive/2007/01/12/
          158079.aspx
```

Richard Miller and Ian Dixon came up with an exhaustive discussion of the ins and outs of trying to get Media Center to record to Windows Home Server — and getting networked computers to "see" the recorded TV shows — on The Digital Lifestyle site at

```
iandixon.co.uk/cs/forums/thread/2608.aspx
```

A newsgroup poster known as `tv` offered one final piece of the puzzle — a batch file that enables Anonymous Logon — at

```
forums.microsoft.com/WindowsHomeServer/ShowPost.aspx?
          PostID=1754294&SiteID=50
```

If you really don't want to use SyncToy (as described in the preceding section), and you're willing to accept the fact that your network will be taxed severely whenever you record TV shows, take a look at Richard and Ian's approach.

Two other partial solutions may appeal to you:

- ✔ Some folks have been able to install the Windows Media Center Edition 2005 user interface on a Windows Server 2003 computer (and thus, by implication, a Windows Home Server box). Microsoft says that doing so constitutes a violation of the End User License Agreement for Media Center Edition 2005. But at least in some cases it appears to work. As noted before, though, this is akin to building a bicycle with one wheel and two crutches, and hoping that the nuts don't fall off. See `thegreen button.com/forums/thread/64051.aspx` for details.

- ✔ WebGuide for Windows Home Server (`www.asciiexpress.com`) has a new version of its popular WebGuide product that works specifically with Windows Home Server (see Chapter 21). WebGuide works through a Web browser, letting you see both live and recorded TV. (It also has hooks into music, pictures, and videos.) It doesn't stick recorded TV inside the Media Center list, but it does make getting at recorded shows on the server very easy, if you have a browser handy.

I think you'll end up deciding that SyncToy ain't such a bad idea after all, and that you can live with mousing to the shared folder whenever you want to watch a recorded TV show. But if rummaging through your Windows Home Server box rings your chimes, have at it!

Viewing TV Shows Stored on the Server

Many hands have been wrung and many brows furrowed about the hassles of dealing with recorded TV shows that are stored in a shared folder on a Windows Home Server server. You'd think it would be easy to tell Windows Media Center to record directly to the server, and to have it retrieve recorded TV shows from the server.

No way.

It's easy to view recorded TV shows sitting on the server — from a PC, anyway — as long as you don't expect Windows Media Center to do any heavy lifting. (The Xbox is a horse of a different, streaming color; see Chapter 8 for details.)

If you're trying to view a recorded TV show from a PC that doesn't have Windows Media Center, navigate to the shared `Recorded TV` folder (hint: start with the Shared Folders on Server icon that's sitting on your desktop), and then double-click the show that you want to watch. As long as the show isn't hermetically sealed with Digital Rights Management restrictions, Windows Media Player 11 should spring to life and start playing your recorded show. It's really that easy.

If you want to use a PC that has Windows Media Center Edition or Vista Home Premium or Ultimate to watch recorded TV shows that reside on the server, you're best advised to put aside that beautiful Media Center TV remote and use your mouse. Follow the instructions in the preceding paragraph, navigate to the TV show and double-click it. Barring ludicrous DRM headaches and other CRAPpy complications (see Chapter 6), Windows Media Center opens up and plays the show. At that point, you can go back to using your TV remote.

Some people feel that Media Center should list TV shows on the server, right next to the TV shows that are stored on the computer, whenever you look at the `Recorded TV` list (see Figure 7-13). I happen to agree with them: if I'm using a TV remote control and I want to play a recorded TV program that's stored on the server, I shouldn't be obligated to haul out a mouse and go click-click-clicking to get into the shared folder on the server and start the show. Unfortunately, Microsoft doesn't agree with me (er, them).

Figure 7-13:
Media Center should list Recorded TV shows that sit on the server next to the ones on the home PC — but it doesn't.

Why WHS Doesn't Back Up Recorded TV

You would think that Windows Home Server would back up your recorded TV programs, eh?

I certainly did. It backs up everything else. The first time I connected my Vista Home Ultimate computer to the WHS server and let Backup run naturally, I was amazed at the size of the backup files — they were so tiny!

I soon discovered why: The built-in backup routine for Windows Home Server doesn't bother to back up recorded TV shows. *My Name is Earl* and *House* and *Lost* sat completely unprotected on the Vista computer: WHS didn't even try to back them up.

I figured I must've done something wrong, so I searched frantically for the "Back up recorded TV" setting. Guess what? It isn't there. You can see the details in Chapter 12 but, trust me, WHS doesn't back up DVR-MS files, and there's not much you can do about it (at least, not by using Windows Home Server).

I checked with Microsoft, and a member of the development team confirmed that WHS doesn't, can't, won't back up DVR-MS files. They gave two reasons:

✔ Recorded TV files are big. If you have a lot of recorded TV files, the first backup may take a long time — a *very* long time — "which is likely to be a sub-optimal experience for our customers."

✔ There are other tools that can sync recorded TV files to the server.

I can certainly sympathize with both of those points. If *my* first WHS backup took 18 hours, I probably would've pulled the plug and never looked back.

The moral of the story: If you want to back up your recorded TV shows, set up a separate sync program to move the shows into a Windows Home Server shared folder (see "Moving recorded TV to the server," earlier in this chapter); or jimmy Media Center to record directly into a Windows Home Server shared folder (see "Recording TV directly to the server," also earlier in this chapter).

As you might guess, the former is considerably simpler than the latter.

Chapter 8

Streaming with the Xbox

. . . .

In This Chapter

▶ Playing files stored on a Windows Home Server with Microsoft's Xbox 360

▶ Opening up the server, to let an Xbox in

▶ Sticking a Media Center PC in the middle and streaming from server to Media Center to Xbox

▶ Getting your Xbox to co-operate

. . . .

Windows Home Server is a server, not a Media Center.

That simple observation carries many ramifications if you own an Xbox 360 or other Media Center Extender-capable contraption.

Foremost among the puzzling consequences: You can play some files stored on a Windows Home Server directly with the Xbox, but in order to play other kinds of files that are stored on the server, you have to use a Vista Premium, Ultimate, or Windows XP Media Center Edition PC as go-between.

Such are the wonders of streaming, Digital Rights Management, and the Media Center shtick.

If you're confused by the bafflegab, don't be. These multimedia gurus talk funny. *Streaming* is a strange name for an old concept. Think of an old-fashioned radio. If you want to hear a particular song on the radio, you have to convince somebody who runs a radio station to play the song. When the DJ spins the song (that's a technical term, *spins*), you tune your radio to that station, and "Blue Suede Shoes" comes pouring out the speaker. You can't play the song yourself on a radio, even if you have the scratchy 45 record in your hand. If you don't have a record player, only the radio station can do it.

Same with streaming. The radio-station analogy isn't perfect because your Xbox can play *some* kinds of music directly. But other kinds of music have to be played by a radio station, er, a Media Center. The Xbox doesn't have the know-how (or, more frequently, the digital-rights authorization) to play the song.

If you've already tried to get your Xbox 360 working with Windows Home Server, no doubt you've encountered problems that can only be solved by sticking a

Media Center computer in the middle. You may have files (such as recorded TV shows or DivX videos) that will only play on the Media Center computer. You may have music that's all tied up in Digital Rights Management restrictions so you have to go through the Media Center PC that originally "bought" it. (Amazing how a computer can buy rights to play music, but you can't, eh?)

This chapter starts with the easy stuff — getting your Xbox to recognize music and movies sitting on the server that it can play directly. It then breaks into the much-more-difficult problem of building a radio station, uh, of sticking a Media Center computer in between the Windows Home Server server and your Xbox.

Using an Xbox in Server Land

As long as you play games and watch TV and movies while connected to a reliable Media Center computer, the Xbox 360 works reasonably well.

At least, it works pretty well until the Xbox breaks (Microsoft is spending an estimated $ 1 billion to repair defective Xbox 360s) or it chews up your DVDs (Xbox 360s are notorious for gouging scratch marks on game and video DVDs). But I digress.

Some people swear that the Xbox 360 rates as the greatest game console ever. I'm sure they're right, but I'm hardly an expert — my thumbs get tied in knots just navigating through the Xbox screens. Where the Xbox 360 excels, without any doubt, is in its ability to play music and videos, whether the media are stored on the Xbox itself, on a networked computer (such as a Windows Home Server server), or streamed through a PC running Windows Media Center.

In this chapter when I use the term *Media Center*, I'm talking specifically about the Media Center program in Windows Vista Home Premium or Vista Ultimate, or the (nearly identical) program in Windows XP Media Center Edition.

Also in this chapter when I use the term *Xbox*, I'm generally referring to any kind of computer that can play music or videos via a Media Center computer. The technical term for that kind of gizmo is "Media Center Extender-compliant." Microsoft's Xbox 360 is a Media Center Extender. Several other manufacturers make Media Center Extender compliant boxes.

The first time you hook up your Xbox, er, Media Center Extender to a Windows XP Media Center Edition computer, you may need to download an update for the MCE computer. It can get pretty hairy. I don't even try to tackle Xbox consternations in this book. If you have an Xbox problem, I strongly recommend Brian Johnson and Duncan Mackenzie's *Xbox 360 For Dummies*, also from Wiley.

One of the top requests for the Windows Home Server development team at this point is to build some sort of Media Center capability into Windows Home Server. If the WHS box could pull double duty as a server and a Media Center, you wouldn't have to go through all the hassle (and expense!) of connecting a Vista Home Premium, Ultimate, or Windows XP Media Center Edition PC in between your server and your Xbox.

It remains to be seen whether Microsoft will come up with some sort of Media Center feature for WHS. So far there's been a great deal of resistance — if nothing else, Media Center isn't the most stable application in the Windows pantheon, and the last thing everyone needs is a server that freezes from time to time for unknown reasons. Rest assured that many, many people have asked for Media Center capabilities in the next version of WHS. In the interim, we have to make do.

Getting Your Xbox to Play with the Server

The Xbox can play certain kinds of files stored on your Windows Home Server server without any help from any other computer on your network.

As of this writing, here's what you can play directly off your server:

- ✔ **mp3 music.** Of course. After all, mp3 is the universal, unrestricted, incorruptible, anti-CRAP option for all your music. (See my tirade about music Content Restriction, Annulment and Protection — otherwise known as Digital Rights Management — in Chapter 6.)

- ✔ **Unprotected WMA music.** Chances are good if you bought a song in WMA format, it's protected. But unprotected WMA music does exist, and if it's sitting on your server, the Xbox can play it.

- ✔ **Unprotected WMV video.** The Xbox doesn't play AVI, DivX, Xvid, or QuickTime video, but it does play WMVs (versions 7, 8, and 9), as long as there are no access restrictions on the file. In my experience, Xbox compatibility is the number-one reason why people who rip their own DVDs save the movies in WMV format.

- ✔ **Some kinds of MPG video files.** The MPG file format is a minefield, and files with a filename extension of .MPG can contain any of dozens of different formats. The Xbox (again, as of this writing, because Microsoft changes things from time to time) supports MPEG-2 files at a maximum resolution of 1080i.

✔ **Unprotected DVR-MS recorded video, maybe.** This is the format that Windows Media Center uses when recording TV. I had nothing but trouble trying to get my Xbox 360 to even list DVR-MS files stored on the server. You may have better luck following the latest advice at The Green Button, thegreenbutton.com. This iffy compatibility is a current source of constant consternation, with many people trying to wrangle WHS and the Xbox into some form of detente.

If you want to play some other kind of media file, chances are good the Xbox can't do it. In particular, if you want to play an AVI, DivX, or Xvid movie stored on your server directly through an Xbox, you have to convert the movie into a format that Xbox understands, such as WMV. The legalities are a bit complex. That's where Google is your friend.

Alternatively, you can try a program that converts file formats on-the-fly. TVersity can play just about anything on any computer. See www.after dawn.com/guides/archive/stream_video_xbox_360_tversity.cfm for a good hands-on introduction.

Here's how to hook things up so your Xbox can play directly from your server:

1. **Go to any computer on your home or office network. Down in the notification area, next to the system clock, right-click the icon marked Windows Home Server and choose the top option, Windows Home Server Console.**

   The Console asks you to log on.

2. **Type your server's password and click the right-pointing arrow.**

   The Windows Home Server Console appears.

Why wouldn't you share media?

It may seem odd to you that Microsoft *doesn't* share all its shared media folders (which is to say, the built-in folders called Music, Photos, and Videos) automatically. There's a reason why: If you turn on Media Library Sharing, as in Figure 8-1, the permission you grant *overrides* WHS's normal access permissions. That may not be what you want.

Say, for example, that you have ribald comedy sketches stored somewhere in the Music folder that you don't want Little Billy to hear. In the

normal course of events, using the methods in Chapter 5, you would set up Billy's account so it has no access to the Music folder.

If you turn on Media Library Sharing for the Music folder, that Sharing setting overrides the restrictions you set elsewhere. Billy may not be able to access the ribald sketches via the Shared Folders on Server link on his desktop. But he will be able to get in via Windows Media Player or Windows Media Center, or play them on the Xbox.

3. **Click the User Accounts tab and make sure that the Guest account is enabled. If it isn't enabled, right-click Guest icon and choose Enable Account.**

   Look in the column marked Status and make sure the Guest account says Enabled.

   The Xbox uses the Guest account to get into your server. You must have the Guest account enabled, with no password, and the Guest account must have Read permission for any folders that you want to get into. (For more details, see Chapter 4.)

4. **In the upper-right corner, click the Settings icon and then, on the left, choose Media Sharing.**

   The Console brings up the Windows Home Server Settings dialog box shown in Figure 8-1.

5. **Make sure that you want to make all the files in your shared media folders available to anybody on your network (see the sidebar "Why wouldn't you share media?"), and if that sounds right for you, select the appropriate On-On-On buttons; then click OK.**

   The contents of the folders you selected should be accessible to any Media Sharing-savvy computer on your network — including, notably, the Xbox.

6. **Fire up your Xbox and go to the Media blade (see Figure 8-2).**

   You get connected to a Media Sharing networked computer on the Media blade. (Yes, Microsoft calls those panels "blades." Gotta be something cool in there that escapes me at the moment.)

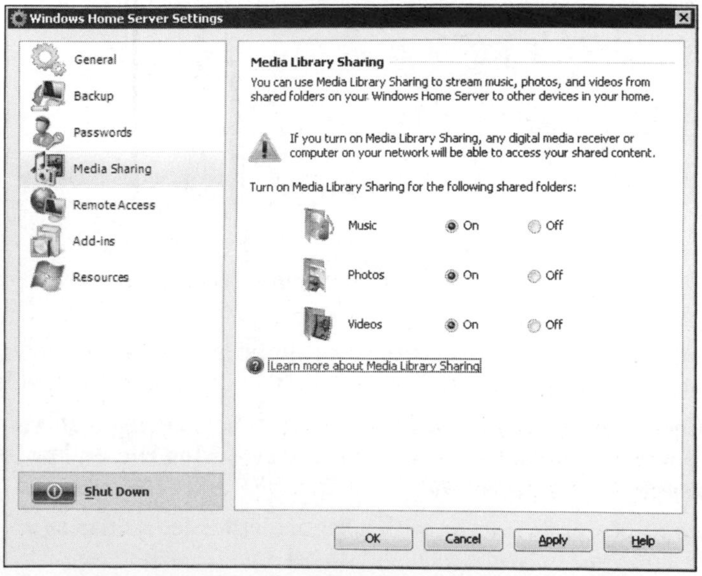

Figure 8-1:
Media Library Sharing is turned on for all the server's built-in media folders.

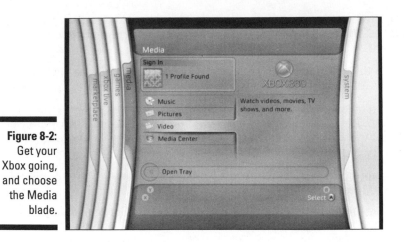

Figure 8-2:
Get your
Xbox going,
and choose
the Media
blade.

7. **On the left, choose Music, Pictures, or Video and click the green "A" Select button.**

   I choose Video and get the screen shown in Figure 8-3.

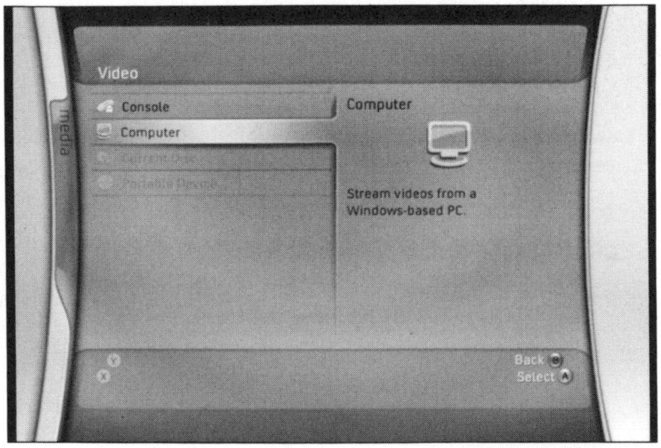

Figure 8-3:
You want
your Xbox to
pull videos
from
another
computer.

8. **On the left, go down to Computer and select the green "A" Select button.**

   The Xbox presents you with a warning that you have to download media sharing software that, in fact, you don't need to download.

9. **Choose Yes, Continue, You Stupid Little Xbox, my Big Bad Windows Home Server Already Has What You're Asking For, and press the green "A" Select button.**

   The Xbox presents you with a list of all the Media Sharing computers on your network, as in Figure 8-4.

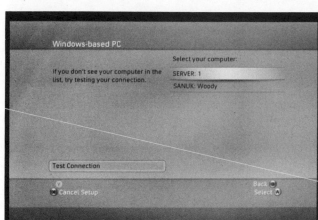

Windows-based PC

If you don't see your computer in the list, try testing your connection.

Select your computer:

SERVER: 1

SANUK: Woody

Test Connection

Cancel Setup

Back
Select

Figure 8-4:
Your server
shows up
as a
Media
Sharing
computer.

If you don't see your Windows Home Server server listed among the Windows-based PCs (it's probably called SERVER, although you may have changed the name when you set up your server), before you freak out, go into the Windows Home Server Console, in the upper-right corner click Settings — and then, in the lower-left corner, click Shut Down. When WHS asks for confirmation, choose Restart. That will reboot your Windows Home Server computer — and chances are good that if you start all over again at Step 5, you'll be able to connect.

If you *still* can't get your Windows Home Server to show up on the list, on the Xbox, move over to the (violently violet) System blade and run through the Network Settings routines, specifically the check called Test Media Connection. That should at least help you identify the problem.

10. **Select your Windows Home Server (it's probably identified as SERVER: 1) and press the green "A" select button.**

   The Xbox reaches into your server and retrieves the names of shared folders that have been earmarked for Media Sharing, and which may contain movies (or music or photos, depending on your choice in Step 6). Your Xbox should show a picture like that in Figure 8-5.

11. **At this point, you're navigating through the shared folders on the server. Only the files that can play directly on the Xbox appear in the lists; other files are ignored.**

   You can click through to subfolders by highlighting them and pressing the green "A" Select button, or go up one level of folders by pressing the red "B" Back button.

   Eventually, if you have any files on your server that will play on the Xbox, you see them listed as in Figure 8-6.

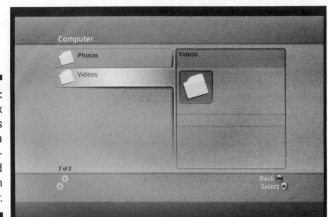

Figure 8-5:
The Xbox shows Media Sharing-enabled folders on the server.

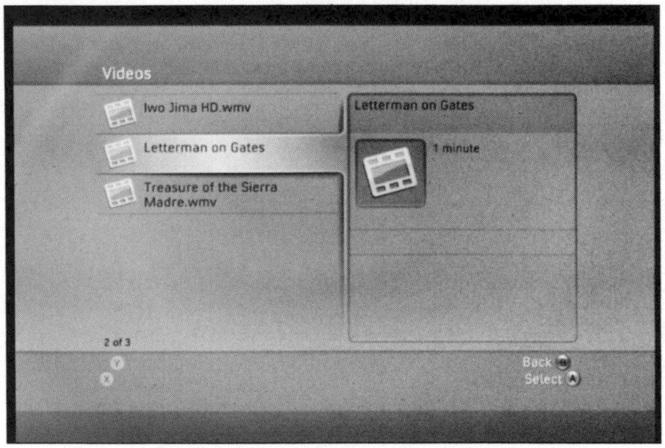

Figure 8-6:
A list of all the files in the current folder that will play on the Xbox.

12. **To play a file (in this case, a movie), highlight the file and press the green "A" Select button. If you then see another screen that gives you a Play option, highlight that option and press the green "A" Play button.**

Your Xbox grabs the movie, video clip, music, or photos (shown as a slide show) that you select — straight off the server — and then plays your selection. The show appears on your TV screen.

Using a Media Center PC to Stream to an Xbox

Ready to set up a radio station (so to speak)?

Good.

If you put things together properly, you can use the Xbox to play files stored on the server, via any computer on your network that has Media Center working. So, for example, you can play recorded TV shows stored on the server by using the Xbox, or by going through a Windows Vista Premium, Ultimate, or Windows XP Media Center Edition PC.

Before you even try to hook up everything, make sure that the Media Center program can pull files off the server; I cover the ins and outs (and very-far-outs) of that subject in Chapter 6. Among other things, you need to point Media Center's Library at the server, and you have to turn on the Guest account on the server. When you're ready, step through the following sections and let the streaming begin. . . .

Connecting an Xbox to a Media Center computer

Next, you need to get your Xbox connected to the Media Center computer. The details of that adventure are really outside the scope of this book, but here it is in a very abbreviated nutshell:

1. **Start your Xbox and go to the Media blade. Highlight Media Center (Figure 8-7) and press the green "A" Select button.**

   The Xbox inundates you with some marketing hype, and then gives you an eight-digit "setup key."

2. **Click the green "A" Select button again and you see instructions for downloading and installing software on your PC. If you have Vista Home Premium or Ultimate (or a fully updated copy of Windows XP Media Center Edition), you can safely ignore the instructions.**

3. **Go to your Media Center computer and start Media Center.**

   In Vista, you click Start⇨All Programs⇨Windows Media Center.

   When Media Center comes up for air, it identifies your Xbox (or other Windows Media Center Extender), and invites you to set it up (per Figure 8-8).

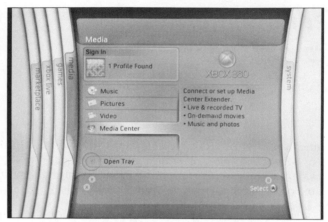

Figure 8-7: The first step in establishing a connection between your Xbox and a Media Center computer.

Figure 8-8: Set up the connection between your Media Center PC and the Xbox by working inside Media Center.

4. **In the Windows Media Center Extender box, click Yes.**

   You may need to monkey around with your TV remote control.

   The setup routine asks you to provide the 8-digit number you retrieved in Step 1.

5. **Type your 8-digit key and then click Next.**

   Media Center pokes through your firewall, asks whether you want to enable Away Mode (which is basically an always-on or almost-always-on power mode), asks whether you want to be able to see media folders on the Xbox (uh, *yeah,* D'OH) and, if you're using Vista, puts you through a User Access Control check.

6. **Make the choices you feel comfortable with (Yes for being able to see media folders) and watch as the Media Center Extender installer does its thing.**

   If you have a lot of shared media on the server, setup can take a long, long time.

   When the installer's done, you see the You Are Done screen in the Extender Setup dialog box.

7. **Click Finish. Then go back to your Xbox and verify that you can see (and work with) Media Center on the PC.**

   If everything's working right, your Xbox displays a Media Center screen like the one in Figure 8-9.

Figure 8-9: Your Xbox, when all works correctly.

If you did everything right, you now have a Media Center computer pulling files off the server (details in Chapter 6), and you have your Xbox hooked into the Media Center computer (details in this section).

Now it's time to bring the two together — as I explain in the next section.

Playing media files with a connected Xbox

After you follow the nostrums in the preceding section, you're ready to see if you can get your Xbox to pull files off your Windows Home Server server, using the Media Center computer as intermediary. If you've gotten this far, it's easier than you think. Here's how:

1. **On your Xbox, navigate to a place in Media Center that uses media files from the server.**

   If you set up your Media Center computer to record TV directly to the server (see Chapter 7), you might go to `TV+Movies/Recorded TV`, as in Figure 8-9. Or you might try `Music/MusicLibrary`. Or, as in Figure 8-10, you could look at `Pictures+Videos/Picture Library`.

2. **Move to folders that are on your Windows Home Server server.**

   They're typically identified as `\\SERVER\`.

3. **Select and play files as usual.**

   For example, in Figure 8-11, using the Xbox, I watch live TV while sorting through photos stored on the server. It's really that easy.

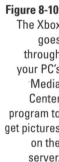

Figure 8-10:
The Xbox goes through your PC's Media Center program to get pictures on the server.

Figure 8-11:
The Xbox can display a live TV show while you look at photos.

Chapter 9

Nailing Down Your Photos

In This Chapter

▶ Organizing photos on the server

▶ Working with both Windows XP and Vista home or office computers

▶ Taking photos off your camera and putting them directly on the server

▶ Using server photos for custom screen savers — the sneaky way

*P*hotos and Windows Home Server go together like Godiva chocolate and chunky homemade peanut butter.

Better, in fact.

Windows Home Server automatically provides a place to store all your photos — a shared folder called, ingenuously, Photos. (Rocket science, eh?) All you have to do is fill 'er up.

Windows XP, Vista, and Microsoft itself provide tools that everybody needs to pull photos off a camera, stick the pics where they belong, stab 'em and slab 'em (er, assign more-or-less meaningful tags to each one) and later on, find and retrieve the pictures you want, when you want them.

With Windows Home Server's readily-enabled Folder Duplication feature, you need never fear losing another photo again — as long as you get your photos onto the server in the first place.

Details, details.

In this chapter, I show you how to hook up the photo-related software you already have so it works better with Windows Home Server. You may be surprised how a nip here and a tuck there can bring your photos back to life.

Using the Windows Tools

Windows has come a long way since the rise of the electronic camera. Many people forget that the original Windows XP was created in an age where electronic cameras weren't nearly as popular as their silver-halide progenitors. That's the main reason why electronic camera support in Windows XP seems rudimentary at best. Even the advances in Windows XP Service Pack 2 feel bolted on.

If you're using the native Windows XP programs to pull pictures from a camera and put them on your Windows Home Server, you get to struggle with the ancient Microsoft Scanner and Camera Wizard. It can be done (see the following section) — the Scanner and Camera Wizard *can* be coerced into playing the middleman — but it's a laborious and painful process. There's a reason why the term "Scanner" appears *before* "Camera."

In a similar vein, Windows XP has few tools for retrieving or displaying photos. Basically, you get these capabilities:

- ✓ Windows Explorer with the View settings (Filmstrip, Thumbnails, and Tiles) that show you picture previews.

- ✓ The moderately capable (but searchless) Windows Picture and Fax Viewer (see Figure 9-1).

- ✓ The bit-blopping octogenarian called Windows Paint.

If you're looking for a good, free Windows Paint replacement, take a gander at Paint.NET (www.getpaint.net). Features galore, well supported, intuitive and slick. Paint.NET runs under the .NET Framework, but if you have the Windows Home Server connector software installed, you already have .NET Framework.

Getting your photos into the server

It's a good idea to move all your photos from your home or office computers onto the server, placing them in the shared Photos folder. The process is quite similar to the method for transferring music from network computers onto the server — and subject to the same caveats. One of those is the sheer size of the individual files; they can gobble up a vast amount of space — even more if you turn on Folder Duplication. For example, if you have 100 GB of photos on a home computer and Windows Home Server has already backed up the computer, then you move the 100 GB of photos onto the server, and turn on Folder Duplication for the Photos folder, the server needs 300 GB of space — the backup copy sticks around until its expiration date has passed.

To get all your network's photos onto the server, follow the steps in Chapter 6, in the section "Sharing from A to Z to PC to PC."

Figure 9-1:
Windows
XP's
Windows
Picture and
Fax Viewer.

You can get Windows XP's tired old programs to work with Windows Home Server, but it takes a bit of effort. (I show you how in the next section.)

Windows Vista, on the other hand, positively teems with picture-handling capabilities, most of which can be used to great effect with your Windows Home Server. At the hub of the hullabaloo: Vista's Windows Photo Gallery (see Figure 9-2).

Photo Gallery includes hooks that can be manipulated to pull pictures off your camera and stick them in your server's `Photos` folder. It can also be trained to include server photos in its giant database, to make scanning and retrieving much easier.

As we went to press, Microsoft was tweaking the interface on a new product called Windows Live Photo Gallery. As things look now, Windows Live Photo Gallery may take the place of *both* the Windows XP photo application lineup *and* Vista's Windows Photo Gallery — it's designed to run on both Windows XP and Vista, and it should run rings around XP's native capabilities. Time will tell if Windows Live Photo Gallery can live up to its hype, but it looks promising. Check `AskWoody.com` for the latest revelations and, if you feel bold (particularly if you're struggling with Windows XP's antiquated picture handling), download and install the new program.

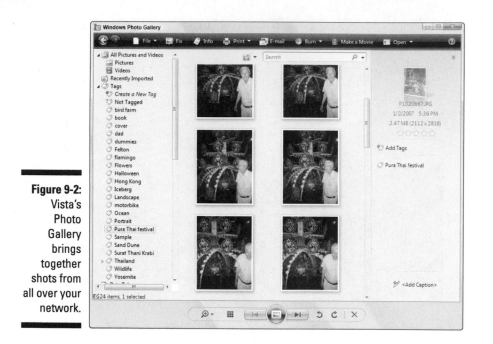

Figure 9-2:
Vista's
Photo
Gallery
brings
together
shots from
all over your
network.

Although Microsoft is still tinkering with the interface as I write this, the precise instructions for modifying Windows Live Photo Gallery to work with Windows Home Server closely parallel the instructions in the section "Modifying Vista for Shared Photos," later in this chapter. Dive in — and if you hit a snag, shoot me an e-mail.

Modifying XP for Shared Photos

When everything's set up properly and working well, Windows XP does a passable job helping you maintain your photo collection. When things get a little bit out of kilter, however, you can waste a *lot* of time and effort trying to sort through the oddities.

Viewing photos in the shared Photos folder

If Windows XP is working right, you should have no trouble seeing the photos stored in your Windows Home Server shared Photos folder, and working with them in the ways the Windows Gods intended. Sometimes, though, Windows XP needs a little, uh, *guidance* — especially when it fails to realize that the shared Photos folder contains photos (*D'oh!*) and (because of the misidentification) fails to give you all the features that are appropriate for a photo-laden folder.

To see whether Windows XP has its story straight — and to make sure that it gets things right in the future — try this:

1. **On a Windows XP computer that's been connected to the server, double-click the icon on the desktop that says Shared Folders on Server.**

   If the password that you used to log on to the Windows XP computer doesn't match any of the logon IDs on the server, you need to provide a user name and password that are valid *on the server.* If you don't know of any valid combinations, try using a user name of Guest and no password at all.

   Once you pass muster, Windows Home Server lets you see all the shared folders on the server, as in Figure 9-3.

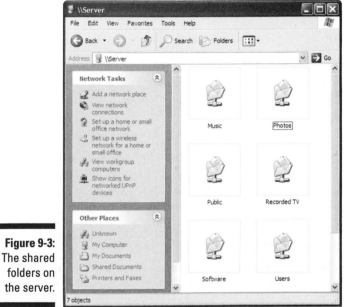

Figure 9-3:
The shared folders on the server.

2. **Double-click the** Photos **folder.**

   Windows XP shows you all the folders that are in the Photos shared folder. (If you haven't yet moved your photos into the Photos shared folder, see the sidebar called "Getting Your Photos into the Server.")

3. **Up on the menu bar, click View, and look at the options on offer.**

   You probably see a list of View options like the one shown in Figure 9-4.

Figure 9-4:
The View
options
available
for the
shared
Photos
folder.
Filmstrip
isn't there.

In my experience, Windows XP doesn't correctly identify the shared `Photos` folder as containing pictures. (Odd oversight, eh?) There are several consequences to that oversight. If XP doesn't officially recognize the folder as a `Pictures` folder, here's the rub:

- You don't get a View as Slideshow option in the task pane on the left.

- You don't see Get Pictures from Camera or Scanner in the task pane, either.

- The most frustrating zapped feature is the lack of a Filmstrip option on the View menu — an option I use all the time. The next step shows you what's missing.

4. **Double-click any folder in the shared `Photos` folder.**

5. **Look for Get Pictures From Camera or Scanner on the left, as well as View as Slideshow. Then click View to see if Windows XP correctly identified the folder as one containing pictures — and therefore placed the Get Pictures and Slideshow option in the task pane, and stuck Filmstrip at the top of the View options.**

In Figure 9-5, you can see the View options for a folder that's been correctly identified by Windows XP as containing pictures. Filmstrip appears at the top of the list. (You can see the effect of Filmstrip View in Figure 9-5.)

Note that the culprit in all this is Windows XP, not Windows Home Server. Windows XP assigns a "folder type" for each folder it encounters. The folder type not only dictates which options are available in the View menu, it also controls what tasks appear on the left, in the task pane. If

XP guesses wrong, you don't get all the tools that are associated with the folder type. In this case, XP misidentifies the shared `Photos` folder as containing `Documents`, so it doesn't offer a Filmstrip View option.

6. **If Windows XP correctly identified the `Photos` folder and you see a Filmstrip option on the View menu (as in Figure 9-4), you're done. Skip to the next section. Congratulations. Your Windows XP is smarter than my Windows XP. But if you don't see Filmstrip on the Photos folder's View list, click the up-pointing arrow twice, to return to the list of shared folders on the server.**

   Your screen should look like Figure 9-3.

7. **Right-click the `Photos` folder and choose Properties. Click the Customize tab.**

   Windows XP shows you the Photos on Server Properties dialog box, as in Figure 9-6.

8. **From the drop-down list, choose Pictures (Best for Many Files). Check the box marked Also Apply this Template to All Subfolders. Click OK.**

   Windows XP marks all the current folders in the shared `Photos` folder as containing Pictures. You should see the correct View options and task-pane entries in every folder.

9. **X-button your way out of the Windows Explorer window.**

   And feel confident that Windows XP will now offer you everything it has to offer for picture folders.

Figure 9-5: Windows XP identifies this folder as one containing pictures, and thus shows the Filmstrip option.

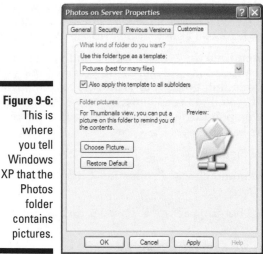

Figure 9-6: This is where you tell Windows XP that the Photos folder contains pictures.

Moving photos from your camera to the shared Photos folder

Most people who buy a new electronic camera immediately install the software that came with it.

Oooh, bad guess.

 Most people spend a few minutes to a few hours futzing with the software — and end up wishing they had never seen it. That's why I recommend — in all my books — that you try to use the built-in Windows software first, *before* you try your luck with the camera manufacturer's CD.

If you haven't yet gummed up the works with a camera manufacturer's programs, setting up Windows XP itself to grab the photos off your camera and stick them in the server's shared Photos folder is pretty straightforward.

 Unfortunately, if you try these steps and the camera's software butts in, you may be in for some way-too-*interesting* times: Some camera manufacturers hook their software so deeply into Windows that it's hard to extract. Start with the instructions for removing the manufacturer's software. If that doesn't work, complain on the camera maker's online support.

Here's how to convince Windows XP to automatically pull photos from your camera and stick them in your Windows Home Server shared Photos folder:

1. **Plug your camera into your Windows XP computer and turn it on. If you see an AutoPlay notice like the one in Figure 9-7, choose Copy Picture to a Folder on My Computer Using Microsoft Scanner and Camera Wizard, and click OK. Then go on to Step 5.**

   Figure 9-7 shows the standard Windows XP AutoPlay notification, as it usually appears for electronic cameras. Unfortunately, there are many ways to divert Windows XP from this version of spiritual bliss, so if you don't see the notice in Figure 9-7, try Plan B, er, Step 2.

Figure 9-7:
The direct route to the Scanner and Camera Wizard.

2. **Double-click the Shared Folders on Server icon on your desktop.**

3. **Double-click the Photos folder. If the top line on the left, in the task pane, says Get Pictures From Camera or Scanner, click it — and when the Scanner and Camera Wizard appears, go on to Step 5.**

   You may need to provide a user name and password to get into the server.

   If you don't see the Get Pictures From Camera or Scanner line, follow the steps earlier in this section to make Windows XP recognize your Photos folder as being a `Pictures` folder.)

   If neither Step 1 nor Step 2 brings up the Scanner and Camera Wizard, there's always Plan C, *to wit* . . .

4. **Click Start ⇨ Control Panel⇨Printers and Other Hardware⇨Scanners and Cameras. If your camera is listed, click once on the camera, and then on the left click Get Pictures.**

   If Steps 1, 2, 3, and 4 don't work — you're stuck with pulling the pictures off your camera manually. Click Start⇨My Computer, double-click the camera's icon (it's probably identified as "Removable Disk"), double-click down to where the pictures are located (look for a folder named `DCIM`), and then click and drag the pictures out of the camera and into your server's shared `Photos` folder.

Windows calls that the "advanced" option. I call it a pain in the neck. There's no easy way to automate the "advanced" option, so resign yourself to copying files by hand, skip down to the next section — oh, and make a note to install Windows Live Photo Gallery just as soon as it's stable.

5. **If you can see the Scanner and Camera Wizard, click Next.**

   The Scanner and Camera Wizard invites you to choose the pictures that you want to copy (or move) from your camera onto the server (Figure 9-8). To do so, check the box next to the pictures that you want to copy or move.

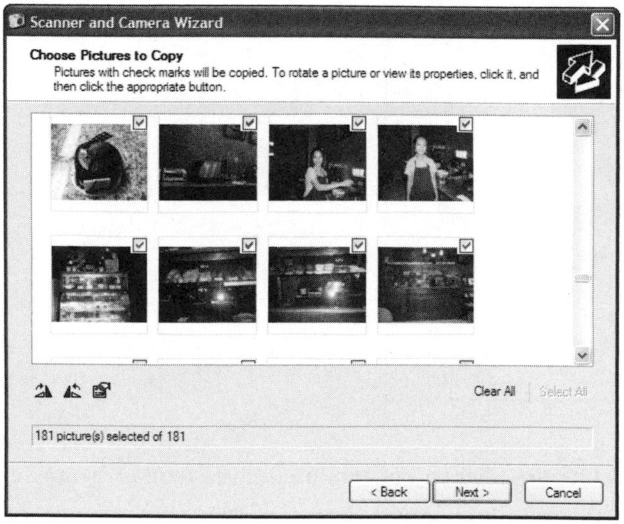

Figure 9-8: Pick the pics you want to stick in the shared Photos folder.

If any of the pictures appear rotated, click the picture once, and then click one of the rotate buttons on the left to rotate the picture a quarter-turn to the right (clockwise) or to the left (counterclockwise).

6. **If this is the first time you've used the Scanner and Camera Wizard since connecting this computer to a Windows Home Server, there's a little trick I'd like to show you. Just this one time:**

   a. Click the Clear All link, and then click the check box next to one picture. Doesn't matter which one.

   We're going to force Windows XP's Scanner and Camera Wizard to remember the location of the server's shared Photos folder. You only need to copy one photo to get the trick to work.

   b. Click Next.

   The Scanner and Camera Wizard invites you to give a name to the pictures, and choose a destination, as in Figure 9-9.

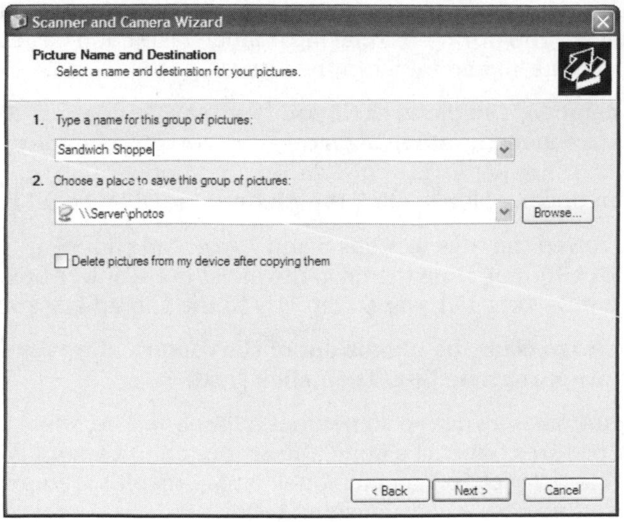

Figure 9-9:
Choose a
name and
location.

c. Click the Browse button and navigate to the `Photos` folder on the
   server.

   You may have to navigate all the way down to `\My Network`
   `Places\Entire Network\Microsoft Windows`
   `Network\Workgroup\Photos`, as in Figure 9-10.

d. Click OK. Then click Next, and let the wizard copy your one chosen
   picture into the shared `Photos` folder.

e. Finally, click Back twice so you can copy the photos from the
   camera "for real," starting all over again at Step 5.

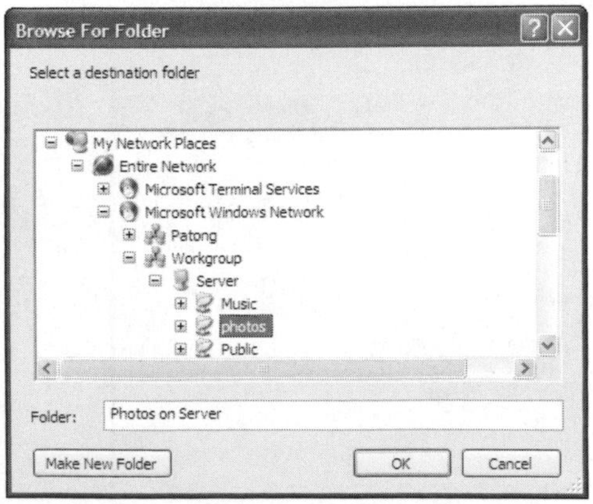

Figure 9-10:
You may
have to
hunt to
find your
server's
Photos
folder.

If you use the shared Photos folder just once, it will appear as a choice in the lower drop-down box, making it much faster and easier to move photos into the shared folder in the future.

7. **Type a name for the pictures (if you type, say,** Sandwich Shoppe, **the pictures are named, rather bizarrely,** Sandwich Shoppe.jpg, Sandwich Shoppe 001.jpg, Sandwich Shoppe 002.jpg, **and so on). Then pick a place to stick the pictures (see Figure 9-11).**

   If you followed the trick in Steps 5 and 7, you can choose \\Server\Photos from the drop-down list in the lower box, and then click Browse — *et voilà*, you go directly to the shared Photos folder.

8. **If you want to clear the photos out of the camera after you copy them, check the appropriate box. Then click Next.**

   The wizard takes awhile — sometimes a loooooooong while — to transfer your pictures. When it's done, the Scanner and Camera Wizard politely offers to let you spend money on Microsoft's Web-publishing or photo-printing sites. (How considerate.)

9. **Click Cancel.**

   Save your money; Microsoft has enough of it already. If you want to publish on the Web, go to flickr.com or any of hundreds of sites that specialize in free photo-posting.

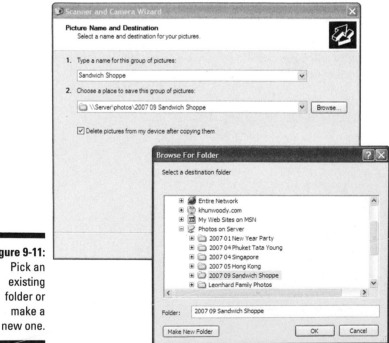

Figure 9-11: Pick an existing folder or make a new one.

Modifying the screen saver to use the shared Photos folder

If you've been using Windows XP for any time at all, you probably know that you can set up the screen saver so it displays a slideshow of pictures in your My Pictures folder.

You may not realize that you can make the screen saver cycle through all the pictures in any folder — including any folder in the server's shared Photos folder, or even *all* the photos in the shared Photos folder. As long as your user name and password on the home or office computer matches up with a logon ID and password on the server, and that user name has permission to look at the files in the Photos folder, it's easy.

Here's how to use your shared Photos folder for a Windows XP screen saver:

1. **Log on to any Windows XP computer using a user name and password that works on your server. Right-click an empty space on the desktop and choose Properties. Click the Screen Saver tab.**

   You see the Screen Saver selection choices shown in Figure 9-12.

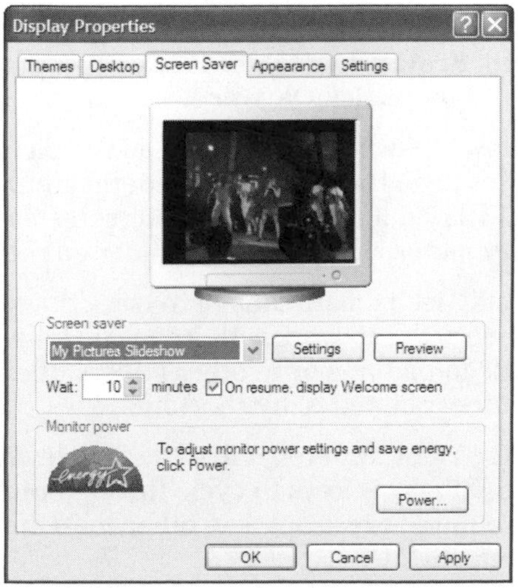

Figure 9-12: Choose My Pictures Slideshow here.

2. **In the drop-down box marked Screen Saver, choose My Pictures Slideshow. Then click Settings.**

   Windows XP shows you the My Pictures Screen Saver Options dialog box, as in Figure 9-13.

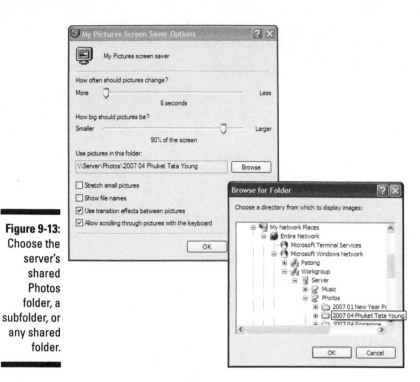

Figure 9-13:
Choose the
server's
shared
Photos
folder, a
subfolder, or
any shared
folder.

3. **Click the Browse button. Browse to a folder that you want to use to create the slideshow, and then click OK twice.**

   Keep in mind that Windows XP will cycle through all the pictures in the folder, and all the pictures in all the subfolders underneath the folder. If you choose the server's shared Photos folder, your screen saver turns into a slideshow of every picture in the Photos folder on the server.

   Unfortunately, Windows XP isn't smart enough to track down shortcuts. So if you set up the screen saver to work with a specific folder and that folder contains shortcuts to pictures or to other folders, the slideshow will not include the pictures pointed to by shortcuts.

4. **To make sure you got the right folder(s), click the Preview button. Then use the left and right arrow keys to cycle through pictures in the slideshow. When you're done, press any key other than an arrow key to stop the preview, then click OK.**

   Windows uses your new slideshow as a screen saver the next time you let your computer sit idle.

Modifying Vista for Shared Photos

If you're working with pictures on Windows Home Server, Vista has many more options — and many fewer roadblocks — than Windows XP.

Take a few minutes to get Vista hooked up, and you'll be amazed at how well it co-operates with Windows Home Server.

Viewing photos in the shared Photos folder

Vista's Windows Photo Gallery has a checkered lineage. It started out (at least conceptually) as a fully functional database system that didn't care much where pictures were located. The original design faded and took several twists and turns as the Vista development team inside Microsoft started missing internal-target release dates. The Photo Gallery that you see inside Vista retains many of its database-style roots, but the old location-dependent navigation system remains. Neither fish nor fowl, Photo Gallery can be confusing at first, especially if you're from the "where did I put that file?" generation.

Providing you have a user name and password on your home machine that matches one on the server, getting Photo Gallery to recognize and catalog photos on your server only takes a few clicks. Here's how:

1. **Log on to a Vista machine using a user name and password that are known to the server.**

   The user name, er, logon ID on the server must have security permission to read the contents of the shared Photos folder. (See Chapter 5 for the details of setting permissions for shared folders.)

2. **Click Start⇨All Programs⇨Windows Photo Gallery.**

   You see the Photo Gallery.

3. **Click File⇨Add Folder to Gallery.**

   The Windows Photo Gallery responds with its Add Folder to Gallery dialog box, shown in Figure 9-14.

4. **Navigate down to the Network's \\Server\Photos folder and click OK.**

   The Photo Gallery asks whether you're really, really sure you want to add \\SERVER\Photos to the Photo Gallery.

5. **Click Add.**

   Some days I wish I had an option to click a button that says, You Silly Computer, I Just Told You I Wanted To Do That, Why Do You Insist On Bugging Me? Just Add It And Be Done With It.

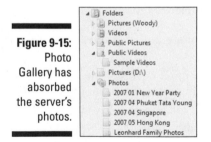

Figure 9-14:
Choose a folder for the Photo Gallery to constantly monitor.

Vista warns you that it can take a long, long time to add large folders to the Photo Gallery. It can. Hours.

You know that Vista has completed its indexing when you can see the server's `Photos` folder at the bottom of the list of folders on the left, as in Figure 9-15.

Figure 9-15:
Photo Gallery has absorbed the server's photos.

Moving photos directly from your camera to the shared Photos folder

Vista's photo-importing technology runs rings around Windows XP's.

In most cases, you don't even need to plug your camera into your Vista computer. All you need to do is stick the camera's memory card into a compatible card reader, and Vista is smart enough to kick in the requisite program.

Here's how to get Vista to unload your pictures directly to the server's shared Photos folder:

1. **Log on to a Vista computer using a user name and password that's known to your Windows Home Server server.**

2. **Take your camera's memory card out of the camera and put it in a compatible card reader.**

   Vista responds with an AutoPlay dialog box like the one in Figure 9-16.

Figure 9-16: Vista's very good at identifying camera memory cards.

3. **Click the link to Import Pictures Using Windows.**

   Vista does a quick scan of the camera's memory card, locates the first picture, and presents you with the Importing Pictures and Videos dialog box (shown in Figure 9-17).

Figure 9-17: Here you tell Vista it's okay to import.

4. **Click the Options link.**

   You see the Import Settings dialog box in Figure 9-18. Vista gives you an opportunity to choose a destination folder.

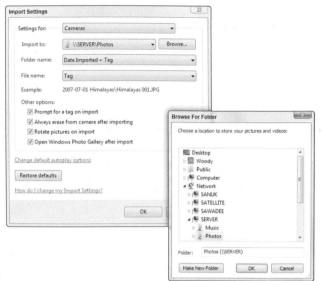

Figure 9-18:
Vista's
surprisingly
limited
Import
Settings
dialog box.

If you ever want to revisit the Import Settings dialog box, bring up the Photo Gallery (Start⇨All Programs⇨Windows Photo Gallery), then click File⇨Options, and choose the Import tab.

5. **Click Browse. Navigate to the server's shared Photos folder (or any other folder you may prefer) and click OK.**

   You go back to the Import Settings dialog box.

6. **Back in the Import Settings dialog box, choose a method for constructing a folder name, a method for constructing file names, and any additional options that may strike your fancy.**

The methods for creating folder names and file names are very restrictive, and they generally hinge on the tag that you type into the Importing Pictures and Videos dialog box (Figure 9-17). In this case, if I use the tag `Sandwich Shoppe`, and choose the Folder Name option called Date Imported + Tag, Vista creates a new folder based on the current date — say, `\\SERVER\Photos\2007-12-31 Sandwich Shoppe`. If I choose the File Name option called Tag, the pictures going into that shared folder are called `Sandwich Shoppe 001.jpg`, `Sandwich Shoppe 002.jpg`, and so on. Each of the files is tagged `Sandwich Shoppe`. Not very elegant, but it gets the job done — quickly.

7. **Click OK, and then click Import.**

If you changed any settings, Vista restarts the Import Pictures and Videos program. You have to click OK and it takes a few seconds.

Depending on the speed of your camera's memory card and the number and size of pictures on the card, importing can take forever.

You can uncheck the box marked Erase after Importing at any time during the glacial import process, and Vista will leave all the pictures on the camera.

Once you have the Import Pictures and Videos program working the way you want it, importing pictures is a snap — take the card out of the camera, plug it into the computer, click the correct AutoPlay item, and click the Import button. Then sit back and cool your heels while Vista pulls all the pictures off the camera, and sticks them in the server's shared Photos folder. Slick.

Creating a screen saver from the shared Photos folder

Like Windows XP, Vista has a screen saver that creates a slideshow out of all the pictures in a folder (and subfolders of the main folder). Like Windows XP, Vista can be told to use pictures stored in the server's shared Photos folder, or any shared folder at all. *Unlike* Windows XP, Vista's slideshow has a few cool options.

Here's how to get your server's shared Photos folder to dish up pics for the screen saver:

1. **Log on to a Vista computer with a user name (uh, logon ID) and password that match a logon ID (uh, user name) and password on the server.**

2. **Right-click any blank part of the desktop and choose Personalize. In the Personalization dialog box, choose Screen Saver.**

Vista brings up the Screen Saver Settings dialog box shown in Figure 9-19.

3. **In the drop-down Screen Saver box, choose Photos. Then click the Settings button.**

Vista shows you the settings for using the Photos folder to feed a screen saver, as in Figure 9-20.

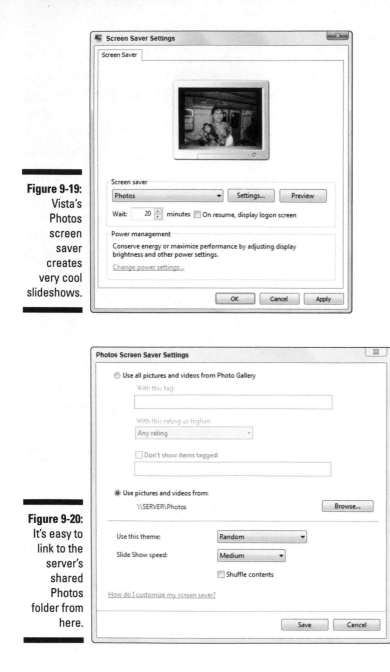

Figure 9-19:
Vista's
Photos
screen
saver
creates
very cool
slideshows.

Figure 9-20:
It's easy to
link to the
server's
shared
Photos
folder from
here.

4. **Vista has an option to draw on pictures from the Photo Gallery with a specific tag. If you choose to show all the pictures with that tag, the screen saver will pull pictures from any location — on your home or office computer, on the server, or anywhere else known to Photo Gallery — and use those for the slideshow.**

   That's a nifty feature if you have the time to add tags to a bunch of files.

5. **Alternatively, to pull pictures from the server's shared Photos folder, click the Browse button, navigate to the** Photos **folder, or any shared folder that you like, and click OK.**

   If you pick a folder, Vista goes through all the pictures in all the subfolders too. So if you choose the server's shared Photos folder, you will see a slideshow of all the shared pictures on the server.

   Unlike Windows XP, the Vista Photos screen saver is smart enough to follow shortcuts, so you can put shortcuts in a folder and have the pictures referenced by those shortcuts appear as part of the slideshow.

6. **Click the Preview button to verify that you've chosen the correct folder(s). You can use the left and right arrows to cycle through the pictures while you're previewing. When you're happy with your choices, click OK, and X-button out of the Personalize dialog box.**

   As you add new pictures to the shared folder, Vista adds them to the slideshow.

Part IV
Sharing in the Wild

In this part . . .

As the computer industry matures, what we do on our own computers becomes less and less important. What we make available to the outside world, and how we interact with the world beyond our homes and offices, holds much greater import.

Why?

There's so much more *out there* than there is *in here*.

> No man is an Iland, intire of itselfe;
> every man is a peece of the Continent, a
> part of the maine.
>
> —John Donne, Meditation XVII of Devotions
> Upon Emergent Occasions, 1624

Chapter 10

Starting Remote Access

In This Chapter

▶ Understanding Remote Access — its benefits and potential problems

▶ Convincing Windows Home Server that you really want to access your network from afar

▶ Poking holes in recalcitrant routers

▶ Poking different holes in pesky Internet service providers' defenses

▶ Getting logged on for the first time

*I*f Windows Home Server's Remote Access feature works for you the first time, you live a charmed life. I've set up Remote Access on many networks, and it seems that no two work the same way.

If it takes you a bit of wrangling (either with your router or with your Internet service provider) to get Remote Access working, take solace in the fact that it's well worth the hassle. Hang in there. You can do it.

With Remote Access enabled and all the pieces put together properly, you can hop onto a computer anywhere in the world, fire up a Web browser, *and* . . .

✓ Upload and download files between your server's shared folders and the computer you're using (see Figure 10-1).

✓ Run the Windows Home Server console, if you know the server's password.

✓ Remotely connect to some of the PCs on your home or office network and take control of the PC as if you were sitting in front of it — plus or minus a (substantial) time lag, anyway. For details (including important, not-so-obvious restrictions), see the next section.

Any way you slice it, Remote Access rates as one of the best Windows Home Server features.

Figure 10-1:
You can use a Web browser to get into your server from anywhere in the world.

Remote Access — the Good, the Bad, and the Really Frustrating

If you decide to enable Remote Access through your Windows Home Server, you can log on to your home or office network from anywhere in the world, using any Web browser, upload and download files, and even "take control" of a PC on the network, pulling its strings like a puppet, in a way that's not too dissimilar to sitting down in front of the computer and typing away.

Except . . . but . . . er . . . well, Remote Access doesn't *quite* work that way, and it can be an absolute monster to set up. There. I warned you.

Remote Access's problems, by and large, aren't Microsoft's fault. They're congenital. By its very nature, Remote Access has to poke through your broadband router (you may call it a "modem," even though it isn't technically a modem), and every router's different. Confounding the problem, many Internet Service Providers play fast and loose with your network's address, making it very difficult to find your network, or they may block incoming connections entirely to keep you from setting up a Web server on your consumer Internet account.

Before you take the plunge and try to get Remote Access working on your network, carefully consider these somewhat embarrassing facts:

✔ **Few Remote Access installations, at least in my experience, go through immediately and without hassles.** There are almost always niggling details. To look at it another way, *almost* all of Windows Home Server works great for an absolute novice, from the get-go, with few required machinations and not that many moving parts. But Remote

Access is a horse of a considerably more complex color. It isn't plug-and-play. Isn't even plug-and-swear. It goes outside the box — literally and figuratively — and, unless you're extremely lucky, getting it to work takes some pushing and pulling.

✓ **Remote Access opens up your network to the outside world.** If you set things properly, there is little security exposure to having your Remote Access enabled network hacked by The Bad Guys. But if you do something stupid — like give away a remote logon ID and password to a friend, who passes it on to another friend — you can kiss your system security goodbye.

✓ **Many people think they can control any computer on their network via Remote Access. Ain't true.** When you're working remotely, you can only take control of PCs that are running Windows XP Pro, XP Media Center Edition, XP Tablet, Vista Business, Enterprise, or Ultimate. That's it. XP Home, Vista Home Basic, and Vista Premium PCs aren't sufficiently endowed to do the "puppet" shtick.

I don't mean to put you off. I love Remote Access and use it all the time, even though it was a bear to set up on my home office network. I also take great care to make sure none of my Remote Access user names leak out — and the passwords would tie your tongue, much less your typing fingers. (Word to the wise there.)

An Overview of Remote Access Setup

Still with me? Good. Remote Access is worth the sweat. No pain no, uh, pain. Something like that.

At the very highest level, and in the best of all possible worlds, here's how you get Remote Access working:

1. **Fire up the Windows Home Server Console and tell WHS that you want it to start responding to inquiries from the great, cold outside world.**

   That part's easy.

2. **Enable Remote Access for one or more user names (er, logon IDs).**

   These user names have to have "strong" passwords, and they're the only ones allowed to log on to the server remotely.

3. **Poke a hole through your router.**

   Aye, there's the rub. Er, hub. You have to set things up so somebody trying to get to your Windows Home Server server from out on the Internet can get past the router far enough to get into the server. Some routers get poked automatically by the Remote Access setup routines. Some routers allow you to poke through manually with relative ease. Many don't.

4. **Get a permanent address for your server.**

   You need a domain name for your server (for example, mine is `AskWoody.homeserver.com`) so folks on the Internet — including you — can find your server. And therein lies a tale: see the sidebar on Dynamic DNS.

   In some cases, using a domain name for your server isn't an absolute requirement. If you know positively, for sure, that your Internet Service Provider will never change the IP address of your server, you can just type the four-number IP address into your Web browser. But having a name that always points to your server makes life much simpler.

   The company that sold you your Windows Home Server may offer a free "Dynamic DNS" (see the nearby sidebar). HP, for example, offers the first year free — you can use Microsoft's Homeserver program, or you can sign up with any of dozens of competitors.

5. **If you want to connect directly to one of the computers on your network, you have to tell the computer that it should accept Remote Desktop connections.**

   Windows Home Server uses Remote Desktop to establish connections to computers in your home or office network. Unless you specifically set up a computer to accept Remote Desktop, it won't respond, won't behave like a puppet.

6. **Test everything.**

   The proverbial proof of the pudding.

7. **If you make a major change to your home network, you may have to repeat Step 3.**

   They don't warn you about this in Remote Access school, but if the internal address of your Windows Home Server server changes (it's an IP address that probably looks like `192.168.1.3` or some such), you have to go back and poke another hole through your router. If you do so, remember to close up the old holes!

Step 3 is the tough one. And if things suddenly stop working today, when they were working the day (or hour) before, you most likely need to concentrate on Step 6.

Forewarned and four- (or six-) armed, you're ready to take on the task. Simply follow the steps in the rest of this chapter in order, and you stand a good chance of getting connected.

Dynamic DNS

The Internet works with numeric addresses, called *IP addresses*, much like the telephone system works with telephone numbers. When you type an address into your Web browser — www.Dummies.com, for example — your browser has to go out and find the numeric address of the Web site, in a process that's very similar to looking up a telephone number in a phone book. The Internet's phone book, called a *Domain Name Server*, translates names like Dummies.com into IP addresses like 208.215.179.139 (which happens to be the Dummies.com IP address). Armed with the numeric IP address, your browser can find the site you seek.

Problems arise when your Internet Service Provider changes your home server's IP address. Big commercial sites like Dummies.com have permanently assigned phone numbers, er, IP addresses. But little guys like you and me may have our phone numbers re-assigned at any moment, at the ISP's whim. If I tried to put my home server entry into the Internet's phone book, the phone number might work for a day or a week or a month, but then it'd get changed, and the phone book entry would suddenly point to the wrong number. Updating the Internet's phone book takes a long time, and it's a hassle.

That's where Dynamic DNS comes into play. Several companies (including Microsoft and HP) maintain their own mini-phone books, their own *Dynamic DNS Servers*. These phone books can be changed automatically in a fraction of a second — and you don't need to lift a finger. By setting up a Dynamic DNS address like AskWoody.homeserver.com, you can fly to the Faroes, fire up Firefox, type in Ask Woody.homeserver.com, and the far-flung Web browser will know how to connect to your server back home, even if your ISP has changed its phone number in your absence.

Setting up the Server

Getting your server ready for Remote Access takes just a few minutes, as long as you know the server's password.

Follow these steps:

1. **Log on to any computer on your home or office network. Double-click the Windows Home Server icon in the notification area, next to the system clock. Type the server's password and press Enter.**

   The server's password is the one you created when you first installed the server. (See Chapter 3 for details, or Chapter 19 if you forgot the password.)

2. **At the top, click the User Accounts icon.**

   Make sure at least one account has Remote Access permission (see Figure 10-2).

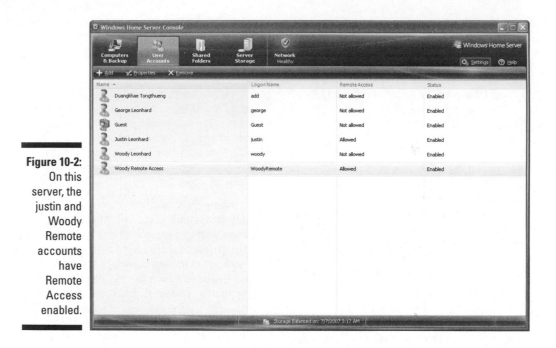

Figure 10-2:
On this
server, the
justin and
Woody
Remote
accounts
have
Remote
Access
enabled.

3. **Scan the column marked Remote Access. If all users have specified Not Allowed (or if you don't know the password(s) for the account(s) that are marked Allowed) refer to Chapter 4 and add a new user with Remote Access enabled.**

Every account with Remote Access enabled must have a "strong" password. (See Chapter 4 for details.)

It wouldn't hurt to write down the precise name of the account, just so you don't forget it.

4. **In the upper-right corner, click Settings. When the Windows Home Server Settings box appears, on the left, click Remote Access.**

You see the Remote Access settings shown in Figure 10-3.

5. **Under Web Site Connectivity, click the Turn On button.**

Windows Home Server goes out to lunch for a few seconds, and when it comes back, it says Web Sites are On.

6. **That finishes preparation work for the server itself. Continue with the next section.**

Now things get interesting.

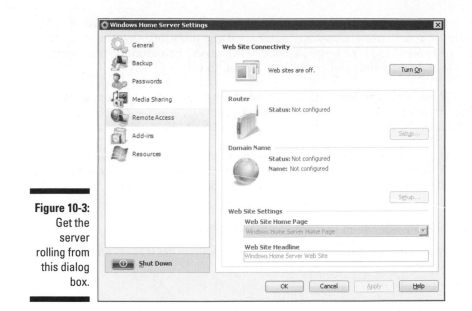

Figure 10-3:
Get the
server
rolling from
this dialog
box.

Configuring Your Router

It's easy to get bogged down in technical gobbledygook. Don't let the weird
names and numbers confuse you. When you set up your router to work with
Remote Access, the goal is clear. It's just that the means can befuddle even
the most grizzled veteran.

Your next task involves poking holes in your router.

At the risk of overstretching a well-worn analogy, think of the inbound part of
your router as a telephone exchange. When something wants to get into your
network from out in the big, bad Internet, the caller not only needs to know
your system's telephone number (the *external IP address*), but also has to
provide an extension number (a *port* in networking parlance).

Under normal circumstances, if an inquiry comes in from the Internet, your
router and/or firewall will simply swallow it — no answer, just stony silence.
That's its job. But if *you're* trying to phone home — as is the case when you
try to run Remote Access on your server — then the shoe's on the other foot.
You want your router to answer the phone, at least long enough for you to
verify that you are who you claim to be.

In order to simplify things a bit, you agree in advance to ask for one of several
specific extension numbers (specifically ports 80, 443, or 4125). You want the
router to let through calls that come in to those specific extension numbers.

At this point, the analogy's stretched mightily. Here's where it breaks down entirely: You want to have your router send any inquiries directed at ports 80, 443, and 4125 *to the server*. That way the server can monitor the incoming traffic and verify that you are who you claim to be.

The Windows Home Server Console makes a valiant attempt to forward traffic that arrives at ports 80, 443, and 4125 to the server; in some cases, it succeeds automatically. Here's how to see whether you live a charmed life:

1. **If you don't already see the Windows Home Server Settings dialog box (refer to Figure 10-3), fire up the Windows Home Server Console, click the Settings button and (on the left) click Remote Access.**

   WHS should tell you that Web Sites are On.

2. **In the router section, click the Setup button.**

   WHS tells you that it will attempt to configure port forwarding, and asks whether you would like to continue.

3. **Click OK.**

   If Windows Home Server can't get your router to recognize its commands, you see a warning that your router doesn't support UPnP and cannot be configured automatically, or you may see a checklist with red Xs like the one in Figure 10-4. At that point, you need to go into your router's settings and make the changes yourself. Continue with Step 4.

   On the other hand, if WHS got your router to respond properly and you see green check marks all the way down the Router Configuration Details checklist, bask in the glory of a charmed life, and go down to the next section. Just give me your autograph the next time I see you, okay?

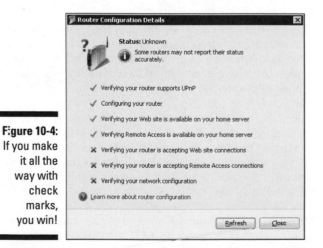

Figure 10-4: If you make it all the way with check marks, you win!

4. **If WHS tells you that your router doesn't support UPnP (either in a dialog box or with a red X in Figure 10-4), go to your router manufacturer's Web site and figure out how to turn on UPnP. Then click the Refresh button on the Router Configuration Details dialog box and try again.**

Usually it's easy to turn on UPnP, but each router is different. On my Zyxel 660R router, the screen for enabling UPnP looks like Figure 10-5.

Next, in order to forward traffic through your router, you need the IP address of your Windows Home Server server.

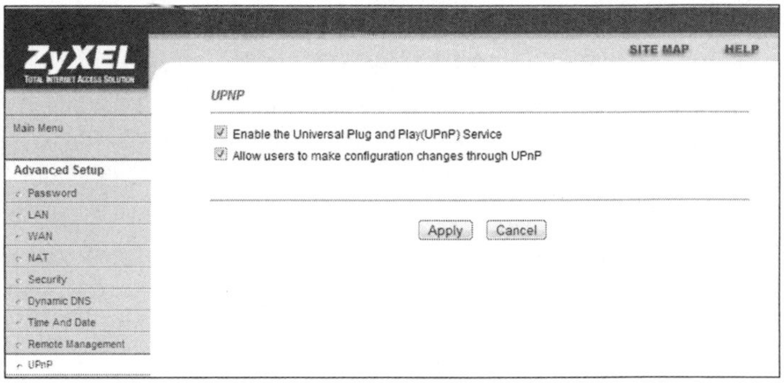

Figure 10-5:
Turning on
UPnP on a
Zyxel router.

5. **There are many ways to retrieve the server's IP address, but a very easy way is to click Start⇨All Programs⇨Accessories⇨Command Prompt. When the command line comes up, type** ping server **(or** `ping` **whatever name you gave the server when you set it up) and press Enter.**

Windows tells you the server's address. In Figure 10-6, the server address is `192.168.1.3`.

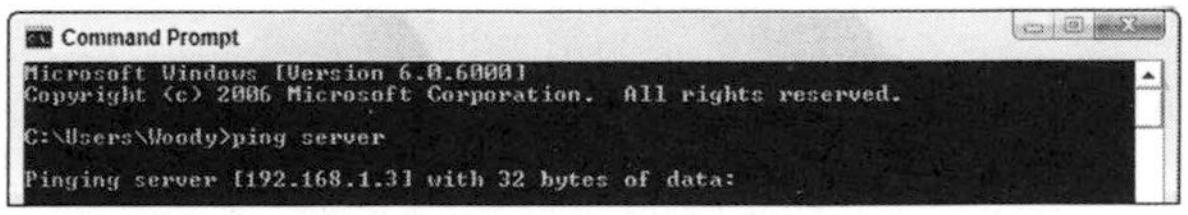

Figure 10-6:
An easy
way to find
the IP
address of
your server.

Most servers automatically pick up their IP addresses from the network's router: If you unplug the server and plug it in again, it may pick up a different IP address. Your router, on the other hand, requires you to provide specific IP addresses when you go poking holes. After you have Remote Access working, you might want to take the advanced course and assign a permanent IP address to your server. That way, you can poke the holes through your router and have the incoming traffic always go to your server — even if you unplug your server and plug it back in again. If you assign the IP address properly, you won't have any conflicts with other computers on your network — but it takes some effort. See Chapter 17 for details.

Or if you're lazy, you can do what I do. See the section "My Encounter with the Seventh Ring," at the end of this chapter.

With the server's IP address in hand, you need to dig into your router and tell it to forward traffic on ports 80, 443 and 4125 to the server. That's easy to say — and devilishly difficult to do because every router is different. I recommend that you go to the site `portforward.com` and look for specific instructions for your router.

Many routers are similar to my trusty Linksys WRT54G, and I present (in the following steps) the method for changing the WRT54G. Your mileage may vary. Be sure to consult `portforward.com` for details applicable to your router.

6. **To get into my Linksys WRT54G, I start Internet Explorer and type the IP address of the router — which I just happen to know is** `192.168.1.1`.

   The router asks me to provide the user name and password for the router.

7. **Type the router's user name and password. Note that these are different from your Windows Home Server user names and passwords. Press Enter.**

   If you don't know the user name and password of your router, `port forward.com` lists the defaults for most major brands. You may need to call whoever installed your router to get those essential bits of info. (I warned you this would be fun, didn't I?)

   When you (finally) get into the router, you see a setup screen. The Linksys WRT54G setup screen looks like Figure 10-7.

8. **Click the tab marked Applications & Gaming.**

   That's where Linksys puts the port-forwarding settings, as shown in Figure 10-8.

9. **You need to forward three ports. In the Application column for each of the three, type** WHS Remote Access.

   Actually, you can type anything you like; the router ignores what you type. But type this anyway; it may help you in the future if you type something that helps you remember why you changed your router so rudely.

10. **In the Start and End boxes, type** 80, 443, **and** 4125 **respectively.**

    See Figure 10-8.

11. **In the three IP Addresses boxes, type the IP address of your server.**

    That's the number you pinged in Step 4.

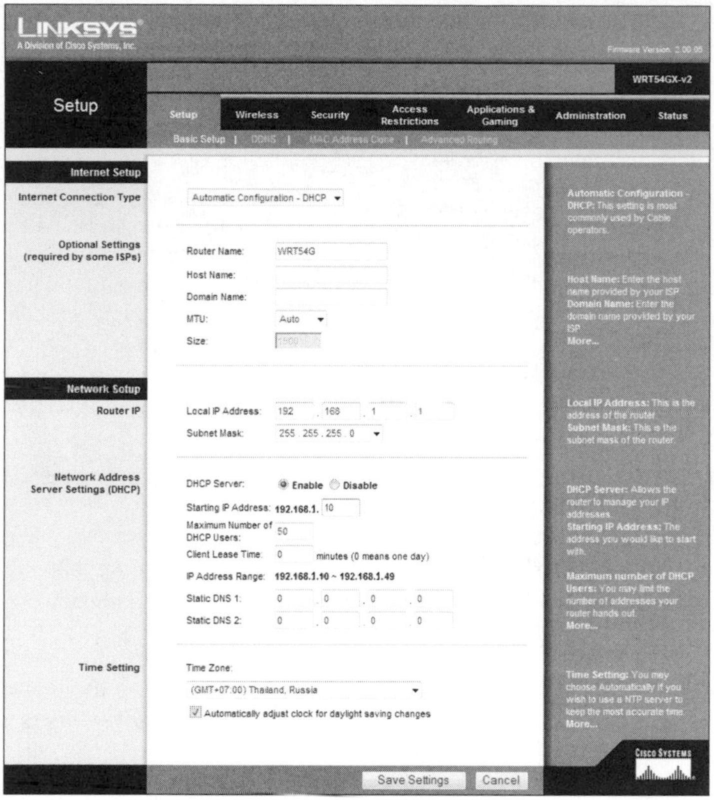

Figure 10-7:
The main setup screen for the Linksys WRT54G router.

Figure 10-8:
Here's where you specify which ports should be forwarded.

What if you have two routers?

Many people have two routers — one connects to the Internet, the other (typically wireless) serves as the main hub for your home or office network. In my experience, Windows Home Server almost never pokes through *two* routers successfully.

The problem is easy to understand, but difficult to fix: First you must poke a hole through the Internet router that allows stuff to get in from the Internet and through to the main (typically wireless) router. Then you must poke another hole through the main (typically wireless) router

that forwards stuff on to the Windows Home Server. Double your pleasure, double your run.

Getting the routers to work together is hard enough. Adding Windows Home Server to the mix can drive you nuts. If you find yourself in a position where you have to get two routers to co-operate well enough to allow Remote Access, take a couple of aspirin and head to `portforward.com/help/double routerportforwarding.htm`.

---

12. **Check the Enable boxes for all three.**

    Don't forget — if the box remains unchecked, the changes won't take effect.

13. **Click Save Settings.**

    Your router goes out to lunch for a while, but when it comes back, it should start forwarding messages sent to those three ports, shuffling them onward to the WHS server.

As you go spelunking through your router, keep the Windows Home Server Console open. If you make a change that you think will finally — finally! — get Remote Access working, flip over to the Router Configuration Details dialog box (Figure 10-4) and click Refresh. The Remote Access setup program will try, once again, to get connected. Your fate hangs in the balance.

Establishing a Permanent Domain Name

With your router suitably trained and playing well with Windows Home Server, you should get a Web address that can move with you.

Therein lies a tale of woe.

Your network (actually, your router) has an address that identifies it uniquely on the Internet — its IP address. If you're curious, you can see your network's IP address by going to `whatismyipaddress.com`. In order to connect to your Windows Home Server network using Remote Access, you have to know the address of your network. You could run to `whatismyipaddress.com`, get your network's IP address and tattoo it to the inside of your eyelids, then type that address into your Web browser — but there's a little problem . . . .

Your IP address can change. Even if you have a DSL router that's "always on," from time to time your Internet service provider may change your IP address, and you won't know a thing about it.

On the Internet, Domain Name Servers are the equivalent of giant, computerized telephone books. You type an address like dummies.com into your Web browser, the browser looks up the name in the Domain Name Server, and comes up with an IP address like 208.215.179.139. That works great for IP addresses that don't change very often. But imagine what would happen if you had to print a telephone book for a city where many phone numbers change *every day*.

The solution? Something called a *Dynamic* Domain Name Server (that's DDNS in alphabet-soup-speak; see the sidebar earlier in this chapter). Here's how to make DDNS work for you:

1. You register with a company that maintains a DDNS, and the company gives you an address like AskWoody.dynDNS.org or SlapMeSilly Willy.homeserver.com.

2. When you want to connect to your Windows Home Server network, you type SlapMeSillyWilly.homeserver.com into your Web browser and the browser goes to homeserver.com.

3. The computer at home server looks up SlapMeSillyWilly's current IP address, and automatically shuffles your browser off to the correct location.

4. When your ISP changes your IP address, a program (possibly Windows Home Server, possibly a program running in your router) notifies the DDNS company that your IP address has changed.

5. The next time you type SlapMeSillyWilly.homeserver.com into your browser, home server knows where your site went.

If you bought an HP SmartServer, HP offers a free-for-the-first-year dynamic domain name. Microsoft also offers dynamic domain names with their home server.com service. DynDNS.com has been in the business for years; they have a free service and several paid ones.

Windows Home Server makes it easy to sign up for a Microsoft homeserver. com dynamic domain name. Here's how:

1. **If you don't already have a Windows Live ID (also known as a Hotmail address, a Windows Live Hotmail address, an MSN Hotmail address, an MSN.com account, a Microsoft Passport, a .NET Passport and/or an**

MSN Passport — they're all the same thing), go to `account services.passport.net` and sign up.

The account is free, and you can make things up along the way. (Hey, your name is William H. Gates III and you live at One Microsoft Way, Redmond WA 99362, don't you? Kidding.)

2. **If you don't already see the Windows Home Server Settings dialog box (refer to Figure 10-3), start Windows Home Server Console, click the Settings button, and on the left, click Remote Access.**

    WHS should tell you that Web Sites are On. The status of your Router may be Unknown. Don't let that deter you yet.

3. **In the Domain Name area, click the Setup button.**

    WHS brings up the Domain Name Setup Wizard.

4. **Click Next.**

    The Domain Name Setup Wizard asks for your Windows Live ID and password.

5. **Type in a valid Windows Live ID and password (for the Windows Live ID account) and click Next.**

    The wizard goes out for a while, verifies your ID and password, and comes back with a warning that the server will periodically phone home to Mother Microsoft. That's to be expected: it's the only way Microsoft's Dynamic Domain Name Server can keep track of your current IP address.

6. **Select I Accept, and then click Next.**

    The wizard asks you to choose a domain name, as in Figure 10-9.

7. **In the left box, type the name you want to reserve.**

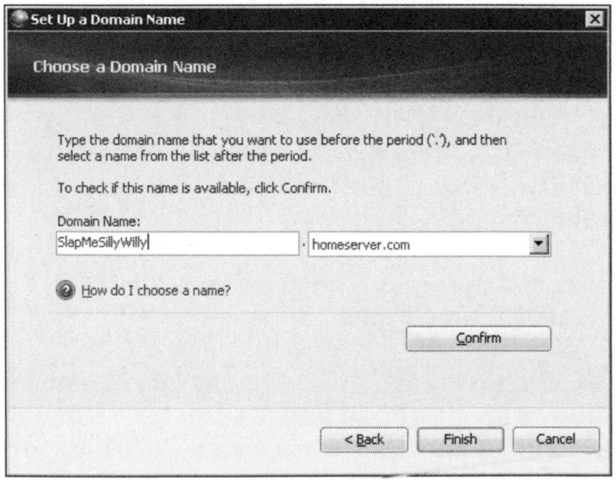

Figure 10-9: Choose your unique domain name.

8. **From the drop-down list on the right, choose the rest of your new domain name from the options on offer.**

   For example, if you type `SlapMeSillyWilly` on the left and choose `homeserver.com` on the right, your new dynamic domain name will be `SlapMeSillyWilly.homeserver.com`. Microsoft will keep it updated, so it points to your network's IP address, no matter what indignities your Internet service provider might inflict.

9. **Click Confirm to make sure your name hasn't been reserved already, and when you're done, click Finish.**

   You probably didn't notice, but Windows Home Server snuck out and grabbed your IP address, sent it to Microsoft's Dynamic Domain Name Server, and associated it with your new domain name.

   WHS advises (Figure 10-10) that you can now access your home server by using `https://` followed by your new domain name.

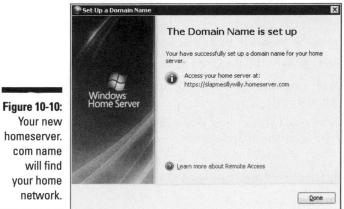

Figure 10-10:
Your new homeserver.com name will find your home network.

Spreading Out the Welcome Mat

I know you're itching to get logged on and try Remote Access. There's one little problem: If you try to use Remote Access from your home network to get on your home network (as any tester worth her salt would try about now), many routers won't let you do it. If you're working on your home or office network, and you've just finished the preceding steps, and you try to use one of your network's computers to log on to `https://slapmesilly willy.homeserver.net` (just like it says in Figure 10-11), chances are very good your router will get all confused and show you the router logon screen.

Bummer.

So hang in there. Follow the last few steps in this section. Then you'll be ready to go somewhere else — knock down your neighbor's door and demand to get on the Internet, or schlep your laptop to Starbucks — and try it all out. Patience, grasshopper.

Here's how to get Remote Access ready to rock:

1. **If you don't already see the Windows Home Server Settings dialog box (Figure 10-11), start Windows Home Server Console, click the Settings button, and (on the left) click Remote Access.**

   WHS should tell you that Web Sites are On. The status of your Router and your Domain Name may be Unknown. Persevere.

2. **In the Web Site Home Page drop-down box, choose between the feel-good Windows Home Server Home Page (shown in Figure 10-12) and the dour Windows Home Server Remote Access home page (shown in Figure 10-13).**

   There's no functional difference between the two. It's all a matter of style. Or lack thereof.

3. **Type some text in the Web Site Headline box and click OK.**

   You can see where the text will appear by looking at Figures 10-13 and 10-14.

4. **On each computer you want to be able to log on to remotely, enable remote connections.**

   By enabling the remote connections, you enable a computer to become a puppet when you connect to them from afar.

Figure 10-11:
Time for the
finishing
touches.

Figure 10-12:
The friendly
face of
Windows
Home
Server's
Remote
Access.

Figure 10-13:
The
buttoned-
down "we
just work
here"
Remote
Access
home page.

While there are several layers of security at work here, it's a good idea to "enable remote connections" *only* on PCs that you'll use frequently. If you have a PC that you may need to get into while you're on a month-long cruise down the Irrawaddy, enable remote connections before you leave — but then close it back down when you get back.

Remember that you can only enable remote connections on PCs running Windows XP Pro, Windows Media Center Edition, Windows XP Tablet, Windows Vista Business, Windows Vista Enterprise, and Windows Vista Ultimate. There's no way to set up a PC to play the puppet if it's running XP Home, Vista Home Basic, or even Vista Home Premium.

- *To enable remote connections on a Windows XP Pro computer,* click Start, right-click My Computer, and choose Properties. On the Remote tab, check the box that says Allow Users to Connect Remotely to this Computer (see Figure 10-14). Then click OK.

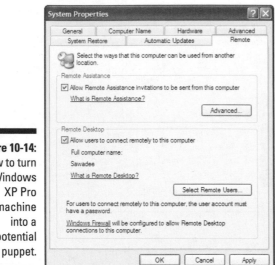

Figure 10-14:
How to turn
a Windows
XP Pro
machine
into a
potential
puppet.

- *To enable remote connections on a Vista Business, Enterprise or Ultimate computer,* click Start, right-click Computer, and then choose Properties. In the Task list on the left, choose the link to Remote Settings. Under Remote Desktop, choose Allow Connections from Computers Running any Version of Remote Desktop (Less Secure).

Vista shows you a warning that the computer goes to sleep when it isn't in use and when it's asleep, people can't connect to it remotely. If you want to change the setting, click on the Power Options link offered in the dialog box.

5. **On Vista PCs, click OK twice, then X-button your way out of the System dialog box.**

You are now *finally* ready to test Remote Access on your home network.

Getting Connected for the First Time — or Maybe Not

If you really want to test Remote Access to your home network, you should log on from a location that isn't on your home network. Go to a neighbor's house and get onto the Internet using her connection, or take your laptop to a local hotspot and log in from there.

Many routers get confused when they see that somebody inside their network is trying to get in through the front door — and they respond by showing a router logon screen in the browser, as if you wanted to get into the router instead of using Remote Access. It's most disconcerting, especially if you don't know that on some networks *it simply works that way* — there's nothing you can do about it.

That said, let me fill you in on a little secret: If you really want to see what Remote Access will be like, even though you're working from a computer that's on your network, you can bring up the Remote Access main page — and do everything Remote Access should be doing — by going to any home or office computer on your network, cranking up a Web browser, and typing this little command:

```
http://server
```

If you gave your server a name other than `server` when you set up Windows Home Server, you should use that name, for example:

```
http://server2
```

When you've finished all the steps in the preceding sections, and you're ready to see if Remote Access will work for you, here's how to proceed:

1. **Go to any computer that's *not* on your home or office network. Bring up Internet Explorer (other Web browsers seem to have problems with Microsoft's prefabricated site from time to time) and type in the dynamic name of your Remote Access Web page.**

   I fire up Internet Explorer, and type

   ```
   https://slapmesillywilly.homeserver.com
   ```

   Sit back and relax. This can take a while — the Web browser has to run to Microsoft's homeserver.com service, retrieve your home server's current IP address, and redirect you to your Windows Home Server — and then the server at your home or business has to respond.

   If all goes well, you see a logon screen (refer to Figure 10-13).

2. **If you can't get through to your Remote Access Web page, go back home and run the diagnostics in the Windows Home Server Settings dialog box (Figure 10-11).**

   You may be in for some interesting times. Follow the tips in this chapter, including the last section which talks about my walkabout with the Dark Side of the Force. If none of the nostrums in this chapter work, hop on the Windows Home Server forum at

   ```
   forums.microsoft.com/WindowsHomeServer
   ```

   and fire away, or drop a line on my site by going to `AskWoody.com` and clicking the tab that says Ask a Question.

What if Your ISP Blocks Port 80?

Some people try and try to get Remote Access to work, and ultimately discover that they can't get into their servers because their Internet service providers won't let them. Some ISPs actively block inbound traffic on port 80 (that's the `http://` port) and port 443 (that's the `https://` port). It's like they put a big, dumb firewall in front of your firewall, just so you can't get any incoming Web traffic.

If you can't get Windows Home Server Remote Access to respond to any requests, check with your ISP. If you find that your ISP is blocking ports 80 and 443, yell real loud. Then hit Google

and figure out how to jimmy your router so it re-routes a different port: For example, you can re-route port 81 to port 80 inside your router. Then, instead of typing

```
https://slapmesillywilly.home
server.com
```

you type

```
https://slapmesillywilly.home
server.com:81/remote
```

It's complicated, but doable, with Google's help.

3. **If you do get through, sign in with a user name and password that have been designated Remote Access Allowed on your server (refer to Figure 10-2).**

   Whether you chose the Windows Home Server Home Page (as in Figure 10-12) or the Windows Home Server Remote Access home page (as in Figure 10-13), you end up on the Remote Access page (refer to Figure 10-1).

4. **Click the Computers tab.**

   For a thorough rundown of the options on offer, see the next chapter. For now, we just want to verify that everything is working, so check to see whether the Computers tab lists all the computers you opened up in Step 4 of the preceding section (see Figure 10-15).

5. **Click the Shared Folders tab.**

   Windows Home Server shows you a list of all the shared folders on the server, as in Figure 10-16.

6. **Double-click on several folders, to see that you have full access to them, just as if you were sitting at your home or office computer.**

   The interface is a little clunky, but it works amazingly well. I take you through all the details in the next chapter.

7. **You can X-button out of Internet Explorer if you like, or you can leave IE sitting there and pick up with our jaunt around the Remote Access interface, in the next chapter.**

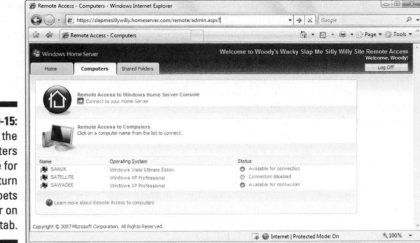

Figure 10-15:
All the computers available for you to turn into puppets appear on this tab.

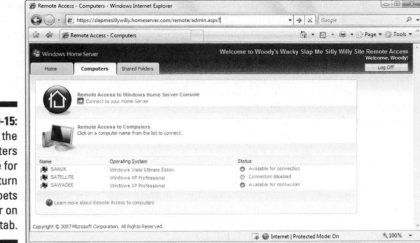

Figure 10-16:
Get into shared folders, just as you would while sitting at home.

My Encounter with the Seventh Ring

Looking back on it, Remote Access sure looks easy, doesn't it?

Let me tell ya something. It isn't. No way.

Networking for the masses is still in its infancy. The fact that normal consumers like you and me have to worry about arcane mumbo-jumbo like IP addresses and Dynamic Domain Name Servers is a sad reflection on the state of the industry. If you don't understand this stuff, don't worry — *nobody* understands all of it. Nobody.

In the course of writing this chapter, I had to reconfigure my entire network dozens of times, looking for the right settings to let Windows Home Server poke through my router. It took many tries and long hours to finally figure out how to do it. My situation is a fairly common one, so I figured I'd take a minute to show you what I had to go through, in the hope that my experience in Dante's Seventh Ring might help you on the road to WHS Enlightenment.

I have two routers. One plugs into my ADSL line. For sake of this discussion, let's call it a "modem." The other router is a Linksys WRT54G — probably the most popular wireless router ever made. Hundreds of thousands (maybe millions) of people have the same setup. I plug the modem into the WRT54G using the jack in the back of the WRT54G that the modem's supposed to use. I plug my other computers into the WRT54G. And I have a handful of computers running with the WRT54G's wireless connection. It's a boring, plain-vanilla setup, with everything put together the way the manufacturers recommend.

A long time ago, I learned that the easiest way to get the modem and the wireless router to work together involved setting them up with completely separate IP address subdomains (there's another inscrutable term for you). I let the modem stay at 192.168.1.1, but I manually switch the WRT54G over to 192.168.3.1 (note the 3). That way all the computers on my network have 192.168.3.x addresses, the modem doesn't conflict with the wireless router, and everybody gets to play nice. I've written about that method in several books, about how to keep the "mother hen" routers from scratching each others' eyes out. It works great.

Except . . . that combination doesn't work at all with Windows Home Server's Remote Access. Or if it does, I never figured out how.

I'll spare you the gory details and cut to the chase.

Here's how I got my system to work. If you have a modem and a separate wireless router, and you've pulled out all your hair, try this approach:

1. **Make sure you know all the account settings that your modem needs, and then reset the modem. Reset the router.**

   Push a little pin into their quivering carcasses. Except for your Internet server provider's account information, everything your modem and router "know" doesn't work with Windows Home Server.

2. **Connect a computer to the wireless router, and log in to the router.**

   Your router's instruction manual should give you directions, but logging in to the router usually involves firing up a Web browser and typing the address **192.168.1.1**.

You may need to manually change the IP address of the computer in order to get it to recognize the wireless router. For example, if the freshly reset wireless router starts with the address 192.168.1.1, you probably need to change the IP address of the computer to, say, 192.168.1.2. See the router's instruction manual for details.

3. **Set the wireless router up with a local IP address like** 192.168.1.250 — **something on the** 192.168.1.*x* **subdomain that won't conflict with any automatically assigned addresses.**

4. **On the wireless router, disable DHCP, disable UPnP, and turn off the firewall.**

   Both of those programs are just in the way here:

   - *DHCP* is the program that assigns IP addresses. Arcane terminology again, eh? Well, *Dynamic Host Configuration Protocol* is worse. By either name, DHCP is a program that hands out IP addresses to all the computers on a network. You can't have both the modem *and* the wireless router assigning IP addresses, so I find it's easiest to shoot the wireless router's DHCP.

   - *UPnP* (Universal Plug and Play) is the method Windows Home Server uses to change stuff inside the modem and router. If you follow the method I outline here, you don't want Windows Home Server to change anything on your wireless router. You want WHS to make all the changes to the modem. If you turn off UPnP on the wireless router, there's no chance that WHS can get confused and start twiddling the wrong box's bits.

5. **If you're going to use the wireless router for wireless access (D'OH! what else?), do whatever you need to do in order to set up wireless security.**

   Might as well secure the router before you set it up. WEP, WPA, WPA 2 — see *Wireless Home Networking For Dummies*, by Danny Briere, Pat Hurley and Walter Bruce, from Wiley, for lots of good advice.

6. **Make sure you save all the settings in the wireless router and then disconnect it from the computer.**

   When you save the settings, the router reboots. That can take a while.

7. **Plug in your modem. Type all the account stuff — password, routing type, VPI, VCI. Make sure the firewall is enabled.**

8. **Make sure that DHCP is enabled *on the modem only,* and that the assigned IP addresses don't conflict with the IP address you put in the wireless router.**

   With DHCP enabled, the modem will assign all the network's IP addresses.

9. **Read the documentation, if necessary, and enable UPnP *on the modem only*.**

   You want Windows Home Server to make its changes to the modem, not to the wireless router.

10. **Make sure you save all the settings on the router, and then unplug it from the computer. Then turn off the modem, the router, and all the computers on the network.**

11. **This is the step that will drive you nuts: *Don't* plug the modem into the modem jack on the back of the wireless router. Instead, plug the modem into one of the jacks that's designed for other computers on the network.**

    You want the wireless router to treat the modem exactly the same way that it treats all the computers on the network. If you plug the modem into the modem jack, all sorts of weird things happen.

12. **Turn on the modem. Wait 30 seconds. Turn on the wireless router. Wait another 30 seconds.**

13. **Turn on the Windows Home Server server.**

    If you turn on the WHS server before any of the other computers on the network, it will always receive the same IP address. That shouldn't make any difference, *but* if you have a hard-wired server address accidentally stuck somewhere, it doesn't hurt to get the same address on the server every time.

14. **Turn on the other computers.**

    If you had to set the IP address manually for one of the computers in Step 2, don't forget to go back into that computer and reset it to retrieve its IP address automatically.

From this point, you should be able to continue with the process described in the section "Configuring Your Router," earlier in this chapter. Oh, and congratulations. You just passed one of the toughest courses in the WHS School of Hard Knocks.

Chapter 11

Using Remote Access

In This Chapter

▶ Logging in to your Windows Home Server from any computer, anywhere in the world

▶ Getting into the server's shared folders

▶ Uploading and downloading data

▶ Logging on to your home or office computers

▶ Customizing the Windows Home Server logon screen

sing Remote Access, Windows Home Server opens up your entire home or office network, so you can get at any shared folder and (in some cases) log on to any computer on your network, from anywhere in the world.

Scary thought, eh?

Windows Home Server's remote interface is a little clunky — you have to click an Upload or Download button to move files around, instead of click and drag, for example. You have to check a box next to a file or folder name before renaming it or downloading the contents of the folder. Definitely retro. But there are redeeming social values. For example, WHS automatically zips files and folders prior to uploading or downloading them. As a first approximation, and for a version 1.0 product from Microsoft, it's quite remarkable.

In the preceding chapter I show you how to set up Remote Access — and (unless you're very lucky) setting up Remote Access is a bear, with technical challenges running amok. (*Two* moks, for that matter.)

If you've reached this stage of Windows Home Server enlightenment, and made it past Chapter 10, you're no doubt ready to plunge in and give Remote Access a try. This chapter takes you on a guided tour of what's on offer.

If you haven't yet finished the steps in Chapter 10, and Remote Access isn't yet running on your network, I feel your pain. But you can't do anything in this chapter until you have Remote Access up and running. Go back and try, try, try again. Perseverance is next to godliness.

Logging on to Your Windows Home Server Remotely

At the end of Chapter 10, you find steps to get you logged on to your server from any computer, anywhere in the world. Here are the high points, from the point of view of someone trying to get onto your system:

- ✔ **Your system at home or the office has to be set up properly,** with Windows Home Server running, appropriate holes poked through your firewall, your Internet connection working, and all the other technical gobbledygook that consumes Chapter 10.

- ✔ **You have to use Internet Explorer to get into your server from afar.** At least as of this writing, Windows Home Server Remote Access doesn't work right with Firefox.

    Why? Remote Access uses a small browser-attached program called an ActiveX control. Only Internet Explorer understands ActiveX — the designers of Firefox figure they'll support ActiveX shortly after Hell, Nevada freezes over. Until somebody comes up with a way to get into Windows Home Server's Remote Access without using an ActiveX control, you're stuck with IE.

- ✔ **You need to know your server's address.** Most people do that by setting up a Dynamic Domain Name Server account with Microsoft, HP, DynDNS, or any of a handful of competitors (see the sidebar in Chapter 10).

- ✔ **For most Windows Home Server networks, you have to get into the network "from the outside."** If you try to use Remote Access from a computer that's on your network, chances are good your router will go bonkers, prevent you from logging on to the server, and try instead to get you to log on to the router.

- ✔ **At most two remote users can be logged on to your home network simultaneously.** That's due to a strange licensing restriction from Microsoft.

- ✔ **You must have a username and password that are recognized on the server and have Remote Access enabled.** When Remote Access gets enabled, Windows Home Server requires that your password must be at least seven characters long, and contain characters that meet at least three of the four "complexity" criteria: uppercase letters, lowercase letters, numbers, or symbols.

If everything looks hunky-dory, here's how to get into your system from Timbuktu (or Philadelphia):

1. **Start Internet Explorer.**

    If you can, use Internet Explorer 7.

2. **Type your Windows Home Server's site address.**

   In Figure 11-1, I type `https://slapmesillywilly.homeserver.com` and *mirable dictu*, my Home Server site appears.

Windows Home Server has had an on-again-off-again spitting relationship with Web-security certificates. Microsoft insists that it has solved all the problems. I remain skeptical. If you receive a warning stating that `the security certificate presented by this website was not issued by a trusted certificate authority` while trying initially to get into your home server, you don't have much choice but to click Continue to this Website (Not Recommended) — and ignore the warning.

3. **When you see the Windows Home Server Home Page (shown in Figure 11-1), click Log On.**

   That takes you to the Remote Access logon screen, shown in Figure 11-2. Depending on which option was chosen in the Windows Home Server Console many moons ago, it's possible that you will bypass the happy page shown in Figure 11-1 and go directly to Figure 11-2.

Figure 11-1: Seeing the Windows Home Server Home Page indicates that you've made it into your home network.

4. **Type a username and password that are known on the server. The username must be for a designated Remote Access user. Click Log On.**

For a discussion of Remote Access users, see Chapter 4.

Note that the server's Administrator account *won't work here*. Even if you know the server's password, there's no way to log on remotely unless you have a designated Remote Access username and password.

You see the Remote Access home page, shown in Figure 11-3.

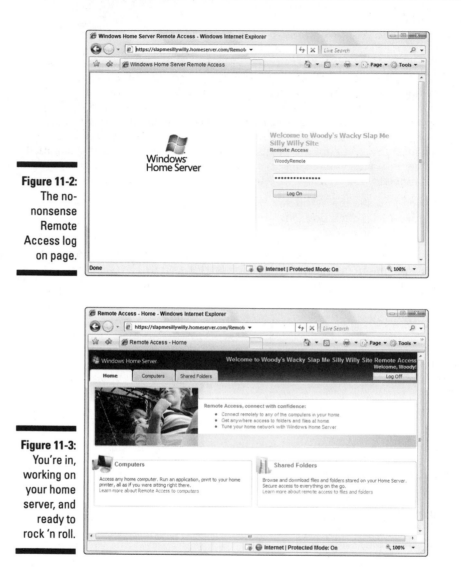

Figure 11-2:
The no-
nonsense
Remote
Access log
on page.

Figure 11-3:
You're in,
working on
your home
server, and
ready to
rock 'n roll.

Congratulations! You're ready to work with your server from far afield.

Accessing Shared Folders

After you've logged on to the Windows Home Server remote access page, you can get into the shared folders on your server.

Maybe.

Just as there are access restrictions for shared folders when you get into the shared folders "normally" (a computer geek would say "locally") — which is to say, while working on your network at home — those same access restrictions apply when you log on to the server from the local Starbucks, your Great Aunt Mabel's house, or Toad Suck, Arkansas.

The server protects access to the shared folders based on permissions granted to the username you used to log on to Remote Access. So if you usually work with the ID Woody, but you connect remotely using the username WoodyRemote, you will only be able to get into folders that have permission granted to WoodyRemote.

Here's how to get around all the shared folders on the server — at least, the folders that you have permission to see:

1. **From the Remote Access home page (Figure 11-3), click the Shared Folders tab.**

   Windows Home Server shows you a list of all the shared folders that you're allowed to get into.

2. **Click one of the folders.**

   In Figure 11-4, I click the Invoices folder, and WHS shows me a list of the files sitting in the Invoices folder.

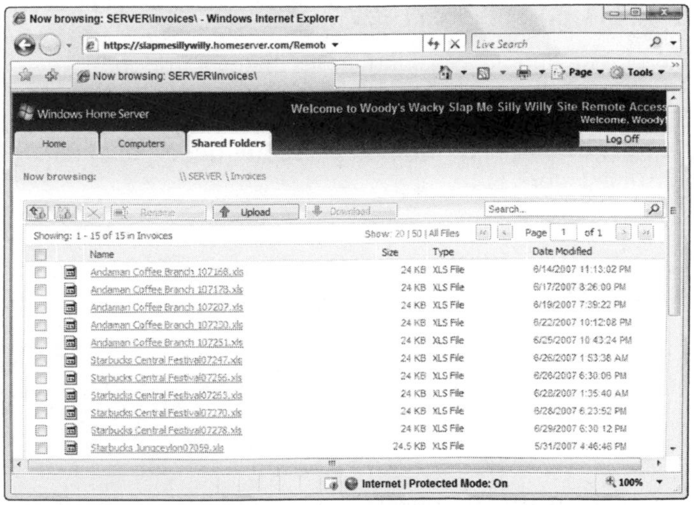

Figure 11-4: Navigate through the folders as you would expect, by double-clicking.

3. **Windows Home Server Remote Access has a "cookie-crumb" navigation system at the top, to the right of the Now Browsing text (in Figure 11-4 it shows \\SERVER\Invoices). Click any folder in the cookie-crumb hierarchy to jump to that folder.**

Hard to believe, but true: Unlike Windows Vista — which (infuriatingly) has no "up one level" navigation button — Windows Home Server *does* have an "up one level" arrow. It's the leftmost icon on the Shared Folders icon bar. Click the icon and you move up one folder level.

Vista's designers could take a hint from Windows Home Server's, eh?

4. **Take a few minutes to work the navigation buttons. Note how you can click on the "star" folder — the second icon on the icon bar — and add a new folder. You can also click a file or folder once, and then click the Rename icon to rename the file or folder.**

It all works pretty much as you would expect.

Uploading files

Transferring data from your remote computer to the Windows Home Server's shared folders works very easily. You can't just drag and drop a file from your Windows desktop into the shared folder (which you can do if you're working at home), but the Remote Access substitute works almost as easily.

Here's how to upload data from your computer in Looneyville, Texas, to your home server:

1. **From the Remote Access home page, click the Shared Folders tab. Then click the folder that you want to upload data into.**

Your screen should look more-or-less like Figure 11-4.

2. **Click the Upload button.**

Windows Home Server brings up a rather odd Upload dialog box that looks like Figure 11-5.

Figure 11-5:
Upload files from your local computer to the WHS server.

The WHS Upload dialog box is a bit odd because it doesn't work like a normal upload dialog box (or at least it doesn't work like *other* upload dialog boxes that I've seen). There's a reason why: Windows Home Server automatically zips any files that you select, transmits them, and then automatically unzips them when they arrive at your home or office network's server. That's a cool capability, very efficient, but it adds to the complexity here just a little bit.

Keep in mind that WHS wants you to select all the files you're going to upload *as a group*. Then, when you're done selecting, WHS uploads them *en masse*. That should help you understand what the upload dialog box is trying to do.

3. **Don't bother trying to type a file name in the Add a File box. WHS won't let you. Instead, click the Browse button.**

   WHS opens a dialog box marked Choose File (see Figure 11-6).

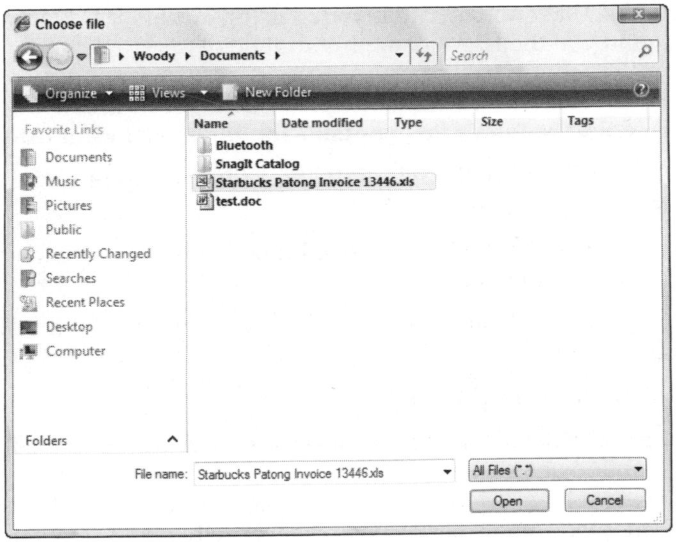

Figure 11-6: Pick the files you want to upload.

4. **Choose the file(s) you want to upload, and click the Open button.**

   Windows Home Server adds the selected file(s) to the Upload list in the bottom box in Figure 11-5.

5. **To add more files to the Upload list, repeat Steps 3 and 4.**

6. **If you want to remove any files from the Upload list, select the file and then click the Remove button.**

7. **When you've selected all the files you want to upload, check the indicated box if you want the server to overwrite any files with the same name, and then click the Upload button at the bottom of the Upload dialog box (Figure 11-5).**

   Windows Home Server notifies you that it's uploading the files, zips the files, sends them back to your home server, unzips them, and sticks them in the current `Shared` folder.

Downloading files

The process for downloading data — which is to say, transferring files from one of Windows Home Server's shared folders to the computer you're using — acts a bit like uploading, but there are a few significant differences.

Here's how to peel a file out of your home or office network's `Shared` folder and stick it on that computer that you're using in, oh, Lizard Lick, North Carolina (and you thought I made this stuff up):

1. **From the Remote Access home page, click the Shared Folders tab. Then click the folder that contains the file(s) you want to snag.**

2. **Check the boxes to the left of the files that you want to download (refer to Figure 11-4).**

   You can click the top box, the one to the left of the word `Name`, to select all the files in the folder.

   Don't click the file name itself, unless you want to open the file on the local computer.

3. **Click the Download button.**

   Windows Home Server puts a message on the screen that asks you to wait while "we prepare your files for download." While you're pondering precisely whom "we" refers to, WHS gathers the selected files from the shared folder on the server, zips them together, and sends them to you via Internet Explorer. Internet Explorer asks whether you want to save the zipped file.

4. **Click Save.**

   IE has you specify a location for the zipped file.

5. **Choose a place to put the single, zipped file and then click Save.**

   Internet Explorer downloads the file and notifies you when the download is complete.

6. **In the Download Complete dialog box, click Close.**

The downloaded zipped file, which contains all the files you requested, can be treated like any other zipped file: You can double-click it to open it and see all the files it contains and select the Extract option to unzip them so you can work with the actual files.

Getting into the Windows Home Server Console

Say you're logged on to your home server via Remote Access, and you suddenly discover that you need to change access permissions for a folder or you want to create a new remote access-enabled user account.

What do you do? Why, bring up the Windows Home Server Console, of course. Surprisingly, it's easy to get into the Windows Home Server Console, as long as you know the server's password.

Here's how to bring up the Windows Home Server Console while you're sitting in an Internet café in, oh, Yeehaw Junction, Florida:

1. **Log on to your Windows Home Server back at home.**

   See the first section in this chapter for details.

2. **Click the Computers tab.**

   You see the Windows Home Server Remote Access computers list, as in Figure 11-7.

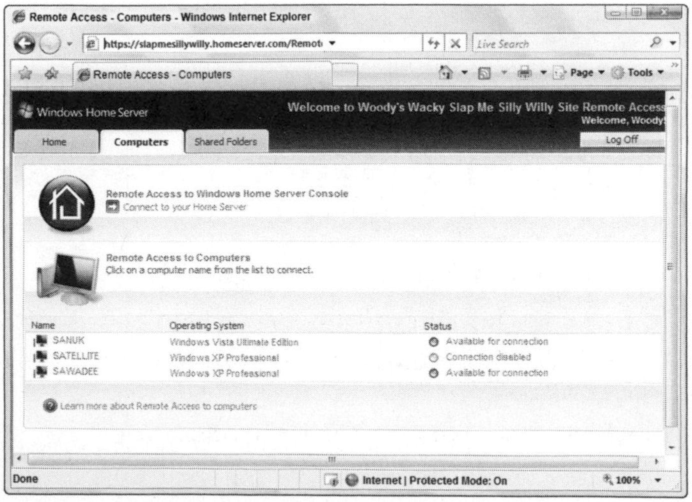

Figure 11-7: To bring up the Windows Home Server Console, start on the Computers tab.

3. At the top, click the link to Connect to Your Home Server.

Windows Home Server asks you to type in your password.

4. Type the server's password and click OK.

Note that you want the Windows Home Server password. That's the password you originally established when you set up the server. It's the password you type whenever you want to get into Windows Home Server Console. It's *not* your user-account password.

Internet Explorer may pop up a box saying you have to add the WHS server's address to your Trusted Sites Zone.

5. If you are required to add your home site address to the IE Trusted Sites zone, inside Internet Explorer:

a. Choose Tools⇨Internet Options and select the Security tab.

b. Click the green check mark that says Trusted Sites and click the Sites button.

c. Make sure your home server site is listed in the top box (it's okay if you have the `https:` version of the site address), and then click Add to add the address to the Trusted Sites zone, as in Figure 11-8.

d. Click Close, click OK, and then go back to Step 4 and start all over again.

Windows Remote Desktop Connection slaps a warning on your screen asking if you trust the computer you are connecting to, and whether you want to allow access to the clipboard on the computer you're using.

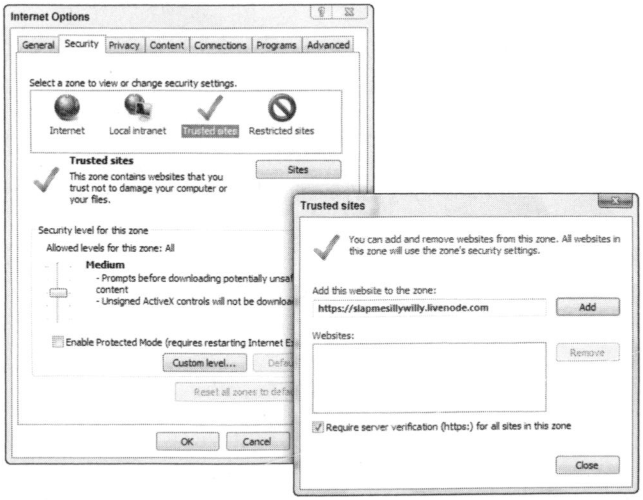

Figure 11-8:
Add your home site to the Trusted Sites zone.

6. **Click Yes.**

   You get a weird floating notice to press the spacebar or Enter to activate and use this control.

7. **Press the spacebar or Enter.**

   The Windows Home Server Console appears (as in Figure 11-9). You can use it any way you would use the Windows Home Server Console while sitting at a home computer.

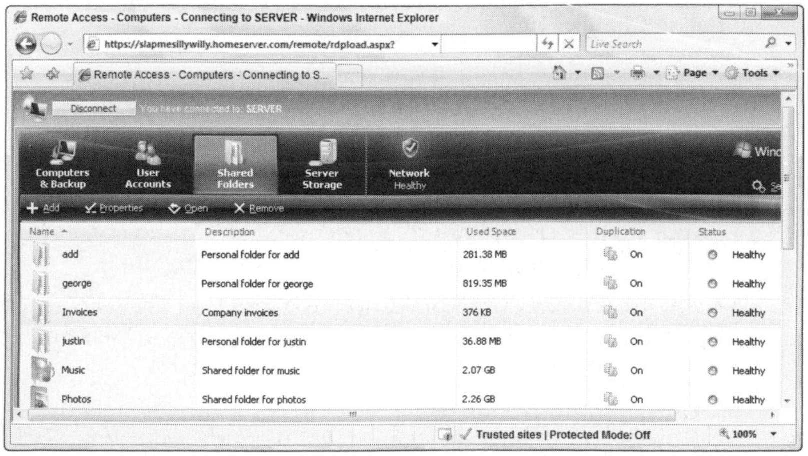

Figure 11-9:
The Console appears, ready to do your bidding from afar.

Pulling Puppet Strings on Your Home Network's Computers

If you've ever used Windows Remote Desktop Protocol, or Remote Assistance — or a third-party program like LogMeIn (basic edition is free, from LogMeIn.com) — you know what it's like to log in to your home computer from a zillion miles away.

Cool. Very cool.

Speeds vary. Screen resolutions vary. Sometimes the connections go bump for no discernible reason. But by and large, remote-control programs — the ones that let you do everything remotely that you can do while sitting at your computer — rate as a lifesaver.

Windows Home Server has a remote-control capability that works respectably well. There are plenty of if's, ands and buts — unlike LogMeIn, which seems to work all the time, no matter what — but if you meet the requirements and you can get into your server via Remote Access, logging on to certain computers on your home network only takes a few clicks.

Reviewing the ground rules

I talk about the limitations of Remote Assistance's puppet-string-pulling capabilities in Chapter 10.

Here's a quick synopsis of all the requirements.

In order to log on to a computer on your home or office network:

✔ Windows Home Server Remote Access must be up and running, and your home network has to be accessible from the computer you're using. (For many people, that's the key missing link.)

✔ You must have a username and password that are recognized by the Windows Home Server server as being Remote Access-enabled. (I talk about Remote Access authorization in Chapter 4.)

✔ The computer you're using to get into your home network — the prospective puppet master — must be running Internet Explorer. I strongly recommend Internet Explorer version 7 (or later) to minimize your chances of hitting unexpected problems. (That's a polite way of saying IE 6 is so buggy and full of security holes that you should drop it like a hot potato . . . but I digress.)

✔ The computer you want to log on to — the prospective puppet — must be connected to your Windows Home Server, and the connection to the server has to be working. If you can get into the server's Shared folders from the computer, you're in good shape.

✔ In general, the computer you want to log on to must be "awake." If it's slipped into Sleep mode, WHS doesn't have any built-in way to wake it up. (See Chapter 21 for a possible solution to this problem, via "Wake on LAN for Home Server.")

✔ The computer you want to log on to must be running Windows XP Professional, XP Media Center Edition, XP Tablet, or Windows Vista Business, Enterprise or Ultimate. In particular, Windows XP Home and Windows Vista Home Basic and Home Premium won't work. They don't have the plumbing.

✔ The computer you want to log on to must have remote access enabled. I explain how to do that in Chapter 10.

Getting logged on

If you're sitting in Knockemstiff, Ohio, and you want to take control of one of your home PCs far away, and you meet all of the (voluminous!) requirements earlier in this section, here's how to get in and start pulling the puppet strings:

1. **Fire up Internet Explorer, type in your home server's address. Log on using a username that's been set up on the server for remote access. Then click the Computers tab.**

   You see a list of all the computers currently active on your home network (refer to Figure 11-7). On the right, under Status, the Available for Connection status indicates the computer is capable of having its strings pulled.

   If a computer is listed as having Connection Disabled, chances are good it isn't running a version of Windows that can accept a connection, or you forgot to turn on remote access on that computer. See earlier in this section for details.

2. **Click the link for the computer whose strings you want to pull.**

   Windows Home Server presents you with several Connection Options, as shown in Figure 11-10.

Figure 11-10: The connection options control both security and speed-related settings.

3. **Follow the advice in Table 11-1 to choose the options that are right for you, then click OK.**

   The Remote Desktop program asks if you trust the computer you are connecting to (in much the same spirit as Figure 11-11).

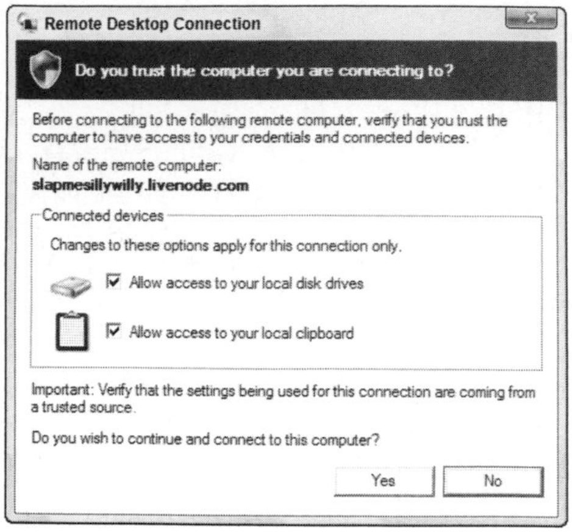

Figure 11-11:
Do you feel lucky? Well, do ya, punk?

4. **In general, you want your home computer to be able to get onto the drives there with you in Knockemstiff, Ohio, so check both boxes and click OK.**

   Wait.

5. **Move your mouse around a bit. If Internet Explorer tells you that you need to** `Click to activate and use this control` **or** `Press SPACEBAR or ENTER to activate and use this Control`, **click a blank place inside the Internet Explorer window, or press the spacebar or Enter.**

   And wait. And wait. Even if you have fast connections at your home or office *and* in Knockemstiff, WHS still takes an age or two to establish the connection.

   Sooner or later you see a Windows logon screen like the one in Figure 11-12.

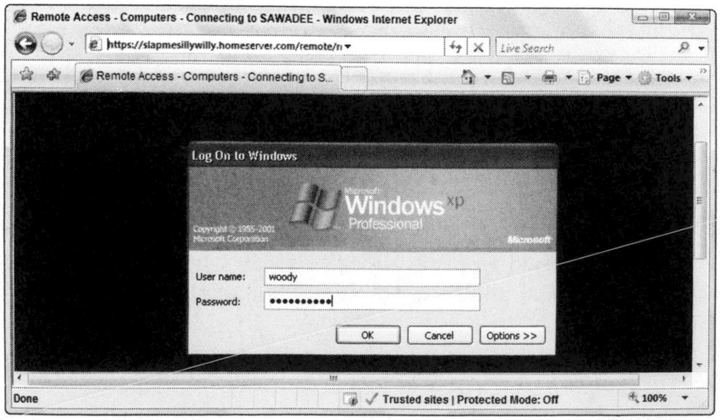

Figure 11-12:
Log on to your home or office computer.

6. **Type a username and password that are valid on the home or office computer that you're trying to get into and click OK.**

You're logging on to the home computer, so you have to provide a user-name and password that will get you in to *that* particular computer. A logon ID for the server doesn't work. The password for the server doesn't work.

At that point, Windows comes up and you can see your desktop, just the way you left it — Windows update notifications and all. If you chose Full Screen in Figure 11-10, a small band appears at the top allowing you to "minimize" the remote desktop or X-button out of Remote Access. If you chose anything other than Full Screen, a slice of the Remote Desktop appears inside the Internet Explorer window (as in Figure 11-13).

Figure 11-13:
In IE, a precise rendition of the screen at home.

If you work at anything less than Full Screen (see Table 11-1) — as long as you stay inside the Internet Explorer window, anyway — Windows behaves pretty much the way it normally does. You can copy files back and forth between machines by right-clicking the file (or folder), choosing Copy, moving to the desired destination, and using right-click Paste. It's a bit diffi-cult to bring up an auto-hiding Windows taskbar down at the bottom of the window, but if you persevere, you'll be able to get the taskbar to appear. It's slow and, at times, painful. But it works. Most of the time.

If you work at full screen, you can copy files from the puppet computer onto your computer in Knockemstiff quite easily: On the puppet machine, right-click the file and choose Copy; click the Minimize button on the full-screen control bar up at the top; then (back on your puppet master) navigate to the proper location, right-click, and choose Paste. Try it and you'll get the hang of it in no time.

You can get at the server's shared folders through this puppet connection: just click the puppet computer desktop's shortcut to Shared Folders on Server, and the Shared folders appear, using the access restrictions in effect for the username that you just used to log on.

Table 11-1	Remote Access Connection Options	
Option	*What It Really Means*	*Recommendation*
Connection Speed	If you have a slow connection, WHS won't try to display some of the detail.	Use the Broadband setting unless your connection is painfully slow.
Select a Screen Size	Tells WHS that it's okay to trim down pieces of the screen, to limit the amount of data that has to be transmitted. If you choose anything less than Full Screen, the remote computer's desktop appears inside an Internet Explorer window on the controlling PC.	Try working at Full Screen if your connection speed will handle it. The view's amazing.
Enable the remote computer to print to my local printer	While you're pulling the puppetstrings on your home, computer do you want to be able to print something on the printer there with you?	If you enable printing this way, Windows has to install the right drivers— a potentially time-consuming process. Only check this box if you expect to need to print hard copy.
Hear Sounds from the Remote Computer	Also requires a driver, but this involves a minimal amount of overhead.	Go ahead.
Enable files to be transferred from the remote computer to this computer	Although you can't drag and drop files between computers, if this box is checked, you can right-click and *copy*— in both directions, from puppet computer to the puppet master and vice versa.	Go ahead and check the box. You never know when you might need a file.

Part V
Backing Up

The 5th Wave — By Rich Tennant

"So far he's called up a cobra, 2 pythons, and a bunch of skinks, but still not the file we're looking for."

In this part . . .

Like the weather, everybody talks about backup, but nobody ever does anything about it.

Until now.

Windows Home Server's greatest claim to fame doesn't lie in its fancy folder sharing, its plucked-from-afar remote-access capabilities, or even the way it takes care of all the details about disks and their care and feeding.

Nope. To me, at least, WHS deserves highest accolades because it makes backups a lead-pipe cinch. No muss, no fuss, plug it in and forget it . . . until your hard drive dies, you accidentally change a file that shouldn't have been changed, or your kids install that wonderful new Breezy the Clown game with its ill-mannered cousin, Rootus Kitus of Troy.

Chapter 12

Running Backups

In This Chapter

▶ Understanding backup basics

▶ Getting the drop on backups

▶ Customizing backups

▶ Turning off all your unnecessary backup programs

▶ Dealing with backup oddities

*N*o doubt you already know that Windows Home Server automatically backs up every computer on your network, every night. That's part of the setup routine — as soon as you run the Connector CD on a home or office computer, the computer gets set up for automatic backups every night. There's no setup wizard. No weird jargon. At the risk of parroting a cliché, it just works.

You may know that WHS uses a clever method for minimizing the size of the backups, that WHS avoids making duplicate copies of pieces of files (even if the same file exists on multiple home or office computers), and that WHS only backs up changes in files. The first time you back up a computer, it can take forever. Afterwards, only the *changes* have to be sent to the server. It's really very smart.

As with anything useful, though, backups come with a few gotchas. This chapter catapults you through the downs and ups of backups. With a little up-front knowledge of the processes and programs working inside the case, your backups — and more importantly, any file restoration you need to do — won't keep you up at night. (At least not too late.) And your hard drives won't become bloated with too many backups that you just don't need, either.

With this knowledge under your belt, you find steps for all the backup tasks you'll likely want to do: keeping Vista and XP backup utilities out of the way, setting the schedule and time, and checking to make sure the backup is working.

If you looking for help with a backup error message, flip to Chapter 16 or Chapter 20.

Mired in Myriad Backups

Windows Home Server introduces three new backup routines to your network: A backup of all the computers, folder duplication (if it's turned on), and previous versions (also known as "shadow copies"). Those three backups operate completely independently of each other; each has its own rules; and you must use different methods to restore each kind of backed-up file.

Adding to the complexity of the matter: Windows Vista has two different backup programs that run automatically, too, and they both operate completely independently of Windows Home Server's *three* different backup programs. On many Vista computers, therefore, you have four or five independent backup programs running — and it can be intimidating figuring out which one to use.

So, to start you off, this section helps you take stock of what backup programs are running on your system, understand the quirks of each program, and (in some cases) decide whether you need the program at all now that Windows Home Server is in place. When you're done with this section, be sure to check out "Unraveling the Mess" later in this chapter as well, for further advice and steps for straightening out the backup mess *before* it gets going.

Backing up files on network computers

Incremental backup. Differential backup. Image backup. Mirror backup. Stack backup. Full backup. Partial backup. RAID type 1, 2, 3, 4, and 5. There must be a dozen different kinds of backup, each with its own subtleties and gotchas.

With Windows Home Server, you don't have to worry about any of that stuff. A straightforward backup — where, to a first approximation, files on your home or office computers get backed up to the server — runs (see Figure 12-1) automatically, every night, and you don't need to lift a finger.

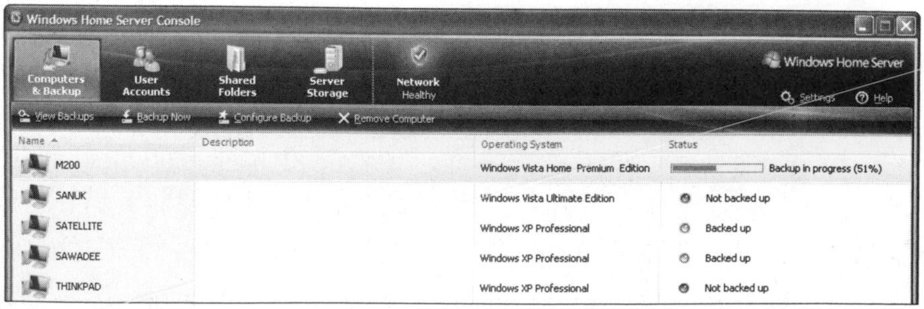

Figure 12-1: Automatic backups are just beginning for a new WHS network.

While Windows Home Server introduces three new backup schemes to your network, it also has several restrictions and a whole lotta nitty-gritty details that you may find most annoying. It would behoove you to be well aware of the problems *before* something goes bump in the night.

Knowing what's backed up

In nittier and grittier detail, here's what really is and isn't backed up:

- **As long as WHS works right and your network holds together, then (with very few exceptions)** *everything* **on** *every* **computer gets backed up** *every* **night.** System files. Programs. Settings. Registry. Data. Aunt Agnes's cute 5GB PowerPoint show of her prize Alapaha Blue Blood Bulldog biting Uncle Billy's butt. It's all there. And you don't need to lift a finger.

- **Some obvious things don't make the cut.** Those would be the Recycle Bin, temporary files, the hibernation file, and "offline" files (see support. microsoft.com/kb/307853).

- **WHS won't back up recorded TV for love nor money.** See Chapter 7.

- **Files you're currently working on are** *not* **backed up as you go.** Say you're working on a spreadsheet that's stored on the server. You get up, take a break, and when you come back, you keep pounding away. A couple of hours or so later, you suddenly realize that what you're doing is all wrong — you zigged with a column when you should've zagged with a row a couple of hours ago. So you madly click the Undo icon, only to discover that Excel (bless its pointed little head) doesn't keep a whole lot of "undo" information. You can't go back to where you were a couple of hours ago.

  Guess what? Unless you're really lucky, Windows Home Server can't help you. While you can probably retrieve a previous version of the spreadsheet as it existed when you first started working on it that morning, and possibly a copy of the way the file looked at noon, there aren't any other intermediate copies to fall back on. You're up the ol' creek without a paddle.

- **If you enable Folder Duplication for a specific shared folder on the server, there are backup copies of files in that folder made all the time, but the copies are only accessible if the server's hard drive dies.** Folder duplication and "previous version" shadow copies are two entirely separate backup techniques, with two entirely different goals.

- **The server is smart enough to back up data that's on several computers only once, reducing overhead.** With the technical magic of Single Instance Storage and an ability to recognize repeated clusters, Windows Home Server knows when you have copies of a file, such as a program, on several computers on the network. For details, see this handy sidebar elsewhere in this chapter: "SIS, clusters, and one finely tuned backup system."

Backing up the server itself is another kettle of fish entirely. If you want to keep a copy of server data so it's stored someplace other than your home or office, you have some work to do. See Chapter 15 for details.

SIS, clusters, and one finely tuned backup system

Windows Home Server uses a technology called Single Instance Storage to efficiently keep all the backups organized. (SIS has been around for quite a while, in various guises; see `en.wikipedia.org/wiki/Single_Instance_Store` for details.) Instead of scanning all the files on all of your computers every night to see what's been changed — the approach most backup programs follow — SIS focuses on what's stored on your hard drives. Physically. And therein lies a white-lab-coat sort of story.

Most NTFS drives store files in 4,096-character bunches called *clusters*. A file consists of one or more clusters. The file system built into your home or office computer keeps track of which clusters belong with what file. The clusters can be scattered willy-nilly all over a hard drive, but Windows XP or Vista knows which clusters go with what file, in what order, and which clusters aren't being used.

Take that concept, move it onto the server, and add an interesting wrinkle or three, and you have Single Instance Storage.

At its heart, Windows Home Server doesn't back up files; it backs up clusters. And it goes to great lengths to ensure that it doesn't store the same cluster twice. So if you have, oh, Halo 3 installed on four of your home computers, Windows Home Server only stores the duplicated clusters once. It keeps track of which clusters go on what computer, and in which file. But the clusters themselves only get stored once. If you install Halo 3 on another computer, when WHS gets around to backing it up, the existing clusters never move onto the server. Instead, WHS updates its list of files and locations, and moves on to the next cluster.

When you change a file — say, you save a new winning score in Halo 3 — the WHS backup program only stores the changed clusters.

It's fast, efficient, and very effective. The only downside? The original backup — the very first one — can take a looooooooooong time. On a big hard drive, it isn't unusual for the initial backup to take 12 hours or more.

Single Instance Storage uses another clever trick to minimize system overhead. Instead of storing clusters as individual units on the server's drives, WHS takes command of the drives — swallows them whole — and manages groups of clusters in 4GB groups. There's no fragmentation on Windows Home Server drives. ("All your drives belong to us.")

A WHS backup session goes like this:

1. The server chooses which PC should go first.

2. The server starts the backup program on your home or office computer.

3. The backup program running on your home or office computer scans your files and decides which, if any, have changed in the past 24 hours. If it finds a changed cluster, it notifies the server, sending the server a "hash" that uniquely identifies the cluster.

4. The backup program running on the server scans all the backed-up clusters to see if that particular cluster is already sitting on the server.

5. If it's a completely new cluster, the program on the home or office computer sends it over to the server (see the following figure); if the cluster's already on the server, no data gets shoved through the network.

(continued)

(continued)

6. The server updates its list of file contents to include the new cluster — and the home or office computer continues on its merry way.

The two programs run asynchronously, so the home or office computer doesn't have to wait for the server, and the server doesn't have to wait for the home computer. You can break the connection at any time a file's being backed up — in fact, either computer can *break down* at any time — and the server can figure out how to put the file-in-process back together.

Setting the stage for smooth backups

The more skeptical among you may have noticed that I said in the preceding list, "As long as WHS works right." And Windows Home Server server does have a few stipulations, above and beyond the setup routine you find in Chapter 3. Follow these tips to make sure backups run smoothly:

✔ You *can* back up a computer over a wireless connection. But if you want to restore a drive on that same computer, you have to connect a wire. That's covered in Chapters 13 and 14, which focus on restoring drives and files.

✔ You can't back up a computer that's turned off. If you want to back up a computer, you have to leave it running normally, or in Sleep or Hibernate mode.

✔ Laptops can be backed up, but Windows Home Server won't start a backup on a laptop unless the power cord is plugged in.

✔ Windows Home Server only backs up disks that are formatted with NTFS. If you have an older computer with FAT32 disks, or a USB thumb drive that's FAT32, those disks aren't even eligible for backup. For an analysis of FAT32 versus NTFS, take a look at www.ntfs.com/ntfs_vs_fat.htm. For instructions on converting FAT32 disks (actually, partitions) to NTFS, see support.microsoft.com/kb/307881.

If you're uneasy knowing that your backups might miss a beat, know that you can review their status by following steps in "Checking That Backups Run Smoothly" at the end of this chapter. Also, Chapter 16 explains how the system-health monitor lets you know when there's trouble with a backup.

Understanding the timing

Backups happen sequentially, in the middle of the night. Windows Home Server normally starts at midnight, backing up each computer, one at a time, until 6:00 a.m. The backup gets stored on the server.

On Sundays, Windows Home Server also runs its cleanup routines, which I discuss in the section "Keeping backups" later in this chapter.

Because Windows Home Sever uses Single Instance Storage and clusters to keep the backups running smoothly, the first backup pokes along like plankton crossing the Pacific. But rest assured, backups progress much faster afterwards. See the sidebar "SIS, clusters, and one finely tuned backup system" for details.

What you need to know about restore

This chapter isn't really about restoring files, but you do need to know a few things about how restoring the backup works before you get started:

- ✔ In order to restore one of the files sitting on your home or office computer, you have to know the server's password.

- ✔ If you *do* know the server's password, you can retrieve any backed-up file from any backup run on any computer — and put a copy of the old file on any other computer. In that sense, retrieving an old version of a backed-up file isn't so much a "restore" as much as it's a simple "copy" operation.

- ✔ Windows Home Server doesn't have a Recycle Bin. If you delete a file on the server and you want to get it back, you have to use Windows XP, or Vista Business, Enterprise or Ultimate. You can't get a deleted file back by using Vista Home Basic or Premium. You can't restore an earlier version of the server file with Vista Home Basic or Premium, either.

    Okay, I lied. Actually, there's a tricky way to restore files in a duplicated folder using Vista Home Basic or Premium. (I explain Folder Duplication in the next section.) The caveat is that you have to establish a Remote Desktop Protocol connection with the server — which ain't just a-whistlin' Dixie. See Chapter 17 for details.

- ✔ You can restore an entire clobbered drive by following the nostrums in Chapter 13. You can restore the files one-by-one using the techniques in Chapter 14.

Backing up shared folders with Folder Duplication

Folder Duplication is Windows Home Server's method for backing up shared files on the server — which is to say, backing up files in shared folders. That's your music, your photos, and whatever else you've put in those folders. Folder Duplication is completely different from, and operates independently of, the method for backing up files on home or office computers, explained in the preceding section.

To set Folder Duplication in motion, you have to turn it on. If you have Folder Duplication turned on, Windows Home Server automatically maintains two copies of every file in the duplicated folder. The duplication isn't instantaneous, but Microsoft promises that it takes at most three minutes to duplicate any file after it's been closed.

Unfortunately, you can't use the duplication feature for those "aw shucks" moments that happen when you want to bring back an old version of a file that you still have open. The duplicated file sits tucked away deep inside the server, and only becomes accessible if you restore an entire drive.

If you turn on Folder Duplication, and your server has more than one hard drive, WHS ensures that the originals and duplicates reside on different drives. If one of the drives dies, you can restore every file in a duplicated folder (plus or minus three minutes) by following along in Chapter 18. But you can't use folder duplication to restore an individual file.

Because the method for backing up shared files on the server works independently of "regular" computer backup, you may find that WHS will store three separate copies of files that you manually copy to the server. (See the sidebar, "Folder Duplication eats disk space" for details.)

Folder Duplication eats disk space

You might think that Microsoft would use the same technology both for its network-wide backups and for shared folder duplication. It doesn't.

If you tell Windows Home Server to duplicate a shared folder, it stores a second copy of every file in the folder; if your server has two or more drives, WHS stores the second copy on a different drive from the original. That way, if one of the drives fails, there's a second copy of the data sitting safely on a different drive.

Although they address similar problems, Folder Duplication and backup work entirely separately, in entirely different ways: Folder Duplication doesn't work at the cluster level, for example — it copies entire files. In addition, backup only occurs once a day, whereas duplication happens almost instantaneously.

Those differences can have a big effect on the amount of disk space required. Say you have 200 GB of photos on a home computer. You connect the computer to your Windows Home Server server, and let backup run overnight. The next morning, you have 200 GB of pictures on the home computer, and 200 GB (less any duplicated clusters) on the server. Now say you move the pictures over to the shared `Photos` folder on the server. The `Photos` folder has duplication turned on. If there's enough hard-drive space available, Windows Home Server creates two copies of each picture in the process of moving the files — one each on two different drives. WHS isn't smart enough to realize that it already has a backup copy of the pictures; Folder Duplication doesn't even consult the backup list of clusters. The net result: You have *three* copies of all your photos on the server.

The solution? See the "Keeping backups" section, later in this chapter — and manually delete the backup copy.

Shadow copies in Windows Home Server

Twice a day — around noon and again around midnight — Windows Home Server makes a backup of everything in all the server's shared folders. (Actually, it makes a copy of every file that's changed since the last run.) You can get at these previous versions, these so-called *shadow copies* if you're running Windows XP or Vista Business, Enterprise, or Ultimate.

Shadow copies are designed to help you bring back old versions of a file that you've munged, but the feature isn't very useful for restoring more than a handful of files. If your hard drive dies, it'll take both your original file and all its shadow copies.

In order to restore a file in a shared folder on the server — the file's shadow copy — you must have available a user name and password that have read permission for the shared folder (see Chapter 5). That's expected. The unexpected part: You must get into the server's Shared folder from a computer that's running Windows XP (any flavor), Media Center Edition, Tablet PC, or Windows Vista Business, Enterprise, or Ultimate. In other words, *you can't restore a file in a duplicated folder on the server by using a computer that's running Vista Home Basic or Premium.* (Bet they didn't teach you that in Home Server school, eh?)

Okay, I lied again. Just a little bit. If you find yourself sitting at a Vista Home Basic or Premium computer, and you absolutely have to restore a previous version of a file in a duplicated folder on the server, use the approach described in Chapter 17 to break into the server and restore the file. It's more than a little scary, but if you're careful, you can do it without any ill effect.

Independently of Windows Home Server, Vista Business, Enterprise, and Ultimate also make shadow copies of files on the home or office computer. See the next section for details about what backup routines are running on Vista.

Understanding what Vista is backing up

In addition to all the backups whirring away on Windows Home Server, Windows Vista has a few backup tricks of its own that run automatically:

- ✔ Vista's **Automatic File Backup,** makes copies of a particular user's data files. If you use any version of Vista other than Home Basic, the first time you start the File and Folder Backup Wizard, Vista automatically sets up nightly backups. Each time the backup runs, only changed files for one specific user get backed up. Each changed file — the whole file — gets placed in a zipped folder where you can get at it directly. You typically store backups on a separate hard drive, or shoot them out to another computer on your network. If you have Vista Home Basic, the first time you run the wizard, Vista runs a backup, but then you have to manually run the wizard again to get another backup. Home Basic doesn't automatically start nightly backups.

Computers running Vista probably have Automatic File Backup running nightly. (Windows Vista Home Basic users have to bend over backwards to get Automatic File Backup running nightly.) In "Unravelling the Mess" (later in this chapter), I show Vista users how to give Automatic File Backup the heave-ho.

✔ Vista's **Previous Versions** (also known as **Shadow Copies**) work in conjunction with the daily System Restore Point runs. These are like the shadow copies that Windows Home Server creates, but they're stored on the Vista computer, not on the server. Vista's shadow copies are generated automatically, once a day, usually just after midnight — but only in Vista Business, Enterprise, and Ultimate versions. You can't get at the previous versions directly — they're stored in a compressed format, smashed in with the nightly Restore Points. Unless you've changed something, the previous versions of a file are stored on the same drive as the file itself, so if the drive goes twisting off into the sunset, you lose both your original file *and* its shadow copy.

Vista also has the ability to create a full backup of a hard drive, called a CompletePC Backup, but that's pretty much obsolete considering Windows Home Server's ability to restore an entire hard drive (see Chapter 13).

I go through the details about Vista backups in both *Windows Vista All-In-One Desk Reference For Dummies* and *Windows Vista Timesaving Techniques For Dummies*.

Checking Windows XP for backup routines

Windows XP also has backup capabilities, to a greater or lesser degree depending on which version of Windows XP you use. Sometimes they work. Sometimes they don't. Seriously.

While most Vista computers have backups running automatically every night, computers running Windows XP may or may not have the old NTBackup program going nightly. (Windows XP Home users have to jump through some extraordinary hoops to get NTBackup working.) In the next section, "Unraveling the Mess," I show you how Windows XP users can turn off NTBackup.

And I hit the high and low points about Windows XP backups in *Windows XP All-In-One Desk Reference For Dummies, Windows XP Timesaving Techniques For Dummies,* and *Windows XP Hacks and Mods For Dummies*, all from Wiley.

Unraveling the Mess

As I explain in the preceding section, at least seven completely different backup programs in WHS, Vista, and XP may be spinning the heads on your hard drives silly, all through the night. After spending a lot of time diving through the various backup programs, I have a few recommendations:

- ✔ **You should have at least one Windows XP or Windows Vista Ultimate, Business or Enterprise PC in your home or office network.** Otherwise, restoring files in shared folders on the server rates as a monumental pain in the posterior. Microsoft's failure to provide a way to restore shadow copies (previous versions) in Windows Vista Home Basic and Premium rates as one of the most serious oversights in Windows Home Server.

- ✔ **If you have WHS, you shouldn't spend a penny on Vista Ultimate for its shadow-copies capability.** In spite of what you may have read, Vista Ultimate's shadow copies/previous versions are only generated once a day. But Windows Home Server makes backups once a day. Ultimate's shadow copies don't work any better than Windows Home Server's standard nightly backup — except they're arguably a little easier to find — and the fact that Ultimate's shadow copies sit on the same hard drive as the original files (ooh, risky, risky) makes WHS's backup far superior.

- ✔ **If a file or an entire drive gets screwed up and you have to resort to a backup, use the server's backup.** Windows Home Server's backup beats all the alternatives, hands down, no question.

A corollary: You can safely disable any Windows Vista or XP backups that you are currently running. They don't bring anything better to the backup party.

If you have Windows Home Server running properly, there's no reason at all why your computer should take the time (and, more to the point, waste the disk space) to run NTBackup on Windows XP or Automatic File Backup in Vista. And if you're running any third-party backup programs, it's probably time to give them their pink slips, too.

To turn off automatic backups in Vista, follow these steps:

1. **Click Start.**

   The cursor appears in the Start Search box.

2. **Type** `backup` **in the Start Search box.**

   Vista shows you at least two backup programs, and possibly a whole lot more.

3. **Click the link to the Backup Status and Configuration Center.**

   You see a Backup Status and Configuration window like the one in Figure 12-2.

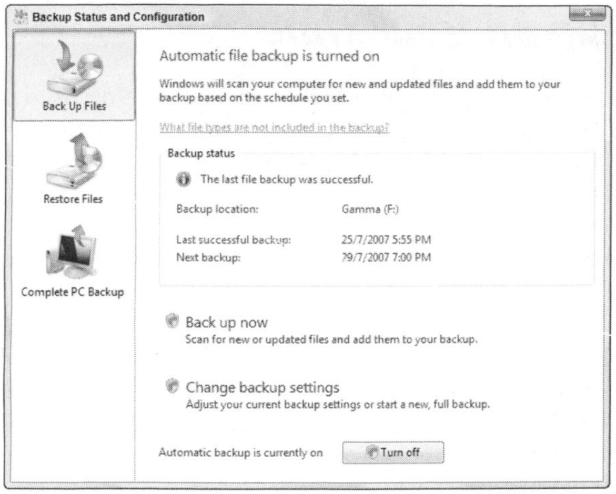

Backup Status and Configuration

Back Up Files

Automatic file backup is turned on

Windows will scan your computer for new and updated files and add them to your backup based on the schedule you set.

What file types are not included in the backup?

Restore Files

Backup status

The last file backup was successful.

Complete PC Backup

Backup location: Gamma (F:)

Figure 12-2:
If Vista is
performing
its own
backups,
turn it off.

Last successful backup: 25/7/2007 5:55 PM
Next backup: 79/7/2007 7:00 PM

Back up now
Scan for new or updated files and add them to your backup.

Change backup settings
Adjust your current backup settings or start a new, full backup.

Automatic backup is currently on   Turn off

4. **If Automatic File Backup is turned off, there's nothing to do. Go on to Step 6.**

5. **If Automatic File Backup is turned on (see Figure 12-2), click the button at the bottom marked Turn Off, then click Continue to get through the User Account Control inanity.**

6. **X-button out of the Backup and Status Configuration Center and kiss Vista's backups goodbye.**

   Automatic Vista backups will never darken your door (or clog your Vista computer's drives) again.

In Windows XP, the simplest approach to getting rid of redundant backup programs is to delete any backup tasks (whether they be NTBackup or some other backup program) from the Task Scheduler. To get into the Task Scheduler, click Start⇨All Programs⇨Accessories⇨System Tools⇨Scheduled Tasks. Look in the list for references to backups. Right-click any likely candidates and choose Delete.

Setting Up Server Backups That Serve You

Windows Home Server lets you set options for when and how it backs up the computers on your network. Not many options, but you do have them. The following sections explain how to get your Windows Home Server beating to your personal backup drummer.

Backing up on your time

Windows Home Server lets you control the window of time used to run back-ups. By default, backups start at midnight and then proceed, computer by computer, until the last computer gets backed up, or the clock hits 6:00 a.m., whichever comes first.

Here's what actually happens:

1. When the backup alarm clock rings (figuratively, of course), WHS chooses a computer randomly and starts running a backup on it.

   The sequence of computers changes from day to day: WHS spreads things around so a different computer starts each time. That helps balance the load if one or two computers see massive changes (requiring many hours of backup time).

2. When the first computer finishes, WHS starts with the next computer, and then the next, and the next.

   If all the computers get backed up before the "stop" alarm rings, WHS jumps down to Step 4.

3. If there's a backup running when the "stop" alarm rings, WHS allows the current backup to finish.

   Yes, even if it takes another 12 hours.

4. WHS downloads and installs any automatic updates for the server itself. If any of the updates require a restart, the server reboots itself.

5. If today is Sunday, WHS runs its Backup Cleanup routines (see the next section).

   And you're ready for a brand new day.

Although you don't have a lot of control over the sequence of backup events, you can control the start and stop times — set the alarm clock as it were. Here's how:

1. **Go to any computer on you network. Right-click the Windows Home Server icon in the notification area, near the clock. Choose Windows Home Server Console. Type the server's password and click the right-arrow.**

2. **In the upper-right, click the Settings icon. Then, on the left, choose Backup.**

   You see the backup settings in Figure 12-3.

3. **Roll either the Start Time or End Time clock forward or backward. When you're done, click OK.**

   The new settings take effect when the next backup starts.

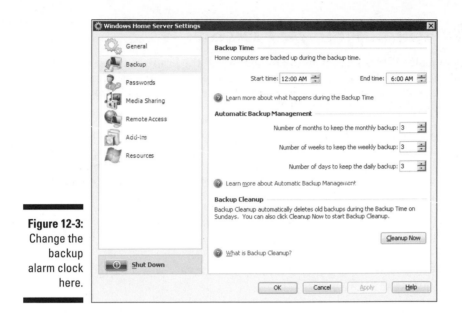

Figure 12-3:
Change the
backup
alarm clock
here.

If you have problems with Windows Home Server running backups at odd times — the drives start whirring an hour or two or five before or after the alarm clock time passes — check to make sure the server's time and time zone are set properly.

To do so, bring up the Windows Home Server Console and click the Settings icon. On the left, choose General. If the Date and Time listed don't match your watch, it's possible that Windows Home Server is synchronizing to the wrong time zone. If that could be your problem, click the Change button, then click the Time Zone tab. Get zoned in (see Figure 12-4), click OK twice, and your backups should march to a local drummer.

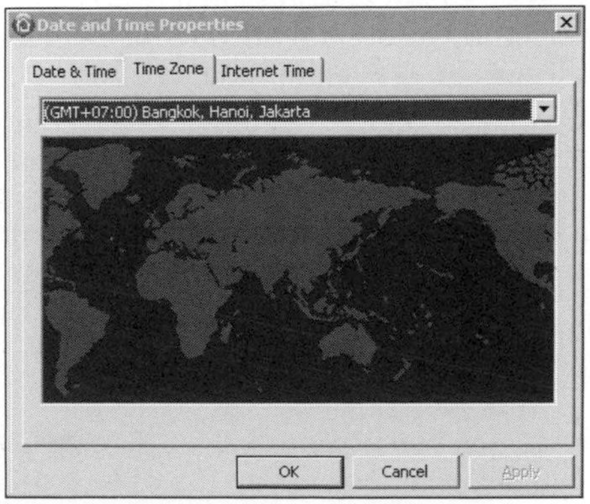

Figure 12-4:
Check your
time zone.

Choosing what gets backed up

By default, WHS backs up all the folders on all the home or office computer's hard drives (both internal and external), passing over a handful of folders that nobody except the terminally persnickety could possibly want, and intentionally ignoring recorded TV programs.

You can tell WHS to ignore specific folders, if you like — but you have absolutely no control over which file types get backed up. Many people have complained about this lack of granularity, but Microsoft's inflexibility in this case has one great benefit: By Keeping It Simple, Server, you can't accidentally exclude a file from backup that you really *should* back up.

The downside? You lose some space on the server to store backup copies of files that you'll never need or want.

The upside? When you suddenly discover that you really *did* need that file you were going to exclude, it's there.

With storage space getting cheaper all the time, and virtually no processing overhead involved in backing up unwanted files (yeah, okay, working on unwanted backups consumes my machine from 4:13 to 4:14 every morning), I have a hard time getting worked up over Microsoft's decision to limit our ability to knock files out of the backup box. I just wish they'd back up recorded TV!

If you have specific folders on a specific computer that you want to exclude from WHS's backups, you must know *the server's password* in order to change backup settings — an administrator password on your home or office machine just won't cut the mustard.

Here's how to knock a specific folder out of the backup box:

1. **Go to any computer on you network. Right-click the Windows Home Server icon in the notification area, near the clock. Choose Windows Home Server Console. Type the server's password and click the right-pointing arrow.**

   The Windows Home Server Console appears.

2. **Click the Computers & Backup icon. Then right-click the computer that contains the folder you want to block, and choose Configure Backup.**

   The WHS Backup Configuration Wizard appears.

3. **Click Next.**

   The wizlet asks which volumes you want to back up. In Figure 12-5, you can see that Windows Home Server offers you the choice of backing up hidden partitions as well as regular partitions (er, volumes).

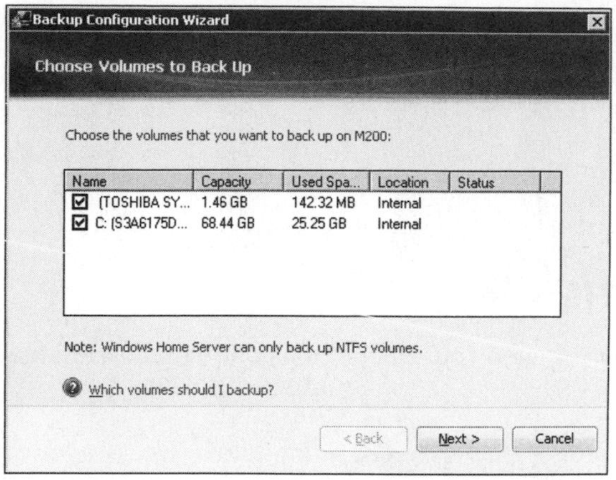

Backup Configuration Wizard

Choose Volumes to Back Up

Choose the volumes that you want to back up on M200:

Name	Capacity	Used Spa...	Location	Status
☑ [TOSHIBA SY...	1.46 GB	142.32 MB	Internal	
☑ C: (S3A6175D...	68.44 GB	25.25 GB	Internal	

Note: Windows Home Server can only back up NTFS volumes.

Which volumes should I backup?

< Back   Next >   Cancel

Figure 12-5:
All your
disks (er,
partitions)
get backed
up by
default.

4. **Choose the volumes that you would like to back up, and click Next.**

   If you don't want to back up this computer at all, uncheck all the boxes next to all the volumes in the list.

   The wizlet shows you a list of all the folders in the chosen volumes that aren't being backed up (see Figure 12-6).

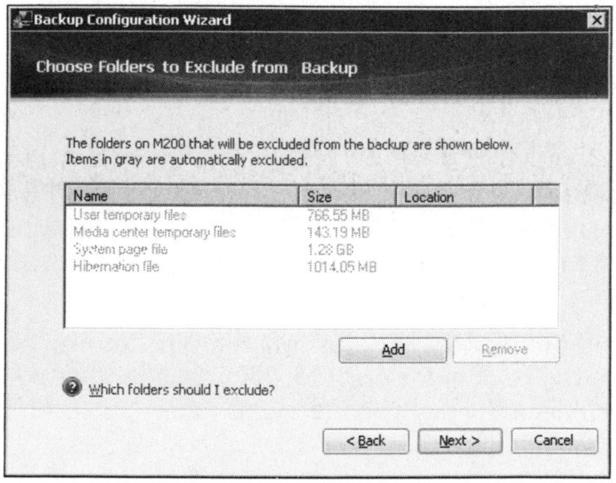

Backup Configuration Wizard

Choose Folders to Exclude from Backup

The folders on M200 that will be excluded from the backup are shown below.
Items in gray are automatically excluded.

Name	Size	Location
User temporary files	766.55 MB	
Media center temporary files	143.19 MB	
System page file	1.28 GB	
Hibernation file	1014.05 MB	

Add   Remove

Which folders should I exclude?

< Back   Next >   Cancel

Figure 12-6:
You can
exclude
additional
folders here.

5. **If you want to exclude more folders, click the Add button, navigate to the folder you want to exclude (by clicking the +/- expand/collapse boxes), highlight the appropriate folder and choose Exclude. When you're done, click OK.**

   Note that you have no control over the types of files that are backed up.

6. **Back at the Choose Folders dialog box (Figure 12-6), confirm that you've excluded all the folders you want to exclude and click Next.**

The wizlet confirms that you're done.

Those are your only options.

Keeping backups

Windows Home Server ages your backups like fine pomegranate juice (er, grenadine).

That way if you discover that a file got munged two weeks ago, you can go rummaging around in the backup from *three* weeks ago and retrieve the right version. It's a very powerful capability.

In fact, some people spend an extra hundred bucks for Windows Vista Ultimate just to get a similar feature — it's one of the few reasons why anyone in their right mind would pay extra for Ultimate. For you, being the savvy Windows Home Server user that you are, it's free.

I've found only one hurdle in dealing with aged backups — Microsoft calls it *Automatic Backup Management*. The technology works fine. The terminology stinks.

Here's what happens:

✔ **Windows Home Server makes a backup every night.**

The WHS dialog boxes, documentation, and help files might lead you to think there are many different kinds of backups — daily, weekly, monthly, during the full moon. Sorry — there aren't. All the backups are just plain-vanilla backups.

WHS could hold on to all its backups forever. Who knows? You might want to look at the backup for April 15, 2007, to see what your spreadsheets looked like on the day you filed your taxes, and then look at April 16, to see what, uh, changed.

✔ **You tell Windows Home Server to save certain backups and throw away the others, the old ones that you'll never use.** Realistically, sifting through a backup a day for the past decade or two would drive you nuts — and take up unnecessary space on your computer.

✔ **Unless you change things, Windows Home Server claims that it keeps backups for the three preceding days, for the first backup on Monday morning in each of the three preceding weeks, and the first backup in each of the preceding three months.**

Those aren't "monthly" or "weekly" backups. They're just regular back-ups that happened to take place on a Monday, or on March 1 or April 1 or May 1. Nothing magical about them.

✔ **Windows Home Server throws away old backups that it no longer needs** at the end of each Sunday's backup run — using the steps I list at the beginning of the section "Backing up on your time," earlier in this chapter. It throws away the indexes. It also throws away the clusters themselves, if they aren't being used. (See the sidebar elsewhere in this chapter if you're curious about clusters.)

Did you notice the discrepancy?

Windows Home Server says it keeps backups for the preceding three days — but it only throws away old backups once a week. So the data has to hang around for a week, whether you can see it or not. That's why I jiggle the backup settings a bit — my approach doesn't consume any more space, but it gives me a little extra cushion in case I clobber something thoroughly — and discover later on that I goofed.

Here's what I do:

1. **Go to any computer on you network. Right-click the Windows Home Server icon in the notification area, near the clock. Choose Windows Home Server Console. Type the server's password and click the right-pointing arrow.**

2. **In the upper-right corner, click the Settings icon. On the left, choose Backup.**

   You see the backup settings (refer to Figure 12-3).

3. **In the box marked Number of Months to Keep the Monthly Backup, tell WHS how many months' worth of backups it should accumulate, saving the first backup of the month.**

   There's no such thing as a "monthly backup." Personally, I keep four months around — so if this is January, I have September 1, October 1, November 1, and December 1 readily available.

4. **In the box marked Number of Weeks to Keep the Weekly Backup, tell WHS how many preceding Mondays it should keep around.**

   I like to keep a little more than one month's worth, just in case.

   There's no such thing as a "weekly backup," either.

5. **In the box marked Number of Days to Keep the Daily Backup, tell WHS how many previous days' backups should be available.**

   I keep a week's worth. Note for posterity: in Windows Home Server, every backup is a "daily backup."

6. **Click OK.**

   Your new settings take effect immediately.

As far as I can tell, there's no way to change the frequency of backup cleanups. You get them every Sunday, at the end of the backup period, whether you want 'em or not.

Checking That Backups Run Smoothly

Here's how to get Windows Home Server to back up a home or office computer:

1. **Hook up the computer to your WHS network using the Connector CD.**

   See Chapter 3 for details.

2. **Do nothing.**

   Wait overnight and — unless something weird happens — you're done.

Backing up computers with WHS is so simple, and so automatic, that you may be worried that the backups aren't running. No need to fear. If WHS ever fails to complete a backup, every computer on the network warns you. The Windows Home Server icon down in the notification area typically glows yellow, warning you about a backup error (see Figure 12-7).

Figure 12-7:
The last backup for M200 didn't complete properly.

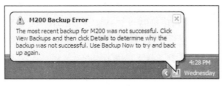

If you follow the Health Monitoring steps in Chapter 16 to start the Windows Home Server Console, you see a notification like the one in Figure 12-8.

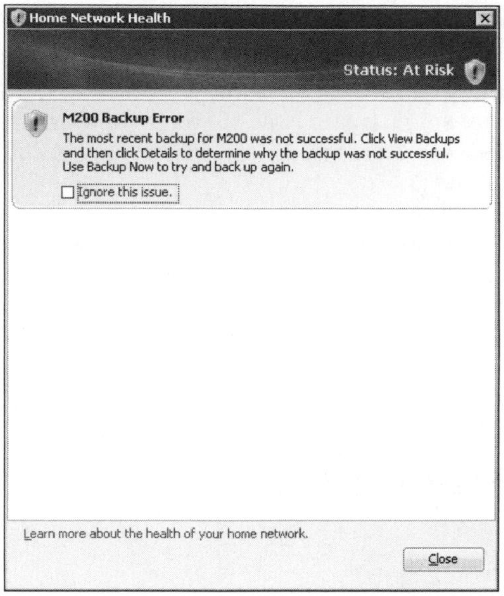

Figure 12-8:
A Windows
Home
Server
health alert
warns you
when a
backup
goes awry.

Here's how to check the current backup status of your home or office computer:

1. **Go to any computer on you network. Right-click the Windows Home Server icon in the notification area, near the clock. Choose Windows Home Server Console. Type the server's password and click the right-arrow.**

   The password was assigned when you first set up the server; see Chapter 3. If you've forgotten the password, see Chapter 19.

   The Windows Home Server Console appears.

2. **In the upper-left corner, click the Computers & Backup icon.**

   You see a list of all the computers known to the server, with their current backup status, similar to Figure 12-1 earlier in this chapter.

3. **If a computer appears as "Not Backed Up" and you wonder why, right-click that computer and choose View Backups.**

   Windows Home Server shows you a list of all the backup runs for that particular computer, as in Figure 12-9.

4. **Click to select the backup that has you concerned, and then click Details.**

   A description of the backup, and what went wrong, appears as in Figure 12-10.

5. **Click OK twice to go back to the Windows Home Server Console.**

    If you're baffled by the reason for the backup's failure, run a manual backup by right-clicking the Windows Home Server icon on the offending computer and choosing Backup Now. If you need more details about why the backup failed, see Chapters 16 and 20 for tips on understanding backup error messages.

Note that a backup will fail if the computer being backed up doesn't have enough room left on the hard drive to create a Windows restore point.

If you ever want to run a manual backup on a particular computer, right-click the Windows Home Server icon in the notification area, near the system clock, and choose Backup Now.

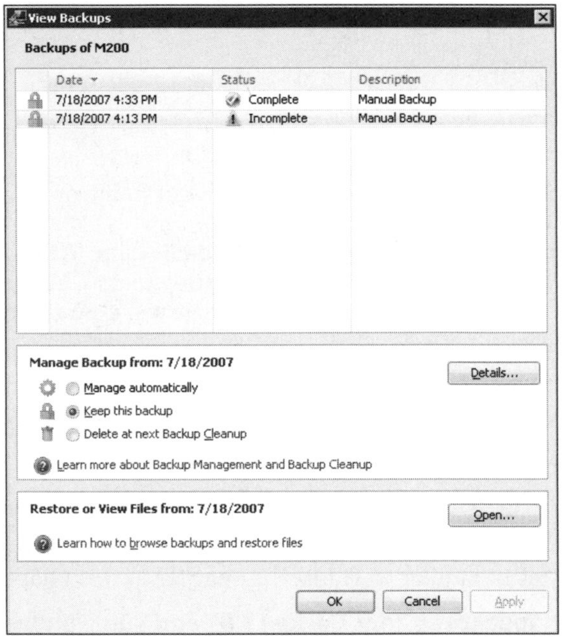

View Backups

Backups of M200

Date ▾	Status	Description
🔒 7/18/2007 4:33 PM	✅ Complete	Manual Backup
🔒 7/18/2007 4:13 PM	⚠ Incomplete	Manual Backup

Manage Backup from: 7/18/2007   [Details...]

⚙ ○ Manage automatically
🔒 ● Keep this backup
🗑 ○ Delete at next Backup Cleanup

❓ Learn more about Backup Management and Backup Cleanup

Restore or View Files from: 7/18/2007   [Open...]

❓ Learn how to browse backups and restore files

[OK] [Cancel] [Apply]

Figure 12-9:
A list of all the backups performed on the chosen computer.

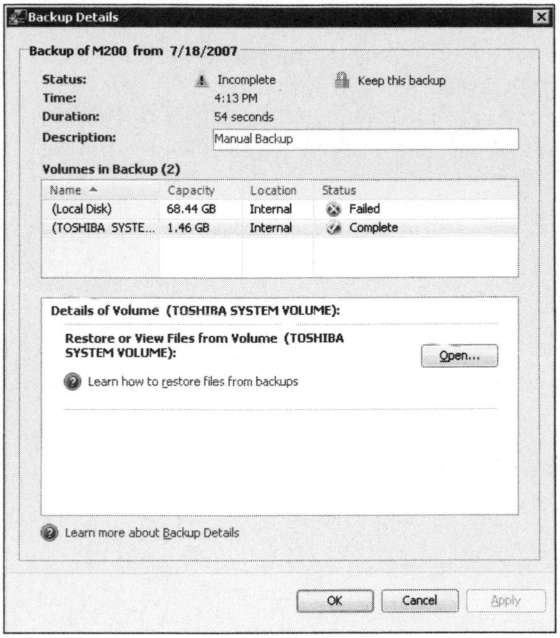

Figure 12-10:
The details about the backup failure, in this case, aren't very informative.

Chapter 13

Restoring a Dead Computer from Backup

In This Chapter

▶ Using the WHS Home Computer Restore CD

▶ Bringing back a broken (or compromised) computer

▶ Reviving a dead disk

▶ Dealing with restore oddities

*I*n the preceding chapter, I take you through the steps to get Windows Home Server's backup working reliably, day after day, night after night.

In this chapter, you get to see why and how those backups can save your bacon.

In order to get WHS's full-disk restore to work, you have to dig out one of the CDs that came with your server (or the software you used to install WHS). It's called the Windows Home Computer Restore CD.

If you ever need it, that CD will be worth its weight in gold.

With a few quibbles, discussed in the next section, the Windows Home Server Home Computer Restore CD brings back the contents of any hard drive on any networked computer. You can use it to

   ✔ **Restore all the data on a hard drive that has crashed.** You simply stick a new drive in the computer, run the WHS Computer Restore CD, answer the questions correctly, and in an hour or two (or three or four), you're back where you started.

   ✔ **Replace a smaller hard drive with a larger one.** It's as simple as unplugging the old drive, plugging in the new one, and running the Computer Restore CD. You can replace a drive that seems to be on its last legs, or you can replace a tiny hard drive with a new monster.

✔ **Wipe out a messed-up drive.** If you think you accidentally installed a rootkit and your computer's been turned into a zombie, you can restore any or all of your computer's hard drives to a previous — presumably pre-zombified — state.

The Windows Home Server Home Computer Restore program even works if the dearly departed drive is the "system" drive (usually the C: drive). It's a very powerful program.

Dealing with Home Computer Restore Restrictions

```
Disk boot failure. Insert system disk and press ENTER.
```

For experienced Windows users, few error messages bring up beads of sweat like that one. Generally, it means your C: drive bit the dust.

If your computer adamantly refuses to start, help is at hand. As long as the offending computer meets WHS's requirements, you should be able to slap a new hard drive in the computer, boot with the Windows Home Server Home Computer Restore CD, and (plus or minus a few hours) have Windows Home Server completely restore your dead hard drive to a previous state.

WHS Home Computer Restore isn't just for dead drives. If the kids "accidentally" installed a program that pushes Internet Explorer to XXX Web sites, or if you got suckered into installing a bogus security patch and it's killing your system, you can roll everything back to a kinder, gentler era. (Yes, you can even roll back Microsoft's Windows security patches that "can't" be rolled back.) Just use the WHS Home Computer Restore CD on your hard drive, and all will revert, without a hiccup. No new drive necessary.

WHS Home Computer Restore does, however, have a couple of sticking points that may surprise you. At least, they surprise me. Before you try to use the WHS Home Computer Restore CD, make sure that your system meets all the following requirements:

✔ **You have to know the server's password.** The Restore Wizard won't let you in without one, no way, no how.

✔ **Your home or office computer — the one that needs the restore — must have a CD-ROM drive, and you must be able to boot from the CD-ROM drive.** Any plain-vanilla, ancient CD-ROM drive will do, as long as you can boot from it.

✔ **If you are replacing a hard drive, the new hard drive must be the same size as, or larger than, the old hard drive.** If you're simply overwriting an existing hard drive, you're fine. But you can't use WHS Home Computer Restore to restore a larger drive onto a smaller drive — even if you only used a tiny fraction of all the space available on the original hard drive.

This is a surprising requirement, made necessary because the WHS Home Computer Restore program works with clusters (see Chapter 12). If there are more clusters on the new drive than there were on the old drive, no problem. But if there are fewer clusters on the new drive than on the old drive, WHS won't budge. Microsoft is looking at relaxing that requirement in a future version of Windows Home Server, but for now, we're stuck with it.

✔ **The home or office computer — the one that needs the restore — must be plugged in to your network.** Although you can make backups over a wireless connection, you can't perform a restore wirelessly. You have to plug the computer in with a LAN cable.

The official maximum length for a LAN cable (CAT5, CAT5e, CAT6, or CAT7) is 100 meters, or 328 feet. That assumes the cable goes from your PC to the network's router without major kinks or hard turns.

In addition, you need to make sure you have working Windows 2003 drivers for both your network interface card and your disk drive controller(s). I show you an easy, thorough way to cover both bases in the next section.

There's a list of all the drivers that ship with the Home Computer Restore CD at

```
forums.microsoft.com/WindowsHomeServer/ShowPost.aspx?PostID=1439157&SiteID=50
```

If the driver's on the CD, the Restore Wizard will find it, and you don't need to do anything.

Restoring a Hard Drive

So your C: drive has gone to meet its maker. My condolences. *Sic transit gloria harddriveri* . . . .

Your system won't boot, or it boots so erratically that you figure it's time to put the system drive out of its blue-screen-induced misery. Maybe your whole system has come down with an infection that simply can't be scanned and removed by normal means. Maybe you did something stupid — perhaps you installed a security patch that locks your computer up tighter than a mosquito's tail stretched over a rain barrel. Lucky for you that you have Windows Home Server up and running, with a recent backup of your main drive. (Well, yeah, that *is* required if the procedures outlined here are going to work.)

Or perhaps you have a D: drive loaded with data that you've backed up with the server but that you didn't want to put in the shared folders on the server: confidential files, maybe, or works in progress. One day the D: drive goes up in a puff of smoke.

Relax. Help is at hand. Here's what you need to do:

1. **If you need a new drive, go out and buy a new hard drive that's at least as large as the one you're replacing. If you don't have a USB key drive, get one of those, too — even a small one will work fine.**

   You need the key drive to store your computer's drivers. Any key drive will do.

2. **If you're replacing the hard drive, tear open the dead computer, yank out the old drive, put in the new one, and screw the computer back together again.**

   Depending on what kind of server you have, you may need to make sure that you unplug everything, ground yourself, sit in a lotus position on a plastic sheet, and/or repeat *Om Mani Padme Hum* with great vigor. If you have an HP MediaSmart Server, replacing a drive is as easy as sliding the holder out of the front of the computer, sticking a new drive in the holder, sliding the holder back into the computer . . . and that's it. Very slick.

   Take care to follow the manufacturer's instructions about cable connections and jumpers on older IDE drives — or just take the monkey-see-monkey-do approach and set your new drive just like your old drive. SATA II drives go in without a hitch. Laugh maniacally as you throw away the hard-drive manufacturer's software setup disk. You won't be needing it.

3. **To retrieve any drivers that you may need to get the restore working, go to one of the functioning computers on the network, right-click the Windows Home Server icon in the notification area next to the system clock, and choose Windows Home Server Console. Type the server's password and click the right-pointing arrow.**

   The Windows Home Server Console appears.

4. **In the upper-left corner, click the Computers & Backup icon. Click once on the computer that you're going to restore. Then, under the Computers & Backup icon, click View Backups.**

   WHS shows you the latest backups of the computer you're about to restore, as in Figure 13-1.

5. **In the View Backups dialog box at the top, click the most recent backup (just once). Then, at the bottom, under Restore or View Files, click the button marked Open.**

   If the computer with the hard drive that you're going to restore has more than one disk (more precisely, more than one volume or partition), WHS asks you to select a volume to open. If that happens to you, choose the system drive — usually the C: drive — and click Open.

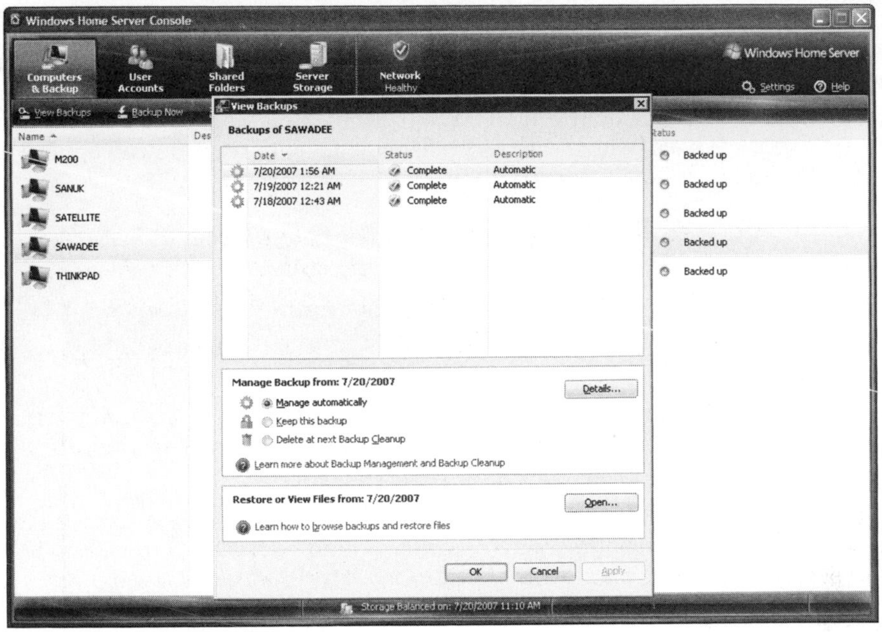

Figure 13-1:
Current backups of the computer that died.

WHS chugs and whirs and Windows may ask you to install device drivers for "Generic Volume" — which is just WHS's way of opening the backup files. Follow the defaults and have Windows install any drivers it needs (it does that automatically). If Windows says it needs to reboot, ignore it. The requisite drivers install all by themselves — no reboot necessary.

Ultimately, Windows shows you a list of all the folders and files in the latest backup, as in Figure 13-2.

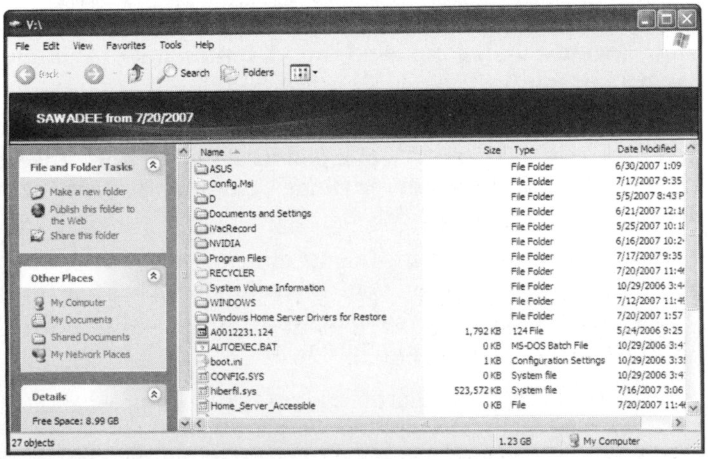

Figure 13-2:
All the backed up folders and files.

6. **Double-click the folder called Windows Home Server Drivers For Restore.**

   This folder (see Figure 13-3) contains all the unusual drivers your computer was using during the last backup. "Normal" drivers don't appear here — they're supplied on the WHS Home Computer Restore CD. But all the odd-balls (which can be devilishly difficult to track down!) appear here.

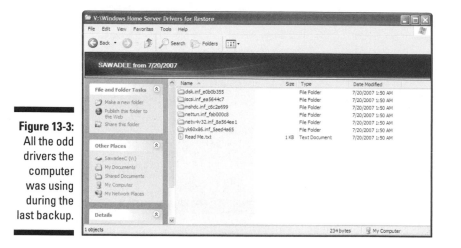

Figure 13-3: All the odd drivers the computer was using during the last backup.

7. **If there are any files in the Windows Home Server Drivers for Restore folder besides one called `Read Me.txt` (which isn't a driver), copy the entire Windows Home Server Drivers for Restore folder over to your USB key drive.**

   You now have all the drivers you need to get your computer restored.

8. **Do whatever you need to do to safely pull the USB drive out of the computer (you may need to go through Windows Safely Remove Hardware program, down in the notification area), Cancel out of the View Backups dialog box, and then X-button out of Windows Home Server Console.**

9. **Move over to the PC with a dead (or soon-to-be-overwritten) hard drive, and be sure the computer's plugged in to the network. Insert the CD called Windows Home Server Home Computer Restore CD into the CD drive, and boot from the drive.**

   If you can't find a copy of the Home Computer Restore CD, there's a version of it tucked away safely on your server's hard drive. See the section "Rolling Your Own Home Computer Restore CD" at the end of this chapter for details on retrieving and burning the CD.

You may spend a long time — ten minutes or more — staring at a blank screen, or a screen that shows just a mouse pointer. Watch the hard drive's blinking light for signs of life. Or sit back and enjoy the silence.

Sooner or later, the Home Computer Restore program tells you that it's launching the Restore Wizard (see Figure 13-4).

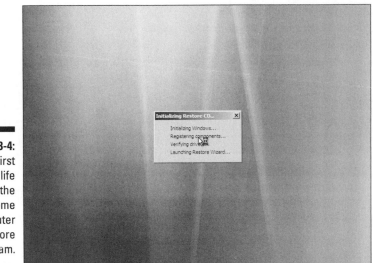

Figure 13-4:
The first
sign of life
from the
Home
Computer
Restore
program.

10. **Sit and wait until you're asked to do something. Until then, you really don't need to do anything. Avoid the temptation to rip the CD out of the drive and stomp on it.**

The Restore program is actually bringing up, and then running, something called the Windows Preinstallation Environment, or WinPE. It's not sprightly, but it's the same environment that runs when you install Windows. Humor it till it's finished doing its thing.

When the Restore Wizard is ready to start, it asks you to verify the time and currency format and your keyboard/input language. (See Figure 13-5.)

11. **Choose your localization settings and click Continue.**

The Restore Wizard looks at your hardware and drivers, and gives you an inventory similar to the one in Figure 13-6.

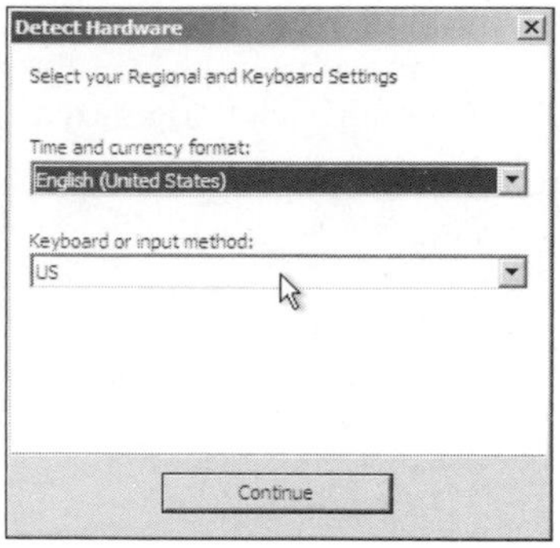

Figure 13-5:
The Restore
Wizard's
first
question.

Figure 13-6:
The wizard
found drive
controllers
but no
network
controllers.

12. **If the wizard found all your hard drive controllers and your network controller, go to Step 14. Otherwise click Show Details.**

    The Restore Wizard lists the drivers that it can find, and urges you to click Install Drivers to install any drivers you may have.

13. **Insert your USB key drive into a convenient USB slot and click Install Drivers. Then click Scan.**

    The wizard scans your USB key drive and installs any drivers it can find. The process can take a long time.

14. **Click Continue.**

    The official Restore Computer Wizard appears, per Figure 13-7.

15. **Click Next.**

    The wizard goes out and looks for your Windows Home Server server. If it has difficulty finding the server, it gives you an opportunity to specify that you have an "advanced network configuration" (geeky translation: a network with two subnets), at which point you can type in the name of the server, and the wizard will look once again.

    When the wizard comes back up for air, it asks you to type in the server's password.

16. **Type the server's password — the one you used when you originally set up the server — and click Next.**

    The Restore Computer Wizard asks you to choose which computer you want to restore.

17. **Select This Computer and click Next.**

    The wizard wants you to pick a backup to restore.

18. **Unless you have a good reason for picking an old backup, choose the latest backup and then click Next.**

    At this point, you have an option to run Disk Manager, if you want to change partitions or do anything strange with your hard drives. If you click the button marked Run Disk Manager, the Windows Server 2003 Disk Management MMC Snap-In starts. That's a rather complex beast, and making changes at this point can break the WHS restore. For help, see support.microsoft.com/kb/323442.

    If more than one drive on the computer has been backed up, you need to choose which drive (er, volume) you want to restore.

19. **Choose the drives you want to restore. If there's more than one drive on offer, and you only want to restore one, choose None from the extra drop-down box(es). Click Next.**

    The wizard tosses up a warning, saying that you will overwrite all the data on the hard drive. Which is what you wanted to do anyway, right?

20. **Click Next.**

    Go out and get a latte. This can take a long time.

    When the Restore Wizard finally gets its act together, it brings up a box that says the restore has been successfully completed.

> **21. Click Finish and the wizard reboots your computer, leaving you with the topside up and ready to roll, with absolutely everything on the drive restored to the chosen backup point.**
>
> It's important to realize that you've just restored a precise cluster-by-cluster backup of your hard drive. Everything's exactly the way it was before your old hard drive started having fits.

Rolling Your Own Home Computer Restore CD

If you can't find the Windows Home Server Home Computer Restore CD, don't sweat it. There's a condensed copy of the CD stored on the server. Here's how to get it, and burn your own version of the Restore CD:

> **1. On any functioning computer, double-click the shortcut on the desktop called Shared Folder on Server.**
>
> If you aren't logged in with a user name and password that are recognized by the server, you have to provide your bonafides.
>
> **2. Double-click the Software folder, and then double-click to open the Home PC Restore CD folder.**
>
> Windows Explorer shows you two files, `Readme.txt` and `restorecd.iso`. (See Figure 13-8.)

Figure 13-8:
A compressed copy of the Home Computer Restore CD.

Name	Date modified	Type	Size
ReadMe.txt	6/6/2007 1:50 AM	Text Document	1 KB
restorecd.iso	7/6/2007 11:26 AM	ISO File	288,132 KB

Software ▸ Home PC Restore CD

Favorite Links · More »
Folders
2 items — Offline status: Online — Offline availability: Not available

The file is an image of a CD, stored in a very specific format that Windows can't handle directly. Microsoft distributes the Home Computer Restore CD that way to make your life miserable, er, to ensure that the CD you create looks precisely like the original Home Computer Restore CD. You can't use Windows to transfer that file onto a CD. You have to use a program that specifically recognizes and burns ISO files.

3. **Double-click the ISO file.**

4. **If Windows recognizes the ISO file (probably because you already have Nero or a competitor's CD-burning software installed on your computer), follow the instructions on the screen to burn** `restorecd.iso` **on a CD.**

   Congratulations. You're done. The CD you just burned is an exact copy of the Windows Home Server Home Computer Restore CD.

5. **If Windows complains that it cannot open the ISO file, head over to** `www.deepburner.com` **and download and install DeepBurner Free, a very competent, free program that recognizes ISO files.**

6. **When you start DeepBurner Free, it asks you to Select Project Type. Choose Burn ISO Image, open the** `restoredcd.iso` **file, stick a CD in your CD burner, and click the Burn icon to burn the CD.**

   That gives you a good Windows Home Server Home Computer Restore CD, too.

With a Restore CD in hand, you're ready to take on the steps in the section "Restoring a Hard Drive," earlier in this chapter.

Chapter 14

Restoring Files from Backup

. . . .

In This Chapter

▶ Finding earlier versions of backed-up files

▶ Restoring backed-up files

▶ Comparing Vista shadow copies with Windows Home Server backups

▶ Restoring previous versions of files in shared folders

. . . .

1 remember when restoring files was pretty simple.

Either you had a backup or you didn't, and 99 percent of the time, you didn't.

With Windows Home Server you should never be at a loss for backups. In fact, your disks should runneth over with backups. Your main problem, when confronted with a file that has gone awry, is figuring out which backup to use — and how to retrieve the old file without clobbering potentially useful recent copies.

As you see in this chapter, the mechanics of retrieving an old copy of a file aren't difficult at all. But the logistics of knowing which copy to retrieve and when — ah, that's a far more difficult challenge.

There's a detailed description of backups, how they're created, and what limitations you can expect, in Chapter 12.

If you need to restore an entire drive — maybe the drive went up in smoke, or your system's been infected with interminable rootkits — look at Chapter 13.

To restore one file at a time, the old-fashioned way, the exact method varies — depending on whether you're restoring a file on your home or office computer, or you're restoring a file that usually sits in one of the server's shared folders. The method for restoring files from shared folders varies depending on whether you're using Windows XP or Vista. Is your head spinning yet?

The next section shows you how to restore a file that was on your home or office computer. The last two sections cover restoring files from the server's shared folders, first from Windows XP, and then from Windows Vista.

Restoring a Backed-Up File

This section discusses the method for retrieving backed-up copies of files and folders that reside on your home or office PC. If you need to restore a file that normally sits on the server, you're in the wrong place: look at one of the next two sections in this chapter, depending on whether you're running Windows XP or Vista. If you want to bring back all the files or folders on a hard disk — that is, restore an entire disk — look at Chapter 13.

To a first approximation, every night, Windows Home Server reaches into your PC and backs up very nearly all the files on the PC. I discuss the details in Chapter 12. Those are the backups you can get at using the Windows Home Server restore capabilities.

If you accidentally delete a file on your own computer, you don't need Windows Home Server. Just look in your computer's Recycle Bin. That's what it's there for.

Use the Windows Home Server back up files if you . . .

- ✔ Really mess up a file and want to go back in time, to work on a copy of the file the way it existed very early this morning.

- ✔ Delete a file on a different computer on your network and you want to get it back. When you delete a file on some other computer, it doesn't get routed to the Recycle Bin. Thus, frequently the only way to bring back a deleted network file involves digging into the Windows Home Server server's backups.

- ✔ Want to compare different versions of a file, over time. The backup copies are only generated once a day, in the middle of the night, so you don't get all the versions of a file. But if you can make do with daily snapshots, then you can restore multiple versions and compare them to see what changed, day to day.

- ✔ Moved a file or folder and you can't find it. (Wish I had a nickel for every time that's happened to me.) It's often faster and much less painful to just dip into the server and make another copy of the file or folder.

You can't bring back, oh, the version of that Word document that you saved at 10:00 yesterday morning, or the version from 3:15 this afternoon. But you can bring back a copy of the file from early this morning, early yesterday morning, early the morning before that, and so on.

Here's how to restore a backed-up copy of a file:

1. **Make sure you know the server's password, and then go to any computer on your home or office network.**

   As long as you know the server's password, you can restore any existing backup of any file from any computer on the network.

2. **Right-click the Windows Home Server Console icon in the notification try, near the clock. Choose Windows Home Server Console.**

   The Console sign-on screen appears.

3. **Type the server's password and press Enter or click the right-arrow.**

   The Windows Home Server Console appears.

4. **In the upper-left corner, click the icon marked Computers & Backup. Then double-click the computer that held the file you want to restore.**

   In Figure 14-1, I double-click the computer called Thinkpad, and the View Backups dialog box for the Thinkpad appears.

5. **Double-click the backup that you want to use.**

   This is where a bit of luck and guessing come into play. You may have a hard time figuring out exactly which day's backup you want to work with, so don't be afraid to guess, take a look, and guess again.

   In Figure 14-2, I double-click the backup for 7/22/2007, and get the Backup Details dialog box you see in Figure 14-2.

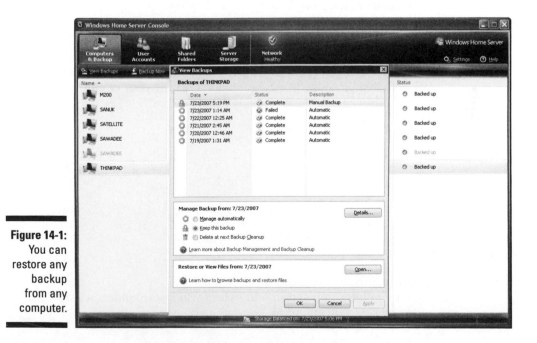

Figure 14-1:
You can restore any backup from any computer.

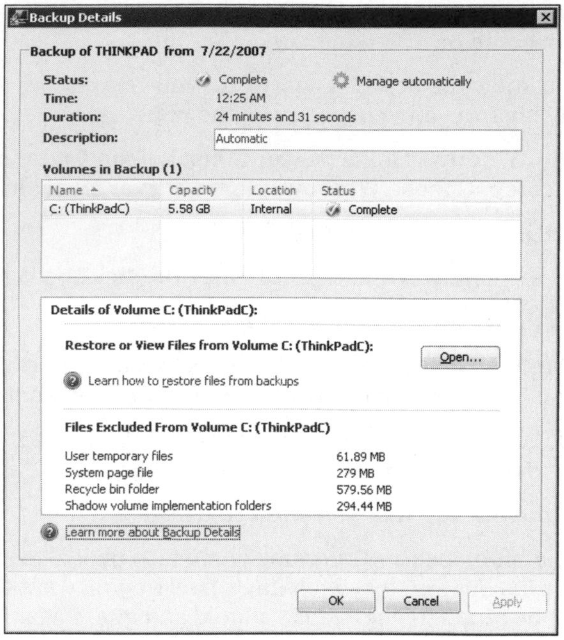

Figure 14-2:
Details for
my chosen
backup.

6. **Click the volume (usually the drive) that contains the file you seek, and then click Open.**

   Windows goes through various gyrations, depending on whether or not you've restored a file before. In some cases it tells you that it needs to install a new driver (see Figure 14-3); in other cases it may tell you that you need to restart your computer. Just take the defaults — yes, it's okay to install a new driver — and don't restart your computer.

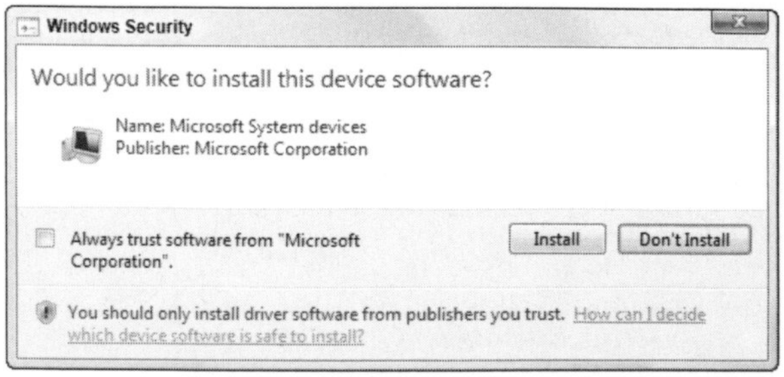

Figure 14-3:
If Windows
wants to
install a new
device
driver, let it.

Sooner or later, you see an odd hybrid Windows Explorer window like the one shown in Figure 14-4.

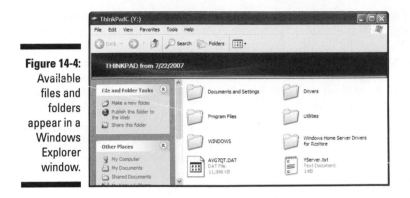

Figure 14-4:
Available
files and
folders
appear in a
Windows
Explorer
window.

> 7. **Navigate to the file or folder that you want to restore (see Figure 14-5), and then use any of the standard Windows ways to copy the file or folder to any location at all.**

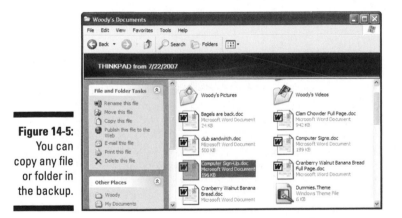

Figure 14-5:
You can
copy any file
or folder in
the backup.

You can copy the file onto your desktop, into one of your computer's folders, into a shared folder on the server, into any allowed location on any other computer on your network, onto your USB key drive, or onto the tip of your tongue if it has a proper receptacle.

You can open one of the backed-up files with an application running on your computer — double-click a backed-up DOC file, for example, and Word appears with the DOC file loaded. You can burn a backed-up file on a CD. You have read-only access to everything in the backup file. In short, you can do just about anything you want with the backed-up file, except you can't delete it, can't change it, can't create a shortcut to it, and you can't put new files inside the backed-up folders.

Even though reaching into the backup like this is properly called a "restore," in fact it's more like a copy. When you restore a file from the Recycle Bin, Windows sticks it back in its original location. In many of the various Windows backup programs, restoring a file frequently overwrites the original, which is an invitation to disaster. Not so with a Windows Home Server restore: you get to put the file (or folder) anywhere you like, and no current files are disturbed.

8. **When you've retrieved all the files and folders you like from the backup, X-button out of the special Windows Explorer window; if you're done with the Windows Home Server Console, X-button out of it.**

Retrieving backups is just that easy.

Restoring a Shared Folder File with Windows XP, Media Center, or Tablet PC

This section focuses exclusively on restoring a previous version of a file stored in a shared folder on the server. At midnight, Windows Home Server makes backups — previous version "shadow copies" — of files in shared folders. (For an introduction to shadow copies, see Chapter 12.)

In several places, Microsoft's documentation says Windows Home Server generates shadow copies twice a day, at midnight and noon. That may be the case on your computer, but in my extensive testing with several different servers, I never found a single noon-time shadow copy — the only previous versions I could find were generated at midnight.

If you want to restore a backup of a file that sits (or used to sit) on a home or office computer, you're in the wrong place. Look at the steps in the preceding section. If you want to restore all the files on a hard drive, check out Chapter 13.

This section only applies if you are sitting at a network computer that's running Windows XP Service Pack 2 (Home or Pro), or XP Media Center Edition, or Tablet PC. If the computer you're running uses Windows Vista Business, Enterprise, or Ultimate, see the next section. If the computer you're sitting at runs a version of Windows XP prior to Service Pack 2, or Windows Vista Home Basic or Home Premium, you're outta luck. You can't restore any files in shared folders on the server. You have to move over to a different computer on your network — one that's running XP SP2, or Vista Business, Enterprise, or Ultimate. (Or you can try to log on to the server directly, using the trick in Chapter 17.)

You can't get finer granularity than Windows Home Server shadow copy backups — that is roughly at midnight. If you seek a version of the file that you saved at 10:00 this morning or 3:30 this afternoon, you don't stand a chance. What you get is a copy of the file as it existed around midnight. Period.

Historically, shared server folder backups are kept until WHS runs out of space, at which point it drops the oldest backups. (I haven't found a precise description of the phrase "run out of space," but WHS appears to reserve a great deal of room for old shared folder backups.) In practical terms, if you change a file in a shared folder on the server once a day, chances are good that you can retrieve old versions of the file that go back months.

WHS has no Recycle Bin. If you want to retrieve a deleted file, you need to know which folder the file resided in prior to being given the axe. There's no central index; it's strictly a hunt-and-peck operation.

You don't need to know the server's password in order to recover previous versions of a file. But you do need Read access to the folder that contains the file. (See Chapter 5 for details on granting Read access to shared folders.)

To restore a previous version (shadow copy) of a file in a shared folder on the server — using a computer running Windows XP Service Pack 2 — follow these steps:

1. **On your Windows XP computer's desktop, double-click the shortcut that says Shared Folders on Server.**

   If you aren't already logged on with a user name and password that's known on the server, you have to provide both. Note that the user name must have read permission for the folder that contains the file you want to restore.

   Windows shows you all the shared folders on the server, as in Figure 14-6.

Figure 14-6:
No need to
use the
Console to
retrieve
files.

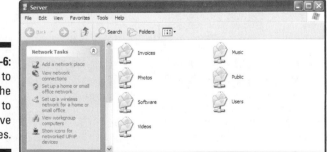

2. **If you want to retrieve an earlier version of a file that's still on the server, navigate down to the file, right-click the file, choose Properties, and then click the Previous Versions tab.**

   Windows Explorer shows you a list of all the available previous versions of the file, as in Figure 14-7.

   Note that the date and time brand on the file corresponds to the time the shadow copy was taken — typically midnight. It doesn't reflect the date and time at which the file was last changed.

3. **Choose the version you want to bring back and click Copy.**

   I strongly recommend that you *don't* use the Restore option. Clicking the Restore button overwrites the current version of the file with the old version. It's always much safer to retrieve a copy of the file first, and *then* figure out whether there's anything in the current version of the file that's worth keeping.

   Explorer shows you a Copy To dialog box.

4. **Navigate to the location where you would like to place the copy (the desktop usually works fine) and click Copy. Then click OK to get out of the Properties dialog box.**

   Windows deposits a copy of the earlier version in the location you specify. From that point you can work with the new and old versions, mash them up any way you like, and extract the best from both.

Figure 14-7:
A list of the previous versions of the file that are available on the server.

5. **If you want to retrieve an earlier version of a folder, or if you've deleted a file and you want to bring it back, navigate to the folder, right-click it, choose Properties, and then click the Previous Versions tab.**

   Windows Explorer displays a list of the previous versions of the folder, as in Figure 14-8.

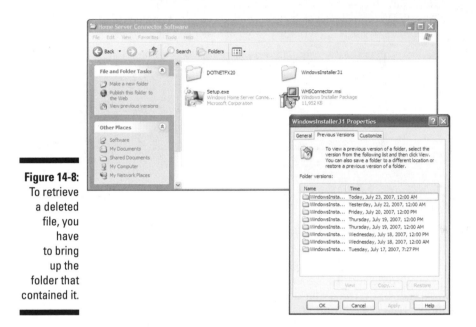

Figure 14-8: To retrieve a deleted file, you have to bring up the folder that contained it.

6. **If you really want to restore the whole folder, select the folder, click the Copy button, choose a location (as in Step 4), click Copy, and then click OK.**

   Here's the alternative if you want to restore a particular file that's been deleted: Click the folder that the file used to be in, and then click the View button.

   Windows shows you a list of the backed-up files in the folder (see Figure 14-9).

   At this point, you can do just about anything with the file — open it with an application, run it, copy it other places on the server, copy it onto your own computer — except you can't modify or delete it.

7. **Restore the folder or file in any way you see fit, and when you're done, X-button out of the Windows Explorer window. Then click OK to go back to Windows Explorer.**

   Your copied file or folder can be treated just like any other.

Figure 14-9:
To see the file(s) that used to be in the folder, click the View button.

Restoring a Shared Folder File with Vista Business, Enterprise, or Ultimate

The process of using Vista Business, Enterprise, or Ultimate to restore a file in a shared folder on the server is similar to what you do if you're using Windows XP to do the same thing. There are, however, a couple of confusing subtleties that you should watch out for if you own a computer that runs Windows Vista.

Before I get into those, however, it's handy to re-state the restrictions:

- ✓ Windows Home Server keeps shadow copies of files and folders stored on the server, but the copies are only made around midnight. (The WHS documentation states that shadow copies are also made around noon, but after months of trying, I never found any.)

- ✓ The process described in this section only applies to backups of files stored on the server. To restore backup copies of files normally stored on your computer, see "Restoring a Backed-Up File" earlier in this chapter. (To restore an entire hard drive, see Chapter 13.)

- ✓ You can use most any computer on your network to restore any backup copy of any file in any shared folder on the server, as long as you log on with a user name and password that have Read access to the folder that contains the file. (See Chapter 5 for a description of access permissions.) Also, the computer must be running Windows XP Service Pack 2, or Vista Business, Enterprise, or Ultimate.

You can't restore a file or folder using Vista Home Basic or Vista Home Premium, as you discover in Step 2 of the following list. (If you have to restore a file using Windows Vista Home Basic or Premium, see Chapter 17 for the trick.)

To restore a previous version (shadow copy) of a file in a shared folder on the server using a computer running Windows Vista Business, Enterprise, or Ultimate, follow these steps:

1. **On the Vista computer's desktop, double-click the shortcut that says Shared Folders on Server.**

    If you aren't already logged on with a user name and password that's known on the server, you have to provide both. Note that the user name must have Read permission for the folder that contains the file you want to restore.

    Windows shows you all the shared folders on the server, as in Figure 14-7 in the preceding section.

2. **If you want to retrieve an earlier version of a file that's still on the server, navigate down to the file, right-click the file, choose Properties, and then click the Previous Versions tab.**

    Here's the reason why you can't use Vista Home Basic or Premium to restore a backed-up file: if you're using Vista Home Basic or Premium, when you right-click a file (or folder) and choose Properties, the Properties dialog box *doesn't have a Previous Versions tab* (see Figure 14-10).

Figure 14-10: Vista Home Basic or Premium doesn't have a Previous Versions tab.

Figure 14-11:
Windows
Vista
Business,
Enterprise,
and Ultimate
have a
Previous
Versions
tab, but the
tab's text is
misleading.

On the other hand, if you are running Vista Business, Enterprise, or Ultimate, you see a Previous Versions tab, as in Figure 14-11.

The text in Figure 14-11 is misleading because previous versions on the server aren't saved on your computer's hard drive. They're saved on the server.

3. **Choose the version you want to bring back and click Copy.**

   Explorer shows you a Copy To dialog box.

4. **Navigate to the location where you would like to place the copy (the desktop usually works fine) and click Copy. Then click OK to get out of the Properties dialog box.**

   Windows deposits a copy of the earlier version in the location you specify.

5. **If you want to retrieve an earlier version of a folder, or if you've deleted a file and you want to bring it back, navigate to the folder, right-click it, choose Properties, and then click the Previous Versions tab.**

   Windows Explorer displays a list of the previous versions of the folder, as in Figure 14-8 in the preceding section.

6. **If you really want to restore the whole folder, click the folder, click the Copy button, select a location (as in Step 4 above), click Copy, and then click OK.**

   If you simply want to restore a file that's been deleted, click the folder that the file used to be in, and then click the View button.

   Windows shows you a list of the backed-up files in the folder (see Figure 14-10 in the preceding section).

7. **Restore the folder or file in any way you see fit, and when you're done X-button out of the Windows Explorer window. Then click OK to go back to Windows Explorer.**

   Your copied file or folder is ready to roll.

Chapter 15

Backing Up the Server

In This Chapter

▶ Why you need to back up your server

▶ What needs to get backed up, and what doesn't

▶ Choosing a backup service

▶ Running server backups

> *Quis custodiet ipsos custodes?*
>
> *Who will guard the guardians?*
>
> — *Juvenal,* Satire VI, *ca. 190 AD*

Windows Home Server does a great job of backing up your entire network. Plug in the WHS box, stick a CD in each home or office computer, click a few times, wait overnight, and you're backed up.

Right?

Well, yes. Sorta.

But then again, not exactly.

In order to understand exactly where your vulnerabilities lie — and what you can do about them — it's important to understand the inner workings of the server. When you know what you're up against, you can choose a server-backup strategy that works best for you.

That's where this chapter comes in.

If one of the hard drives on your server has failed, you're too late to use any of the advice in this chapter. Lick your wounds and proceed to Chapter 19.

Mapping Out Windows Home Server Storage

You *can't* back up your whole server. Although backing up the home or office computers on your network is a lead-pipe cinch, Microsoft didn't build the hooks into Windows Home Server to allow you to run a full backup of the server itself. There's no CompletePC backup (as in Windows Vista), no NTBackup (the backup program in Windows XP), Norton Ghost won't do the trick, Acronis True Image can't, either. Try running any of those programs and the program may *say* it has a good backup after it finishes its work — when it doesn't.

Drive Extender, the technology that makes managing storage on your server so simple — no drive letters, no running out of space on individual drives, no hassles adding a new hard drive — also makes it impossible for traditional backup programs to do their jobs. You can't back up your D: drive when there *is* no D: drive!

Your server's storage (like all of Gaul) is divided into three parts (*Machina est omnia divisa in partes tres?*):

- ✔ **The Windows Home Server operating system itself.** Think of it as your C: drive and you won't be too far off. (In fact, physically, the operating system *is* on your C: drive, but you can only get at it if you're prepared to jump through some doggedly difficult hoops.) Other programs get tossed in with the operating system when they're installed — add-in programs, antivirus programs, basically any program that runs on the server gets lumped in with the operating system.

  You don't need to back up the operating system or your programs. If your server's main hard drive dies, reinstalling programs may take a long time, but you shouldn't lose any sleep over it.

- ✔ **Backed-up data from your home or office computers.** This includes the clusters and the map that specifies which clusters belong to what files on which computers. (I talk about the cluster backup method in Chapter 12.)

  As of this writing, there is no program that will successfully back up the server's backed-up data. For some people, that's no big deal — if the server (or hard drive on the server) goes kablooey, simply installing a new server (or hard drive) and running a regular nightly backup will restore the backed-up files.

  For some people, though, the lack of a backup for the nightly backups causes real heartburn. They're concerned about recovering data if their house or office burns down and *all* the PCs on the network get fried. Windows Home Server doesn't have a handy solution for that kind of fiery scenario. If you can ensure that all your important files are stored in shared folders on the server, backing up the shared folders will suffice. But if you have key files sitting in PCs on the network, you have to use some other form of offsite storage to guard against the chance that everything will burn down. The situation is no different from your exposure if you don't have Windows Home Server.

✓ **Files in shared folders, shadow copies of files in shared folders, and (if Folder Duplication is turned on) exact duplicates of files in shared folders.** As long as you have two or more hard drives, and Folder Duplication is turned "on" (see the next section), Windows Home Server is very clever about spreading out copies among available hard drives. This is the key data on the server that isn't backed up anywhere else.

The bottom line? You don't have to be worried about losing a single hard drive on the server — WHS can rebuild itself. But if your computer gets hit by lightning and two or more drives die simultaneously, or your three-year-old decides the cool blue box should go for a swim, you're going to wish you had a backup somewhere.

Many people who have been dealing with backups for eons take consolation in the fact that if your Windows XP or Vista computer suddenly starts acting flakey, you can always rip the hard drive out of one machine and put it in another: instant after-the-fact backup. But be advised: *Windows Home Server doesn't work that way.* If your server's motherboard dies, you can't simply remove the hard drive from the brain-dead machine and plug it into another PC. Windows Home Server won't survive the transfer in workable form.

Moral: In the brave new world of Windows Home Server, it pays to be prepared.

Using Folder Duplication

Unless you're running out of disk space, you should turn on Folder Duplication for all your important shared folders, even if you only have one hard drive. Permit me to explain why.

If you have a file in a shared folder, and that folder has been designated "Duplication On" (see Figure 15-1), Windows Home Server maintains an exact duplicate of the file. When you change a file and close it, WHS takes at most three minutes to create the duplicate copy.

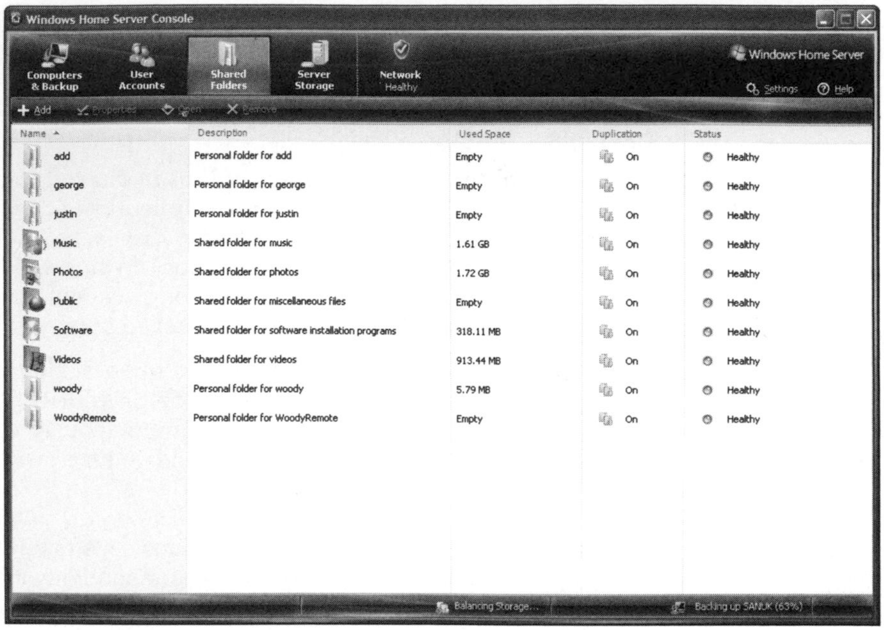

Figure 15-1:
Duplication
is turned
"On" for all
of my
shared
folders.

If you have more than one hard drive on your server, and you have room, WHS is smart enough to store the duplicate on a different drive from the original. That way, if one of the hard drives on your server bytes the dust (ahem), you can get the data back — automatically and quite readily (see Chapter 19).

But even if you only have one hard drive on your server, if you have Folder Duplication turned on, WHS can recover from part of the drive going bad — a *bad sector*, in computer lingo — and restore your shared files, and you don't have to do a thing.

You don't need to turn on Folder Duplication for any shared folder that stores stuff you don't care about — copies of installation discs, redundant data that's already stored on CDs, Donny Osmond albums. But any shared folder that holds worthwhile data — data you need to keep — should have Folder Duplication turned on.

I explain how to turn on Folder Duplication in Chapter 5. In order to adjust the duplication setting, you must know the server's password.

Making Offsite Backups of Shared Files

Anything short of a major catastrophe can be handled directly with Windows Home Server's built-in restore features and programs. Need to recover a munged file? Look at Chapter 14. Lose a computer on the network, or a hard drive on one of your home or office computers? No problem — follow the steps in Chapter 13 and you'll be back and running in minutes. (Or hours. Maybe many hours.)

If one of the hard drives on your server takes a permanent snooze, you have my permission to scoff. Run out and buy a bigger drive than the one that died, plug it into your server, and follow the procedure in Chapter 19. Providing Folder Duplication was turned on for all your important folders, restoration runs faster than a two-bit horse in a three-bit race.

If you lose all your computers to a fire or flood, or a rampaging Pamplona Bull Run re-enactment, Windows Home Server can't help. You have to rely on backups of the individual computers on the network, which you probably didn't create, did you?

I didn't think so. Bend over and kiss your smarter half good-bye.

Between the extremes of trivial restoration and impossibly bad luck sits a middle backup path that you should seriously consider following: run periodic backups of the files in your shared folders, and store the backups someplace far removed from your server. That approach protects you and the important data on your server if your dog suddenly decides to relieve himself on both of your server's hard drives simultaneously.

If you opt for offsite backup, you can avail yourself of two general approaches:

- ✔ **You can copy the server's shared files to an external drive, and store the drive someplace away from your house or office.** Big external drives are cheap and easy to use. But the backup programs that come with many external hard drives won't work with Windows Home Server, and remembering to schlep the disk offsite can be a burden, especially if you're rememberationally challenged like me. (See the next section for some tricks.)

- ✔ **You can get an account with an online storage facility, and back up by copying files into the online vault.** You shouldn't trust the online company's backup program to reach into your server and extract what you need, but you can usually work around it. (See the last two sections in this chapter for details.)

Copying files to an external drive

The cheapest, easiest, and fastest way to make an offsite copy of all the data in your server's shared folders is just about as low-tech as you can get: External hard drives — drives that sit outside your computer, typically plugging into a USB port — have been around for ages.

When you buy an external hard drive for backing up your server, take these factors into account:

✔ The drive likely connects to a computer via a USB cable, or possibly an eSATA cable if your computer can handle it. If you use USB, make sure you get a USB 2.0 drive. (It's hard to imagine that USB 1.0 drives are still around, but you can find them in discount places. USB 2.0 is about 40 times faster than USB 1.0.)

✔ The rotational speed of the drive — 4,200 rpm or 5,400 rpm or 100,000 rpm — doesn't mean much.

✔ Don't worry about any built-in backup programs. You can't use them anyway.

✔ I prefer the kind of drive that you have to plug into an electrical outlet. I know it's all cool and hip to have external drives that draw their power off the USB connection, but I've seen too many wimped-out USB ports that can't handle high levels of power consumption for extended periods of time — which is precisely the situation with a long backup like the one you'll be performing.

✔ Go cheap. Look for the lowest price per byte. If you want a fashion accessory, buy a designer humidifier.

To back up your server's shared folders to an external drive, follow these steps:

1. **Go to any convenient home or office computer on your network and log in using a user name and password that has read permission on the server for all the files you want to back up.**

   You can only back up files if you log on with a user name that has permission to read the files.

2. **Plug in the external drive to the USB port of the computer you just logged on to.**

   Do NOT plug the drive into your server. If you do, Windows Home Server will try to absorb the drive into the Drive Extender Borg-equivalent and wipe out all the data on it (see Chapter 18). Note the following:

   It may take a noticeable while for Windows to recognize the drive, particularly the first time. While that's going on, note:

   • You may be put on hold while Windows installs drivers for the new drive.

   • You may have to Just Say NO to any built-in backup programs on the drive that try to install themselves; you don't want them gumming up the works.

   • You should certainly *not* reboot your computer.

   In the end, you should see an AutoPlay notification like the one in Figure 15-2.

Figure 15-2:
AutoPlay
detects your
external
hard drive.

3. **Click Open Folder to View Files using Windows Explorer.**

   Windows Explorer appears, and shows you whatever folders may be on
   the external hard drive.

4. **If you want to put this backup in its own folder, right-click an empty
   spot inside Windows Explorer and choose New↪Folder. Type in the
   name of the new folder and press Enter.**

5. **On the desktop, double-click the icon that says Shared Folders
   on Server.**

   If you didn't log on to Windows with a user name and password that are
   recognized on the server, Windows Home Server presents you with a
   challenge, and you have to provide legitimate credentials.

   Windows Explorer appears with a list of all the shared folders on the
   server, as in Figure 15-3.

6. **One by one, right-click any folders on the server that you want to
   back up and choose Copy. Then go over to the list of folders on the
   external hard drive, right-click wherever you want the backup to go
   and then choose Paste.**

   You can select high-level folders, or you can drill down and back up only
   folders of specific interest. Or you can select multiple folders (use
   Ctrl+click to select individual folders, Shift+click to pick a bunch, or
   "lasso" whichever folders you like) and copy them *en masse*.

   Note that you don't need to wait for one copy to end before you begin
   another.

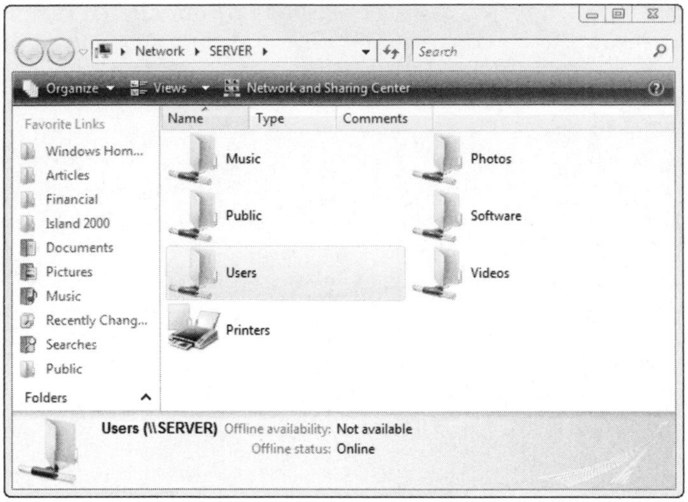

Figure 15-3:
Shared
folders on
the server,
ready to
back up.

7. **If you try to copy a folder but you don't have Read permission for that folder on the server, you see a warning box like that in Figure 15-4. Click Skip, and realize that the protected folder hasn't been backed up.**

   If you're using Windows XP, you simply get an inscrutable error message.

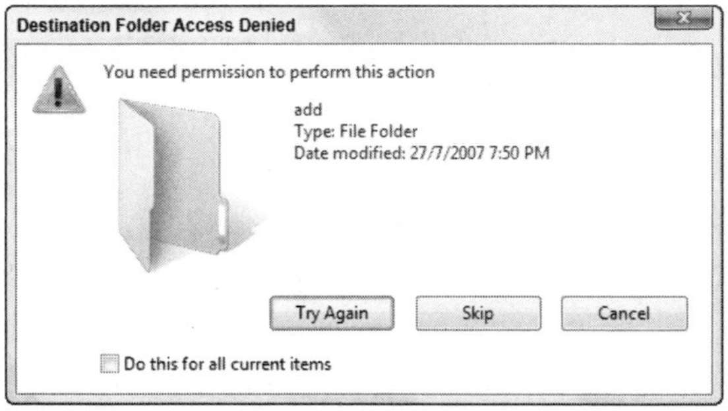

Figure 15-4:
You don't
have read
permission
for the
shared
folder.

8. **Grab a latte.**

   By the time you come back, a copy of all the contents of all the folders should be on your external hard drive.

9. **Disconnect the external hard drive (you may want to first click the Safely Remove Hardware icon in the system notification area, next to the clock).**

10. **Store the external hard drive offsite and you can sleep easy at night, knowing that if your house burns down, you still have copies of all of your tax returns and music files.**

There's a significant advantage to backing up your shared folders using simple drag-and-drop copying, as in the preceding steps: the backups can be used on any computer, running any operating system. You don't need any special software to get at the data. In almost all cases, all you have to do is plug in the drive.

You can use SyncToy to back up shared folders to an external drive, but in my experience, SyncToy frequently encounters problems that it doesn't report. The end result: a backup that isn't complete, for reasons that aren't at all immediately clear. Also, if you schedule SyncToy to run nightly, you have to plug your external drive into your computer nightly — which isn't much consolation if your house burns down in the middle of the night, eh?

If you want to give SyncToy a try, see Chapter 7.

Choosing an online backup provider

Few online services are going through such tumultuous change right now as the online-backup sector. Everybody and his brother, it seems, is stumbling around trying to provide enormous amounts of free (or very-low-cost) online backup space. With Microsoft' Windows Live Folders and Google's GDrive not yet released to the general public (as of this writing), we're going to see a lot of competition in the free online-backup realm. Prices are going down — I figure Microsoft should pay you to store your data on its servers, doncha think? — and storage capacity is headed up.

That's great, particularly because online backup makes so much sense for Windows Home Server shared folders.

On the downside, online backups can really clog up an Internet connection. Depending on how much data you want to back up and how often, they can also get expensive. You may fear storing your data on some big company's servers, for all sorts of good reasons. And unless the online site has software specifically designed for backing up Windows Home Server, you may be in for a rocky ride.

On the plus side, if you store your backups online, you don't have to worry about your house burning down and taking your shared folders with it, or schlepping that external hard drive with you to Aunt Gertrude's every afternoon. You don't have the (significant) initial expense buying the drive. And you don't have to tell your cat for the umpteen-thousandth-time to stop gnawing on the power cord.

All in all, online backup is a good choice.

Philip Churchill has been testing various online backup products, specifically trying them with Windows Home Server, and posting the results on his Windows Home Server blog. For an example, see

```
mswhs.com/2007/06/25/online-offsite-whs-backup-solutions
```

At this moment, Philip recommends Idrive-E (`www.idrive.com` — tutorial at `mswhs.com/2007/06/27/tutorial-how-to-backup-whs-using-idrive-e`), but there are new products and significant revisions to old products coming fast and furious.

If you're in the market for a (possibly free) online backup solution, check out Philip's site.

Part VI
Staying Alive and Well

The 5th Wave   By Rich Tennant

"They can predict earthquakes and seizures, why not server failures?"

In this part . . .

Ask not what your home server can do for you.

Ask what you can do to your home server.

This part digs into the server itself — reading the tea leaves, breaking into the server, adding and removing hard drives, and recovering the server if a drive takes a dive. Real nitty-gritty stuff.

Think of it as the advanced course.

Although it's built on top of the venerable Windows Server 2003, Windows Home Server is a new product. Getting help with WHS isn't like getting help with Windows XP or Vista; you can't rely on gurus who steep themselves in the experiences of hundreds of millions of users.

WHS cognoscenti are a much rarer breed, although you can find one if you know where to look. If you find yourself out on a Home Server limb and can't figure out what to do next, try posting a question on the Windows Home Server forum at

```
forums.microsoft.com/
windowshomeserver
```

Chapter 16

Monitoring System Health

• •

In This Chapter

▶ Reading your network's health report

▶ Knowing why a "Critical" report may be okay and a "Healthy" report may hold surprises

▶ Identifying network health problems

▶ Solving the problems

• •

*I*t happens to everybody, sooner or later.

Your home network's all set up, Windows Home Server is sitting in the closet doing its thing on a nightly basis, all is well in your networking world, and suddenly the Windows Home Server icon on one of your machines turns red. The icon informs you (as in Figure 16-1) that one of the computers on your network is about to melt down in a colorful but smelly medley of sparks, flames, and gooey plastic blobs.

Or something like that.

Figure 16-1: A bad health report.

No spyware protection

SANUK has antispyware software turned off or out of date.

If you've been using WHS for more than a day or two, you probably know that Windows Home Server constantly monitors all the computers on your network and gives you a concise, centralized "health report" in the Windows Home Server Console. The health report stays on top of the current status of patches, virus signature-file updates, whether backups are up to date, and how much hard-drive space you've almost run out of. Bad health reports result in red (or occasionally yellow) Windows Home Server Console icons appearing in the notification area of all the home and office computers on your network.

What you may not know is that some health reports are more accurate than others. In the sections that follow, you discover how to find and read health reports and what to do about them.

Understanding the Network Health Indicator

The Network Health Indicator — the Windows Home Server Console icon in your system tray, down near the time — takes on one of three colors: green, yellow, or red. The official designations (Healthy, At Risk, and Critical respectively) don't add much intellectual weight to the obvious assessment — green is good, red is bad, and you can step on the gas and race through on a yellow.

In fact, Windows Home Server's designers are a little cleverer than the color-based triage might lead you to believe. Here's a finer breakdown:

- ✔ **Green** means Windows Home Server hasn't detected any problems, although some computers (specifically Windows XP computers) may have non-functional firewalls, out-of-date spyware, and/or nonfunctional antivirus programs.

- ✔ **Yellow** means WHS has hit a problem, but it isn't particularly severe. You should take a moment to look at the full Network Health report, but your immediate assistance isn't necessary.

    For example, if one of your machines misses a backup (perhaps the computer was turned off, or another backup ran so long that it took up the entire midnight-to-6:00-a.m. window), you get a yellow alert.

- ✔ **Red** doesn't necessarily mean that the sky is falling, but you should stop what you're doing and see why your server has a bee in its bonnet.

    For example, if you don't allow Windows Home Server to update itself automatically, then you see a red Network Health Indicator every time Microsoft "pushes" a security patch to you. I call it a Drama Queen Warning. On the other hand, a red Network Health Indicator *can* reflect serious problems with your server, such as the Backup Sever Error shown in Figure 16-2.

Figure 16-2:
This red "critical" alert reflects serious problems.

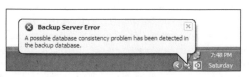

When Windows Home Server wants to whup you upside the head, it shows you a red Network Health Indicator. Sometimes the "red alert" warning's justified. Many times it isn't. Regardless, when you see it, you're best off if you check the full network health report — at any time — which you can see by following these steps:

1. **From any home or office computer, right-click the Windows Home Server Console icon in the notification area, next to the time, and choose Windows Home Server Console.**

   The Windows Home Server Console logon page appears.

2. **Type the server's password and click the right-pointing arrow.**

   Windows Home Server Console appears.

3. **At the top, click the Network icon (which should say Healthy, At Risk, or Critical).**

   Windows Home Server shows you the full Network Health report. Figure 16-3 shows a clean bill of server health. I dedicate the rest of this chapter to explaining how you interpret alerts and fix server health problems.

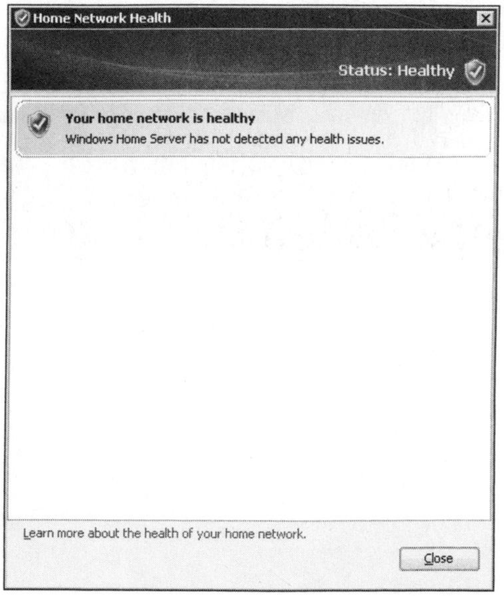

Home Network Health   ✕

                                              Status: Healthy ✓

✓ **Your home network is healthy**
   Windows Home Server has not detected any health issues.

Learn more about the health of your home network.

                                                        [Close]

Figure 16-3:
A "green"
clean bill of
health.

A Windows Update two-step

Personally, I have Vista check for updates but let me decide whether I want to download or install them. The reason: I don't trust that the updates will install smoothly, and I don't want to break my machine with updates that don't work right. For those who share my skepticism, I report on updates at my site, `AskWoody.com`, noting which are important, which are safe, and which have reportedly caused havoc on people's machines.

You can turn off automatic updating in Windows Vista without raising any alarm in Windows Home Server. (You can turn off automatic updates in Windows XP, and Windows Home Server will never know the difference.)

To get rid of automatic updating in Vista without upsetting the Windows Home Server applecart, follow these steps:

1. **Click Start⇨Control Panel. Click the Security link.**

   You see Vista's Security Settings homepage.

2. **Under the icon marked Security Center, click the link to Turn Automatic Updating On or Off.**

   Vista shows you the Choose How Windows Can Install Updates dialog box, shown in the following figure.

3. **If you want to keep Windows Home Server's Network Health Indicator to stay off your back, choose any option *other* than Never Check for Updates (Not Recommended).**

4. **Click OK. If you get a User Account Control message, click Continue. X-button out of the Security Settings dialog box.**

   It may take Windows Home Server a few minutes to recognize your new settings.

See *Windows Vista All-In-One Desk Reference For Dummies*, from Wiley, for details about keeping Microsoft's mitts off your machine.

Choose how Windows can install updates

When your computer is online, Windows can automatically check for important updates and install them using these settings. When new updates are available, you can also install them before shutting down the computer.

Understanding Windows automatic updating

- **Install updates automatically (recommended)**
  Install new updates:
  Every day ▾ at 3:00 AM ▾

- Download updates but let me choose whether to install them

- Check for updates but let me choose whether to download and install them

- Never check for updates (not recommended)
  Your computer will be more vulnerable to security threats and performance problems without the latest updates.

Recommended updates

☑ Include recommended updates when downloading, installing, or notifying me about updates

Note: Windows Update might require an update before you can install updates for Windows or your programs. For more information, see our privacy statement online.

OK   Cancel

What Can Go Wrong?

Windows Home Server's health assessment relies on three broad categories of monitoring:

- **The server monitors itself.** If your server's running low on hard drive space, if there isn't enough room to store a duplicated folder (see Chapter 5), if the server's backup program isn't running or it isn't running correctly, if there's a problem validating your copy of Windows Home Server, or if one of your hard drives is failing repeatedly, the server raises a red flag.

- **Windows XP and Vista computers monitor backups.** While the server keeps tabs on backups from its side, each of your networked computers watches from its end, too. Individual computers on the network can report a problem with the last backup(s), and that problem can trigger a yellow or red alert.

- **Vista computers (and *only* Vista computers) report their Security Center status.** Every Vista computer hooked up to your network reports to the server on its firewall status, and raises an alarm if your antivirus or antispyware programs are out of date. Unfortunately, WHS isn't smart enough to interrogate Windows XP machines. (More accurately, Windows XP Home, Pro, Media Center, and Tablet PCs don't report their Security Center status to the server.)

These are the same tests that Vista normally runs all the time, whether it's connected to a network or not. If a Vista PC fails one of the tests, you see a yellow or red Security Center "shield" icon in the notification area. If the Vista PC is connected to a WHS server, Windows Home Server picks up the problem and modifies the Network Health Indicator in the notification area of every computer on the network.

Table 16-1 summarizes the most common Windows Home Server health problems.

Table 16-1	Common Health Problems	
Type of Problem	*Yellow ("At Risk") Warning*	*Red ("Critical") Warning*
Backups	A home or office computer's last backup failed.	A specific home or office computer hasn't been backed up for 15 days.
Available disk space on the server's hard drives.	Less than 7% on 500GB systems, 4% on 1TB systems.	Less than 2% on systems with 200 GB to 1 TB.

(continued)

Table 16-1 *(continued)*

Type of Problem	Yellow ("At Risk") Warning	Red ("Critical") Warning
Shared folder duplication	One or more folders aren't being duplicated because there isn't room.	
Server drive failure	SMART drive reports failure(s); run a repair (see Chapter 19).	Complete failure(s); run a repair.
Automatic updates	An update on a Vista computer is waiting for your approval.	An update on the server is waiting for your approval, or a Vista computer has update notifications turned off.
Firewall		A Vista computer has the firewall turned off (same as Security Center status).
Antivirus		A Vista computer doesn't have up-to-date antivirus software (same as Security Center status).
Antispyware		A Vista computer doesn't have up-to-date antispyware software (same as Security Center status).
Server software		An important WHS program didn't start correctly.

How to Fix Health Problems

If you get a yellow or red Network Health Indicator warning, you may be inclined to panic. Don't worry. Be happy. Few problems that trigger Network Health Indicator reactions are fatal.

If you get a yellow or red icon, follow these steps:

1. **From any home or office computer, right-click the Windows Home Server Console icon in the notification area (next to the time), and choose Windows Home Server Console.**

Even though Windows XP computers don't report their full status to the server, you can use any computer on the network to get the whole low-down on your network's health.

The Windows Home Server Console logon page appears.

2. Type the server's password and click the right-pointing arrow.

Windows Home Server Console appears.

3. At the top, click the Network icon (which should say Healthy, At Risk, or Critical).

You see the latest health report, as in Figure 16-4.

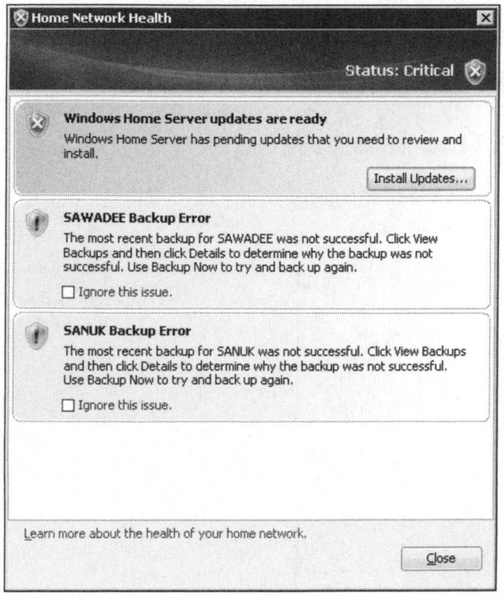

Figure 16-4:
Although it appears dire, this "Critical" network health report bears few tidings to cause immediate concern.

> **Home Network Health** ☒
>
> Status: Critical ☒
>
> ☒ **Windows Home Server updates are ready**
> Windows Home Server has pending updates that you need to review and install.
>
> [Install Updates...]
>
> (i) **SAWADEE Backup Error**
> The most recent backup for SAWADEE was not successful. Click View Backups and then click Details to determine why the backup was not successful. Use Backup Now to try and back up again.
> ☐ Ignore this issue.
>
> (i) **SANUK Backup Error**
> The most recent backup for SANUK was not successful. Click View Backups and then click Details to determine why the backup was not successful. Use Backup Now to try and back up again.
> ☐ Ignore this issue.
>
> Learn more about the health of your home network.
>
> [Close]

4. When in doubt, follow the instructions.

Most health warnings, most of the time, include instructions for resolving the problem. For example, in Figure 16-4, you can click the Install Updates button and Windows Home Server takes you through the steps to install Microsoft's latest patches.

If the Network Health report tells you to run Repair on a finicky hard drive, do so immediately (see Chapter 19). If you have to run a Repair more than once on the same hard drive, get a new hard drive and install it just as soon as you can — before the old one comes to a grinding halt. Having an extra hard drive never hurts.

TIP

Don't sweat the small stuff. If you miss a backup or two, the sky isn't falling. If you feel strongly that Windows Home Server should back up a hard drive that wasn't automatically backed up, follow the instructions in Chapter 12 to run a manual backup. (Short version: In the Windows Home Server Console, click the Computers & Backup icon, right-click the computer you want to back up, and choose Backup Now.)

5. **When you're done, click Close to return to the Windows Home Server Console.**

Unfortunately, not all health warnings include information about recovering from the problem. For example, in Figure 16-5, there isn't even the beginning of a clue about how to start the Backup Service, even though its absence triggered a "Critical" health warning.

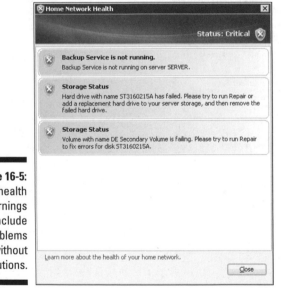

Figure 16-5:
Some health warnings include problems without solutions.

ASKWOODY.COM

Whenever I encounter a health warning without a clear cause or solution, my first reaction is to reboot the server, unless the warning seems to be related to a potential hard drive failure on the server. Re-booting doesn't always work, but it's easy and relatively fast. At the very least, if the problem persists, you know you started from a clean slate.

If I get a warning that one of the server's hard drive is about to head south, I try to retire the problematic drive gracefully, using the steps in Chapter 18. I don't re-boot immediately, in the (unlikely) event that the drive's so far gone the system won't re-boot.

Here's how to reboot your Windows Home Server server:

1. **In the upper-right corner of the Windows Home Server Console, click the icon marked Settings.**

   You see the Windows Home Server Settings dialog box, as in Figure 16-6.

2. **On the lower left, click Shut Down.**

   WHS gives the option of shutting down entirely or rebooting.

3. **Click Restart.**

   Your server goes out to lunch, and you receive a notification that the connection has failed.

4. **Wait a few minutes, right-click the Windows Home Server Console icon in the notification area, choose Windows Home Server Console, and take it from there.**

   Chances are good you want to check your network's health — that's what got you here in the first place — so click the Network icon at the top.

If you hit a problem that you can't solve, start by looking in this book's index, and then try using the Windows Home Server Console's Help button. If that doesn't work, get online and post a question on the Windows Home Server forum, forums.microsoft.com/WindowsHomeServer.

Chapter 17

Breaking into the Server

In This Chapter

▶ Understanding Rule #1: Never, ever break into your server.

▶ Figuring out when you have to ignore Rule #1

▶ Getting into your Windows Home Server server without monitor, keyboard, or mouse

▶ Knowing what to do — and what *not* to do — while you're in the server

*T*his is the most dangerous chapter in the book.

Almost everything that you need to do with your server you can do through the Windows Home Server Console. That's what it's there for.

But sometimes you want to do things with your server (defenestration doesn't count) that you can only accomplish if you get into the server itself. Windows Home Server Console only goes so far. Logging on to the server with an Administrator account gives you full access to essentially everything in the server, and everything that Windows Server 2003 has to offer.

One little problem: You really *can* mess up stuff while you're rummaging around inside the server. Even simple things like moving a file can have dire consequences if you aren't extremely careful.

Be afraid. Be very afraid.

Most Windows Home Server servers run *headless* — no monitor, no keyboard, no mouse — and you might be intimidated into thinking that you can't work directly with a server that has no head. In fact, using *any computer on your network* to get into the server isn't difficult at all. Don't let that put you off. Just *make sure you know what you're doing* once you get inside, and don't go changing things indiscriminately.

Deciding to Break In

Windows Home Server runs on top of Windows Server 2003 — in many respects, it's a program, just like any other program. But it has very deep ties into the internal workings of Windows Server.

If you can accomplish what you need to accomplish without breaking into your server, by all means do so. The Windows Home Server Console, which forms a common thread throughout this entire book, covers most of the bases. It's a safe, insulated, supportive, nearly bulletproof environment that does everything most people need to do, most of the time.

Okay, okay. So I didn't scare you away yet, did I?

Here's another way to look at it: Windows Home Server, when used the way it was intended, is a remarkably solid and reliable program. But if you sneak into the server and go messing around with just about anything, you can break your system entirely. A broken Windows Home Server system rates high on the pain-o-meter, right up there with root canals and proctologist's exams. If you can't get the system working again, your data's basically hosed. (That's a technical term.) You can't pluck a hard drive from your lifeless ex-server, stick it in another computer, and expect to get your data back. All the backup capabilities and stability and peace of mind that you paid for when you bought your Windows Home Server goes right out the, uh, window if you start messing around inside the server.

In particular, Microsoft warns that monkeying around with any of these common Windows Server 2003 tasks can do irreparable harm to Windows Home Server:

- ✔ **Changing files in Windows Explorer.** If you go into your server and start clicking around on your C: or D: or E: drive, you may think that you know where you are, and where your files have gone, but you don't. Trust me. To get into the server's shared folders, always type the address into Windows Explorer's address bar like this: `\\server\Photos` or `\\server\SharedFolder` (as shown in Figure 17-1).

- ✔ **Setting access permissions.** Don't even think about setting folder or file-access permissions by going directly into a folder on the server with Windows Explorer and using the Properties tab (this particular no-no is shown in Figure 17-2). You'll end up locking everybody out of everything. If you can't set the permissions you need with Windows Home Server Console, take my advice and throw away WHS.

- ✔ **Doing *anything* with Disk Manager.** The official warning, "Almost any change you make in Disk Manager will cause the storage system on your home server to fail, possibly resulting in data loss." Don't mess with Mother Nature. Or Disk Manager.

✔ **Create new shared folders or modify existing ones.** Windows Home Server is very persnickety about how shared folders get set up, and how they are maintained. Trying to do any of that manually is folly.

✔ **Changing users, user groups, or adding or deleting users.** Windows Home Server keeps its own groups in its own way, and you don't stand a snowball's chance of getting all the details right. If you need to do something with users, work with Windows Home Server Console. If the Console can't do what you need to do, then you've outgrown Windows Home Server.

Figure 17-1: To get to shared folders, always type the address in the address bar.

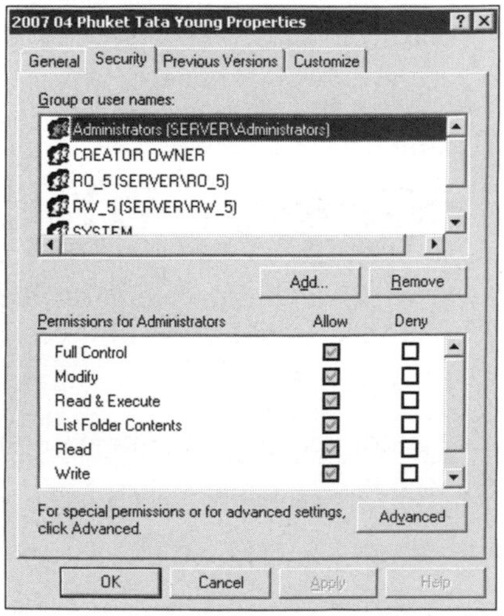

Figure 17-2: Setting access permissions manually will drive you nuts — and may lock out everybody.

That said, there are some things you have to do directly, that require you to go *mano a mano* with your server. For example:

✔ **If you need to install a driver,** you can't do it through the Windows Home Server Console; you need to wrestle directly with the server. You may need a driver that doesn't ship with Windows 2003, particularly if you stick a printer on your server, or add some weird new hardware.

✔ **If you want to install (or sometimes even run) a program that wasn't designed for Windows Home Server,** a trip to the server is in order. While programs designed to run under WHS can be installed and run using the Console, other programs generally can't be installed (or sometimes even run) through the Windows Home Server Console. To install (run) those programs, you need to get into the server.

✔ **If your network's router doesn't play properly with others,** you may need to assign a permanent address — a *static IP address* — to your server. The only way to do that involves breaking into the server and uttering the proper magic incantations.

✔ **If you don't have easy access to a Windows XP or Vista Business, Enterprise or Ultimate computer on your network, and you need to restore a previous version of a file in one of the server's shared folders,** you have to dig into the server. As I describe in Chapter 14, you can't get at previous versions of shared files using Windows Vista Home Basic or Premium.

If you're still hell-bent on breaking into your server, you're most likely to find success using a Windows feature known as the Remote Desktop Protocol. Newbies call it "Remote Desktop," but you can sound cool and refer to it by its guru's nickname, "RDP."

Logging On to the Server with RDP

If you're convinced that the only way to solve your problem involves breaking into the server, you'll be pleasantly surprised to discover how easily you can do it.

Here's how to log on to the Administrator account on your Windows Home Server server:

1. Go to any computer on your network.

2. **Start RDP in the way that works for your operating system.**

   - If the computer is running Windows XP, click Start⇨All Programs⇨Accessories⇨Communications⇨Remote Desktop Connection.

   - If the computer is running Windows Vista, click Start⇨All Programs⇨Accessories⇨Remote Desktop Connection.

   The Remote Desktop Connection dialog box (see Figure 17-3) asks you which computer you wish to log on to.

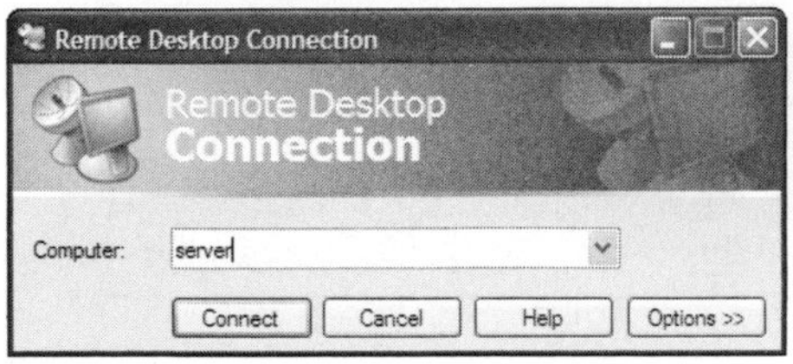

Figure 17-3: RDPing to your server starts with specifying the server's name.

3. **Type the name of the server in the box marked Computer and click Connect.**

   Unless you changed it, your server is probably called SERVER.

   Remote Desktop whines and whirs for a few seconds, and then shows you the logon screen in Figure 17-4. It's important to realize that the logon screen you see involves logging on to Windows Server 2003, on your Windows Home Server server.

4. **In the box marked User Name, type** Administrator. **In the box marked Password, type the server's password. Then click OK.**

   That's the same password you use to log on to the Windows Home Server Console. You chose it when you first set up Windows Home Server.

   When Windows Server 2003 is ready for your command, Windows Home Server butts in and shows the screen in Figure 17-5.

Once you see the screen shown in Figure 17-5, you're running Windows Server 2003.

Be careful. Don't run with scissors.

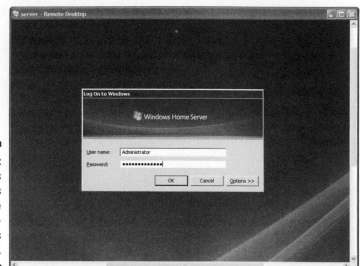

Figure 17-4:
The server's
password is
also the
Admini-
strator's
password.

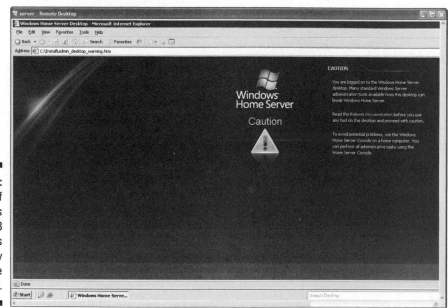

Figure 17-5:
All of
Windows
Server 2003
lurks
directly
beneath the
surface.

Where's the log file?

If you're spelunking inside your server because of an error that you can't possibly understand, you may need to look at the Windows Server 2003 log file (variously called an "error log file" or a "system log file" or a "system event log"). The log file contains an overwhelming mass of detail about every action Windows Server takes, what worked, what didn't, and why.

To get into the log file, once you've RDPed into the server, click Start➪Control Panel➪Administrative Tools➪Event Viewer. Windows Server offers four different filters to make it easier to find what ails you:

✔ **Application,** which contains status messages from various applications

✔ **Security,** in which lies a full security log, including the times that various machines on your network log on to the server)

✔ **System,** where you're most likely to find information about hardware that isn't working

✔ **Home Server,** which includes details about backups and other Windows Home Server activities

Simply click the filter that interests you, and double-click any event to see the details.

Attaching a Printer with RDP

Windows Server 2003 ships with printer drivers for hundreds of printers — but chances are awfully good that the printer you own isn't among them. Printer manufacturers work hard to create and maintain drivers that plug and play well with Windows Vista and Windows XP — but Windows Server 2003 drivers seem to get the short end of the stick.

If you want to attach a printer to your Windows Home Server server (which would certainly seem to be a reasonable goal), be aware that you're going to need a driver that works with Windows Server 2003. Sometimes Windows XP drivers work fine under Windows Server 2003. Frequently, however, they produce weird random errors, which can be daunting if you have to solve printer problems on a server without a monitor or keyboard.

In general terms, here's how to get a printer attached to your server:

1. **Go to the printer manufacturer's Web site and download the latest Windows 2003 Server version of the printer's driver.**

In my case, I wanted to hang an older printer/scanner/fax machine (specifically an HP PSC 2410) off the server, so I went to the HP site and looked for a driver. HP doesn't have a Windows Server 2003 driver for the PSC 2410. So I checked several Web sites and forums, and discovered that the Windows XP driver seems to work with Windows Server 2003, although the scanner won't work right across a network. Undaunted, I downloaded the Windows XP driver from HP's site.

2. **Double-click the Shared Folders on Server icon that's sitting on your desktop. Then copy the driver into the server's shared Software folder.**

   In Figure 17-6, I double-click the Shared Folders on Server shortcut, double-click the Software folder, create a new folder called HP PSC 2410 Driver, and then click and drag the downloaded driver (drv_gc _w01_ENU.exe) into the folder.

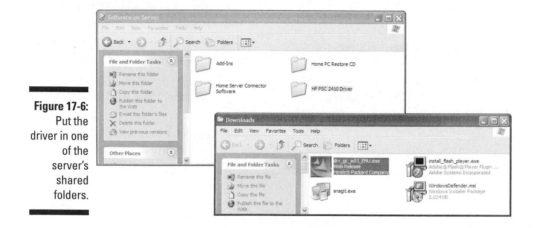

Figure 17-6: Put the driver in one of the server's shared folders.

3. **Using the steps in the preceding section, log on to the server using RDP.**

   When you're done, you are logged in to the Administrator account, and you see the Windows Home Server Desktop page, viewed through Internet Explorer, shown earlier in this chapter in Figure 17-5.

4. **In Internet Explorer, click File➪Close.**

   The remote Windows Home Server desktop, which is a modified version of the Windows Server 2003 desktop, appears as in Figure 17-7.

5. **On the Windows Home Server desktop, double-click the shortcut that says Shared Folders on Server. Then double-click Software, and double-click the folder that holds your new printer driver.**

   You should see the driver installer file that you downloaded, as in Figure 17-8.

6. **Double-click the printer driver and run the installer.**

   If you encounter warnings, read them, but don't be overly intimidated; printer drivers designed for Windows XP, for example, can and do work with Windows Server 2003.

   Depending on how the installer behaves, you may go through several steps in the wizard. In the end, the driver should be installed on your server, and the printer should work.

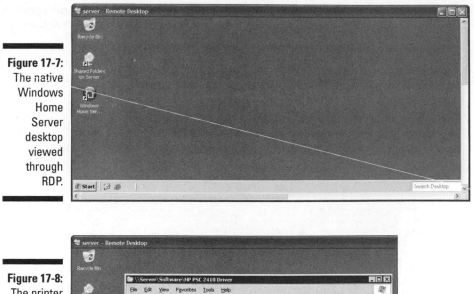

Figure 17-7:
The native
Windows
Home
Server
desktop
viewed
through
RDP.

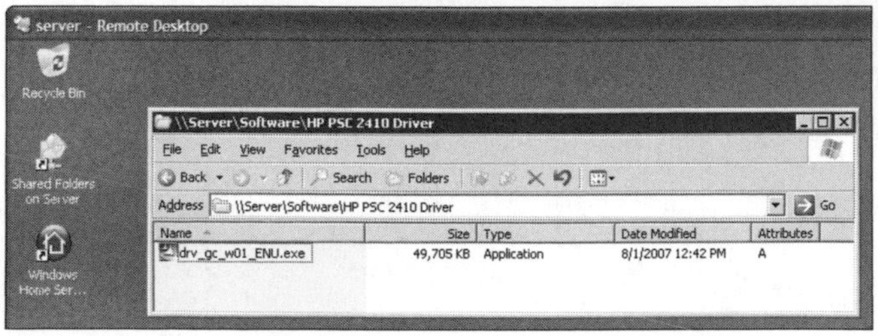

Figure 17-8:
The printer
driver is
right where
you put it.

7. **When you're satisfied the printer is working properly — try running a few test sheets from the Remote Desktop — click the X in the upper-right corner of the server – Remote Desktop box.**

   Windows advises that This will disconnect your Windows Session. Your programs will continue to run while you are disconnected. You can reconnect to this session later by logging on again.

8. **Click OK.**

   That breaks your Remote Desktop connection, and returns the server to its normal, headless state. (Scary thought, that.)

9. **One by one, go to each computer on your network and add the new printer.**

   • **In Windows XP,** click Start⇨Control Panel⇨Printers and Other Hardware, and then click the link to Add a Printer.

   • **In Vista,** click Start⇨Control Panel, under the Hardware and Sound icon click the link marked Printer, and then at the top click Add a Printer.

10. **In either case, you go through a very simple wizard that should recognize your new printer, although you may need to tell the wizard to browse the network location** `\\server` **(see Figure 17-9).**

The printer should work from every computer on your home or office network.

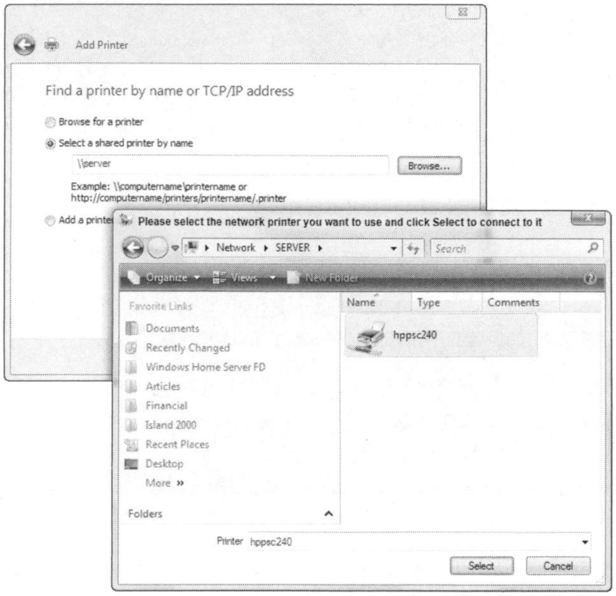

Figure 17-9:
The Add a
Printer
Wizard may
have a hard
time auto-
matically
finding the
printer. If so,
browse
starting at
\\server.

Certain scanners may work across a network — but don't count on it. I couldn't get any Windows XP or Vista computers to recognize the scanner that comes with the PSC 2410. If you figure out how to get an HP PSC to scan across a Windows Home Server network, drop me a line, okay?

Restoring a Previous Version of a Shared File with RDP

Windows Home Server's "previous versions" capability allows you to bring back earlier versions of a file stored in a shared folder on the server. You can't get back just any old copy. WHS takes snapshots of all the files in the shared folders on the server every day around noon and midnight. If you suddenly discover that you messed up (or deleted) a file on the server, you can retrieve one of the older copies.

Cool. But there's a gotcha.

In Chapter 14, I kvetched (that's a polite way of saying it) about the fact that you can't use Windows Home Server's "previous versions" capability to restore an earlier version of a shared file, if you're running Windows Vista Home Basic, or Home Premium.

Microsoft's decision to short-change Vista Home users has more to do with marketing goals and product differentiation than with user-friendliness or customer satisfaction. The previous versions' capability is built into Vista Business, Enterprise, and Ultimate — and it works for every file on your home or office computer, not just files in shared folders on the server. Apparently somebody decided that Vista Home Basic and Premium users would have to pay more for Vista Ultimate to get the feature, even if they've paid for Windows Home Server.

If you sit down at a computer on your network and that computer's running Windows XP Home, Pro, Media Center, Tablet PC, or Windows Vista Business, Enterprise, or Ultimate, restoring a previous version of a shared file is as simple as right-clicking the file, choosing Properties, and then bringing up the Previous Versions tab (shown in Figure 17-10). I talk about the method in Chapter 14.

If you sit down at a Windows Vista Home Basic or Home Premium computer, bring up a file in a shared folder on the server, right-click it and choose Properties, *there's no Previous Versions tab*, much less a Previous Versions feature (as shown in Figure 17-11).

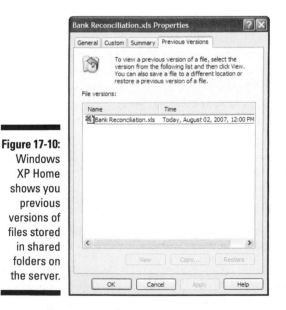

Figure 17-10: Windows XP Home shows you previous versions of files stored in shared folders on the server.

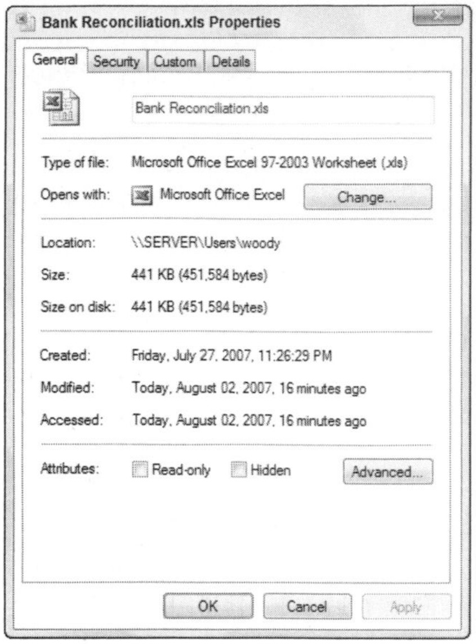

Figure 17-11:
In Vista
Home
Premium,
you aren't
even offered
a Previous
Versions
tab.

To get back a previous version of a file in a shared folder on the server, you can use RDP this way:

1. **From any computer on your network (Windows XP, Vista Home, whatever) follow the steps in the section "Logging on to the Server with RDP," earlier in this chapter, to log on to your server.**

   You are logged in to the Administrator account on the server. You may see the Windows Home Server Desktop page, viewed through Internet Explorer (refer to Figure 17-5); or you may just see the server – Remote Desktop screen shown (refer to Figure 17-7).

2. **If you see the Windows Home Server Desktop running inside Internet Explorer, click File⇨Close to get to the server – Remote Desktop screen in Figure 17-7.**

3. **Working in the RDP session (which is a geeky way of saying, "working in the server – Remote Desktop screen in Figure 17-7"), double-click the Shared Folders on Server shortcut.**

   The server brings up a list of all the shared folders on the server.

4. **Navigate to the file you want to retrieve. Right-click the file and choose Properties. Then click the Previous Versions tab.**

   Windows Server 2003 brings up a list of all available previous versions of the file in question, as in Figure 17-12.

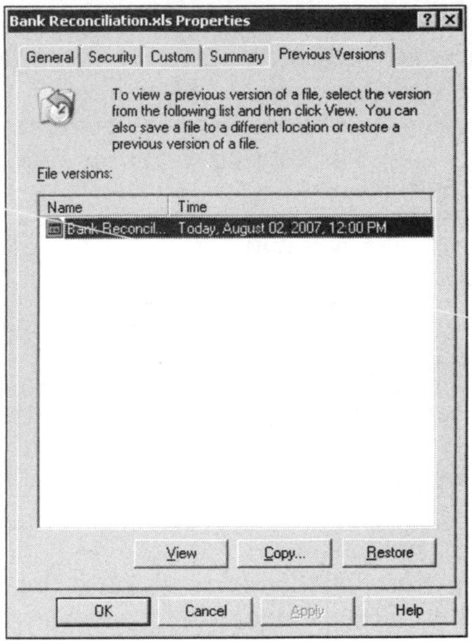

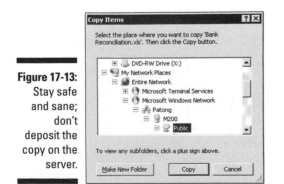

Figure 17-12: Via RDP, you see the Previous Versions tab, no matter which version of Windows you use.

5. Click Copy. No, don't click Restore. Click Copy.

Working inside Windows Home Server gives me the willies. If you click Restore, chances are good everything will work fine, but why take a chance? It's far better to Copy the previous version onto your home or office computer. If you decide later that you want to replace the original version in the server's shared folder, you can copy the previous version from your home or office computer back into the Shared folder on the server. Besides, you may be able to recover something worthwhile from the messed-up copy of the file, too. Think of it as "two logs crossing" (with thanks to Walter Edmonds).

Windows Server 2003 offers to copy the file anywhere you like (see Figure 17-13).

Figure 17-13: Stay safe and sane; don't deposit the copy on the server.

6. **Unless you have a very good reason for copying the file back onto the server, avoid using Desktop or the C: drive (SYS) or any other drive on the server — those are forbidden places that can only lead to ruin. Instead, choose a location on one of your network computers. If you must put the copy on the server, stick it in a different shared folder. Click Copy.**

   In Figure 17-13, I copy the previous version into the Public folder on the computer that I'm using to break into the server.

7. **Click OK in the Copy dialog box, then click the X in the upper-right corner of the server – Remote Desktop box.**

   Windows displays this message: This will disconnect your Windows Session. Your programs will continue to run while you are disconnected. You can reconnect to this session later by logging on again.

8. **Click OK.**

The Remote Desktop connection disappears, and everything goes back to normal. You can open your copied file and treat it like any other file. If you want to use it on the server, make sure you have the version of the file that you want, and then manually copy it back into the appropriate place in Shared Folders on Server.

Giving Your Server a Permanent IP Address

It isn't supposed to work this way, but on some networks, you just can't get your Internet connection to work (or you can't get all the computers talking with each other) unless you manually assign an address — an *IP address* — to the server. I talk about the vicissitudes of rowdy routers in Chapter 10. Manual IP addressing is a problem that should've been solved about two decades ago, but we computer consumers are still stuck with it. If your server won't work any other way, you have to dig into it to set a hard-wired IP address.

If you change your server's IP address, you may have to re-run the Home Server Connector CD on all the computers on your network.

If you get to the point where you know that you absolutely *must* assign an IP address to your Windows Home Server server, it's pretty easy to do the dirty deed. Here's how:

1. **From any computer on your network, follow the steps in the section "Logging On to the Server with RDP," earlier in this chapter, to log on to your server.**

   That logs you on to the server with the Administrator account. You may see Internet Explorer showing the Windows Home Server Desktop "let's scare them away" page (refer to Figure 17-5); or you may just see the RDP server – Remote Desktop screen (refer to Figure 17-7).

2. **If you see Internet Explorer running, click File⇨Close to get to the server – Remote Desktop screen in Figure 17-7.**

3. **Click Start⇨Control Panel⇨Network Connections⇨Local Area Connection.**

In some unusual cases, you may see an entry for your local area connection that has a name other than "Local Area Connection." Basically you're looking for the connection between your server and the network itself — typically a Network Interface Card of some sort. It may help to hover your mouse over each of the connections shown, if you have an obfuscated choice.

Windows Server 2003 (which is in command) shows you a Local Area Connection Status dialog box.

4. **Click Properties.**

You see the Local Area Connection Properties dialog box shown in Figure 17-14.

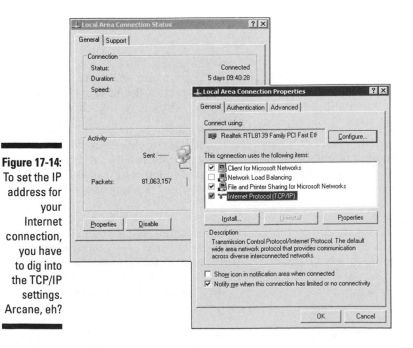

Figure 17-14:
To set the IP address for your Internet connection, you have to dig into the TCP/IP settings. Arcane, eh?

5. **At the bottom of the box, click once on Internet Protocol (TCP/IP). Then click the Properties button.**

Windows Server 2003 shows you the Internet Protocol (TCP/IP) dialog box shown in Figure 17-15.

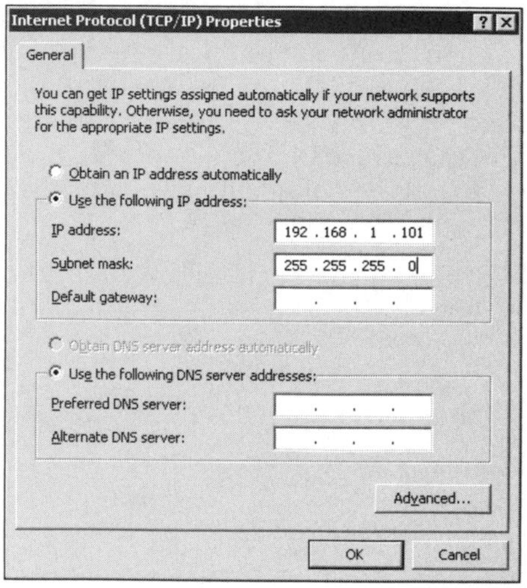

Figure 17-15:
Set the server's IP address manually here.

Internet Protocol (TCP/IP) Properties

General

You can get IP settings assigned automatically if your network supports this capability. Otherwise, you need to ask your network administrator for the appropriate IP settings.

○ Obtain an IP address automatically

● Use the following IP address:

IP address: 192 . 168 . 1 . 101

Subnet mask: 255 . 255 . 255 . 0

Default gateway: ___ . ___ . ___

○ Obtain DNS server address automatically

● Use the following DNS server addresses:

Preferred DNS server: ___ . ___ . ___

Alternate DNS server: ___ . ___ . ___

Advanced...

OK   Cancel

6. **If you're absolutely, totally, completely, unreservedly sure that you want to change your server's IP address, click the button marked Use the Following IP Address, and type the address you've chosen and the subnet mask in the indicated boxes.**

Be painfully aware of the fact that changing your server's IP address manually can render it completely incommunicado on the network. You may have to plug a keyboard, mouse, and monitor into your server to get it talking again. *If you don't know what you're doing, don't do it.*

7. **Click OK.**

Your RDP connection gets broken immediately, but if you're lucky, when the server comes back up for air, it'll be able to connect to the Internet and to your network, although you may have to re-run the Windows Home Server Connector CD on every computer on your network, to help your home or office computers "find" the newly relocated server.

Chapter 18

Adding and Retiring Drives

• •

In This Chapter

▶ Understanding Windows Home Server disk management

▶ Spotting what matters with a new hard drive — and what doesn't

▶ Adding new hard drives

▶ Removing old hard drives without screwing up your system

• •

*W*indows Home Server takes care of disk management behind the scenes so you don't have to.

You'll never even know (or care) which drive on the WHS computer holds what folders, or which files go where. Backups get mirrored automatically. Volumes and folders get extended as needed, and you don't have to lift a finger.

When the WHS server starts running out of disk space, it tells you. Install another drive and it's absorbed into the Borg-equivalent: More space becomes available, and you don't need to care about any of the details.

Someday, all computers will be that simple. For now, for those of us accustomed to Windows' whining and whining, the Windows Home Server approach to disk management — called Drive Extender — feels like a breath of fresh air.

Keep a few rules of thumb in mind:

✔ The first drive on the system — the System hard drive, which probably came preinstalled with your Windows Home Server box — is notoriously difficult to upgrade. You can replace it if you have to (see Chapter 19), but given a choice, don't bother trying to change the System hard drive to a larger or faster model.

✔ The best way to upgrade a hard drive goes in three steps:

1. Install the new (presumably larger) drive.

2. Wait a day or two.

3. Remove the old drive.

I go into much more detail in the last section of this chapter.

✔ When you add a new hard drive to Windows Home Server's pool, *everything* on that new hard drive gets obliterated. You don't have any choice. No data on the drive survives — it's all wiped out. That's the price the drive pays for being absorbed into the Windows Home Server Borg-collective.

✔ Don't unplug an external hard drive (or remove an internal hard drive) until you've told Windows Home Server, in advance, that you intend to remove it. While the results may not be totally catastrophic if you have Folder Duplication turned on, you still may end up losing the data on the drive. It ain't nice to fool Mother Home Server.

✔ If you add more than one USB hard drive, don't have any two of them share an external USB hub, unless the hub is a fancy one that reserves full bandwidth for each port. Those cheap hubs are mighty handy when you need extra USB ports. But hard drives need to run quickly, and plug-in hubs create bottlenecks worse than O'Hare in a snowstorm.

Knowing When and What to Feed the Maw

Windows Home Server lets you know, loud and clear, when it wants more hard drives. It's as subtle as Audrey II in *Little Shop of Horrors*. "Feed Me, Seymour!"

As soon as your main hard drive, the System hard drive, gets down to 5 GB of free space, you see a warning like that in Figure 18-1 every time you log on to any computer on your home or office network.

Figure 18-1:
It's time to get more storage.

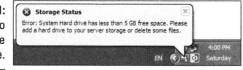

If you see a message like the one in Figure 18-1, head over to the Windows Home Server Console and take a look at your current (not yet desperate!) status:

1. **On any computer that's hooked up to your Windows Home Server server, double-click the (now red!) Windows Home Server icon in the notification area, near the system clock.**

   Windows Home Server invites you to log on to the Console.

2. **Type the server's password, and press Enter.**

   The Windows Home Server Console appears.

3. **Up at the top, click the icon that says Network Critical.**

   The Console shows you why it's gone ga-ga. At a minimum, it tells you that the System hard drive is running out of space. In addition, you may see (as in Figure 18-2) that backups have failed.

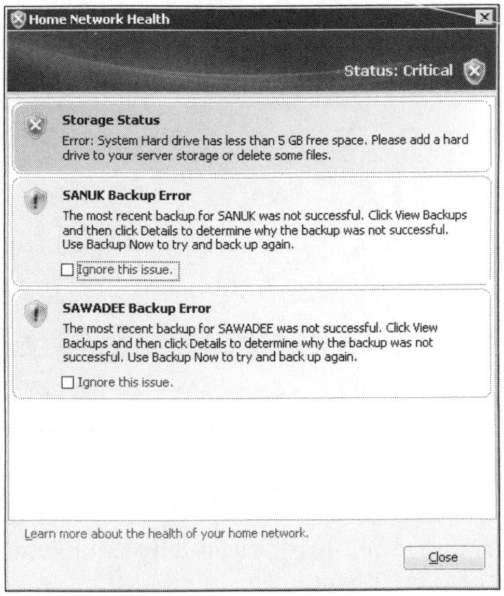

Home Network Health

Status: Critical

Storage Status
Error: System Hard drive has less than 5 GB free space. Please add a hard drive to your server storage or delete some files.

SANUK Backup Error
The most recent backup for SANUK was not successful. Click View Backups and then click Details to determine why the backup was not successful. Use Backup Now to try and back up again.
☐ Ignore this issue.

SAWADEE Backup Error
The most recent backup for SAWADEE was not successful. Click View Backups and then click Details to determine why the backup was not successful. Use Backup Now to try and back up again.
☐ Ignore this issue.

Learn more about the health of your home network.

Close

Figure 18-2: The System hard drive's too big for its britches.

4. **Don't panic. You still have room for essential activities. In fact, if you wait a day, the warning may go away (Drive Extender is smart enough to balance things out, if the situation isn't too dire). But resign yourself to the fact that you need another hard drive.**

You can try to delete data in the shared folders, but if those folders are duplicated (see Chapter 5), the duplicate copies stick around. In my experience, trying piecemeal solutions to reduce server-side data bulge only delays the inevitable — and usually not very long. Save up your shekels and go buy a drive.

Even if everything is working fine (as it is in Figure 18-3), Windows Home Server raises the alarm when the System hard drive has less than 5 GB available.

Figure 18-3:
A perfectly healthy drive that's dipped below the 5GB-free-space mark.

What makes drives fail?

At the February 2007 Usenix conference, researchers at Carnegie-Mellon released a study on the Mean Time Between Failure (MTBF) rates for various kinds of hard drives (www.usenix.org/events/fast07/tech/schroeder.html). Their conclusion: The number-one cause of hard-drive failure is age. There's very little difference between brands, and the manufacturer's MTBF ratings are laughable. Drive-failure rates rise when you get to around five years of service, and after seven years the rate goes way up. It doesn't matter whether you're using SATA, SCSI, or some more-esoteric technology. The environment doesn't mean much. When drives get old, they die. It's that simple.

Vendor MTBF ratings didn't correlate with the experienced failure rates. Drives with an MTBF rating of 1 million hours should (in theory) fail, on average, after 110 years of service. In practice, they fail after six or seven years, on average.

Google published a paper at the same conference (el-in-f132.google.com/papers/disk_failures.pdf), based on data from 100,000 hard drives, that shows heat doesn't kill hard drives, nor does overwork! You can let a drive go up to 100 degrees Fahrenheit with impunity. Making a hard drive work all the time doesn't make it fail. Failure rates during the first three months of use are high, regardless of the type of drive, but if your drive makes it through the first three months, it'll take a beating and keep on ticking. Or twirling at least. Go figger.

Moral of the story: buy drives based on price-per-gigabyte, and don't be afraid to use them heavily, in a relatively hot environment.

When you go shopping for another hard drive, keep a few points in mind:

- ✔ If you have an old drive lying around, use it! Windows Home Server recognizes drives as small as 8 GB. As long as heat isn't a major concern, using an old drive makes a lot of sense. (Stick too many drives in a small space and your server may turn into a chip-cookhouse.) But remember, all the data on the old drive will be wiped out.

- ✔ Drive speed doesn't mean much, and when you're backing up in the middle of the night, it doesn't mean anything at all. Go for capacity.

- ✔ Hard drives, at least among major brands, are a commodity. No single manufacturer makes better (or worse) drives than the others, although the length of the warranty may be important to you. Compare drives using bucks-per-byte.

- ✔ When it comes to performance and overnight backups, there's very little noticeable difference between internal and external drives, as long as you don't use USB 1 drives (ancient technology that runs at one-fortieth the speed of USB 2) and you attach each drive to its own USB port, instead of ganging them up on a cheap external USB hub. If you frequently bang around big files in shared folders on the server, though, SATA drives (internal or external) are hard to beat.

    If you run out of USB ports on your server, and the computer supports eSATA (external SATA), that's the fastest and most reliable way to attach external drives. Check with your hardware manufacturer for details.

    Failing eSATA, buy a generic PCI card with four (or more) ports. They're cheap, they drop into the computer easily, they rarely have any driver problems, and they're fast.

- ✔ External drive enclosures are cheap, and they work fine. If there's a significant price difference between internal and external drives of the same capacity, buy the internal drive (which should always be cheaper) and put it in an external drive enclosure. You can do it yourself in just a few minutes with nothing more complicated than a screwdriver.

Adding a New Internal Hard Drive

If you've ever struggled with adding a new hard drive to a Windows machine, your first experience adding an internal hard drive to a Windows Home Server server should have you dancing in the streets.

Here's how:

1. **Shut down the server. From the Windows Home Server console (see the preceding section), in the upper right, click the Settings icon, and then at the lower left click Shut Down (see Figure 18-4).**

   Wait a few minutes for all the lights to go out on the server. The Windows Home Server icon in the notification area grays out as the server goes gentle into that good night.

Windows Home Server Settings

General	**Date & Time**
Backup	6/19/2007 12:50 PM Change...
Passwords	**Region**
Media Sharing	English (United States)
Remote Access	**Windows Update**
Add-ins	⦿ On (recommended) Update Now...
Resources	✓ Install updates automatically.
	○ Off (not recommended)
	✗ Do not check for updates.
	? How does Windows Update help protect my home server?
	Customer Experience Improvement
	☐ Help make Windows Home Server better. Sign up for the Customer Experience Improvement Program.
	Read our Privacy Statement
	Windows Error Reporting
	☐ Turn on Automatic Windows Error Reporting (recommended)
	Learn more about Windows Error Reporting
Shut Down	
	OK Cancel Apply Help

Figure 18-4:
Shut down the server via the Windows Home Server console.

2. **Crack open the server's case and install the hard drive.**

   Any data on the drive will be nuked. Zapped. Sent to the big bit bucket in the sky. If you need any data on the drive, copy it to another computer before you stick it in the server!

   If you're using older IDE technology, you have to be careful to get the jumper on the drive set right. Follow the manufacturer's recommendations for the jumper setting ("Cable Select" is a good first guess) and for the best place to hook up the drive's cable connection. Note that you probably don't have a CD drive on your server, so any IDE controller that's normally used for the CD drive is fair game.

   If you have newer SATA-II drives, you don't need to worry about cable orientation or jumpers. Just get them plugged in and screwed down.

3. **Don't follow the manufacturer's instructions for installing drivers.**

   At least 99 percent of the time, you don't need them. (If it ends up that you absolutely must install a driver manually, scream at the hard drive manufacturer, and refer to Chapter 17 for instructions on digging into the server.)

4. **Put the server back together and turn it on.**

   Wait a few minutes for the connections to re-establish. The icon in the notification area goes back to red when the server's ready for action.

5. **Double-click the Windows Home Server icon in the notification area, type in the server's password, and press Enter.**

   The Windows Home Server Console appears, with your new hard drive identified as a "Non-Storage Hard Drive." I think that's like having a "non-seating chair," but I digress. (See Figure 18-5.)

6. **Right-click the hard drive's id number (WHS hard drives don't have names) and choose Add.**

   The Add a Hard Drive Wizard appears.

7. **Click Next.**

   The wizard warns you, with absolutely no waffling, that the data on the drive is going to be wiped out, utterly, completely.

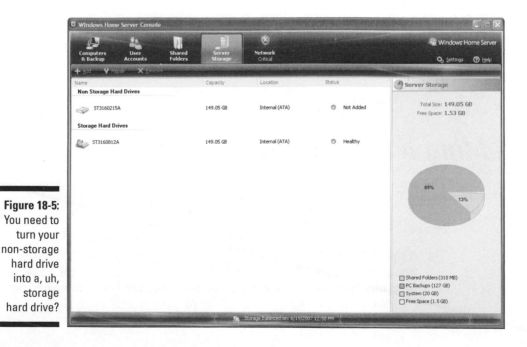

Figure 18-5:
You need to turn your non-storage hard drive into a, uh, storage hard drive?

8. **If you're ready, click Finish.**

It may take a while, but when your hard drive's been absorbed into the Windows Home Server Borg-equivalent, you see a message like that in Figure 18-6.

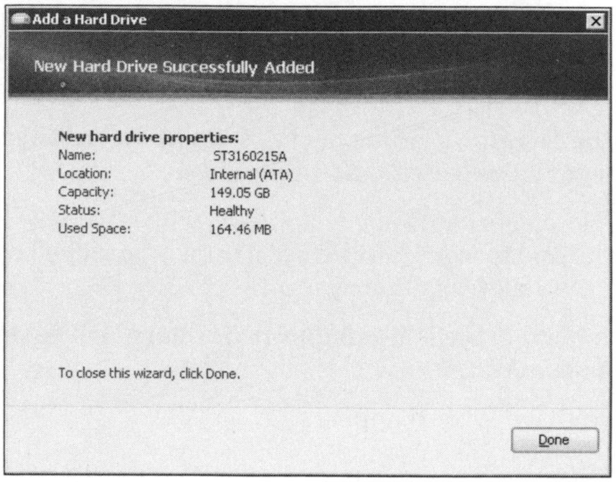

Figure 18-6:
(Burp!) The server has finished absorbing your new drive.

9. **Click Done.**

Go back into the Windows Home Server console, click the Server Storage icon, and your new drive now appears in the Storage Hard Drive area. It may take awhile — maybe even overnight — for the server to make full use of the new drive, but when it's done, you don't have to worry about a thing.

Easy, eh?

Adding a New External Hard Drive

The procedure for adding a new external, USB- (or, rarely, FireWire-) attached hard drive is so easy you could probably do it in your sleep.

Here's how:

1. **Go to any computer on your home or office network, double-click the Windows Home Server icon in the notification area, type the server's password, press Enter and, up at the top, click the Server Storage icon.**

2. **Plug the new drive's USB cable into the server.**

   You've probably heard this before: *Any data on the drive will be nuked. Zapped. Sent to the big bit bucket in the sky.* If you need any data on the drive, copy it to another computer before you plug it into the server!

   Your new drive appears as a Non-Storage Hard Drive in the drive list.

3. **Right-click the hard drive's number and choose Add.**

   The Add a Hard Drive Wizard appears, the same one shown at the end of its work in Figure 18-6 (earlier in this chapter).

4. **Click Next.**

   The wizard warns you that the data on the drive is going to be wiped out, utterly, completely.

5. **If you're ready, click Finish.**

   When Windows Home Server finishes formatting the drive, you see a message that tells you the deed is done.

6. **Click Done.**

   The USB drive appears in the storage list, ready for action (see Figure 18-7).

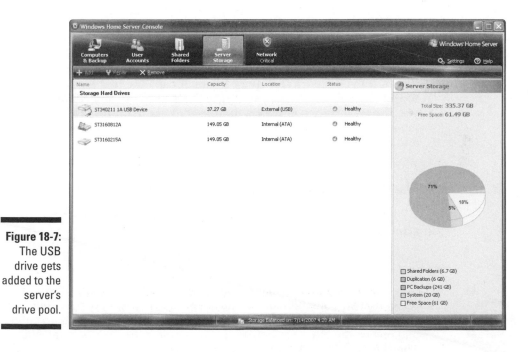

Figure 18-7:
The USB drive gets added to the server's drive pool.

Retiring an Old Drive Safely

If you want to upgrade a hard drive on your server, it's safest to install the new hard drive first, let Windows Home Server take overnight to get things balanced out, and then remove the old hard drive.

But if you can't install the new hard drive in advance (for example, if you don't have enough internal hard-drive slots), you can try removing the old hard drive first. If you go that route, Windows Home Server does its level best to get the data shuffled off, minimizing your chances of losing anything, and warning you of the consequences. If you can get the old drive off and then install a new one, WHS will automatically balance things — dumping all the data on the new hard drive when it's installed.

Windows Home Server can't magically stuff data in places that don't exist — and it isn't smart enough to copy data from the server onto the network's other computers — so it's important that you follow the Remove a Hard Drive Wizard's instructions quite precisely.

If you want to remove a hard drive that's currently attached to your Windows Home Server server — maybe it's starting to smoke and screech like a banshee, or you really need the hard drive to stick in a different computer — the process is easy, as long as you have enough space.

Here's how to put a drive into forced retirement:

1. **Wait until you have a few spare hours. It can take that long, or longer, to remove a drive. When you've got the time, go to any computer on your home or office network, double-click the Windows Home Server icon in the notification area, type the server's password, press Enter and, up at the top, click the Server Storage icon.**

   You see a list of the drives on the server, much like the one in Figure 18-7.

2. **Right-click the drive you want to retire and choose Remove.**

   Windows Home Server cranks up the Remove a Hard Drive Wizard.

3. **Click Next.**

   The wizard checks the drive to see if any users on the network have files on the drive open. You see a report like the one in Figure 18-8.

Note that media folders may be open for no apparent reason. If you go to the computers mentioned and check, though, you will probably find that the offending users are running Windows Media Player or Media Center, and one or the other (or both) is set to monitor the folders in question. The solution: Close Media Player or Media Center.

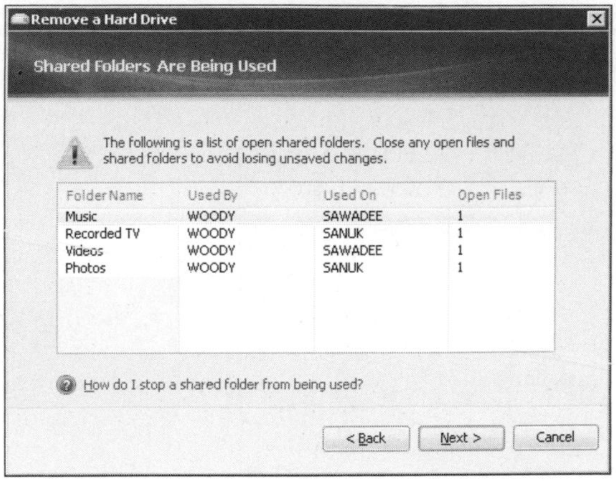

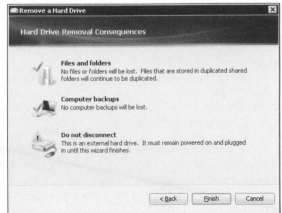

Figure 18-8:
Several
users (all
mysteriously
named
WOODY)
have open
files on the
drive.

4. **Go to the identified computers and close the offending folders. If you can't get the folder closed, reboot the computer. Once you have all of the open folders closed, click Next.**

   The wizard looks at the drive you want to remove, and analyzes whether the data on the drive will fit on the remaining drives.

   - If you have enough room, you see an analysis like the one in Figure 18-9.

   - If you *don't* have enough room, you get the warning shown in Figure 18-10.

Figure 18-9:
Everything
is ready for
the drive to
be removed.

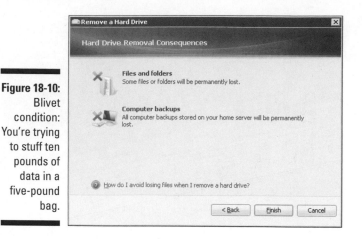

5. **If you're very, very sure that you still want to remove the drive, click Finish.**

   Windows Home Server slowly, methodically moves data from the removed drive to other drives on the server, discarding backups if necessary. The process can take hours. Many hours, for a large drive. When it's done, the wizard hoists a `Hard Drive Successfully Removed` message into view.

6. **Click Done.**

   Now you can remove the drive. If it's an external drive, simply pull the plug and disconnect the drive. If it's an internal drive, crack open the server and take it out.

It's important to understand that Windows Home Server removes the *drive*, it doesn't remove the *data*. The data on the drive can be recovered. In some cases, it's in an odd compressed format; in many cases it's in simple, everyday folders and files.

If you suddenly get that "oops" sensation — you should've pulled some files off the drive before removing it — plug the drive into another computer and take a look. You may be pleasantly surprised.

On the other hand, if you store sensitive data anywhere on your network — *please* tell me you don't have millions of veterans' names and Social Security numbers (www.epic.org/privacy/vatheft) — you better wipe that disk clean before you even think of selling it at a flea market. Check out DBAN at dban. sourceforge.net for pointers.

Chapter 19

Repairing and Recovering the Server

....

In This Chapter

▶ Knowing what to do if you lose the server password

▶ Repairing Windows Home Server without wiping out all your data

▶ Recovering from a broken hard drive

▶ Rebuilding your Windows Home Server server if the main drive fails

....

*C*hances are good, if you're reading this chapter, that you're standing neck-deep in a swamp of alligators.

Whether you lost your server's password, you think Windows Home Server has given up the ghost, or one or another of the drives on your server has spun its last, this chapter fills you in on the gory details.

Be of good cheer.

It probably ain't as bad as you think.

The folks who designed Windows Home Server built in hooks for precisely these problems. As long as you know where and how to latch onto the hooks, chances are very good you can get your server back up and running, with no lost data. It may take quite a few hours, but sooner or later you should be back on your feet.

Although Microsoft built a set of specific restore capabilities into Windows Home Server, different hardware manufacturers may have different ways of restoring the server — and your hardware manufacturer's method may *not* rely on Microsoft's approach.

> ✔ If you received three discs with your server, and one of the discs is marked "Windows Home Server Installation DVD" or something similar, *and* your server has a bootable DVD drive, the methods in this chapter will work.

✔ On the other hand, if you bought a server with Windows Home Server preinstalled, and you didn't get any CDs, you need to *check with your server's manufacturer* before manually running any repair or recovery routines. You should be able to find the recovery information on the manufacturer's Web site. Chances are good that the manufacturer has a recovery disc image stuck away somewhere — possibly in a hidden place on one of the drives inside the server. There may be some other magic incantation necessary to get your server password reset, or to RebuildPrimary — rebuild the main drive inside the server.

Dealing with Lost Passwords

If you forgot the password for your account on the server, resetting it is easy — as long as you know the server's password.

I go into detail in Chapter 4, but here's the short version:

1. **Log on to any home or office computer. Right-click the Windows Home Server icon in the notification area, near the clock, and choose Windows Home Server Console. Type the server's password and press Enter.**

   The Windows Home Server Console appears.

2. **Click the User Accounts icon at the top.**

   A list of users defined on the server appears, as in Figure 19-1.

3. **Double-click the account you want to change and click the button marked Change Password.**

   The Change Password dialog box appears.

4. **Type the new password twice and click OK.**

   You *don't have to type in the old password*, which means anyone who knows the server's password can change any user's password at any time.

Resetting a forgotten user password is easy. But if you forgot the server's password, you're in for some interesting times.

When you originally typed in the server's password — back when you set up the first computer on the network — you had to type in a password hint. If you can't remember the server's password, make sure you check the hint (if you haven't already) to see if it jogs your memory:

1. **Log on to any home or office computer. Double-click the Windows Home Server icon in the notification area.**

   The Windows Home Server logon screen appears.

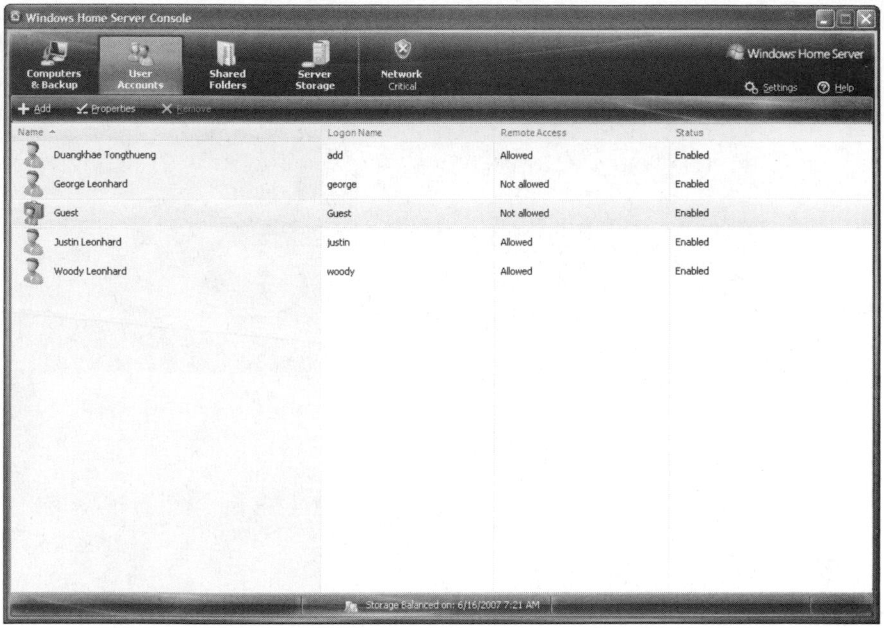

Figure 19-1:
Changing a
user's
password is
easy, if you
know the
server's
password.

2. **Click the down-wedge to the right of Options and choose Password Hint.**

   Windows Home Server shows you the password hint you typed when
   you originally set up the password. (See Figure 19-2.)

If the password hint doesn't help you remember the password, you only have
one alternative — reinstall Windows Home Server. Because your server's
hard drives are intact, you won't lose any data during a reinstallation, but
you will lose some other things:

- ✔ **All your Windows Home Server settings.** Basically everything you set in
  the Options part of the Windows Home Server Console is irretrievably
  clobbered.

- ✔ **All the server's user names ("logon IDs") and passwords.** Re-establishing
  the user names and passwords is a pain in the neck, but if you go to
  each computer on your network and methodically add all the existing
  users, one by one, you'll get there.

- ✔ **Any add-ins you may have installed.** If you put the add-in installation
  file(s) in a shared folder, such as the one called `Software`, those files will
  survive the reinstallation of Windows Home Server. But you'll have to go
  back and reinstall each add-in individually after the WHS reinstallation is
  complete.

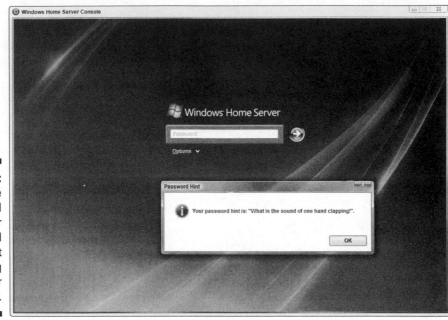

Figure 19-2:
If you chose
a good
server
password
hint, it
should jog
your
memory.

In addition, after you reinstall Windows Home Server, you need to go to each computer on your network and reinstall the Windows Home Server Connect CD. The second time around, the steps are the same, so see Part II of this book, which explains the basics of setting up your server.

If your Windows Home Server server came with three discs, I show you how to reinstall WHS in the section "Repairing the primary drive," later in this chapter. If the company that sold you Windows Home Server didn't send you three discs, you need to get on the Internet, visit the vendor's site, and find out how they recommend you proceed.

Fixing a Broken Server Hard Drive

Three-alarm time. Smoke's pouring out of your server, and it smells like the starting line at Lions Drag Strip. Maybe you start hearing the unmistakable snap, crackle, and pop of a hard drive dying, or the wimpy click-click-click-it of one already gone.

Hey, it happens. What spins up must spin down.

As long as you have Folder Duplication enabled (see Chapter 5) for all your important shared folders on the server, you probably won't lose any data. It may take a day or two to recover completely — restore the server's data, get all your home or office computer backups running again — and you have to jump through several hoops to get there, but almost all the time, Windows Home Server has the smarts to heal itself.

Primary versus secondary drives

Windows Home Server uses a system called Drive Extender to manage all hard drives on the server — internal drives, external drives, any and all drives get absorbed into the Drive Extender Borg-equivalent.

The first drive in your server — the one that holds the Windows Home Server system files — is different from all the others. Variously known as the *primary drive*, *primary disk*, *system drive*, and other (less printable) appellations, the first drive is what Drive Extender splits into two partitions:

 ✔ The smaller partition (known as the C: drive, and you can see that its name is SYS if you dig deep enough into the server) holds system files, system details (like the list of users and passwords), certain housekeeping files, and add-in programs you've installed. If you're curious about the kind of housekeeping files involved, read about *tombstones* at

    `msmvps.com/blogs/ulfbsimonweidner/archive/2005/10.aspx`

    Windows Home Server allocates 20 GB for this system partition.

 ✔ The larger partition (known as the D: drive, called DATA, if you look hard enough) holds data. No system files, no internal housekeeping files. Just plain data.

If you have more than one drive, all the other drives hold data. Some of the data (particularly backups of your home or office computers) may be completely illegible. Some of the data may be duplicated, if you have folder duplication enabled for any shared folders on the server. But it's all data.

The big difference between the primary drive and all the other drives is the presence of the Windows Home Server program and supporting files. If one of your other drives dies, Windows Home Server knows enough to kick in, restore missing data, and get on with doing server stuff. If your *primary* hard drive dies, though, it takes along Windows Home Server itself. As you might expect, if your primary hard drive heads south in a hand basket, you need to reinstall Windows Home Server before you can do anything else.

What if you don't know primary from secondary?

Hey, I only work here.

At least, that's how you might feel if you don't know whether the drive that just died is the primary drive (the one with Windows Home Server on it), or a secondary drive. I mean, it isn't like the drives have the words "Primary" and "Secondary" painted on them in Day-Glo orange.

If you aren't sure whether the dead drive is a primary or secondary drive, don't sweat it. Replace the drive. Turn on the server. Wait a few minutes, and then try to bring up the Windows Home Server Console. If the Windows Home Server Console comes up (see Step 3 in the "Replacing a broken secondary drive" section), you just replaced a secondary drive. If the computer sits there staring at you with a dumb expression on its face — it doesn't boot, and you can't get into the Windows Home Server Console — you know you just replaced the primary drive, and you have to use the more complex procedure in the "Repairing the primary drive" section.

Replacing a broken secondary drive

If one of your secondary hard drives turns into a jagged bucket of broken bits, replacing it and restoring your data couldn't be simpler — as long as you had folder duplication enabled for your shared folders. Here's all you have to do:

1. **Turn off your server, remove the dead drive, and stick in a new one.**

   You can use internal or external drives, IDE or ATA or SATA or SATA II or SATA III or PATA or IATA (well, you get the idea). There's no reason at all to replace a dead drive with another drive that's even remotely similar — although it never hurts to stick in a bigger hard drive than the old one. See Chapter 18 for my recommendations on buying new hard drives for Windows Home Server.

2. **Turn on the server.**

   Give it a few minutes to get re-established.

3. **Log on to any home or office computer. Double-click the Windows Home Server icon in the notification area, near the clock. Type the server's password and press Enter.**

   You see the Windows Home Server Console.

4. **Click the icon marked Server Storage.**

   Windows Home Server reports, per Figure 19-3, that the old, dead drive is Missing (not surprising because you just threw it on the ground as hard as you could and stomped on it), and that the new drive is available, but Not Added.

Figure 19-3:
The dead drive is Missing, and the new drive appears as Not Added.

5. **Right-click the Not Added drive and choose Add.**

   The Add a Hard Drive Wizard appears. I take you through the steps for adding a new hard drive in Chapter 18. The wizard is quite simple; it mostly exists to remind you that any data on the hard drive will be wiped out.

6. **In the wizard, click Next, then Finish. When the wizard's done formatting the hard drive, click Done.**

   Immediately after you click Done, Windows Home Server moves all the data in duplicated folders onto the new hard drive. You see an icon at the bottom of the screen that says `Balancing Storage`.

7. **Back in the Server Storage listing (Figure 19-3), right-click the Missing dead drive and choose Remove.**

   Windows Home Server brings up the Remove a Hard Drive Wizard (which I also discuss in Chapter 18).

8. **Click Next.**

   Not realizing that you have already eviscerated the offending dead drive and seriously contemplated subjecting it to a blowtorch disk-wipe, Windows Home Server ventures the opinion that the hard drive is not connected (see Figure 19-4).

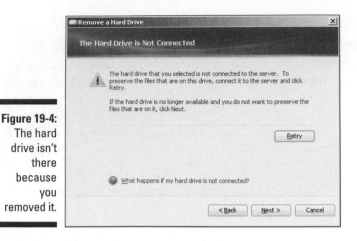

Figure 19-4:
The hard drive isn't there because you removed it.

The warning in Figure 19-4 — If the hard drive is no longer available and you do not want to preserve the files that are on it, click Next — is a bit of a red herring. In fact, unless you have been contending with "Storage Status" health warnings (see Chapter 20), all the important files that were on the hard drive — which is to say, the files stored in shared folders on the server that had folder duplication enabled — will come through just fine if you click Next. It's true that relatively unimportant files (such as the ones in shared folders without duplication, and backed-up files from your home and office computers) may not survive, but the important ones always will.

9. Click Next.

If you're lucky, Windows Home Server reports, as in Figure 19-5, that you won't even lose any backups from your home and office computers.

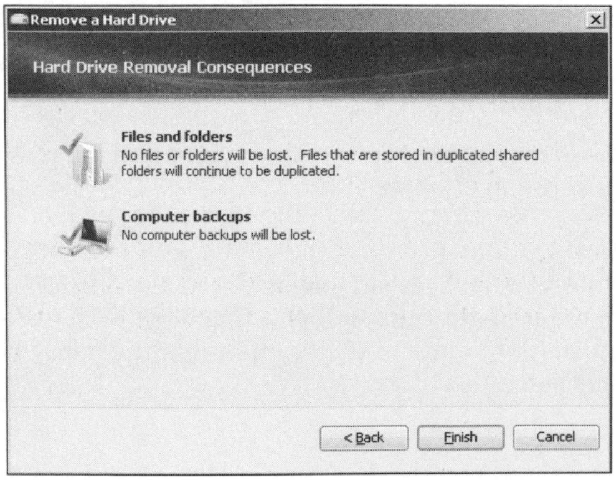

Figure 19-5:
You got lucky: Absolutely no data will be lost, although the original drive is simmering on the floor.

10. **Click Finish.**

    Although the wizard may warn you that it can take several hours to remove the missing hard drive, it rarely takes anywhere near that long.

11. **When the wizard says that your hard drive was successfully removed, click Done. Then wait.**

    It may take awhile for WHS to copy all the duplicated folders over to the new hard drive — to "balance" its storage. And the process will certainly take overnight — maybe several nights — to replenish any missing backups of your home or office computers. But sooner or later, with absolutely no additional effort on your part, everything that was on the old, dead drive (with the exception of the contents of unduplicated shared folders on the server) gets copied to the new whippersnapper.

This has to be one of the smoothest restores in the computer business, right up there with hot-swappable RAID systems that cost a fortune. Quite remarkable.

Repairing the primary drive

So what happens if your server's primary hard drive — the one that contains Windows Home Server's files — disappears?

The answer: not much.

In official Microsoft parlance, you need to *reinstall* Windows Home Server. You have to run a Server Reinstallation when the hard drive containing the system dies. You may also be told to run a Server Reinstallation if something really bad happens to your system. (More often than not, WHS gets blasted irreparably if you happen to screw something up while breaking into your server, per Chapter 17.) Perhaps surprisingly, you also need to perform a Server Reinstallation if you forget the server's password. There's no magic reset disk. No royal road to changing the server's password. You have to reinstall and create a new password.

That'll teach ya to remember your password.

When you reinstall Windows Home Server, the Server Reinstallation routine basically wipes out everything in the 20GB primary disk partition (discussed earlier in this chapter in the section "Primary versus secondary drives"). You can think of it as reformatting the C: drive and reinstalling from scratch.

Note, however, that the primary disk partition *doesn't hold any data*. So if you reinstall Windows Home Server, you don't wipe out any data at all. Many people find that hard to believe, so it bears repeating: reinstalling Windows Home Server knocks out a few of your settings (such as user names and passwords), and it clobbers your add-ons, but you don't lose *any* data. The Server Reinstallation routine is smart enough to avoid touching anything on the second partition on the first disk (the "D: drive"), and it doesn't do anything to any other drives, if they exist. The reinstaller wipes the primary partition clean, reinstalls Windows Home Server, and then runs a program called *RebuildPrimary* that scans all the data on the second partition and any other hard drives, reconstructing the internal tables necessary to keep Windows Home Server alive and well.

Follow the upcoming steps if . . .

- ✔ **You forgot your server's password.** This time pick a better hint and write the password down and stick it in the safe, OK?

- ✔ **Windows Home Server starts acting really flakey.** If you can't get the Windows Home Server Console to come up on any home or office computer, and you've tried restarting the server and restarting the network computers many times, you may need to run a Server Reinstallation. Ditto if Windows Home Server starts crashing or locking up for no apparent reason.

You might want to run the hard drive manufacturer's diagnostic routine on the flakey primary drive, but it's probably best to retire the drive, stick it in a Windows Vista or XP computer, run the diagnostic, and then reinstall the drive from scratch in your server.

- ✔ **The primary hard drive on your server dies.** In that case, tear out the old drive, stick in a new one, brace yourself for several hours of down time, and follow along here.

In order to run a reinstall, you must . . .

- ✔ **Have the "Windows Home Server Installation DVD" in your hand, along with its product key.** If your server manufacturer didn't give you an Installation DVD, you can't use Microsoft's method for reinstalling the server. Get on the manufacturer's Web site, and seek divine guidance.

- ✔ **Be able to boot your server from a DVD.** For most systems, that means you either have a DVD drive in the server, or you attach a DVD drive via a USB cable and tell your server's BIOS that it needs to boot from the DVD. For instructions on changing the BIOS so the server boots from DVD, check the manufacturer's Web site.

- ✔ **Attach a monitor and keyboard (and usually a mouse) to your server.** You can't run a reinstall on a headless computer.

✔ If you're reinstalling Windows Home Server on a working hard drive, you don't need to worry about this part, but **if you replaced the primary hard drive, the new hard drive must be recognized as the "first" hard drive by your server's BIOS.** Again, check your hardware manufacturer's site for BIOS instructions.

So you have a monitor, keyboard and mouse hooked up to your server, and you can boot from a DVD. Here's how to reinstall Windows Home Server:

1. **Turn the server off. Place the Windows Home Server Installation DVD in the DVD drive, and turn on the server.**

   The Windows installer loads its files, initializes setup, and the Windows Home Server Setup Wizard appears.

2. **Click Next.**

   You see a hard drive list like the one in Figure 19-6. If you're reinstalling Windows Home Server and you want to keep your data intact, it's *vital* that WHS correctly identify all your hard drives. Your primary drive should have a 20GB partition called SYS (that's where WHS puts its programs and settings), and the rest of the first drive and all subsequent drives should be called DATA.

   If the hard-drive list in Figure 19-6 isn't correct, stop everything that you're doing and make sure you get the correct drivers installed so WHS will "see" all your hard drives. (Refer to Chapter 18 for tips on getting the drivers right.)

3. **Verify that WHS sees all your hard drives correctly, and click Next.**

   The Setup Wizard asks you to select an installation type (see Figure 19-7).

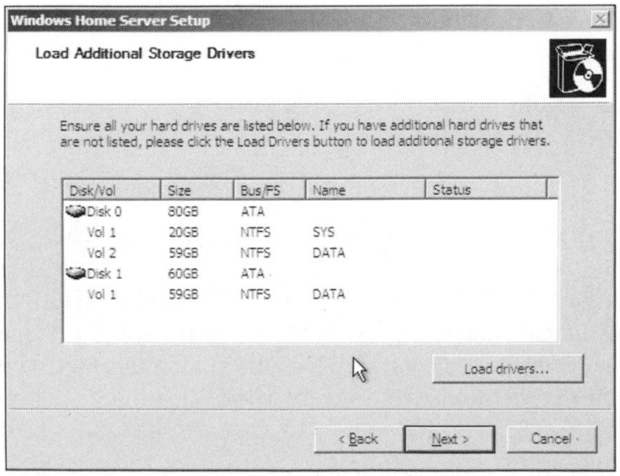

Figure 19-6: Be very sure that WHS correctly identifies your hard drives.

Figure 19-7:
If you
want to
save
your server
data, always
choose
Server
reinstal-
lation.

Windows Home Server Setup

Select an Installation Type

What type of install do you want to perform?

Installation Type: Server Reinstallation

Choose this option to reinstall your Windows Home Server operating system.

IMPORTANT: Your installed programs and settings will be lost.

Your Computer Backups and Shared Folder content will be preserved.

< Back   Next >   Cancel

4. **Choose Server Reinstallation. Click Next.**

   Don't choose the other installation type, which is called "New Installation." A "New Installation" wipes all the data off all your drives, and you can't ever get it back.

   The Server Reinstallation routine asks you to pick your time and currency format and your keyboard language. Then it asks you to read a 10,000-word legal document "carefully." (Hey, the folks who built this installer certainly had a sense of humor.)

5. **Make the obvious choices, type in your product key, and keep clicking Next.**

   The Server Reinstallation routine asks you to pick a memorable name for your Windows Home Server.

6. **Unless you have a good reason for changing it, stick with the name** SERVER **and click Next.**

   The Server Reinstallation program tells you that it's ready to install Windows Home Server (see Figure 19-8).

7. **Click Start.**

   Although the Setup screen warns you that it can take hours to install Windows Home Server, in fact you're not *only* reinstalling WHS — and the whole thing can take a long, long time. The Server Reinstallation routine kicks in after the reinstallation finishes and runs a program called RebuildPrimary that scans every piece of data on every drive in your server, rebuilding all the internal tables that WHS needs to keep the server running, the shared files sharing, and the backups backing. The process can take many, many hours.

Figure 19-8:
The Server
Reinstalla-
tion routine
can take it
from here.

8. **Wait.**

When Windows Home Server is finally reinstalled, many reboots later, you see the Windows Home Server Caution page (it's actually a page displayed using Internet Explorer) showed in Figure 19-9. That tells you the reinstallation went without a hitch.

Figure 19-9:
This page
shows
when the
reinstalla-
tion finishes
properly.

9. **Turn off the server — and then disconnect the monitor, keyboard, and mouse. Move the server to its usual home, and turn it back on again. Wait a few minutes for it to stabilize.**

   You're ready to set up your network again.

10. **Follow the steps in Chapter 3 and, one by one, run the Windows Home Server Connector CD on each computer on your network.**

    This step establishes the backup connection with the newly refurbished server.

11. **Follow the steps in Chapter 4 and add users to the server, setting passwords, and synchronizing passwords between the server and individual computers.**

12. **Follow the steps in Chapter 5 to set access permissions for shared folders.**

    Don't forget to turn on Folder Duplication. As you know by now, it's important.

Congratulations. You just passed the advanced course.

Any time you feel enormously frustrated, ready to throw your server out the window, try to think of how life used to be, before you had all those backups. Whooooooo-eeee.

Part VII
The Part of Tens

The 5th Wave   By Rich Tennant

ⒸRICHTENNANT

"I'm not saying I believe in anything. All I know is since it's been there our server is running 50% faster."

In this part . . .

Dan Gookin's pioneering work *DOS For Dummies* — the first, legendary *For Dummies* book that spawned an entire book-writing genre — included a section in the back devoted to Dan's "top ten" lists of all sorts of things, from advice to arcana to admonishments, incantations, and invocations.

In that same spirit, I offer you two of my own top ten lists: a quick reference for Windows Home Server health alerts, and a handful of interesting starting points for new and different things you can do with your own Home Server.

Windows Home Server is a fascinating product that can keep the twiddler in you going for weeks. This part points the way to the future — and shows you what to do if your network gets the hiccups along the way.

Chapter 20

Top Ten Health Traps Triaged

In This Chapter

▶ The most likely causes of Network Health Indicator warnings, and some solutions

▶ Warnings from Vista computers only — antivirus, antispyware problems

▶ When backups go bad

▶ Notices that your server is having difficulties — and what you can do about it

*I*n Chapter 16, I talk about the Network Health Indicator — the Windows Home Server icon that sits in the notification area, near the clock, of every computer on your network. When all is well network-wide, the iconic house glows green and all is right in the world. But when things start getting a bit shady, the icon turns yellow or red, and may start sprouting annoying Chicken Little pop-up messages like the one in Figure 20-1.

Figure 20-1:
In spite of the pop-up message, the sky probably isn't falling.

> ⊗ Your home network health is critical.
> To open the Windows Home Server Console, click here.
> Then click the Network Health button to view the details.

If you get a Chicken Little message, double-click the Windows Home Server icon, type the server's password in the indicated box, and press Enter. The Windows Home Server Console appears. Click the Network health icon and, if Chicken Little has gone yellow or red, you see a status report like the one in Figure 20-2.

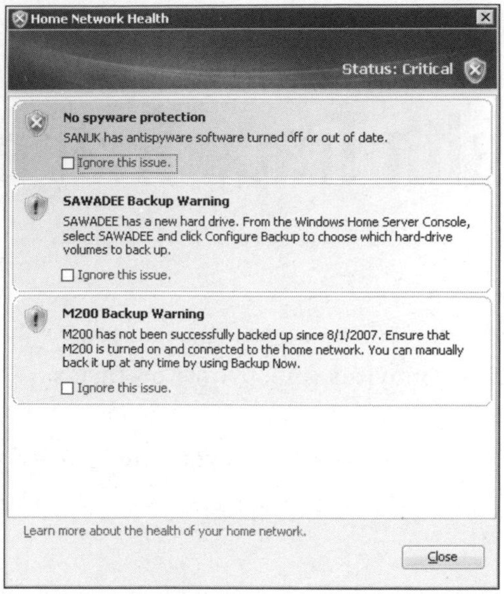

Home Network Health

Status: Critical

No spyware protection
SANUK has antispyware software turned off or out of date.
☐ Ignore this issue.

SAWADEE Backup Warning
SAWADEE has a new hard drive. From the Windows Home Server Console, select SAWADEE and click Configure Backup to choose which hard-drive volumes to back up.
☐ Ignore this issue.

M200 Backup Warning
M200 has not been successfully backed up since 8/1/2007. Ensure that M200 is turned on and connected to the home network. You can manually back it up at any time by using Backup Now.
☐ Ignore this issue.

Learn more about the health of your home network.

Close

Figure 20-2:
A fairly common health report is full of sound and fury, signifying little.

With apologies to Douglas Adams, DON'T PANIC. Problems listed in the Network Health report usually have mundane causes and simple solutions. Usually.

This chapter lists the ten health "issues" I've encountered most often, shows you the likely cause of each "issue," and gives you a quick suggestion for correcting the problem.

Microsoft loves to use the word "issue" because it doesn't sound as intimidating as "problem" or "this is screwed up" or "horked" or any of a few hundred other phrases that are far more descriptive (only some of which are printable). Personally, I avoid the word "issue" unless I'm talking about a magazine. You could say I have an issue with "issue."

No Spyware Protection

Likely cause: Windows Defender hasn't been updated in the past day or two (see Figure 20-3). The message may appear when other antispyware programs don't get updated, but I've only seen it to refer to Microsoft's Windows Defender.

Figure 20-3:
A critical error.

No spyware protection
SANUK has antispyware software turned off or out of date.

As mentioned in Chapter 16, you only get this warning for Vista computers. Windows Defender could turn belly-up and swim in circles for weeks on a Windows XP computer, and Windows Home Server wouldn't be any the wiser.

Likely solution: Go to the computer reporting the problem (in Figure 20-3, it's the computer called SANUK) and log on. If the Windows Defender icon (which looks like a castle wall; refer to Figure 20-1) has an exclamation point on it, double-click the icon, and then click the button that says Check For Updates Now. Click Continue on the User Account Control warning, let Windows Defender update itself, and your Windows Home Server icon should revert to green in a few minutes.

Windows Defender running on Vista has a nasty habit of not updating itself automatically. Nobody seems to know why, but on some machines, Windows Defender just stops applying the updates it downloads. The Windows Defender Help file says, To help keep your definitions up to date, Windows Defender works with Windows Update to automatically install new definitions as they are released. Unfortunately, demonstrably, that isn't always the case.

Backup Warning

Likely cause: Windows Home Server hasn't backed up the specified computer (refer to Figure 20-2 earlier in this chapter) in several days. In my experience, there are four likely causes:

- **The computer is a laptop, and it isn't plugged into the wall.** Windows Home Server backs up a laptop only if it's physically plugged into a power supply.

- **The computer's turned off.** In some circumstances, Windows Home Server can "wake up" a computer if it's in Hibernate mode or sleeping (see the section about Wake on LAN in the next chapter), but if the computer is turned off, there's nothing WHS can do.

- **Other computers are taking up all the allotted backup time.** Unless you change settings, WHS only runs backups between midnight and 6:00 a.m. If other computers on your network take up all the time — not unusual when you first install Windows Home Server — you keep getting these backup warnings until *all* the computers on the network have a chance to finish running their backups.

- **The network connection isn't working well enough.** If a cable's unplugged, or if your wireless connection has the hiccups, WHS can't make the connection and thus can't perform the backup. If you have a computer with lots of data, running with a wireless connection, you can expect to see this warning until the first big backup finishes.

Likely solution: If you get the warning for a laptop computer, make sure it's plugged into the wall and going into Hibernate or Sleep mode. If you just can't get the laptop to backup while it's asleep, follow the instructions in the next chapter to install Wake on LAN for Home Server.

If other computers are grabbing all the time between midnight and 6:00, you can always run a manual backup. To do so, follow these steps:

1. **Log on to the computer you want to back up.**

   You can do this backup even if you don't know the server's password

2. **Right-click the Windows Home Server icon in the notification area, near the clock, and choose Backup Now.**

   The Backup Now dialog box appears (see Figure 20-4).

Figure 20-4:
You can back up any computer on the network at any time.

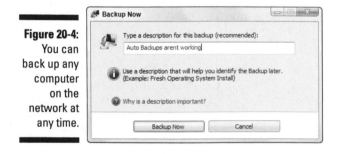

3. **Type a good description of the backup in the top box and then click the button marked Backup Now.**

   Windows Home Server starts the backup. Note that the backup could take quite awhile, but when it's done, you have a *full* backup.

If you're trying to perform a big backup on a computer with a wireless connection — the first backup run on any computer is always a "big" backup — go to your friendly local computer shoppe and pick up the longest LAN cable you can find (they max out at 100 meters, or about 330 feet). Just this once, disable the wireless connection (usually it's easiest to turn off the wireless antenna using a switch on the computer, but sometimes you have to remove the PCMCIA card or the USB adapter). Then plug the recalcitrant computer into your network, and run a manual backup. Big backups over wired connections are far, far more reliable than over wireless.

Backup Warning, New Hard Drive

Likely cause: You installed a new hard drive on one of your home or office network computers, and you didn't tell Windows Home Server to back it up. That's the cause of the Backup Warning you see earlier in this chapter in Figure 20-2.

Likely solution: It's entirely possible that you don't want Windows Home Server to back up the new drive. If that's the case, in the Home Network Health dialog box, click the box marked Ignore this Screw-up, er, Ignore this Issue, and then click Close to make sure you aren't warned again.

If you do want to back up the drive, follow the steps in Chapter 12 (in the section that explains how to choose what gets backed up) to tell Windows Home Server precisely what you want to back up on the new hard drive.

Backup Error

Likely cause: Something bad happened in the middle of your last backup — the power may have flickered, a LAN cable might've hiccupped, or your wireless connection might've been scrambled by an orbiting UFO. You get a Home Server Health report like the one in Figure 20-5.

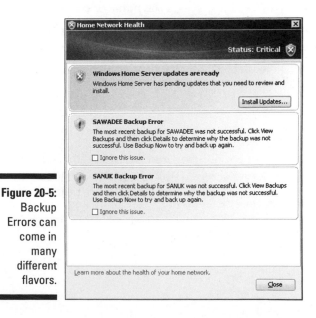

Figure 20-5:
Backup Errors can come in many different flavors.

Likely solution: Crank up the Windows Home Server Console to see what happened and why. To do so, follow these steps:

1. **Log on to any home or office computer. Right-click the Windows Home Server icon in the notification area next to the time, and choose Windows Home Server Console. Type the server's password and click the right-arrow.**

   The Windows Home Server Console appears.

2. **In the upper-left corner, click the Computers & Backup icon.**

   You see a list of all the computers on your network.

3. **Right-click the computer that's having problems and choose View Backups.**

   Windows Home Server shows you a list of all recent backups for that computer.

4. **Click the latest backup that didn't work.**

   WHS shows you details for the backup. In most cases, it should be obvious what problem the backup program encountered — for example, if there's a corrupted file on the home or office computer, or if there isn't enough space on the server to store the whole backup, the detail listing explains what happened.

   A backup will also fail if there isn't enough room on the home or office computer's hard drive(s) to create a restore point. In that case, you need to delete files or otherwise free up space on the home or office computer.

5. **Fix the problem indicated, and then click OK twice to get back to the Windows Home Server Console.**

   It's a good idea to run a manual backup (see the preceding section) just to make sure that the fixes you made work.

Backup Server Error

Likely cause: Windows Home Server screwed up (er, had an issue). Usually this error means that one of your hard drives is rapidly degenerating and about to croak. See Figure 20-6.

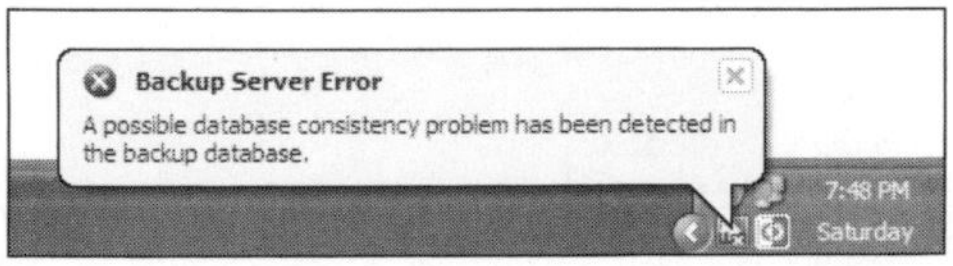

Figure 20-6: A Backup Server error.

Backup Server Error ✕
A possible database consistency problem has been detected in the backup database.

7:48 PM
Saturday

Likely solution: Alas, with this error, there isn't much you can do. It would be worth the effort to check your manufacturer's support page, and/or ask around on the Windows Home Server forum at

```
forums.microsoft.com/windowshomeserver
```

to see whether there's a specific, known problem that's cropped up. In general, though, you probably have a hard drive that's going to keep giving you problems.

Make sure you have at least two hard drives in your server (three wouldn't hurt), and double-check to make sure that Folder Duplication is turned on for all your shared folders (see Chapter 5 and Chapter 12). You might want to reboot your server so it can try to straighten things out automatically (see Chapter 16). Or you can go through the server's hard drives and try to run a manual repair (from the Windows Home Server Console, Server Storage tab, click each drive, one by one, and choose Repair). Other than that, it's a waiting game.

Storage Status, Not Enough Room

Likely cause: You're running out of room and need to add a hard drive to the server.

Windows Home Server has an odd quota system for its hard drives. You see a yellow or red Health Indicator warning according to the criteria in Table 20-1.

Table 20-1	Server Storage Health Indicator	
Amount of storage on server	% of space available triggers Red warning	% of space available triggers Yellow warning
100 GB or less	under 12%	under 3%
101 GB to 200 GB	10%	3%
201 GB to 500 GB	7%	2%
501 GB to 1 TB	4%	2%
> 1 TB to 2 TB	3%	1%
> 2 TB	2%	1%

Note that running out of storage space can have a cascade effect on other Network Health Indicators. You may receive separate warnings that there isn't enough space to duplicate shared folders, or to store backups.

Likely solution: Get another drive and follow the steps in Chapter 18 to install it.

Storage Status, Failing Hard Drive

Likely cause: One or more of the hard drives on your server is dead. See Figure 20-7. Note that failed hard drives can cause other critical problems, too, including the early demise of Backup Services.

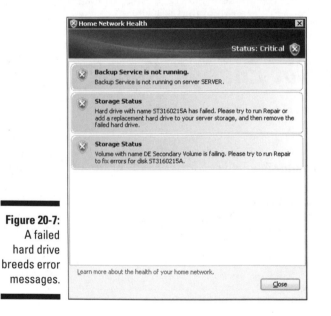

Figure 20-7: A failed hard drive breeds error messages.

Likely solution: Sometimes you get this error message when a hard drive starts to fail its S.M.A.R.T. tests. (For a details description of SMART tests see, for example, www.seagate.com/docs/pdf/whitepaper/enhanced_ smart.pdf.) In that case, running the manufacturer's diagnostic tools will tell you what you probably guessed already — your drive's about to spin its last, and you need to replace it (see Chapter 18).

The only other time I've seen this Network Health Indicator is after a hard drive on the server has turned belly-up and won't work at all. The only solution I know is to buy a new hard drive, install it using the hints in Chapter 18, and pray that all your data makes it through intact.

Passwords Do Not Match

Likely cause: This warning (see Figure 20-8) appears frequently when you first install Windows Home Server. After the initial stab, you see it only if you change your password on the server and forget to change it on your home or office computer, or vice versa.

Figure 20-8:
Server and
computer
passwords
are out of
synch.

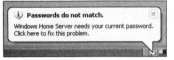

Passwords do not match.
Windows Home Server needs your current password.
Click here to fix this problem.

Likely solution: Assuming you want to synchronize passwords between your work computers and the server (it really does make life easier), Windows Home Server has a handy wizard that makes synchronizing passwords quick and relatively painless — providing you know the server's password (see Chapter 4 for details).

Updates Are Ready

Likely cause: You set Windows Home Server to notify you when updates are available, but not to install them automatically. Guess what? If you see this red Network Health Indicator, Microsoft is trying to push a patch onto your server (see Figure 20-9).

Likely solution: Check my Web site, AskWoody.com, to see whether there are any known horrendous problems with the latest Windows Home Server patch(es). If you feel comfortable installing the patch(es), click Install Updates and pray for the best.

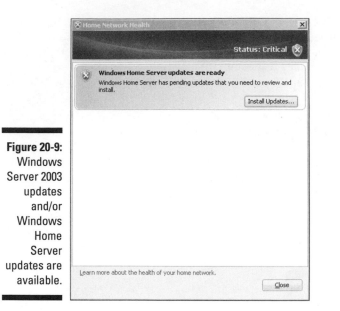

Figure 20-9:
Windows
Server 2003
updates
and/or
Windows
Home
Server
updates are
available.

Antivirus Out of Date

Likely cause: The antivirus package on one of your home or office computers hasn't been updated in several days. Depending on which antivirus package you use, there are many reasons why it may not be updating.

As mentioned in Chapter 16, you only get this warning for Vista computers. If the antivirus program on a Windows XP computer goes bonkers, Windows Home Server won't even know about it. Also, Windows Home Server doesn't keep track of antivirus programs running on Windows Home Server. Something like the cobbler having no shoes . . . .

Likely solution: Log on to the computer that's having problems, and crank up the antivirus program. (Don't bother using Windows Home Server or the Windows Security Center — they all play second fiddle to the antivirus package itself.) If you can't figure out why the AV program isn't getting updated, go to the manufacturer's Web site and see if there's something wrong that you can fix.

If all else fails, take the advice that I've been doling out for years: Dump your expensive antivirus package and use AVG Free. It works just as well as any other AV package, and it's absolutely free for home use. Drop by `free.grisoft.com`, or read the details in my *Windows Vista All-In-One Desk Reference For Dummies*, from Wiley.

Chapter 21

Ten More Tricks with Windows Home Server

In This Chapter

▶ On Beyond Zebra — expanding and extending your server's capabilities

▶ Finding new programs for your server

▶ Installing the new goodies correctly

▶ Running new programs without messing up your server

W indows Home Server runs on top of a specially modified version of Windows Server 2003 — one of the most powerful operating systems ever invented.

The folks who designed Windows Home Server knew that everybody and his brother (not to mention his sister, aunt, and long-suffering astrologer) would have cool new ideas for programs that could run on a server: home automation stuff, multimedia stuff, downloading stuff, picking and packing and poking and stuffing stuff.

Think of it this way: You have this hunk of iron sitting in your closet or nestled precariously on your desk, without a monitor, without a keyboard, without any mundane traditional Windows applications, but with acres of disk space, wide-open data channels, unfettered access to the Internet . . . and a whole lotta time on its hands.

Your Windows Home Server server works its headless head off for an hour or two a day, and the rest of the time it mostly just sits there.

Might as well use it, eh?

This chapter scratches the surface of the new applications being built specifically for Windows Home Server. It's a huge potential market, with all sorts of bright ideas coming on stream every day. After all, Windows Home Server isn't just a server. It's an ecosystem.

Installing (and Uninstalling) Add-Ins

Microsoft made it easy for developers to install new applications on your Windows Home Server server, as long as you know the server's password.

If you find a new Windows Home Server add-in that you really want (see the last section in this chapter for tips), follow these simple steps to download and install it:

1. Go to any home or office computer on your network and download the application's installation file.

Every application designed to be installed with Windows Home Server comes in a specific kind of file called an `.msi` file. (If you can't see the `.msi` at the end of the downloaded file's name, follow the instructions in Chapter 3 to make Windows XP or Vista show you filename extensions.)

2. Double-click the icon on the desktop marked Shared Folders on Server. Double-click the Software folder, and then double-click the folder called Add-Ins.

Windows Explorer should look like Figure 21-1.

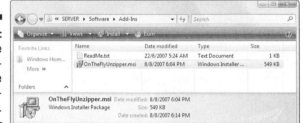

Figure 21-1:
The OnTheFly-Unzipper file in the Add-Ins folder.

3. Copy the installation file (the `.msi` file) into the Add-Ins folder. Then X-button out of Windows Explorer.

4. Double-click the Windows Home Server icon in the notification area, near the time. When the Windows Home Server logon dialog box appears, type your server's password and click the right-pointing arrow.

5. When the Windows Home Server Console appears, at the upper right, click the Settings icon.

Windows Home Server Console shows you the Settings dialog box.

6. On the left, click Add-Ins. Then click the Available tab.

You see a list of available add-ins, as in Figure 21-2. Not surprisingly, the list of available add-ins corresponds one-to-one with the `.msi` files in the Add-Ins folder. Rocket science.

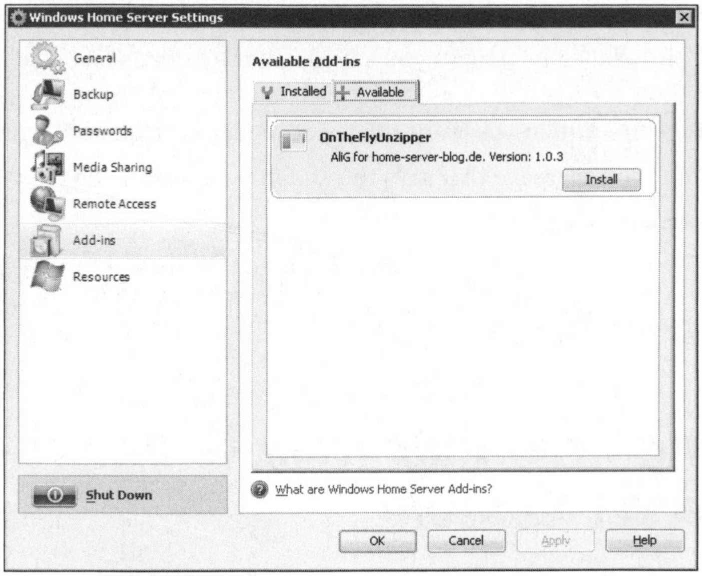

Figure 21-2:
Windows
Home
Server lists
the
available
add-ins.

7. **Find the add-in you want to install, and click its Install button.**

   Windows Home Server installs the program by running the .msi file.
   When it's done, you see the Installation Succeeded message.

8. **Click OK.**

   Windows Home Server advises that the computer has lost its connection to
   the server, and the Windows Home Server logon dialog box appears again.

9. **Type the server's password and click the right-arrow.**

   The Windows Home Server Console appears again. If the add-in put a new
   tab on the Console, you can see the new tab. Your new add-in is running.
   Take it for a spin.

Finding the right add-ins can be a daunting task. If you ever change your mind
about a particular add-in, uninstalling it couldn't be simpler, if you know the
server's password. Here's how:

1. **Log on to any computer on your network. Double-click the Windows
   Home Server icon in the notification area, near the time. When the
   Windows Home Server logon dialog box appears, type your server's
   password and click the right-arrow.**

2. **When the Windows Home Server Console appears, on the upper right,
   click the Settings icon.**

   Windows Home Server shows you the Settings dialog box.

3. **On the left, click Add-Ins.**

   The Installed tab shows you a list of all the Add-ins installed on your server.

4. **Pick the Add-in you want to axe, and click its Uninstall button.**

   You see a message that says the add-in was uninstalled.

5. **Click OK.**

   The connection with the server is broken. If you want to log back in to the Windows Home Server Console to verify that the add-in isn't running anymore, by all means do so.

Launching Programs from Windows Home Server Console

Dan Forsyth from Red D Solutions has written a simple, fast add-in for Windows Home Server that's worth its weight in gold if you want to launch programs on the server from the WHS Console. That allows you to run programs like the Task Manager or Windows Explorer without breaking into the server.

His WHS Program Launcher (see Figure 21-3) puts a new Program Launcher icon on your Windows Home Server Console that lists programs you can run at any time.

Figure 21-3:
Dan Forsyth's WHS Program Launcher.

If you want to add a new program to the list, simply click the Add icon at the top.

Of course, if you start Windows Explorer by using Dan's program and start moving files around willy-nilly, you can break your server. Permanently. So don't, okay? (See Chapter 18 for details.) This add-in only makes it easier to shoot yourself in the foot; it doesn't prevent you from pulling the trigger.

To get the program, go to

```
www.danno.ca/blog/Quick+WHS+AddIn+Program+Launcher.aspx
```

and click the link for WHS Program Launcher. That will take you to a download page. Download the .msi installer file and install it using the instruction in the preceding section.

Works like a champ.

Changing Your Remote Access Page with Whiist

Andrew Grant has a fantastic program, called Whiist, that lets you create your own Remote Access pages, or link to existing pages from your Windows Home Server page.

It's so easy to use (see Figure 21-4) that anybody — absolutely anybody — can modify a WHS Remote Access page in minutes.

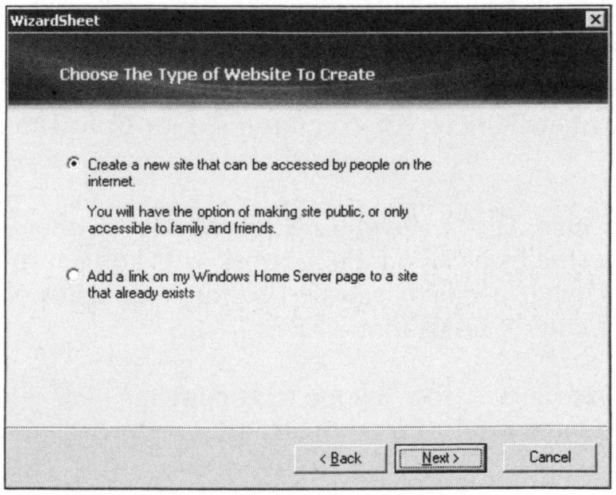

Figure 21-4:
The Whiist Setup Wizard makes customized Remote Access pages easy.

WizardSheet

Choose The Type of Website To Create

○ Create a new site that can be accessed by people on the internet.

You will have the option of making site public, or only accessible to family and friends.

○ Add a link on my Windows Home Server page to a site that already exists

< Back   Next >   Cancel

To get Whiist running on your server, go to www.andrewgrant.org/whiist and download the .msi file installer. Get it going using the instructions in the first section in this chapter.

TIP

Andrew's blog even has instructions for creating a Windows Home Server online photo album, using Bertrand LeRoy's Album Photo Handler (see www.codeplex.com/PhotoHandler).

Running uTorrent on the Server

If you work with *torrents* — the person-to-person file sharing technology pioneered by BitTorrent and uTorrent — you're probably wondering how you can use that almost-always-idle server to download torrents.

Not to worry. Many other people have that same idea. It's a match made in bit heaven: You can continue to download and share torrents even if all the other computers on your network have gone to sleep.

As this book went to press, a veritable, uh, torrent of activity surrounded porting uTorrent applications to Windows Home Server. Marcel Nouwens came out with the first well-known uTorrent add-in for WHS, documented at

```
forums.microsoft.com/WindowsHomeServer/ShowPost.aspx?
            PostID=1717779&SiteID=50
```

To keep up on the latest, I suggest you drop by Philip Churchill's MS Windows Home Server blog, www.mswhs.com, and search on utorrent.

Wake on LAN for Home Server

You might think that it would be easy to reach out and "wake up" any computer on your network, whether you're trying to get in from another network computer, or if you're knocking on the computer's door from Timbuktu using Remote Access.

It isn't as easy as it seems. The "wake on LAN" capability — where a computer wakes up when prompted by a call on the network — is subject to all sorts of restrictions, both with the specific hardware you might be using, and with the operating system, whether it be Windows XP or Vista.

Usually, Windows Home Server does a good job of jingling network computers to life in order to run backups. But sometimes it doesn't manage to wake the slumbering beast.

If you find that one of your network computers runs in Rip van Winkle mode, and won't wake up for love nor money, there are at least two server add-ins designed specifically to increase your chances of waking up sleeping computers. They put a "wake up" function inside the Windows Home Server Console, where it's easy to find — regardless of whether you're working from inside your network or logged in from Timbuktu.

For details, go to

```
forums.microsoft.com/WindowsHomeServer/ShowPost.aspx?
        PostID=1545562&SiteID=50
```

or

```
forums.microsoft.com/WindowsHomeServer/ShowPost.aspx?
        PostID=1717857&SiteID=50
```

Both add-ins work similarly, and both work well.

Uploading Photos to Flickr with PhotoSync

Ed Holloway, Chief Technology Office of Field2Base in Raleigh, North Carolina, has been developing a tremendous program that automatically uploads all the pictures in your shared Photos folder (or any other folder on your server, for that matter) to Flickr.

You need to set up an account with Flickr (www.flickr.com) if you don't already have one. As soon as you install PhotoSync, it automatically contacts Flickr. You need to log on to Flickr, and give your okay to authorize the application WHS Photo Sync to access your Flickr account.

There's a full description of the process on Ed's site at www.edholloway. com. To make sure you find the latest version of PhotoSync, use the site's Search box to search on PhotoSync.

Streaming Away from Home with WebGuide

Long a mainstay of the Windows Media Center Edition crowd, AsciiExpress's WebGuide has been adapted to work with Windows Home Server.

WebGuide streams your music and videos (including DVDs and recorded TV) from the server to any computer on the network, or any computer connected to the network via Remote Access, using a Web browser. It also lets you remotely schedule TV recording sessions and manage music and videos. It's an extraordinary product with tens of thousands of fans.

WebGuide is available in a free demo version, with the full version currently priced at $18. Many people think it's the best media investment they've ever made.

Details at www.asciiexpress.com/webguide.

Streaming to Your TiVo

Do you own a TiVo personal video recorder?

Durfee.net Software has an add-in called TiVo Publisher for WHS that makes all your server-based videos, music, and photos available from any TiVo that supports home networking.

As we went to press, specifics on availability or pricing were unavailable, but TiVo Publisher for WHS appears to be a very useful add-in, if you have a TiVo with home networking. See durfee.net/software/2007/07/tivo-publisher-for-whs.html for details.

Streaming to Your Phone with LobsterTunes

Do you own a Windows Mobile Phone?

Can't get enough of those MP3s?

With LobsterTunes, you can stream music directly from your Windows Home Server to any Windows Mobile Phone. All it takes is a Wi-Fi connection with your server, or a 3G telephone link. The part of LobsterTunes that runs on your phone (see Figure 21-5) can Shuffle, Repeat, or randomly select playlists.

Figure 21-5: Music from WHS to your Windows Mobile Phone.

It's a perfect way to stream the Smothers Brothers' "Crabs walk sideways and lobsters walk straight . . . ." Details at `www.lobstertunes.com`.

Finding More Add-Ins

The number, quality, and capabilities of Windows Home Server add-ins continue to grow by leaps and bounds. Two Web sites specialize in keeping track of the latest:

✔ Terry Walsh's **We Got Served** Windows Home Server Site, based in Milton Keynes (that's near London, if you didn't know already) maintains a big list of the latest add-ins at `www.wegotserved.co.uk/whs-add-ins/`. Terry's at the forefront of breaking Windows Home Server news, too.

✔ Christoph Dommermuth and Bastian Schulte's German-language **Homeserver Blog** has an extensive list of add-ins at `www.home-server-blog.de/category/addins/`. Even if you don't speak a word of German, you'll find the reviews and notices most valuable.

✔ Many Windows Home Server add-in developers first post news of their latest creations on the official Microsoft Windows Home Server forum, `forums.microsoft.com/windowshomeserver`. It's a great place to hang out and catch up on all the latest.

Enjoy!

Index

• Symbols •

+ Add icon, 62, 86

• A •

AAC audio files, 101
Access Denied errors, 84
access permissions, 83–84, 87, 89–90,
  117, 278
Acronis True Image, 256
ActiveX control program, 190
Add a Hard Drive Wizard, 299, 311
Add a Printer Wizard, 286
Add a Shared Folder dialog box, 86–87, 116
Add Folder dialog box, 104–105, 108
Add Photo to Gallery dialog box, 156
Add to Library dialog box, 104–106
Add User Account dialog box, 62
adding hard drives
  external, 300–302
  internal, 297–300
  knowing when, 294–297
  overview, 293–294
add-ins
  finding, 339
  installation files, 307
  installing/uninstalling, 332–334
Add-Ins folder, 332
Administrator account
  accessibility, 277
  automatically generated user folder, 79
  changing passwords, 71–73
  if user name already exists, 61
  versus Limited account, 60
  logging on, 280–281
  Remote Access, 191
  WHS interference, 56

advanced network configuration, 236
Anonymous Logon, 124
Antivirus Out of Date warning, 330
Apple
  DRM, 101
  iPods, 108
  iTunes, 110–111
  Macs, 17
Application filter, 283
applications
  ActiveX control, 190
  Dynamic Host Configuration Protocol
    (DHCP), 187
  Home Computer Restore
    burning CD from server, 238–239
    overview, 229–230
    restoring hard drive, 231–238
    restrictions, 230–231
  LogMeIn, 199
  Program Launcher, 334
  RebuildPrimary, 314, 316
  Windows Safely Remove Hardware, 234
Are you sure? dialog box, 104
AskWoody.com, 5
At Risk network health reports, 273
audio files, 101, 108–109, 131
Automatic Backup Management, 222
automatic backups, 208
Automatic File Backup, 214
automatic updating feature, 51–52
AutoPlay dialog box, 47, 156
AutoPlay notification, 261
AVG Free, 330

• B •

Backup Configuration Wizard, 220–221
Backup Details dialog box, 243

Backup Error warning, 325–326
backup locations, 19
Backup Now dialog box, 324
Backup Server Error warning, 326–327
backup session process, 210–211
Backup Status and Configuration
    window, 216
Backup Warning, 323–324, 325
backups. *See also* Home Computer Restore
    program; restoring files
  automatic, 208
  changing settings, 223–224
  changing start/stop times, 218–219
  checking current status, 224–227
  choosing files, 220–222
  conflicting programs, 216–217
  defining locations, 19
  error messages, 224
  external drives, 259–260
  Folder Duplication, 91, 212–213, 257–258
  laptops, 20, 211
  large, 324
  mapping out storage, 256–257
  on network computers, 208–212
  offsite of shared files, 258–264
  overview, 10–11, 207–208, 255
  removing folders, 220
  saving old, 222–224
  shadow copies, 214
  Sleep/Hibernate modes, 211
  television programs, 126–127
  timing, 218–219
  Windows Vista, 214–215
  Windows XP, 215
bad sectors, 258
Balancing Storage line, 92
Basic Input/Output System (BIOS), 29–30
Berlind, David, 101
BIOS (Basic Input/Output System), 29–30
blades, 133
Blivet condition, 304
booting from CD, 29
breaking into server
  deciding to, 278–280
  overview, 277
  permanent IP addresses, 290–292

RDP
  attaching printers with, 283–286
  logging on with, 280–282
  restoring previous versions of shared
    files with, 286–290
broadband, 40
broken hard drives
  overview, 308–309
  primary, 309, 313–318
  secondary, 309–313
Browse for Folder dialog box, 107
buttons
  Create New Folder Pair, 119–120
  Delete From Library Only radio
    button, 104
  Library, 103
  Load Drivers, 33
  Preview, 122
  Properties, 109
  Start, 35
  Start Rip, 109
  Upload/Download, 189
  Welcome arrow, 35, 49
buttons, KORVUE, Enable Account, 66

• *C* •

C: drive (SYS), 309, 315
cables
  crossover, 22
  LAN
    length, 26, 231
    Wake on LAN capability, 336–337
Camera Wizard, 149–150
cameras, 148–152, 156–159
capitalization, 62
Change Password dialog box, 72, 306
checkboxes
  Enable Folder Duplication, 87, 92, 99, 117
  Enable Remote Access for this User, 62
  Use Error Correction, 109
Chicken Little messages, 321
Choose File dialog box, 195
Choose Folders dialog box, 220–221
Churchill, Philip, 264

Click Here to Add Items to the Library
   link, 104
clusters, 210
columns
   Description, 88–89
   Duplication, 88–89, 92–93, 99
   Name, 88
   Status, 88–89, 99
   Used Space, 88–89
CompletePC Backup, 215, 256
Computers tab, 184
configuring
   routers, 171–176
   WHS, 49–54
Connect to server dialog box,
   68–69, 78–79, 100
Connection Disabled status, 201
Connection Options panel, 201
Connector CD, 17–19, 30, 39–49
Connector Software CD. *See* Connector CD
Console, Windows Home Server,
   99, 115–116
   controlling shared folders from, 84–90
   getting into with Remote Access, 197–199
   launching programs from, 334–335
   overview, 16–18
   setting up, 17
Content Restriction, Annulment, and
   Protection (C.R.A.P.), 101, 110–111,
   113, 125–126
Contribute option, 121
controlling WHS, 16–19
cookie-crumb navigation system, 193
cooling, 24, 26
C.R.A.P. (Content Restriction, Annulment,
   and Protection), 101, 110–111, 113,
   125–126
crash logs, 53
Create New Folder Pair button, 119–120
Create New Folder Pair dialog box, 119–120
Critical network health reports, 273
crossover cables, 22
currency settings, 34
Customer Experience Improvement
   Program, 52, 119

• *D* •

D: drive (DATA), 232, 309, 315
DDNS (Dynamic Domain Name Servers),
   169, 177
Deauthorize Computer dialog box, 111
Defender, 322, 323
Delete From Library Only radio button, 104
deleting shared folders, 85
Description column, 88–89
Devices tab, 108
DHCP (Dynamic Host Configuration
   Protocol) program, 187
dialog boxes
   Add a Shared Folder, 86–87, 116
   Add Folder, 104–105, 108
   Add Photo to Gallery, 156
   Add to Library, 104–106
   Add User Account, 62
   Are you sure?, 104
   AutoPlay, 47, 156
   Backup Details, 243
   Backup Now, 324
   Browse for Folder, 107
   Change Password, 72, 306
   Choose File, 195
   Choose Folders, 220–221
   Connect to server, 68–69, 78–79, 100
   Create New Folder Pair, 119–120
   Deauthorize Computer, 111
   Folder Options
      Windows Vista, 46–47
      Windows XP, 43
   Home Network Health, 325
   Import Settings, 157, 158
   Internet Protocol (TCP/IP), 292
   Local Area Connection Properties, 291
   My Pictures Screen Saver Options, 153–154
   New Windows Home Server Found,
      44–45, 48–49
   Options, 107–108
   Properties, 83, 92
   Properties for Guest, 66
   Remote Desktop Connection, 281
   Settings, 275

dialog boxes *(continued)*
  Update Password, 70–71
  Upload, 195
  User Access Control, 73
  User Accounts, 73
  View Backups, 232–233
dial-up Internet connections, 23, 40
Digital Lifestyle site, The, 124
Digital Rights Management (DRM),
    101, 110–111, 113, 125–126
Disk Manager, 237, 278
disks, hard
  adding, 293–302
  backing up, 11
  broken, 308–318
  disk management, 12–13
  eSATA, 25, 297
  external, 259–263, 297, 300–302
  failed, error messages, 328
  Folder Duplication, 90–93, 98–99, 117,
    141, 208, 212–213, 257–258, 309
  heat sensitivity, 24
  media file space, 98, 117
  MTBF rates, 296
  multiple, 24, 31
  replacing, 229, 231
  restoring, 231–238
  retiring, 302–304
  speed, 297
  USB, 24, 31
Display Properties panel, 153
Dixon, Ian, 124
Domain Name Servers, 177
Domain Name Setup Wizard, 178
domain names, 176–179
Dommermuth, Christoph, 339
downloading
  files with Remote Access, 196–197
  SyncToy, 118–119
Drive Extender, 256, 293
drive speed, 297
drivers, Windows 2003, 23, 30
drives
  DATA (D: drive), 232, 309, 315
  Drive Extender, 256, 293
  DVD, 23, 29

FAT-formatted, 20
hard
  adding, 293–302
  backing up, 11
  broken, 308–318
  disk management, 12–13
  eSATA, 25, 297
  external, 259–263, 297, 300–302
  failed, error messages, 328
  Folder Duplication, 90–93, 98–99, 117,
    141, 208, 212–213, 257–258, 309
  heat sensitivity, 24
  media file space, 98, 117
  MTBF rates, 296
  multiple, 24, 31
  replacing, 229, 231
  restoring, 231–238
  retiring, 302–304
  speed, 297
  USB, 24, 31
  NTFS-formatted, 20
  speed of, 297
  thumb, 20
DRM (Digital Rights Management),
    101, 110–111, 113, 125–126
duplicating shared folders, 90–93
Duplication column, 88–89, 92–93, 99
dust, 26
DVD drives, 23, 29
DVR-MS files, 113–114, 118, 127, 132
Dynamic Domain Name Servers
    (DDNS), 169, 177
Dynamic Host Configuration Protocol
    (DHCP) program, 187

• E •

eMusic.com, 111
Enable Account button, 66
Enable Folder Duplication checkbox,
    87, 92, 99, 117
Enable Remote Access for this User
    checkbox, 62
End User License Agreement (EULA),
    34, 44, 47–48, 118, 125

error log file, 283
error messages, 328
error reporting feature, 53
errors
  Access Denied, 84
  Use Error Correction checkbox, 109
eSATA (external SATA), 25, 297
Ethernet, 25
EULA (End User License Agreement),
    34, 44, 47–48, 118, 125
Explorer. *See* Internet Explorer browser;
    Windows Explorer
external hard drives
  adding, 300–302
  for backups, 259–263
  enclosures, 297
external IP addresses, 171
external SATA (eSATA), 25, 297

• *F* •

fans, 24
FAT-formatted drives, 20
features
  automatic updating, 51–52
  error reporting, 53
  previous versions. *See also* shadow
      copies
    versus Folder Duplication, 91
    overview, 21–22, 208, 214
    Windows Vista, 250–253
    Windows XP, 246–250
  Remote Access
    accessing shared folders, 192–197
    changing page with Whiist, 335
    connection options, 204
    cookie-crumb navigation system, 193
    getting into Console, 197–199
    home page, 181
    interface, 189
    logging on to WHS remotely, 190–192
    logon page, 192
    new users, 63
    overview, 14–15, 19
    passwords, 56, 58, 72

    required Windows versions, 20–21
    setting up, 165–169, 169–171, 171–176,
        176–179, 179–182, 182–185, 185–188
    Sleep mode, 200
    Windows XP versions, 42
    working with home network's
        computers, 199–204
  shadow-copy, 21
file name extensions, 43, 46
files
  .msi, 332
  add-in installation, 307
  audio, 101, 108–109, 131
  changing in Windows Explorer, 278, 334
  choosing for backup, 220–222
  downloading with Remote Access, 196–197
  DVR-MS, 113–114, 118, 127, 132
  log, 283
  media
    Folder Duplication, 98–99
    hard drive space, 98, 117
    moving, 98
  organizing with shared folders, 76–77
  previous versions, 21–22
  restoring
    backups, 212, 242–246
    overview, 10–11, 241
    with RDP, 286–290
    shared folders, 246–253
  retrieving from Recycle Bin, 211, 242
  ripping, 107–109
  ripping to server, 107–109
  shadow, 211
  shared
    offsite backup of, 258–264
    restoring previous versions
        with RDP, 286–290
  system log, 283
  uploading with Remote Access, 194–196
  video, 101, 131
Filmstrip View option, 147
filters
  Application, 283
  Home Server, 283
  Security, 283
  System, 283

filters, log file, 283
finding shared folders, 77–80
Firefox, 190
FireWire-connections, 31
flashing BIOS, 30
Flickr, 337
Folder Duplication, 90–93, 98–99, 117, 141,
    208, 212–213, 257–258, 309
Folder Options dialog box
  Windows Vista, 46–47
  Windows XP, 43
folders. *See also* files
  creating subfolders, 81
  Folder Options dialog box
    Windows Vista, 46–47
    Windows XP, 43
  Music, 76, 80–82, 98–100, 102–104,
      106–107, 109
  My Music, 98, 100
  My Pictures, 153
  My Videos, 98, 100
  Photos, 76, 80–82, 99, 141, 146
  pre-defined, 11
  Public, 76, 80–82, 99
  Public\Public Music, 98, 100
  Public\Public Videos, 98, 100
  Recorded TV, 115–117, 120, 125
  shared
    access, 56, 63–64, 80–84, 193
    characteristics of, 88–89
    controlling access to, 80–84
    controlling from Console, 84–90
    duplicating, 90–93
    finding, 77–80
    Folder Duplication, 212–213, 257–258
    Guest account, 67
    linking to, 19
    media, 19, 97–111, 115–117
    modifying, 279
    navigation buttons, 194
    offsite backups of, 258–264
    organizing files with, 76–77
    overview, 11–12, 75–76
    Photos, 144–154, 155–161
    Remote Access, 192–197
    restoring files, 246–253

  Software, 76–77, 80–82, 99
  TempRec, 123
  Users, 77, 79–83, 90
  Videos, 77, 80–82, 98–100, 106
Format box, 108
Formatting Hard Drives panel, 34–35
Forsyth, Dan, 334
FTP servers, 14
Full access permission level, 83–84, 117
Full Screen option, 203

• *G* •

General tab, 83
Generic Volume, 233
Grant, Andrew, 335
Green Button site, The, 124
Green network health reports, 268
Guest account, 56, 65–67, 78–79, 99, 133

• *H* •

hard drives
  adding, 293–302
  backing up, 11
  broken
    overview, 308–309
    primary, 309, 313–318
    secondary, 309–313
  disk management, 12–13
  eSATA, 25, 297
  external
    adding, 300–302
    for backups, 259–263
    enclosures, 297
  failed, error messages, 328
  Folder Duplication, 90–93, 98–99, 117, 141,
      208, 212–213, 257–258, 309
  heat sensitivity, 24
  media file space, 98, 117
  MTBF rates, 296
  multiple, 24, 31
  replacing, 229, 231

restoring, 231–238
retiring, 302–304
speed, 297
USB, 24, 31
hardware requirements, 22–24, 29
headless computers, 16
headless servers, 277
Healthy network health reports, 273
heat, 24, 26
histograms, 85
Holloway, Ed, 336
Home Computer Restore program
  burning CD from server, 238–239
  overview, 229–230
  restoring hard drive, 231–238
  restrictions, 230–231
Home Network Health dialog box, 325
Home Network Health reports. *See also*
    Network Health Indicator
  fixing problems, 272–275
  health assessment categories, 271–272
  Network Health Indicator, 268–270
  overview, 15, 267–268
  Windows XP, 20
Home Server filter, 283
home server names, 34, 49–51
Hotmail addresses, 177–178
How to Create a Strong Password link, 73
HP MediaSmart Servers, 27
hubs. *See also* routers
  USB, 24

• *I* •

icons
  + Add, 62, 86
  Network, 121
  Network Critical, 295
  Shared Folders, 86, 92, 99, 116
  Shared Folders on Server, 77–78, 80–82,
    88, 100, 103–104, 125, 251
  User Accounts, 72
  Windows Home Server Console, 118

Import Settings dialog box, 157, 158
Installation DVD, 30, 32, 314–315
installing
  add-ins, 332–334
  .NET Framework, 44
  two servers on one network, 42
  WHS software, 27–36
    need for, 28–29
    overview, 27–28
    preparing for, 29–31
    preparing network for, 39–42
    Windows Vista, 46–49
    Windows XP, 42–45
  Windows Vista temporarily, 30
internal hard drives, 297–300
Internet connection speed, 25, 40
Internet Explorer browser
  Remote Access feature, 190, 196, 198,
    200–204
  Trusted Sites zone, 198
Internet Protocol (IP) addresses
  external, 171
  finding, 173
  giving server permanent, 290–292
  whatismyipaddress.com, 176
Internet Protocol (TCP/IP) dialog box, 292
Internet service providers (ISPs), 184
IP (Internet Protocol) addresses
  external, 171
  finding, 173
  giving server permanent, 290–292
  whatismyipaddress.com, 176
iPods, 108
ISPs (Internet service providers), 184
iTunes, 110–111

• *K* •

Keep My Password on the Home Server
    option, 70
Keep My Password on This Computer
    option, 70
keyboard settings, 34

• L •

LAN cables
  length, 26, 231
  Wake on LAN capability, 336–337
laptops
  backups, 20, 211, 323
  WHS on, 20, 29
Library button, 103
Limited account, 60, 71
links
  Click Here to Add Items to the
    Library, 104
  How to Create a Strong Password, 73
Linksys WRT54G routers, 175
Linux PCs, 17
Live Hotmail addresses, 177–178
Live ID, 177–178
Live Photo Gallery, 143
Load Additional Storage Drivers panel, 32
Load Drivers button, 33
LobsterTunes, 338–339
Local Area Connection Properties
    dialog box, 291
log file, 283
logging on
  automatically, 61
  with RDP, 280–282
  remotely, 190–192, 201–204
LogMeIn program, 199
logon accounts
  adding new users, 60–64
  Guest account, 65–67
  overview, 55–57
  passwords
    changing, 71–73
    policies, 57–59
    synchronization, 68–71
Logon Name box, 62
logon names. *See* user names
lost passwords, 306–308

• M •

Macs, 17
management, disk, 12–13

Mean Time Between Failure (MTBF)
    rates, 296
media
  photos, 141–161
    overview, 141
    shared Photos folder, 144–154, 155–161
    uploading to Flickr with PhotoSync, 337
    Windows tools, 142–144
  television programs
    backing up recorded, 19, 126–127
    Guest account, 99
    overview, 113–115
    storing on server, 115–117, 118–123,
      124–125, 125–126
  Xbox 360
    accessing media files, 114–115
    Guest account, 65, 99
    overview, 129–131
    playing with WHS, 131–136
    streaming media, 16
    using Media Center PCs
      to stream to, 137–140
Media blades, 133–134
Media Center, 113–127, 130, 137–140,
    246–250. *See also* Windows XP
    Media Center
Media Center Extenders, 130, 138. *See also*
    Xbox 360
media files
  Folder Duplication, 98–99
  hard drive space, 98, 117
  moving, 98
Media Library Sharing, 97, 114, 132
Media Player
  setting up to play from Music folder,
    102–106
  setting up to rip music, 107–109
  television programs, 114, 125–126
  versions, 103
media streaming. *See* streaming media
medium password policies, 57–58
memory requirements, 23
messages. *See also* error messages
  Access Denied, 84
  Chicken Little, 321
  User Account Control, 47
M4P video files, 101

Microsoft Passport, 177–178
Microsoft's Customer Experience
 Improvement Program, 52
Mike's Digital Home blog, 124
Miller, Richard, 124
mirroring backup data, 11, 90
mobile phones, streaming
 media to, 338–339
monitoring networks, 271
moving media files, 98
MP3 audio files, 101, 108–109, 131
MP4 video files, 101
MPG video files, 131
.msi files, 332
MSN Hotmail addresses, 177–178
MSN Passport, 177–178
MSN.com accounts, 177–178
MTBF (Mean Time Between Failure)
 rates, 296
multimedia. *See* photos; shared folders;
 television programs; Xbox 360
Music folder, 76, 80–82, 98–100, 102–104,
 106–107, 109
music sharing, 97–111
My Music folder, 98, 100
My Pictures folder, 153
My Pictures Screen Saver Options dialog
 box, 153–154
My Pictures Slideshow option, 153
My Videos folder, 98, 100

• *N* •

Name column, 88
names. *See also* shared folders; user
 names
 domain, 176–179
 home server, 34, 49–51
.NET Framework, 18, 42, 44
.NET Passport, 177–178
Network Critical icon, 295
Network Health Indicator. *See also* Home
 Network Health reports
 overview, 268–270
 warnings, 321–330
Network icon, 121

networks (workgroups)
 backups, 208–212
 configuring WHS, 49–54
 connection backup warning, 323
 installing two servers on, 42
 installing WHS Connector
  on Windows Vista machines, 46–49
  on Windows XP machines, 42–45
 overview, 39
 preparing for WHS installation, 39–42
 Remote Access, 199–204
 requirements, 22, 39
 sharing music on, 110–111
 size of, 20, 40
 visibility of PCs on, 40
New Installation option, 34, 316
new users, 60–64
New Windows Home Server Found dialog
 box (wizard panel), 44–45, 48–49
No spyware protection warning, 322–323
None access permission level, 83–84
Norton Ghost, 256
Nouwens, Marcel, 336
NTBackup, 256
NTFS-formatted drives, 20

• *O* •

offsite backups of shared files, 258–264
online backup providers, 263–264
options
 Contribute, 121
 Filmstrip View, 147
 Full Screen, 203
 Keep My Password on the Home Server, 70
 Keep My Password on This Computer, 70
 My Pictures Slideshow, 153
 New Installation, 34, 316
 Options dialog box, 107–108
 Password Hint, 307
 Show Hidden Files and Folders
  Windows Vista, 46–47
  Windows XP, 43
 Update Password, 118
 View, 146
Options dialog box, 107–108

• P •

panels
 Connection Options, 201
 Display Properties, 153
 Formatting Hard Drives, 34–35
 Load Additional Storage Drivers, 32
 Photos on Server Properties, 148
 Remote Desktop Connection, 281–282
 Select an Installation Type, 33
 View Backups, 226
Passport, Microsoft, 177–178
Password Hint option, 307
passwords
 changing, 71–73, 313
 Guest account, 65–67
 hints, 51
 lost, 306–308
 most common, 59
 playing music and, 102–103
 policies, 57–59, 72
 shared folders, 80–81, 85–86
 strong, 51, 59–60
 synchronizing, 56–57, 68–71, 328
Passwords do not match warning, 329
Passwords pane, 57–58
PCI cards, 297
permanent domain names, 176–179
permission levels
 Full access, 83–84, 117
 None access, 83–84
 Read access, 83–84, 99, 102, 117, 247, 251
permissions, shared folder, 80–84, 89–90
phones, streaming media to, 338–339
Photo Gallery, 155
photos, 141–161
 overview, 141
 shared Photos folder
  Windows Vista, 155–161
  Windows XP, 144–154
 uploading to Flickr with PhotoSync, 337
 Windows tools, 142–144
Photos folder, 76, 80–82, 99, 141, 144–161
Photos on Server Properties panel, 148
PhotoSync, 337
portforward.com, 174

ports
 blocked by ISPs, 184
 configuring routers, 171
PowerToys, 123
Preview button, 122
previous versions feature. *See also* shadow
  copies
 versus Folder Duplication, 91
 overview, 21–22, 208, 214
 Windows Vista, 250–253
 Windows XP, 246–250
Previous Versions tab, 288–289
primary hard drives, 309, 313–318
printers, 283–286
product keys, 17, 34
Program Launcher program, 334
programs. *See also* television programs
 ActiveX control, 190
 Dynamic Host Configuration Protocol
  (DHCP), 187
 Home Computer Restore
  burning CD from server, 238–239
  overview, 229–230
  restoring hard drive, 231–238
  restrictions, 230–231
 LogMeIn, 199
 Program Launcher, 334
 RebuildPrimary, 314, 316
 Windows Safely Remove Hardware, 234
Properties button, 109
Properties dialog box, 83, 92
Properties for Guest dialog box, 66
Public folder, 76, 80–82, 99
Public\Public Music folder, 98, 100
Public\Public Videos folder, 98, 100

• R •

RAID (Redundant Array of Inexpensive
  Disks) technology, 13, 91
RDP (Remote Desktop Protocol)
 attaching printers with, 283–286
 logging on with, 280–282
 restoring previous versions of shared
  files with, 286–290

Read access permission level, 83–84, 99, 102, 117, 247, 251
read-only access, 81
read-write access, 81, 100
RebuildPrimary program, 314, 316
recorded television. *See* television programs
Recorded TV folder, 115–117, 120, 125
recovering lost passwords, 306–308
Recycle Bin, 211, 242
Red network health reports, 268
Redundant Array of Inexpensive Disks (RAID) technology, 13, 91
Remote Access feature
  accessing shared folders, 192–197
  changing page with Whiist, 335
  connection options, 204
  cookie-crumb navigation system, 193
  getting into Console, 197–199
  home page, 181
  interface, 189
  logging on to WHS remotely, 190–192
  logon page, 192
  new users, 63
  overview, 14–15, 19
  passwords, 56, 58, 72
  required Windows versions, 20–21
  setting up
    configuring router, 171–176
    connecting for first time, 182–185
    difficulties with, 185–188
    establishing permanent domain name, 176–179
    finalizing, 179–182
    overview, 165–169
    server setup, 169–171
  Sleep mode, 200
  Windows XP versions, 42
  working with home network's computers, 199–204
Remote Assistance, 199–200
remote controls, 126
Remote Desktop Connection dialog box, 281
Remote Desktop Connection panels, 281–282

Remote Desktop Protocol (RDP)
  attaching printers with, 283–286
  logging on with, 280–282
  restoring previous versions of shared files with, 286–290
Remove a Hard Drive Wizard, 302
repairing broken hard drives, 308–318
  primary, 309, 313–318
  secondary, 309, 310–313
reports, health. *See* Home Network Health reports
Restore CD, 30
Restore Computer Wizard, 236–237
Restore Wizard, 235–236
restoring files
  backups, 212, 242–246
  overview, 10–11, 241
  with RDP, 286–290
  shared folders
    Windows Vista, 250–253
    Windows XP, 246–250
retiring hard drives, 302–304
Rip Music to This Location box, 107
Rip tab, 107–109
ripping music files, 107–109
Rogers, Ian, 101
Router Configuration Details checklist, 172
routers
  configuring, 171–176
  Linksys WRT54G, 175
  multiple, 176
  portforward.com, 174
  requirements, 22, 25, 26, 40
  wireless, 186–187

● *S* ●

saved backups, 222–224
SBS (Small Business Server), 1–2
SBS (Windows Small Business Server), 1–2
Schulte, Bastian, 339
screen savers, 153–154, 159–161
screens
  Full Screen option, 203
  setup, 41
  Welcome, 61

secondary hard drives, 309–313
sectors
  bad, 258
security
  logon accounts
    adding new users, 60–64
    Guest account, 65–67
    overview, 55–57
    passwords, 57–59, 68–71, 71–73
  passwords
    changing, 71–73, 313
    Guest account, 65–67
    hints, 51
    lost, 306–308
    most common, 59
    playing music and, 102–103
    policies, 57–59, 72
    shared folders, 80–81, 85–86
    strong, 51, 59–60
    synchronizing, 56–57, 68–71, 328
  permission levels
    Full access, 83–84, 117
    None access, 83–84
    Read access, 83–84, 99, 102, 117, 247, 251
  user names
    adding, 62–64
    capitalization, 63
    number of, 20
    playing music and, 100
    shared, 60
    synchronizing passwords, 68–69
Security filter, 283
security updates, 44
Select an Installation Type panel, 33
Server Caution page, 317
Server Reinstallation, 313
Server Storage Health Indicators, 327
servers, defined, 27
service packs, 44
setting up
  Remote Access feature
    configuring router, 171–176
    connecting for first time, 182–185
    difficulties with, 185–188
    establishing permanent domain
      name, 176–179
    finalizing, 179–182
    overview, 165–169
    server setup, 169–171
  Windows Home Server Console, 17
  Windows Media Player, 102–109
settings
  currency, 34
  Import Settings dialog box, 157, 158
  keyboard, 34
  time, 34
  user access, 83–84, 87, 89–90, 117, 278
Settings dialog box, 275
Settings icon, 57
setup screen, 41
Setup Wizard, 315
shadow copies. *See also* previous
    versions feature
  overview, 21–22, 214
  Windows Vista, 250–253
  Windows XP, 246–250
shadow-copy feature, 21
shared files
  offsite backup of, 258–264
  restoring previous versions
    with RDP, 286–290
shared folders
  access, 56, 63–64, 80–84, 193
  characteristics of, 88–89
  controlling access to, 80–84
  controlling from Console, 84–90
  duplicating, 90–93
  finding, 77–80
  Folder Duplication, 212–213, 257–258
  Guest account, 67
  linking to, 19
  media, 19, 97–111, 115–117
  modifying, 279
  navigation buttons, 194
  offsite backups of, 258–264
  organizing files with, 76–77
  overview, 11–12, 75–76
  Photos
    Windows Vista, 155–161
    Windows XP, 144–154
  Remote Access, 192–197
  restoring files, 246–253

Shared Folders icon, 86, 92, 99, 116
Shared Folders on Server icon, 77–78,
    80–82, 88, 100, 103–104, 125, 251
Shared Folders tab, 184
Shared Photos folder, 142
Show Hidden Files and Folders option
  Windows Vista, 46–47
  Windows XP, 43
Single Instance Storage, 210
Sleep mode, 200
Small Business Server (SBS), 1–2
Software folder, 76–77, 80–82, 99
spyware, 323
Standard account, 60, 71
Start button, unresponsive, 35
Start Rip button, 109
Status column, 88–89, 99
Storage Status, Failing Hard Drive
        warning, 328–329
Storage Status, Not Enough Room
        warning, 327–328
storage, WHS, 256–257
straightforward backup, 208
streaming media
  overview, 16, 97
  to phone with LobsterTunes, 338–339
  to TiVo, 338
  with WebGuide, 337–338
  to Xbox 360, 137–140
strong password policies, 57–58
subfolders, 81
switches. *See* routers
synchronizing passwords, 56–57, 68–71, 328
SyncToy, 118–125, 263
SYS (C: drive), 309, 315
System filter, 283
system health. *See* Home Network Health
        reports
system log files, 283
System Restore Point, 215

tabs
  Computers, 184
  Devices, 108

General, 83
  Previous Versions, 288–289
  Rip, 107–109
  Shared Folders, 184
  User Access, 83
  User Accounts, 62, 66, 99
Task Scheduler, 217
TCP/IP (Internet Protocol) dialog box, 292
television programs
  backing up recorded, 19, 126–127
  Guest account, 99
  overview, 113–115
  storing on server
    creating shared folder, 115–117
    moving to server, 118–123
    recording TV directly to server, 124–125
    viewing, 125–126
TempRec folders, 123
Test Media Connection check, 135
thumb drives, 20
time settings, 34
timing, backup, 211–212, 218–219
TiVo, 338
Tom's Hardware, 25
torrents, 336
Trusted Sites zone, 198
TweakUI PowerToy, 61

• *U* •

uninstalling add-ins, 332–334
uninterrupted power supplies
        (UPSs), 24, 26
Universal Plug and Play (UPnP), 173, 187
Unix PCs, 17
Update Password dialog box, 70–71
Update Password line, 69–70
Update Password option, 118
updates are ready warning, 329
updating BIOS, 30
Upload dialog box, 195
Upload/Download button, 189
uploading
  files with Remote Access, 194–196
  photos to Flickr with PhotoSync, 337
UPnP (Universal Plug and Play), 173, 187

UPSs (uninterrupted power
   supplies), 24, 26
URGE site, 103, 109
USB hard drives, 24, 31
USB hubs, 24
USB key drives, 108
USB 2 controllers, 25
Use Error Correction checkbox, 109
Used Space column, 88–89
User Access Control dialog box, 73
user access settings, 83–84, 87,
   89–90, 117, 278
User Access tab, 83
User Account Control message, 47
user accounts. *See* logon accounts
User Accounts dialog box, 73
User Accounts icon, 72
User Accounts tab, 62, 66, 99
user names
   adding, 62–64
   capitalization, 63
   number of, 20
   playing music and, 100
   shared, 60
   synchronizing passwords, 68–69
users. *See also* logon accounts
   changing/deleting, 279
   new, 60–64
Users folder, 77, 79–83, 90
uTorrent, 336

• V •

video files, 101, 131. *See also* shared
   folders
Videos folder, 77, 80–82, 98–100, 106
View Backups dialog box, 232–233
View Backups panel, 226
View options, 146
visibility of network computers, 40
Vista
   accounts, 56, 60, 61
   antivirus out-of-date warning, 330
   Automatic File Backup, 214
   automatic updating feature, 52

backup tools, 214–215
changing passwords in, 73
checking updates, 270
connector software, 40
health report feature, 15, 20
installing temporarily, 30
Photo Gallery, 143
Photos screen saver, 160–161
previous versions feature, 21–22, 215, 288
Recorded TV folder, 120
removing redundant backup
   programs, 216
restoring shared folder files, 250–253
shadow-copy feature, 21, 215
shared Photos folder, 155–161
slideshows, 159
spyware warnings, 323
SyncToy, 118
Welcome screen, 61
WHS installation on, 46–49
Vista Business
   Previous Versions tab, 252
   Remote Access feature, 181
   Remote Assistance, 200
   restoring shared folders, 250–253
   shadow-copy feature, 21, 211
Vista Enterprise
   Previous Versions tab, 252
   Remote Access feature, 181
   Remote Assistance, 200
   restoring shared folders, 250–253
   shadow-copy feature, 21, 211
Vista Home Basic
   Automatic File Backup, 215
   previous versions feature,
      22, 216, 280, 287
   Remote Assistance, 200
   restoring shared folders, 246, 251
Vista Home Premium
   previous versions feature,
      22, 216, 280, 287
   Remote Assistance, 200
   restoring shared folders, 246, 251
Vista Ultimate
   Previous Versions tab, 252
   Remote Access feature, 181

Remote Assistance, 200
restoring shared folders, 250–253
shadow-copy feature, 21, 211
Vogon International, 13

• *W* •

Wake on LAN capability, 336–337
Walsh, Terry, 339
warnings
  Antivirus Out of Date, 330
  Backup Error, 325–326
  Backup Server Error, 326–327
  Backup Warning, 323–324, 325
  No spyware protection, 322–323
  Passwords do not match, 329
  Storage Status, Failing Hard Drive,
    328–329
  Storage Status, Not Enough Room,
    327–328
  updates are ready, 329
weak password policies, 57–58
WebGuide, 125, 337–338
Web-security certificates, 191
Welcome arrow button, 35, 49
Welcome screen, 61
Whiist, 335
WHS (Windows Home Server)
  computer needs, 24–26
  control of, 16–19
  forum, 327
  functions of, 10–16
  hardware requirements, 22–24
  Home Page, 181
  installing, 27–36
  limitations of, 19–22
  overview, 1–5, 9–10
  positioning in home or office, 26
Windows 2003 drivers, 23, 30
Windows Defender, 322, 323
Windows Explorer
  automatic updating, 52
  changing files in, 278, 334
  View settings, 142

Windows Home Computer Restore CD, 229
Windows Home Server (WHS)
  computer needs, 24–26
  control of, 16–19
  forum, 327
  functions of, 10–16
  hardware requirements, 22–24
  Home Page, 181
  installing, 27–36
  limitations of, 19–22
  overview, 1–5, 9–10
  positioning in home or office, 26
Windows Home Server CD. *See*
    Connector CD
Windows Home Server Connector. *See also*
    Connector CD
  installing
    Windows Vista, 46–49
    Windows XP, 42–45
Windows Home Server Console,
    99, 115–116
  controlling shared folders from, 84–90
  getting into with Remote Access, 197–199
  launching programs from, 334–335
  overview, 16–18
  setting up, 17
Windows Home Server Console icon, 118
Windows Home Server Console
    screen, 64, 82
Windows Home Server Drivers For Restore
    folder, 234
Windows Live Hotmail addresses, 177–178
Windows Live ID, 177–178
Windows Live Photo Gallery, 143
Windows Media Center, 113–127
Windows Media Player
  setting up to play from Music folder,
    102–106
  setting up to rip music, 107–109
  television programs, 114, 125–126
  versions, 103
Windows photo tools, 142–144
Windows Preinstallation Environment
    (WinPE), 235
Windows Remote Desktop Connection,
    198, 281–282

Windows Safely Remove Hardware
      program, 234
Windows Small Business Server (SBS), 1–2
Windows Vista
  accounts, 56, 60, 61
  antivirus out-of-date warning, 330
  Automatic File Backup, 214
  automatic updating feature, 52
  backup tools, 214–215
  changing passwords in, 73
  checking updates, 270
  connector software, 40
  health report feature, 15, 20
  installing temporarily, 30
  Photo Gallery, 143
  Photos screen saver, 160–161
  previous versions feature, 21–22, 215, 288
  Recorded TV folder, 120
  removing redundant backup
      programs, 216
  restoring shared folder files, 250–253
  shadow-copy feature, 21, 215
  shared Photos folder, 155–161
  slideshows, 159
  spyware warnings, 323
  SyncToy, 118
  Welcome screen, 61
  WHS installation on, 46–49
Windows Vista Business
  Previous Versions tab, 252
  Remote Access feature, 181
  Remote Assistance, 200
  restoring shared folders, 250–253
  shadow-copy feature, 21, 211
Windows Vista Enterprise
  Previous Versions tab, 252
  Remote Access feature, 181
  Remote Assistance, 200
  restoring shared folders, 250–253
  shadow-copy feature, 21, 211
Windows Vista Home Basic
  Automatic File Backup, 215
  previous versions feature,
      22, 216, 280, 287
  Remote Assistance, 200
  restoring shared folders, 246, 251

Windows Vista Home Premium
  previous versions feature, 22, 216, 280, 287
  Remote Assistance, 200
  restoring shared folders, 246, 251
Windows Vista Ultimate
  Previous Versions tab, 252
  Remote Access feature, 181
  Remote Assistance, 200
  restoring shared folders, 250–253
  shadow-copy feature, 21, 211
Windows XP
  accounts, 56, 60, 61
  antivirus out-of-date warning, 330
  automatic updating feature, 52
  AutoPlay notification, 149
  backups, 215
  changing passwords in, 72–73
  connector software, 40
  drivers, 30
  Home Network Health reports, 15, 20
  NTBackup, 215
  Picture and Fax Viewer, 143
  Previous Versions feature, 21, 287
  Recorded TV folder, 120
  removing redundant backup
      programs, 217
  restoring shared files, 246–250
  Service Pack 2, 250
  shared ***Photos*** folder, 144–154
  spyware warnings, 323
  SyncToy, 118
  Welcome screen, 61
  WHS installation on, 42–45
  Windows Media Player, 103
Windows XP Home
  Remote Access feature, 167, 181
  Remote Assistance, 200
Windows XP Media Center. *See also*
      Media Center
  Connector CD, 19
  restoring shared folders, 246
  Xbox 360, 129–131, 137
Windows XP Pro
  Remote Access feature, 167, 181
  Remote Assistance, 200

Windows XP Tablet PC, 181
  Remote Access feature, 167
  restoring shared folders, 246–250
  shadow-copy feature, 214
WinPE (Windows Preinstallation
    Environment), 235
wireless network connections, 22, 40
wizards
  Add a Hard Drive, 299, 311
  Add a Printer, 286
  Backup Configuration, 220–221
  Camera, 149–150
  Domain Name Setup, 178
  Remove a Hard Drive, 302
  Restore, 235–236
  Restore Computer, 236–237
  Setup, 315
WMA audio files, 101, 108
WMA music, 131
WMV video, 101, 131
workgroups (networks)
  backups, 208–212
  configuring WHS, 49–54
  connection backup warning, 323
  installing two servers on, 42
  installing WHS Connector
    on Windows Vista machines, 46–49
    on Windows XP machines, 42–45
  overview, 39
  preparing for WHS installation, 39–42
  Remote Access, 199–204
  requirements, 22, 39
  sharing music on, 110–111
  size of, 20, 40
  visibility of PCs on, 40

• *X* •

Xbox 360
  accessing media files, 114–115
  Guest account, 65, 99
  overview, 129–131
  playing with WHS, 131–136
  streaming media, 16
  using Media Center PCs
    to stream to, 137–140

XP
  accounts, 56, 60, 61
  antivirus out-of-date warning, 330
  automatic updating feature, 52
  AutoPlay notification, 149
  backups, 215
  changing passwords in, 72–73
  connector software, 40
  drivers, 30
  Home Network Health reports, 15, 20
  NTBackup, 215
  Picture and Fax Viewer, 143
  Previous Versions feature, 21, 287
  Recorded TV folder, 120
  removing redundant backup
    programs, 217
  restoring shared files, 246–250
  Service Pack 2, 250
  shared ***Photos*** folder, 144–154
  spyware warnings, 323
  SyncToy, 118
  Welcome screen, 61
  WHS installation on, 42–45
  Windows Media Player, 103
XP Home
  Remote Access feature, 167, 181
  Remote Assistance, 200
XP Media Center. *See also* Media Center
  Connector CD, 19
  restoring shared folders, 246
  Xbox 360, 129–131, 137
XP Pro
  Remote Access feature, 167, 181
  Remote Assistance, 200
XP Tablet PC, 181
  Remote Access feature, 167
  restoring shared folders, 246–250
  shadow-copy feature, 214

• *Y* •

Yellow network health reports, 268

Notes

Notes

Notes

BUSINESS, CAREERS & PERSONAL FINANCE

0-7645-9847-3   0-7645-2431-3

Also available:
- Business Plans Kit For Dummies
  0-7645-9794-9
- Economics For Dummies
  0-7645-5726-2
- Grant Writing For Dummies
  0-7645-8416-2
- Home Buying For Dummies
  0-7645-5331-3
- Managing For Dummies
  0-7645-1771-6
- Marketing For Dummies
  0-7645-5600-2

- Personal Finance For Dummies
  0-7645-2590-5*
- Resumes For Dummies
  0-7645-5471-9
- Selling For Dummies
  0-7645-5363-1
- Six Sigma For Dummies
  0-7645-6798-5
- Small Business Kit For Dummies
  0-7645-5984-2
- Starting an eBay Business For Dummies
  0-7645-6924-4
- Your Dream Career For Dummies
  0-7645-9795-7

HOME & BUSINESS COMPUTER BASICS

0-470-05432-8   0-471-75421-8

Also available:
- Cleaning Windows Vista For Dummies
  0-471-78293-9
- Excel 2007 For Dummies
  0-470-03737-7
- Mac OS X Tiger For Dummies
  0-7645-7675-5
- MacBook For Dummies
  0-470-04859-X
- Macs For Dummies
  0-470-04849-2
- Office 2007 For Dummies
  0-470-00923-3

- Outlook 2007 For Dummies
  0-470-03830-6
- PCs For Dummies
  0-7645-8958-X
- Salesforce.com For Dummies
  0-470-04893-X
- Upgrading & Fixing Laptops For Dummies
  0-7645-8959-8
- Word 2007 For Dummies
  0-470-03658-3
- Quicken 2007 For Dummies
  0-470-04600-7

FOOD, HOME, GARDEN, HOBBIES, MUSIC & PETS

0-7645-8404-9   0-7645-9904-6

Also available:
- Candy Making For Dummies
  0-7645-9734-5
- Card Games For Dummies
  0-7645-9910-0
- Crocheting For Dummies
  0-7645-4151-X
- Dog Training For Dummies
  0-7645-8418-9
- Healthy Carb Cookbook For Dummies
  0-7645-8476-6
- Home Maintenance For Dummies
  0-7645-5215-5

- Horses For Dummies
  0-7645-9797-3
- Jewelry Making & Beading For Dummies
  0-7645-2571-9
- Orchids For Dummies
  0-7645-6759-4
- Puppies For Dummies
  0-7645-5255-4
- Rock Guitar For Dummies
  0-7645-5356-9
- Sewing For Dummies
  0-7645-6847-7
- Singing For Dummies
  0-7645-2475-5

INTERNET & DIGITAL MEDIA

0-470-04529-9   0-470-04894-8

Also available:
- Blogging For Dummies
  0-471-77084-1
- Digital Photography For Dummies
  0-7645-9802-3
- Digital Photography All-in-One Desk Reference For Dummies
  0-470-03743-1
- Digital SLR Cameras and Photography For Dummies
  0-7645-9803-1
- eBay Business All-in-One Desk Reference For Dummies
  0-7645-8438-3
- HDTV For Dummies
  0-470-09673-X

- Home Entertainment PCs For Dummies
  0-470-05523-5
- MySpace For Dummies
  0-470-09529-6
- Search Engine Optimization For Dummies
  0-471-97998-8
- Skype For Dummies
  0-470-04891-3
- The Internet For Dummies
  0-7645-8996-2
- Wiring Your Digital Home For Dummie
  0-471-91830-X

* Separate Canadian edition also available
† Separate U.K. edition also available

Available wherever books are sold. For more information or to order direct: U.S. customers visit www.dummies.com or call 1-877-762-2974.
U.K. customers visit www.wileyeurope.com or call 0800 243407. Canadian customers visit www.wiley.ca or call 1-800-567-4797.

SPORTS, FITNESS, PARENTING, RELIGION & SPIRITUALITY

0-471-76871-5

0-7645-7841-3

Also available:
- Catholicism For Dummies
  0-7645-5391-7
- Exercise Balls For Dummies
  0-7645-5623-1
- Fitness For Dummies
  0-7645-7851-0
- Football For Dummies
  0-7645-3936-1
- Judaism For Dummies
  0-7645-5299-6
- Potty Training For Dummies
  0-7645-5417-4
- Buddhism For Dummies
  0-7645-5359-3

- Pregnancy For Dummies
  0-7645-4483-7 †
- Ten Minute Tone-Ups For Dummies
  0-7645-7207-5
- NASCAR For Dummies
  0-7645-7681-X
- Religion For Dummies
  0-7645-5264-3
- Soccer For Dummies
  0-7645-5229-5
- Women in the Bible For Dummies
  0-7645-8475-8

TRAVEL

0-7645-7749-2

0-7645-6945-7

Also available:
- Alaska For Dummies
  0-7645-7746-8
- Cruise Vacations For Dummies
  0-7645-6941-4
- England For Dummies
  0-7645-4276-1
- Europe For Dummies
  0-7645-7529-5
- Germany For Dummies
  0-7645-7823-5
- Hawaii For Dummies
  0-7645-7402-7

- Italy For Dummies
  0-7645-7386-1
- Las Vegas For Dummies
  0-7645-7382-9
- London For Dummies
  0-7645-4277-X
- Paris For Dummies
  0-7645-7630-5
- RV Vacations For Dummies
  0-7645-4442-X
- Walt Disney World & Orlando
  For Dummies
  0-7645-9660-8

GRAPHICS, DESIGN & WEB DEVELOPMENT

0-7645-8815-X

0-7645-9571-7

Also available:
- 3D Game Animation For Dummies
  0-7645-8789-7
- AutoCAD 2006 For Dummies
  0-7645-8925-3
- Building a Web Site For Dummies
  0-7645-7144-3
- Creating Web Pages For Dummies
  0-470-08030-2
- Creating Web Pages All-in-One Desk
  Reference For Dummies
  0-7645-4345-8
- Dreamweaver 8 For Dummies
  0-7645-9649-7

- InDesign CS2 For Dummies
  0-7645-9572-5
- Macromedia Flash 8 For Dummies
  0-7645-9691-8
- Photoshop CS2 and Digital
  Photography For Dummies
  0-7645-9580-6
- Photoshop Elements 4 For Dummies
  0-471-77483-9
- Syndicating Web Sites with RSS Feeds
  For Dummies
  0-7645-8848-6
- Yahoo! SiteBuilder For Dummies
  0-7645-9800-7

NETWORKING, SECURITY, PROGRAMMING & DATABASES

0-7645-7728-X

0-471-74940-0

Also available:
- Access 2007 For Dummies
  0-470-04612-0
- ASP.NET 2 For Dummies
  0-7645-7907-X
- C# 2005 For Dummies
  0-7645-9704-3
- Hacking For Dummies
  0-470-05235-X
- Hacking Wireless Networks
  For Dummies
  0-7645-9730-2
- Java For Dummies
  0-470-08716-1

- Microsoft SQL Server 2005 For Dummies
  0-7645-7755-7
- Networking All-in-One Desk Reference
  For Dummies
  0-7645-9939-9
- Preventing Identity Theft For Dummies
  0-7645-7336-5
- Telecom For Dummies
  0-471-77085-X
- Visual Studio 2005 All-in-One Desk
  Reference For Dummies
  0-7645-9775-2
- XML For Dummies
  0-7645-8845-1

HEALTH & SELF-HELP

0-7645-8450-2   0-7645-4149-8

Also available:
- Bipolar Disorder For Dummies
  0-7645-8451-0
- Chemotherapy and Radiation
  For Dummies
  0-7645-7832-4
- Controlling Cholesterol For Dummies
  0-7645-5440-9
- Diabetes For Dummies
  0-7645-6820-5* †
- Divorce For Dummies
  0-7645-8417-0 †

- Fibromyalgia For Dummies
  0-7645-5441-7
- Low-Calorie Dieting For Dummies
  0-7645-9905-4
- Meditation For Dummies
  0-471-77774-9
- Osteoporosis For Dummies
  0-7645-7621-6
- Overcoming Anxiety For Dummies
  0-7645-5447-6
- Reiki For Dummies
  0-7645-9907-0
- Stress Management For Dummies
  0-7645-5144-2

EDUCATION, HISTORY, REFERENCE & TEST PREPARATION

0-7645-8381-6   0-7645-9554-7

Also available:
- The ACT For Dummies
  0-7645-9652-7
- Algebra For Dummies
  0-7645-5325-9
- Algebra Workbook For Dummies
  0-7645-8467-7
- Astronomy For Dummies
  0-7645-8465-0
- Calculus For Dummies
  0-7645-2498-4
- Chemistry For Dummies
  0-7645-5430-1
- Forensics For Dummies
  0-7645-5580-4

- Freemasons For Dummies
  0-7645-9796-5
- French For Dummies
  0-7645-5193-0
- Geometry For Dummies
  0-7645-5324-0
- Organic Chemistry I For Dummies
  0-7645-6902-3
- The SAT I For Dummies
  0-7645-7193-1
- Spanish For Dummies
  0-7645-5194-9
- Statistics For Dummies
  0-7645-5423-9

Get smart @ dummies.com®

- **Find a full list of Dummies titles**
- **Look into loads of FREE on-site articles**
- **Sign up for FREE eTips e-mailed to you weekly**
- **See what other products carry the Dummies name**
- **Shop directly from the Dummies bookstore**
- **Enter to win new prizes every month!**

* Separate Canadian edition also available
† Separate U.K. edition also available

Available wherever books are sold. For more information or to order direct: U.S. customers visit www.dummies.com or call 1-877-762-2974.
U.K. customers visit www.wileyeurope.com or call 0800 243407. Canadian customers visit www.wiley.ca or call 1-800-567-4797.